VOICES FROM THE PEACE CORPS

KENTUCKY REMEMBERED: AN ORAL HISTORY SERIES

James C. Klotter,
Terry L. Birdwhistell,
and
Doug Boyd,
Series Editors

BOOKS IN THE SERIES

Conversations with Kentucky Writers
edited by L. Elisabeth Beattie

Conversations with Kentucky Writers II
edited by L. Elisabeth Beattie

Barry Bingham
Barry Bingham

This Is Home Now: Kentucky's Holocaust Survivors Speak
Arwen Donahue and Rebecca Gayle Howell

*Freedom on the Border: An Oral History
of the Civil Rights Movement in Kentucky*
Catherine Fosl and Tracy E. K'Meyer

Bert Combs the Politician
George W. Robinson

Tobacco Culture: Farming Kentucky's Burley Belt
John van Willigen and Susan C. Eastwood

Food and Everyday Life on Kentucky Family Farms, 1920–1950
John van Willigen and Anne van Willigen

Voices from the Peace Corps: Fifty Years of Kentucky Volunteers
Angene Wilson and Jack Wilson

VOICES

FROM THE

PEACE CORPS

FIFTY YEARS OF
KENTUCKY VOLUNTEERS

ANGENE WILSON

AND

JACK WILSON

FOREWORD BY
FORMER SENATOR CHRISTOPHER J. DODD

THE UNIVERSITY PRESS OF KENTUCKY

Scholarly publisher for the Commonwealth,
serving Bellarmine University, Berea College, Centre College of
Kentucky, Eastern Kentucky University, The Filson Historical Society,
Georgetown College, Kentucky Historical Society, Kentucky State
University, Morehead State University, Murray State University, Northern
Kentucky University, Transylvania University, University of Kentucky,
University of Louisville, and Western Kentucky University.
All rights reserved.

Editorial and Sales Offices: The University Press of Kentucky
663 South Limestone Street, Lexington, Kentucky 40508-4008
www.kentuckypress.com

15 14 13 12 11   5 4 3 2 1

Library of Congress Cataloging-in-Publication Data

Wilson, Angene Hopkins.
  Voices from the Peace Corps : fifty years of Kentucky volunteers /
Angene Wilson, Jack Wilson.
      p. cm. — (Kentucky remembered)
  Includes bibliographical references and index.
  ISBN 978-0-8131-2975-4 (hardcover : alk. paper)
  ISBN 978-0-8131-2982-2 (ebook)
  1. Peace Corps (U.S.)—History. I. Wilson, Jack. II. Wilson, Jack.
III. Title.
  HC60.5.W493 2011
  361.6—dc22   2010042385

This book is printed on acid-free recycled paper meeting
the requirements of the American National Standard
for Permanence in Paper for Printed Library Materials.

Manufactured in the United States of America.

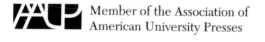 Member of the Association of
American University Presses

Contents

Series Foreword   vii

Foreword   ix

Preface   xi

Map of Peace Corps Host Countries   xx

1. Why We Went   1

2. Getting In   35

3. Training   59

4. Living   95

5. The Toughest . . .   129

6. . . . Job You'll Ever Love   155

7. Telling Stories   199

8. Friends Can Become Family   227

9. Coming Home   247

10. Making a Difference   269

11. Citizens of the World for the Rest of Our Lives   285

Postscript: Our Story   327

Appendix: Interviewee Information   345

Notes   351

Selected Bibliography   359

Index   363

Photographs follow page 186

Series Editors' Foreword

In the field of oral history, Kentucky is a national leader. Over the past several decades, thousands of its citizens have been interviewed. The Kentucky Remembered series brings into print the most important of those collections, with each volume focusing on a particular subject.

Oral history is, of course, only one type of source material. Yet by the very personal nature of recollection, hidden aspects of history are often disclosed. Oral sources provide a vital thread in the rich fabric that is Kentucky history.

Voices from the Peace Corps: Fifty Years of Kentucky Volunteers is the ninth volume in *Kentucky Remembered: An Oral History Series*. Angene and Jack Wilson, former Peace Corps volunteers themselves, conducted eighty-six interviews for this project and used twelve others to present the oral history narratives of Kentuckians whose Peace Corps experiences became central to their adult lives. Oral history draws from individual memory and, like other forms of historical inquiry, is heavily shaped by culture and worldview. By design, the Peace Corps as an institution links the individual to the collective. Through these recordings, the Wilsons link individual narratives to the collective experiences of fellow volunteers. These narratives demonstrate vividly how the lives of individual Kentuckians can be shaped by global experiences in remarkable and meaningful ways.

James C. Klotter
Terry L. Birdwhistell
Doug Boyd

Foreword

As the Peace Corps reaches its fiftieth anniversary, it is a time for celebration. We celebrate one of the most radical ideas I know—that a great nation should send its people abroad not to extend its power, not to intimidate its enemies, not to kill and be killed but to build, to dig, to teach, and to ask nothing in return.

The Peace Corps allows the world to know America and America to know the world. It sends dedicated and industrious people to the far corners of the world to deliver much-needed assistance to countries and communities in the spirit of peace and friendship. It allows the world to see Americans' values, ideals, and hearts firsthand—which are worth more than their weight in gold.

It was a wild notion, so breathtakingly outrageous that it could only have been born out of idealism, youthful energy, and the era of the 1960s. It was two in the morning, and Senator John F. Kennedy was running hours late for a campaign stop at the University of Michigan, where he challenged the crowd. "How many of you," he asked, "who are going to be doctors, are willing to spend your days in Ghana? Technicians or engineers, how many of you are willing to work in the Foreign Service and spend your lives traveling around the world?" It is fair to say that the answer to that question—are you willing to serve your country by serving the world?—was an overwhelming yes.

Like those featured in this book, I also answered yes to the call to service. I was a twenty-two-year-old English major from Providence College when I arrived in the small village of Monción in the Dominican Republic. I barely knew any Spanish, and I had no idea what I was doing. I certainly didn't know that more than forty years later I'd be a U.S. senator, or that the Peace Corps would give me the richest two years of my life.

Jack and Angene Wilson have captured the experiences and sentiments of so many volunteers, from their initial steps in the application process to their homecoming as returned Peace Corps volunteers.

Reading through the experiences of Harold Freeman (Ethiopia 1965–1967) or Rona Roberts (Philippines 1973–1975) brought back many powerful memories and emotions for me, but most of all, it reiterated the transformative power of the Peace Corps. I have witnessed the good the Peace Corps has accomplished, and we have all seen communities transformed, opinions changed, smiles shared, and lasting friendships formed.

I commend and am grateful to Jack and Angene for their tremendous work in bringing the stories of so many volunteers together in such a moving and meaningful book. I also want to extend my heartfelt thanks and gratitude to all the Kentucky volunteers, for without their service, this book and many improvements in lives around the world would not be possible.

Finally, I ask that we, as former volunteers, strive to inspire future generations to walk the path of service and exploration, the one that led me to the Dominican Republic and then, years later, to the U.S. Senate. And I ask that we never lose the spirit, idealism, and ambition that led a young president of a young nation to ask a generation to serve.

Former Senator Christopher J. Dodd of Connecticut
(Dominican Republic 1966–1968)

Preface

What do an architect, a community organizer, a doctor, a forester, a judge, a limnologist, a novelist, a nurse, a photographer, a social worker, a teacher, and many more individuals—all Kentuckians—have in common? With about 200,000 other Americans, they all served as Peace Corps volunteers sometime in the past five decades. They taught English in secondary schools and universities in Turkey and China, worked with primary school teachers in Liberia, developed environmental education materials in Jamaica, and wrote a proposal for the Bikol River Basin Development Project in the Philippines. Like current Peace Corps volunteers, they also promoted a better understanding of Americans in their host countries and brought their new knowledge, cross-cultural sensitivity, and global perspective back to the United States—what has been called "bringing the world back home."

The Peace Corps began as and remains an idealistic face of U.S. foreign policy. In *From Colony to Superpower, U.S. Foreign Relations since 1776,* University of Kentucky Professor Emeritus George Herring writes, the "Peace Corps provided a powerful and enduring example of Kennedy's practical idealism."[1] Summarizing Elizabeth Cobbs Hoffman's conclusions about the Peace Corps and the spirit of the 1960s, he continues: "The Peace Corps' impact on Third World development was negligible. But its contributions in the realm of the spirit were enormous. It helped other peoples to understand the United States and Americans to understand them. It conveyed the hope and promise that represented the United States at its best. It confirmed the nation's values and traditional sense of mission."[2] Wendy Chamberlin, American ambassador to Pakistan on September 11, 2001, and a twenty-eight-year State Department veteran, said more recently of the Peace Corps: "It wasn't a program measured properly in irrigation canals that were dug. No, it was an idea, an idea that reached the people of the world. It was simply that we, who have been given so much, care about you."[3] And it is still such an idea.

As returned Peace Corps volunteers ourselves (Liberia 1962–
1964), we wanted to add to readers' knowledge not only of the Peace
Corps' beginning but also of the fifty-year history of Peace Corps
volunteers and their enduring practical idealism and concern for
people in other parts of the world. We wanted future researchers
and the twenty-first-century public, especially young people, to hear
from returned Peace Corps volunteers not only what it was like to be
in Afghanistan or Armenia or Mali or Micronesia but also why young
and older Americans decided to serve, what training was like, and
what difference the experience made in their host countries and in
their own lives when they returned home—in this case, to Kentucky.
So, as a retirement project, we offered to interview some of the Kentuckians who had served as Peace Corps volunteers for the University of Kentucky's Louie B. Nunn Center for Oral History. We knew
the center had already interviewed, among others, Kentucky public
figures, black ministers, and Vietnam veterans, collecting memories
of their experiences. Why not Peace Corps volunteers?

In spring 2004 we talked with Terry Birdwhistell, then director of the center, who accepted our idea immediately, provided us
with tapes and tape recorders, promised help in transcription, and
encouraged us to think about a book. He also suggested to his summer intern that he interview a relative and one of his professors who
had both been in the Peace Corps. We thank Terry and subsequent
directors Jeff Suchanek and Doug Boyd for believing in and sup-
porting this project. Doug was helpful in getting the last third of
the interviews transcribed by a professional; we also thank the student workers who transcribed the first two-thirds of the interviews.
We appreciated Doug's enthusiasm and his ideas for broadening the
scope of the project—making most of the interviews available online
to listen to and read, soliciting letters and other documentary evidence from Peace Corps volunteers for the University of Kentucky's
Special Collections, and making the Kentucky Peace Corps Oral
History Project a model that other states might emulate. We are particularly grateful to Fran and Will Irwin, Angene's sister and brother-
in-law, who met as Peace Corps volunteers in Afghanistan in 1966
and who read three of the multiple drafts of the manuscript, at the
beginning, in the middle, and toward the end. We thank them for
their thoughtful suggestions and encouragement; we are privileged
to share with them the experience of being Peace Corps volunteers
and a passion for the world.

Before we began interviewing, we developed a list of general questions. We asked about lives before the Peace Corps, motivations for joining, the process of applying and getting accepted, training, the living situation in-country, the difficulties of being a volunteer, the job, memorable stories, friendships, coming home, and the impact of their experiences on the host country and on their lives since the Peace Corps. Because of our own experiences as Peace Corps volunteers, Jack's five years as a Peace Corps administrator, and our subsequent activities as returned volunteers, we were often able to ask pertinent follow-up questions. We tell our own story in the book's postscript and occasionally add examples from our own experiences in the chapters. Especially for recently returned volunteers who were bursting to tell about their experiences and even share pictures on their laptops, we were willing and empathetic listeners. One returned volunteer who had been back two years said, "I could go on and on for days about Bulgaria. It's two years in my life that I feel like I could spend the rest of my life telling about." As most of us have learned, however, few people really want to listen to us "go on and on" about our life-changing experiences in the Peace Corps. Because we asked about the volunteer's lives before and after the Peace Corps, our interviews have some of the characteristics of life histories as well as oral histories about a historically significant organization and time.

To find returned volunteers in Kentucky, we used a list of about 300 generated by Jules Delambre (Cameroon 1965–1967), who, until his death in 2007, was the dedicated keeper and updater of postal and e-mail addresses and a Listserv. We also approached volunteers at meetings of the two formal groups of volunteers in the state at the time and learned about recently returned volunteers through the Peace Corps grapevine.

Understandably, some people are particularly interested in focusing on the organization and on the volunteers who served in the 1960s when the Peace Corps began, received lots of publicity, and reached its peak in terms of number of volunteers (about 15,556 in 1966).[4] Even the youngest of those volunteers are now approaching sixty. However, since we knew volunteers of all ages who served in all decades and wanted the archives to include a broader and ongoing Peace Corps story that demonstrated some of the changes as well as the similarities over time, we decided to interview volunteers from all five decades. Thus, one difference among the interviewees was the individual's distance from the experience. Some recounted events of more than forty years ago, while a few had been back for only several months. Several reread letters written or journals kept during their time in the Peace Corps in preparation for the interview, but for most, the interview itself triggered the memories. What the returned volunteer said in the interview, therefore, might well be different from what he or she reported in a letter at the time or in a twenty-first-century telephone call or e-mail. We also recognize that current events, such as the Afghan and Iraq wars and the foreign policy of the George W. Bush administration, influenced the answers of some volunteers, since the interviews took place between May 2004 and November 2008.

Our major questions for each interviewee were the same. However, volunteers chose to focus on what they thought was most important about their training or which of their stories was most memorable. Our last question was usually "Is there a question we haven't asked that you want to answer?" The interviews from all decades were interesting and insightful. We discovered commonalities, such as reentry or reverse culture shock when returning home, as well as differences, such as modes of communication between the host country and home. We were also reminded that each volunteer had his or her own individual experience, even those who served in the same group at the same time in the same country.

Again, because we wanted to discover the larger story, we interviewed returned volunteers who had served in all regions of the world. In early 2010 the Peace Corps was active in seventy-six countries and had been active in sixty-three others. We were interested in experiences from Eastern Europe and the former USSR as well as Africa, Central and Latin America and the Caribbean, and all parts of Asia and the Pacific. We interviewed returned volunteers who had served in early Peace Corps countries such as India, Malaysia, and Nigeria, as well as those who had gone to former Soviet bloc countries such as Bulgaria, Russia, and Ukraine, which the Peace Corps entered in the 1990s. We interviewed returned volunteers who went as single men and women, and we interviewed, individually, those who went as married couples or who later married. We listened to those who volunteered right out of college and those who joined at thirty, forty, fifty, or sixty. All the volunteers we interviewed talked for at least an hour, even those who initially said, "I'm not sure I have much to say." Most talked for an hour and a half or more. Almost all the volunteers had completed their two years of service, about 10 percent extended for a third year or did a second tour, and a few came home early. We assume that our group of interviewees was skewed toward those who had fairly good experiences and wanted to talk about them. We could have conducted many more interviews with willing participants. We traveled to Berea, Frankfort, Louisville, Morehead, and Murray for interviews. Many others were conducted sitting at our dining room table in Lexington.

Our definition of Kentuckian was deliberately broad and did not specifically match the Peace Corps definition. In January 2010 the Peace Corps counted 1,346 individuals who had applied from Kentucky and served as volunteers since 1961, 64 of whom were currently serving.[5] A little more than a quarter of the volunteers we interviewed were born or grew up in Kentucky and returned to Kentucky when their Peace Corps service ended. The others migrated to Kentucky after their Peace Corps service, as we did, and a few have moved elsewhere since the interviews.

The "small world" of the Peace Corps brought us two of our last interviews. On New Year's Day 2008 Oghale and Sarah Cross Oddo (Jamaica 1994–1996 and 1993–1995) surprised us at the Kentucky Returned Peace Corps Volunteers potluck. We had known Sarah as a high school student in Lexington, and just before joining the Peace Corps, she had been at our house in 1992 for a Kentucky Derby brunch for visiting Peace Corps director Elaine Chao. The Oddos were returning from Fiji, where Oghale was concluding his tour as Peace Corps director—and where we had lived more than twenty-five years earlier when Jack had been Peace Corps director there.

By the end of November 2008 we had interviewed eighty-four returned volunteers—twenty-eight from the 1960s (including ourselves), thirteen from the 1970s, nine from the 1980s, fourteen from the 1990s, and twenty from the first decade of the twenty-first century. We also read the interviews of twelve volunteers who had served in the 1960s, which were conducted by Edward Wardle between 1993 and 1996, and two interviews conducted by Will Jones in 2004, both of volunteers from the 1970s. In addition, we interviewed two staff members, one a doctor, both of whom had married volunteers we interviewed. Altogether, these one hundred interviews represent more than fifty countries of Peace Corps service. We are profoundly grateful to our interviewees for their memories and their reflections. What a history they have provided!

Although we had a vague idea about using the interviews to develop a book that would be published for the Peace Corps' fiftieth anniversary, we did not become serious about that possibility until fall 2007. At that point we began reading and analyzing the transcripts—Jack usually reading the interviews Angene had conducted, and vice versa. We developed categories and subcategories, took careful notes, and then began to draft chapters. Angene read a first draft to Jack as we drove a truck and trailer, fourteen hours each way, to Dallas, Texas, and back in March 2008, taking family furniture to our older daughter Miatta. Angene read a later draft to Jack as we drove to and from Washington, DC, in January 2009 to march with about 175 other returned Peace Corps volunteers in the parade for Barack Obama's inauguration. From June to December 2009 we listened to the more than 150 hours of tapes as we traveled by car—visiting Peace Corps friends out west and on other trips—in order to edit the transcripts and prepare them to go online. Listening to the tapes was another check on our material; for instance, we found a perfect chapter epigraph we had previously missed.

The book chapters are structured around our basic questions, beginning with "Why did you join the Peace Corps?" through "What was the impact of your service on the host country and on yourself, including your career, your family, your worldview, and our own country?" We chose returned volunteers with strong Kentucky connections to represent the five decades; the 1960s are represented by a couple, for a total of six volunteers. Excerpts from their interviews begin each chapter and provide six profiles that continue through all eleven chapters. Other volunteers are quoted in the epigraphs at the beginning of each chapter, and long quotations from volunteers constitute the heart of the narrative of each chapter as we consider and expand on the answers to our questions. We, of course, are responsible for choosing which quotations and stories were included. The interviews were edited for readability; for instance, phrases such as "you know" and repetitious material were deleted (without using ellipses), and sometimes relevant sentences from different paragraphs of a transcript were combined for clarity. We tried to spell correctly place names, proper names, and words in languages other than English, and we appreciated our interviewees' quick responses to our "how do you spell?" queries. Volunteers' countries and years of service are always included, because this is the basic, crucial information that volunteers always share when meeting other volunteers. They constitute our Peace Corps identity.

We chose to use chronology as an organizer in two ways. First, we organized the chapters chronologically through the Peace Corps experience—from motivation and application through returning home and impact—so that readers can gain a sense of how the volunteers' before and after Peace Corps lives bookend the on-the-ground in-country experience in important ways. Second, we followed the chronology of five decades to show change over time in three chapters: Getting In, Training, and Coming Home. We recognize that some readers may be particularly interested in volunteer jobs, for example, or how volunteers made a difference. We also recognize that readers may want to follow a particular volunteer or look up a particular country. The index makes it possible to do that.

We want to make several points about what this book is not. It is not a history of the Peace Corps as an organization or an analysis of its policies or a litany of its successes and failures, although organizational history and policies are sometimes relevant. We consulted our shelf of books about the Peace Corps (both institutional histories and individual memoirs), our collection of Peace Corps publications and articles about the Peace Corps (including the invitation packets we received in 1962), and Jack's papers from his years as a Peace Corps administrator in Sierra Leone, Washington, and Fiji, as well as the Peace Corps Web site. Our own later experiences with the Peace Corps and returned volunteers were very helpful. We participated in and still have the report of the first Returned Peace Corps Volunteer conference in March 1965, which was addressed by Sargent Shriver, the first Peace Corps director; Vice President Hubert Humphrey; Secretary of Defense Robert McNamara; Chief Justice Earl Warren; and Special Assistant to the President Bill Moyers. We have gone to various reunions for all Peace Corps volunteers and for Liberia volunteers over the years—in places ranging from St. Paul, Minnesota, and Portland, Oregon, to Southern California and Washington, DC. As associate director of international affairs from 1990 to 1996, Angene supervised the Peace Corps recruiters at the University of Kentucky. As a professor from 1975 to 2004, she used Peace Corps training materials and literature by Peace Corps writers in her cross-cultural education course; her area of research was the impact of international experience on students, schools, and teachers, including several studies of returned Peace Corps volunteers.

Since 1997, Jack's four years as president of the Kentucky Returned Peace Corps Volunteers and his membership in the national Group Leaders Forum, Angene's six years on the board of the National Peace Corps Association, plus our recent years as members of the Directors' Circle of the latter organization, mean that we are aware of at least some of the current Peace Corps policies and issues. Because of our own experiences, then, we were able to add context to what the interviewees told us. Although we deal with some Peace Corps policies raised by interviewees, we recognize that other relevant issues are not addressed.

This book is not a collection of loosely connected memories and stories, and no one volunteer's entire experience is included, although the six volunteers in five decades represent fairly complete portraits. Many volunteers have written their own compelling memoirs, and there are excellent anthologies of individual cross-cultural stories.[6] We have included many stories that the volunteers told us. In fact, "What is a memorable story from your Peace Corps service?" was one of our questions. However, we have tried to connect these stories to specific points about volunteers' lives and what they experienced and learned.

Finally, this book is not only Kentucky history. Although Kentucky was our geographic touchstone, the returned volunteers we interviewed were born or grew up in twenty-eight other states as well as five other countries—Cuba, England, Japan, Mexico, and Nigeria. To a great extent, these interviews are a microcosm of a larger national and international story. The experiences and reflections of the 100 individuals quoted in this book will be recognizable to most of the 200,000 volunteers who have served in the Peace Corps, wherever they live today. Still, Kentucky is the common thread that binds these interviews and this book together.

When current and past volunteers read this book, we hope they will see something of their own experience. We hope potential volunteers and their families and friends will be intrigued by the variety of Peace Corps experiences. We hope others who want to learn more about the Peace Corps will enjoy both the good stories and the rest of the story. We hope all readers will understand the contributions of these Kentucky-connected volunteers to the Peace Corps, to bringing the world back home, and to the concepts of practical idealism and caring about the world as part of American foreign policy. For us, the years of interviewing and writing have been pure pleasure and even pride.

The famous Nigerian writer Chinua Achebe has described the work of African literature as an *mbari,* a celebration through art of the world and of the life lived in it. He writes: "Whether the rendezvous of separate histories will take place in a grand, harmonious concourse or be fraught with bitterness and acrimony will all depend on whether we have learned to recognize one another's presence and are ready to accord human respect to every people."[7]

We offer this book as a celebration of people who have participated in a very special organization, people who know about separate histories and desire a harmonious future because they recognize the presence of other people in the world and accord them respect. We have learned so much from these other people, people in "our" countries who became not "others" but friends. They taught us how to be citizens of the world for the rest of our lives, and we dedicate this book to them. A portion of the proceeds from the sale of this book will be donated to projects in Peace Corps countries.

Angene and Jack Wilson (Liberia 1962–1964)
Lexington, Kentucky

Peace Corps host countries. (Map by Dick Gilbreath, University of Kentucky Cartography Lab)

Interviewees' host countries

Other Peace Corps host countries

Nations represented by interviewees

Afghanistan
Armenia
Bangladesh
Bulgaria
Cameroon
Central African Republic
Chile
China
Colombia
Costa Rica
Côte d'Ivoire
Democratic Republic of Congo/Zaire
Dominican Republic
Ecuador
Eritrea
Ethiopia
Fiji
Gabon
The Gambia
Ghana
Guatemala
Guinea
Honduras
India
Jamaica
Jordan
Lesotho
Liberia
Malawi
Malaysia
Mali
Micronesia
Morocco
Mozambique
Nevis
Niger
Nigeria
Peru
Philippines
Russia
Senegal
Sierra Leone
Slovakia
South Africa
Sri Lanka
Swaziland
Thailand
Tonga
Turkey
Ukraine
Zambia
Zimbabwe

Other Peace Corps host countries

Albania
Antigua and Barbuda
Argentina
Azerbaijan
Bahrain
Belize
Benin
Bolivia
Bosnia-Herzegovina
Botswana
Brazil
Burkina Faso
Burundi
Cambodia
Cape Verde
Chad
Comoros
Cook Islands
Cyprus
Czech Republic
Dominica
East Timor
El Salvador
Equatorial Guinea
Estonia
Georgia
Grenada and Carriacou
Guinea Bissau
Guyana
Haiti
Hungary
Indonesia
Iran
Kazakhstan
Kenya
Kiribati
Kyrgyz Republic
Latvia
Libya
Lithuania
Macedonia
Madagascar
Malta
Marshall Islands
Mauritania
Mauritius
Mexico
Moldova
Mongolia
Namibia
Nepal
Nicaragua
Niue
Oman
Pakistan
Panama
Papua New Guinea
Paraguay
Poland
Republic of Congo
Romania
Rwanda
Samoa
Sao Tome and Principe
Solomon Islands
Somalia
South Korea
St. Kitts
St. Lucia
St. Vincent and the Grenadines
Sudan
Tanzania
Togo
Tunisia
Turkmenistan
Tuvalu
Uganda
Uruguay
Uzbekistan
Vanuatu
Venezuela
Yemen

Chapter 1

Why We Went

I remember talking with my father about the Peace Corps when
Kennedy became president. I was ten. The idea fascinated me.
My father had written a novel called *No Time for Sergeants*, which
was a satire against war. He was disgusted with the Korean War
so he was thinking in terms of Peace Corps and taking things in a
different direction.
—Gwyn Hyman Rubio (Costa Rica 1971–1973)

Back in the eighties when I was a kid they had all those TV
ads, the toughest job you'll ever love TV ads, and you'd see
these people in some exotic-looking locale. I'm sure it made an
impression on me.
—Ashley Netherton (Senegal 2003–2005)

SIX VOLUNTEERS IN FIVE DECADES

Martin and Patsy Tracy (Turkey 1965–1967)

Martin grew up in Murray, Kentucky, where his father was head of
the Speech Department and debate coach at Murray State University. Martin's Kentucky roots grow deep. He is a direct descendant
of Jane Kenton, sister of pioneer settler Simon Kenton, who came
to Kentucky in 1783 and gave Kenton County its name. After high
school graduation in 1958 Martin joined the army to do something
different and to travel; he was stationed at a missile base in New
Jersey for three years, working as a guidance system and computer
operator. Then he returned to Murray for college.

Patsy grew up in western Appalachian North Carolina, where her
family expected her to get a good education for the "greater good of

1

the community." Berea College was her second choice after a scholarship to Wake Forest was withdrawn. Patsy remembered her time at Berea:

> You joined the debate team to get off campus and to travel and meet guys at other universities. At the end of my freshman year I was at a Kentucky intercollegiate debate at Morehead University. My partner and I were just terrific, and we came up against two young men from Murray State, and we beat them. They asked us out for hamburgers and to go bowling. That's how I met my husband. We married at the end of our sophomore year. I had to transfer to Murray State. And then we were young, struggling, poor married folks. That was a wonderful lesson in looking at our own poverty; we realized that poverty wasn't so bad if you had fun and you had some culture and you had some opportunity. So we became dedicated to being antipoverty. We decided to devote our lives to service. We joined the debate team and the poetry club and the international club and were very fond of meetings with international students. We probably became educated more by our peers who were challenging each other and students from other countries who were challenging us as having a life quite luxurious as compared to the rest of the world. So we decided we'll find out some way to keep our marriage together and we'll have some adventures along the way.

Martin remembered that in the spring of their senior year, "I thought it would be interesting to do something unusual. I saw the advertisement for Peace Corps. I was a very strong devotee of Kennedy and even more of Hubert Humphrey. So I thought this would be something that would really be interesting and would also give us an opportunity to travel overseas. I had always wanted to have an international experience. In junior high when I was asked what I wanted to do, I put down diplomat. I wanted to travel abroad, I wanted to learn languages. I've always had a fascination with how other people live and a sense of adventure."

Patsy admitted, "Martin was more international than I was. I had a firsthand living experience with hard times. Martin was more middle class, and he wanted to find out what the world of service in a rural or poor international community would be like. It wasn't my idea; it was Martin's idea to explore the Peace Corps."

Rona Roberts (Philippines 1973–1975)

Rona, the third of four children, grew up on a 450-acre working farm on a dirt road in Wayne County, Kentucky. When she was in about the third grade, her parents both became teachers; then her mother became a school librarian in order to pay for her older brother's college costs.

Mother was the person to whom the books were shipped when they [the fledgling public library] wrote away asking for remainders from publishers. And the books all came to our house. One of the books that meant an incredible amount to me as a kid was Richard Halliburton's *Book of Marvels*, which was a travel book and had the marvels of the world with those old fuzzy gray pictures, and it made me want to be out in the world and see things and go from this little head of a hollow in Wayne County. One of my memories of myself as a child is standing at the kitchen sink washing jars for canning and dreaming I could be in Rome in the Colosseum.

So travel was a big pull and it was accelerated by an interesting happenstance. My mother was involved in the Farm Bureau Women, and they got involved in a placement program for German young people because of the belief that the two wars in Germany had happened because of the Germans' lack of exposure to other cultures. We could take a lesson for our own culture from this, and Peace Corps is probably part of that lesson. So a young woman who had graduated from high school in Germany was scheduled to come to Kentucky to stay with the head of the Kentucky Farm Bureau Women, but the host got sick and asked Mother to be the host instead. And Mother said, "Well, we don't have running water and a bathroom, but if she's willing to live in those conditions, then we'll take her." So that began a lifelong—now into its third generation—friendship with this German family. Renate went through the last year of high school at Wayne County High School, graduating with my sister Paula. I was tiny, between one and two. I don't remember her at that stage, but there were always letters from Germany. She would send books from Germany and there would be pictures, a lot of pictures of the destruction from the war and then gradually we would get books about rebuilding. She would write in this very distinctive, small blue ink script in English, translating the captions on the pictures.

Jump forward to the Vietnam War era. I always had a stubborn sense about fairness and equity. And I believed strongly that women should be drafted if men were going to be drafted. I had a strong sense about service. I believed that national service was extremely important, and I still do. I had already applied for VISTA [Volunteers in Service to America], but my boyfriend wanted very much to be in the Peace Corps.

Rebecca Roach (Liberia 1988–1989)

The fourth of five children, Rebecca also grew up on a farm, located near Middletown, Ohio. The family grew all their own crops and had cattle and chickens. When Rebecca was in second grade, her mother got her GED (general equivalency diploma) and went to college. Rebecca graduated from Morehead State University in Kentucky and considers herself a southerner.

My family was very religious. We were raised Pentecostal and my grandmother always wanted a missionary in the family. When she conceived my mother, she dedicated her to missions. My mother never went on to be a missionary, but she really pushed me toward international travel, though not with a religious mission in mind. She always felt like I had a gift for working with people. So she was behind me from the time I was about thirteen years old to join the Peace Corps.

I saw a movie called Bush Doctor on television, and I saw photographs of Africa and I just fell in love with it. I went to my mother and said, "I just will die if I don't go to Africa." I remember my mother so clearly saying, "When you're a girl and you're thirteen you know exactly where your heart is." And she was right. I just had a calling to go. I was on the Peace Corps track from thirteen on. When I was a freshman in high school I went to see my guidance counselor and I started getting information on the Peace Corps. They said I needed a skill in health or education or rural development. I went into education at Morehead State University. I got engaged while I was there, but my fiancé said, "No, you can't go to Africa. I've decided you can't go." And I said, "Well, then I'm not engaged."

Sarah Cross Oddo (Jamaica 1993–1995)

Sarah was born and raised in Lexington, Kentucky. In high school she was in the International Club and had friends who were exchange students. She also met some returned Peace Corps volunteers. At the University of Kentucky as an undergraduate, she majored in environmental geology. After her sophomore year she worked as a maid in Yellowstone National Park, her first experience of having to make it on her own. That same year she had a roommate who was applying to the Peace Corps.

> We lived in Lexington because my dad taught at the university. My parents lived in the same house before I was born, and they still live in the same house. I had a very stable childhood. I always lived in the same place, I never had to move, I never had to make new friends—it was all very consistent for me. We traveled a lot in the States because my parents weren't from here, and when we would go visit family, it was a very rural environment. I always enjoyed that very much, and I always wanted to live in the country. So I sort of had this fantasy about living the rural lifestyle, I guess.
>
> When I was a kid I remember seeing the [Peace Corps] commercial where people were all fishing, and I always thought that looked like great fun. I thought that I wanted to go to a village in Africa and fish with all the villagers. I just thought it looked like a fantastic life.

Aaron Shraberg (China 2004–2006)

Aaron grew up Jewish in Kentucky. Family on his father's side came from Lithuania in 1910 and settled in Somerset, Kentucky, and his great-grandfather opened a scrap metal company in Lexington. His mother's family came from England to Maryland in 1668 and got a land grant in Rineyville, Kentucky, after the American Revolution. "In fact, my great-great-grandfather Zachariah Riney was Abraham Lincoln's schoolteacher. So you could say my family is pretty steeped in Kentucky history. My father had worked in Louisiana, and that's where I ended up being born." Aaron attended elementary and middle school in Lexington and high school in New Orleans. He received a BA in English with a concentration in creative writing from the University of Kentucky in May 2004. As a senior, he considered his options: law school, a job, or "leave the United States and see what else was out there."

> I really wanted to broaden my perspective, wanted to see what it was like to live in another culture. So my thought process was, I'm young; I have many years to do graduate studies or to begin working. There's got to be an opportunity out there where I can leave the country, live

abroad, get some perspective, be challenged, and learn something new. And I also wanted some adventure. So I began doing some research on the Internet. I talked with one of my friends who was at Princeton at the time, and he said he was considering the Peace Corps, and we had this idea that we would go into the Peace Corps together. He ended up doing something else, but I still applied. As I researched more and more about the Peace Corps, I found it was something I wanted to be a part of because of its history, because of its mission, its goals, and because of the stories I read about the volunteers who'd served.

These six volunteers in five decades illustrate the diverse motivations for serving in the Peace Corps. In the twenty-first century, Aaron got excited about the Peace Corps because of its history, mission, goals, and stories. President John F. Kennedy is an important part of that history, and he inspired early volunteers like Martin. The mission and goals of helping others and promoting cross-cultural understanding were attractive to others. Patsy and Rona talked about service. Rebecca saw the Peace Corps as a calling. Both she and Sarah were fascinated by Africa and eager for their first cross-cultural experience. Sarah and Martin—and Ashley, quoted in the epigraph—remembered the Peace Corps commercials.

Like volunteers in a 1962 study that analyzed the first applicants' responses to the question, "What do you hope to accomplish by joining the Peace Corps?" these volunteers offered more than one reason. Their motives were complex and mixed.[1] "Why did you join?" is a question many volunteers tire of answering, and Vice President Lyndon Johnson's suggestion to trainees in Puerto Rico in 1962 remains apropos. The next time someone asked, Johnson said, they should turn the "why" question around, "like Thoreau turned Emerson's question around when Emerson paid a visit to his friend in the Concord jail. 'My dear Thoreau,' Emerson said, 'Why are you here?' To which Thoreau replied, 'My dear Emerson, why are you not here?'"[2] Our interviewees from all decades were generally more willing to talk about their reasons for joining the Peace Corps when we asked more specific questions about the life experiences and the people that influenced their decisions.

This chapter focuses first on volunteers from the 1960s and the influence of President Kennedy's call to service. We then deal with the Peace Corps' relationships to the war in Vietnam in particular and to the military in general. That relationship became almost moot after Vietnam, the end of the draft, and the rise of a volunteer army, until controversy about a new connection erupted in the early twenty-first century. By the end of the first decade of the Peace Corps, other influences took the place of Kennedy's call and a looming draft. Some volunteers considered the Peace Corps valuable for their future careers. In the 1990s and early 2000s the Peace Corps attracted young people who were put off by the widespread emphasis on jobs in the investment sector. Peace Corps volunteers themselves became formal and informal recruiters and added their influence to mentors and family members. More and more volunteers came to the Peace Corps with previous international and service experiences.

Always underlying these parsed apart influences are the short yet complex answers to the "why did you join" question, such as those offered by Glen Payne (Gabon 1989–1992)—"I would say my interest in the world and travel and a sensitivity to the plight of other people"—and by David Goodpaster (Malawi 2005–2007)—"I've always been a restless person and a bit idealistic and adventurous." We conclude the chapter with an explanation of "practical idealism" as one way to encompass these mixed motivations in a single phrase.

THE KENNEDY FACTOR

In the minds of many 1960s volunteers and later volunteers who grew up in the 1960s, the Peace Corps was intimately linked to President John F. Kennedy, who established the new agency by executive order on March 1, 1961. Many 1960s volunteers can quote the famous lines from his inaugural address: "And so my fellow Americans, ask not what your country can do for you, ask what you can do for your country." Although quoted less frequently, the sentence that followed threw out a further challenge: "My fellow citizens of the world, ask not what America will do for you, but what together we can do for the freedom of man."

Suddenly peace became patriotic. In June 1962 Kennedy said: "Well, they may ask you what you have done in the sixties for your country, and you will be able to say, 'I served in the Peace Corps.'"[3] At the dedication of the Peace Corps exhibit at the Kennedy Library, a 1960s volunteer was quoted as saying, "I'd never done anything political, patriotic or unselfish because nobody ever asked me to. Kennedy asked."[4]

Two older women who joined the Peace Corps in the twenty-first century described themselves as Kennedy people in the 1960s; they would have joined if they hadn't married and had families. One of them, Peg Dickson (Ukraine 2000–2002), said, "Growing up in the sixties when John Kennedy started Peace Corps, it was something that I had always dreamed about doing."

One older volunteer who joined in the 1960s was Bill Bridges (East Pakistan [now Bangladesh] 1963–1965). He was almost fifty, a widower, processing disability applications for the state of Kentucky. "I remember the morning after President Kennedy announced at my alma mater, the University of Michigan, that he was going to initiate a Peace Corps, I said, 'That's for me!' I kept trying to find out how young you had to be to go into the Peace Corps, and they said 'any age,' so I immediately volunteered." Bill then became concerned about whether he was qualified for the Peace Corps and put the application away for a year. "At last I decided I was overly modest, that I could give the Peace Corps something. I volunteered and I was sent to East Pakistan."

Most of those who cited Kennedy as a reason for joining were 1960s volunteers. "I was a fan of John Kennedy," recalled Dan Sprague (Colombia 1963–1965). "The Peace Corps was a very new thing. I thought it was a very exciting and challenging call to service by the president." He also remembered that Kennedy was assassinated during his Peace Corps training. "We were just in absolute shock and stunned, but I think in the end we said, 'Okay, we're his people and we're going to fulfill what he wanted us to do,' so we bonded together and renewed our commitment to moving forward." "Kennedy was killed," Tom Samuel (Liberia 1965–1967) said, "and it seemed like a good idea to go into Peace Corps." In fact, the week after Kennedy's assassination in November 1963, the all-time record number of applications was received: 2,550.[5]

Carol Conaway (Jamaica 1965–1966) remembered quoting Kennedy ("Ask not . . . ") on her application. Others who served during the same years also talked about Kennedy. Terry Anderson (Ghana 1965–1967) said, "I was taken by John Kennedy and his Peace Corps idealism, and that's why I did it." Jules Delambre (Cameroon 1965–1967) recalled, "When Kennedy announced the Peace Corps in his campaign it caught my imagination." According to Nancy Dare (Malaysia 1965–1967), "Both of us [she and her husband, Phil] were Kennedy people, and we were answering the call, thinking that maybe we could do something to help." Phil Dare remembered, "I was in the classroom teaching at Midway College when the word came that Kennedy had been shot. So there was the feeling that one had to do something in response. There was a real positive atmosphere, certainly for young people, in those days. And we were doing the ethical things and the moral things that we should have been doing a long time ago to get the country to live up to its ideals. It was an exciting time and we wanted to jump into the mix."

Like the Dares, other 1960s volunteers were motivated by Kennedy plus other influences. "It was in my senior year of college I decided to apply to the Peace Corps," Jim Archambeault (Philippines 1966–1968) explained. "I'm sure that part of my desire to at least apply to the Peace Corps was my earlier desire to work as a missionary. And then I was a great admirer of John Kennedy, who started the Peace Corps, and he was assassinated before I applied. Also it would have been an experience, an adventure. And I could have, idealistically perhaps, made a contribution to wherever I went."

Judy Lippmann (Morocco 1966–1968) wanted to see more of the world: "After one year of dental hygiene, I thought this isn't really what I want. And it was the mid-1960s, and John Kennedy had been talking about digging wells and saving the world, and I thought that just sounded wonderful." She had read in *National Geographic* about the blue men of the Sahara and put Morocco down as her first choice. "I thought, I want to see people who are so different from me that I can't imagine what it's like. And the concept of the blue men of the Sahara, it was just fantasy."

In the late 1960s the Kennedy factor became tied to Vietnam and civil rights protests for some volunteers. Like many others, Fred Cowan (Ethiopia 1967–1969), who grew up in Louisville and started college at Dartmouth in the fall of 1963, remembered where he was when JFK was shot.

That was an earth-shattering event for the nation and for everyone. As I progressed through school the other big thing that started to really weigh on everyone's mind was, of course, the Vietnam War. By 1966 there were increasing protests. Sometime in 1966 I became an antiwar advocate. I participated in some campus protests, and I went to some of the national marches in New York. And there was a student protest I participated in having to do with divestments of the college in companies that had business in South Africa. I was not a radical; I was a sort of mainstream protester. I had to think about alternatives to going to war, and certainly at that time the Peace Corps was an alternative. So I was drawn to the Peace Corps I think in part because it was a good way to not go to Vietnam; in part because I had a genuine interest in trying to serve our community, our world, trying to make it a better place; and in part because I was twenty-one years old and I thought this would be a lot of fun. It would be kind of an adventure.

When we interviewed Bill Sweigart (Liberia 1967–1970), he had just found an essay he had written as a high school junior explaining that he was so impressed by Kennedy's inaugural address he was thinking about joining the Peace Corps. As he talked forty years later, Bill cited his "powerful sense of injustice. I think that's one of the things that drew me immediately to the idea of a Peace Corps." In college he was involved in civil rights marches, and much to the dismay of the mayor and the college president, he was quoted in a Pittsburgh newspaper as saying that his black friend could not get a haircut in Indiana, Pennsylvania.

I was very caught up with the meaning of that [social justice] in America. And then I extended the idea to going to the Peace Corps and doing something in my mind that was meaningful that had to do with social justice and development. I think the idea of going 6,000 miles away was just very, very appealing to me because I also grew more and more disenchanted with the society I lived in, the culture I lived in, wanting to get out of it. But at the same time I think a lot of people like me had a real love-hate relationship with this culture in the sixties, yet did not become so negative as to want to completely eschew American social values altogether or whatever democracy supposedly stood for. So the Peace Corps was really a wonderful kind of compromise, and of course, the Vietnam War was on, and I had cousins who were drafted. But that was not my primary motivation.

Vietnam, the Peace Corps, and the Military

Like Fred Cowan and Bill Sweigart, young men in the 1960s and early 1970s had to think about Vietnam. An earlier book based on oral history interviews includes a chapter entitled "A Haven for Draft Dodgers," which concludes that although the Peace Corps "probably accounted for a very small percentage of those who evaded the draft," it "nevertheless resulted in a preponderance of volunteers who were motivated more by opportunism than altruism."[6] Our interviews provide scant support for the second half of that generalization. The relationship between Peace Corps service and military service has always been complex. Experience with the military, before or after the Peace Corps, whether volunteer or drafted, affected individuals in different ways, depending, to some extent, on the years they served in Peace Corps.

In the early and mid-1960s some of our interviewees considered both the armed services and the Peace Corps as options. For example, Paul Winther (India 1961–1963) had been accepted by the U.S. Navy for cadet training. He had his heart set on becoming a navy pilot, but four days before he was to sign his contract, he was also accepted by the Peace Corps. He asked the navy, "Can I take a two-year break, go into the Peace Corps, and then come back and still be eligible?" The navy said yes. After college graduation in 1964, Tom Boyd (Colombia 1964–1966) had been accepted by the Peace Corps and by both the U.S. Navy and Marine Corps Officer Candidate Schools, he had a job offer from Goodyear Tire and Rubber Company, and he was on the waiting list for graduate school at Ohio State. He said, "There was no question I was going to join the Peace Corps simply because it was the biggest adventure." Tom Samuel (Liberia 1965–1967) joined the army reserves in 1963 before becoming a Peace Corps volunteer; when he returned from Liberia there were so many veterans that all the reserve units were full, and in 1969 he got an honorable discharge.

Some volunteers, such as John Skeese (Nigeria 1961–1964) and Martin Tracy (Turkey 1965–1967), had been in the army before their Peace Corps service. Likewise, Bill Davig (Peru 1965–1967) served in the navy for two years. Richard Parker (Côte d'Ivoire 1973–1974, Morocco 1976–1978) "grew up in a navy family, traveling from pillar to post, living different places. The most fascinating experience was when I was eleven and we lived on the navy base at Guantanamo in Cuba, before the revolution." After graduating from high school in 1961, Richard enlisted in the air force, got electronics training, and served for three years. Older volunteer Gary Griffin (Thailand 2004–2006) also grew up in a military family and lived in Germany when he was thirteen, just before his father went to Vietnam for a year. Gary spent three and a half years in the coast guard in the 1970s, where, like Richard, he worked in electronics;

he lived in Turkey, Italy, and Hawaii before going to Indiana University on the GI bill.

Occasionally, volunteers enlisted in the army after their Peace Corps service. Bob Leupold (Indonesia and Thailand 1963–1965) joined the Peace Corps after graduating from college in Morehead, Kentucky, with a degree in physical education and history. He coached basketball and swimming in East Java, the center of the Communist Party in Indonesia, until the Peace Corps canceled the project because of safety concerns (see his story in chapter 4). After the Peace Corps transferred him to Thailand, where he trained teachers for six months, he traveled home through India, Egypt, and Europe and then enlisted in the army. Bob was in Vietnam for three years; after being in the field for six months, he ended up in public information, writing division histories and taking care of reporters. He came home in 1969 still committed to the war.

Sometimes volunteers were drafted after their Peace Corps service. Ron Pelfrey (Ethiopia 1966–1968) thought that if he was going to be a good teacher, he needed to broaden his horizons and see more of the world, so he joined the Peace Corps. Some of his friends were evading the draft by going to Canada, and one of his high school friends was involved in breaking into the office of the draft board in East Lansing, Michigan, and was immediately reclassified by the Lexington draft board and drafted. As a college junior, Ron wrote a letter of protest about the treatment of his friend that was published in a Lexington newspaper. Before completing his service with the Peace Corps in Ethiopia, Ron was accepted into a new graduate program in international education at Columbia Teachers College. He traveled through Europe on his way home to Lexington, and when he arrived he found an official letter stating that he had been reclassified 1-A.

I went immediately to the draft board to meet the lady. She opened my file. And there's the letter to the editor right on top of my file, the actual newspaper clipping. I said, "I was in the Peace Corps. I'm going to school. Both of those are deferments." She said, "Well, you're not in graduate school right now. When we reclassified you, you weren't in the Peace Corps." So I appealed, and long story short, I finally was notified in my last week of basic training that I had been drafted illegally. Since I had been overseas, I had sixty days to appeal my reclassification once I received it, but my lawyer didn't know that. Once you're in, it doesn't

make a difference. Once you accept and report, you lose your appeal. So
I never made it to Columbia. I went to Vietnam in the army and served for
fourteen and a half months in the artillery.

Harold Freeman (Ethiopia 1965–1967) was also drafted a year
after he returned from Peace Corps service. "As long as I taught,
there was a teaching deferment, but I thought it would not be a matter of the highest integrity to stay there doing something I didn't
really want to do and didn't think I was truly qualified to do just to
keep me safe. I got called up for my physical and was declared 1-A,
which meant prime draft meat. I spent my twenty-sixth birthday,
which was the cutoff date for being drafted, in basic training in the
army at Fort Campbell." Before basic training, Harold had some
concerns:

I went to the draft center in Nashville and asked for the oath you had to
take when you went in [the army], because I was kind of iffy about what
I could promise to do. They wouldn't give it to me, and furthermore, they
threatened to have me arrested if I didn't leave. So I did leave, but then
I wrote to the senior Al Gore, who was a senator from Tennessee at that
time, and told him of my experience and said that I thought I should be
able to find out the contents of the oath. He thought so, too, and sent
it [the request] on, and I got a letter from a colonel at the Pentagon
who told me I was entitled to such information, and here it is. So when
I was indeed drafted, I had to show up at this same induction center,
and they knew who Harold Freeman was because they'd heard of me
from the Pentagon. I did not take the oath, and even though the My Lai
incident had not yet come to light, I was not comfortable saying I would
do anything they told me to do. So I just got inducted without taking the
oath, which kept them from giving me a security clearance but didn't
keep them from giving me three jobs that required security clearances.
So I have been in the Peace Corps and I've been in the war corps, and I
prefer the Peace Corps to a high degree over the war corps.

Harold was a "paperwork warrior" for a year in Vietnam, working with a civil affairs company that helped the military coordinate
with local governments for public engineering, education, health,
or public safety projects. Harold noted, "Some folks have heard of
civil affairs companies now in Iraq and Afghanistan. Mostly it was
a make-work job, saying we had achieved our goals. I've said only

somewhat facetiously that if one Peace Corps volunteer hadn't accomplished more than my whole company did in Vietnam, the Peace Corps would have died before 1970."

The Peace Corps tried to be clear about military service and the draft in its applications and handbooks. Volunteers usually received deferments during their Peace Corps service, but that service did not exempt them from the draft, and young men had to deal with their local draft boards individually. Bill Miller (Dominican Republic 1968–1970) remembered having to get approval from his local selective service board to go into the Peace Corps. He had been in the air force Reserve Officers' Training Corps (ROTC), discovered he wasn't cut out for drilling, and decided there were other ways to serve his country. He was very polite when he went for his preliminary physical for the military because he knew the doctor had said some unkind things about the Peace Corps, but in the end the doctor wished him good luck.

Most deferments were granted only after the potential volunteer had successfully completed Peace Corps training. Deferments lasted one year, and volunteers were required to request an extension before the end of each year of Peace Corps service. Volunteers were also advised to keep their local draft boards informed of their whereabouts at all times and to notify them of any change in status, such as the end of their service. The 1967 *Peace Corps Handbook* stated that future deferment depended on considerations such as age, physical condition, marital status, selective service regulations, and manpower quotas.[7] One author reported that between July 1969 and July 1970, 150 of 7,800 male volunteers were drafted directly from their Peace Corps assignments.[8]

A sad event for us occurred when Jack was Peace Corps director in Fiji. We were visited by the parents of a young man who had been drafted and then killed in Vietnam the year after he returned from the Peace Corps. Angene flew with them by seaplane to take the ashes of their only child to his Peace Corps site, the remote and beautiful island of Ono-i-lau.

Don Stosberg (Malawi 1965–1966) got his draft notice in Rome on the way home. He recalled, "I wasn't quite radical enough in those days to run to Canada, but I felt that I'd done my service to the country and I didn't want to do another two years in the army. So I was going through my physical. My eyes didn't show up very good, so they pulled me aside and sent me in to an optometrist, I presume for a second round of tests. I made sure I told the optometrist that I'd just come back from the Peace Corps, and I don't know if he ran the numbers up or not, but I was put in whatever category that meant if the war got really bad, they'd pull you in. I ended up not getting drafted because my eyes were bad enough. I always like to think that the optometrist gave me some good numbers, but I don't know."

Frank Gemendin (Dominican Republic 1968–1969) stayed in the Peace Corps for only a year because he preferred to "face the issue rather than avoid it. I came back and filed for and received conscientious objector status and was all set to do alternate service, but I got a high number in the lottery, so the problem was resolved." He said volunteers in his group were motivated to be in the Peace Corps "because it was a trip to Vietnam if you left."

The first lottery was held on December 1, 1969, to determine the order in which men born in 1944 through 1950 would be called to report for induction in the military, and lotteries were held in subsequent years until the draft was suspended in 1973. The lottery affected Angel Rubio (Costa Rica 1971–1973), who graduated from college in 1971 and had a low number. He recalled his dilemma: "Was I going to get drafted, was I not? Would I go to Canada? Would I try to apply for CO [conscientious objector] status? I actually went back to my high school for some draft counseling. Really, the war was just consuming our thoughts. And then I was drafted, got the letter from selective service, and within three to four weeks I got my acceptance to the Peace Corps. I had to actually fight with the draft board clerk because she didn't like the idea of that [being deferred]. And she said, 'I'm going to get you when you come out.' But she didn't. I had picked up literature about the Peace Corps over the years and sort of toyed with it in a romantic sense, but finally I realized that I was going to have to make a decision."

Women were concerned about the war in Vietnam, too. Sally Spurr (Ecuador 1975–1977) first applied for the Peace Corps when she graduated from Western Kentucky University in 1971. "I wanted to do something different out of the country," she said, "and I loved the idea of helping others to give my life some meaning. I was very much into the political side of the antiwar movement and very much a peacenik." Sally lived with a couple of guys who had returned from Vietnam, and she knew people who were going to Canada to avoid the war. "When I was in college it was the Vietnam era, so there were a lot of people trying to get in Peace Corps at that time. It was kind of a cool thing." Sally was not accepted in 1971. "I was too much of a generalist. I didn't have the specific skills they were looking for at that time."

It is important to point out that small numbers of veterans have always served in the Peace Corps, such as those mentioned earlier: John Skeese, Bill Davig, Martin Tracy, Richard Parker, and Gary Griffin. Even high-ranking officers have become Peace Corps volunteers; for instance, retired Rear Admiral Francis Thomas, a decorated hero during the Japanese attack on Pearl Harbor, was an older Peace Corps volunteer in Fiji in the early 1970s, and the Peace Corps Web site in 2008 featured a retired colonel who was doing medical training in El Salvador.

The relationship between the Peace Corps and the military became controversial in the twenty-first century when the National Call to Service program became law in 2002. The law allowed soldiers who had completed fifteen months of active duty and twenty-four months with the Army Reserve or National Guard to serve the remainder of their eight-year obligation in one of three ways—one of those was to join a national service program such as AmeriCorps or the Peace Corps. The Peace Corps community felt very strongly that the Peace Corps should not be directly linked with a military obligation and engaged in an intensive campaign against the law. The National Peace Corps Association and its members "feared that any blurring [of] the line between the Peace Corps and the military would jeopardize the independence of the Peace Corps and put volunteers at risk if it became widely known that some volunteers were doing Peace Corps service as part of their military obligation."[9] As a result, President George W. Bush signed the 2006 Defense Authorization Act, which removed references to the Peace Corps.

Still, both the Peace Corps and the military remain ways to serve our country. As Lloyd Jones (Colombia 1973–1975) noted, he grew up with a sense of civic duty, "so there was that altruistic motivation in a sense that I didn't mind being a volunteer, but I would have been a volunteer if I'd gone into the military, too."

Preparation for a Career and Other Opportunities

Although very few volunteers mentioned it in their interviews, preparation for a career became a motivation for joining the Peace Corps, particularly after the 1960s. Chapter 11 documents that the Peace

Corps experience frequently had an impact on volunteers' careers. One difference between 1960s volunteers and those who came later seems to be that some early volunteers decided to apply to the U.S. Foreign Service or to work for U.S. or nongovernmental aid agencies *after* their Peace Corps experience, whereas later volunteers often understood beforehand that the Peace Corps would be a useful step on their career paths. In a 2009 survey, volunteering in the Peace Corps was "formally recognized by undergraduate college students as #7" in a list of experiences that would meet their career goals.[10]

In fact, in the twenty-first century, the Peace Corps markets its benefits, including reminding volunteers that there is no fee to participate in the Peace Corps, unlike some other international volunteer programs. A glossy recruiting brochure published in 2005 entitled "Life Is Calling. How Far Will You Go?" states that "volunteers gain valuable cross-cultural experience and improve their foreign language skills, providing a foundation for successful careers in today's global marketplace, receive access to individuals and companies that seek their skills through a variety of job search resources, and have an advantage in applying for certain federal jobs."[11] The benefits page handed out by recruiters in fall 2009 lists the following: full medical and dental coverage while abroad; $6,075 upon completion of service; a monthly living allowance; a passport and work visa; twenty-four vacation days a year; three months of language, technical, and cultural training; free international travel to and from the country of service; two years of international work experience and international contact; and fluency in a foreign language. At the bottom of the page, under "Don't Forget," are "travel adventure, international friendships, and great memories."

For Ben Worthington (Costa Rica 1973–1975), the link between the Peace Corps and career was very clear, even in the early 1970s. In February 1973 he was looking for a job in forestry, and the market "wasn't really that great. I happened to be going in for an interview with a recruiter from the U.S. Forest Service. One of the things he said is that if somebody had gone through the Peace Corps he would hire them directly, without going through all of the competition. So the next week there was a Peace Corps recruiter on campus, and I went over and signed up. About six months later I was working in northern California in the Sierra Mountains, and I got a job offer from the Peace Corps to go to Costa Rica."

Thirty years later, Joshua Mike (Nevis 2004–2006) wanted a

career in international development and considered the Peace Corps a great introduction to development work and diplomacy and a great opportunity for international exposure and language training; in addition, "the financing aspect was incredible because you didn't have to pay to do it." After his post–Peace Corps master's degree at the University of Kentucky's Patterson School of Diplomacy and International Commerce, he was pleased to land a job with the U.S. Agency for International Development (USAID) in Bangkok, Thailand. Abby Gorton (Jordan 2005–2006) completed her master's degree at the Patterson School first; then she saw the Peace Corps as an opportunity to learn Arabic and a step toward a possible career with the Foreign Service. Elizabeth Greene (Niger 2003–2005) studied for a semester in Kenya and then changed her major at the College of Wooster in Ohio from anthropology to international relations, with a focus on development in Africa. "That," she said, "was one of the main reasons why I decided to go into the Peace Corps." Two decades earlier, Kay Roberts (Ecuador 1982–1984) convinced the University of Missouri to count her first year in Ecuador as practical training for her master's in community international development. Her interest began when, as a teenager, she traveled by bus from St. Louis, Missouri, to Guatemala on a Presbyterian Church mission trip; she then studied in Colombia as part of her BA in Latin American studies.

Peace Corps Commercials

Even during the first few years of the Peace Corps, commercials were an important inspiration for joining. They provided catchwords and, on television, a picture of the possibilities. Some of the slogans became well known, especially "the toughest job you'll ever love." Television ads showing a Peace Corps volunteer fishing with people in an African village captured the imagination of some future volunteers.

Marlene Payne (Malaysia 1967–1969) saw the commercials and thought the Peace Corps sounded "intriguing and interesting." William Salazar (Guatemala 1972–1973) remembered the commercials, too. "The ads for Peace Corps were very effective," he said. "I just thought it was an adventure I couldn't pass up." Almost three decades later, Audrey Horrall (Zambia 2000–2002) explained, "When I was in seventh or eighth grade, I saw a television commercial for the

Peace Corps. It piqued my interest because it was traveling to exotic places, which, when I was younger, always fascinated me. I always fantasized about going to different countries and seeing all those different places that you read about and see on television. When I started college I really felt like the next step after college would be the Peace Corps."

Radio was effective, too. Robin Sither (Cameroon 1996–2000) described how he got the Peace Corps inspiration "sitting in my car in Asheville [North Carolina] waiting to go punch the clock for this telemarketing job. I heard a radio advertisement for Peace Corps, and I'd never given Peace Corps a thought. I was like, 'Peace Corps. Okay, I'm going to look into that.'" After he spent six months hiking the entire Appalachian Trail and thinking about the Peace Corps, he applied. Robin was a "military brat," and his "first memories were when we were stationed in Frankfurt, Germany, and we lived in this giant apartment complex, and looking out over the skyline you could still see bombed-out buildings from the war." His mother is Korean, and she barely escaped the atomic bomb because her family was living in Japan during the war. His father served in Vietnam and then learned to fly helicopters and was assigned to South Korea, where he met Robin's mother. However, Robin has strong Kentucky roots. "I've got a lot of cousins and uncles and aunts all over, scattered to the four winds but the epicenter is pretty much Kentucky and Lexington."

Posters at universities were another recruiting tool. Ken Wilson (Malawi 1997–1998) tried to join the Peace Corps as a college freshman in 1982. "I saw a poster saying 'the toughest job you'll ever love.' I thought Peace Corps is exactly what I want to do. I'd been thinking about it since I was fourteen. I tore the little postcard off and filled it out and mailed it off and received a reply about two weeks later saying, 'Thank you very much, but most of our Peace Corps volunteers are college graduates. Call us in three years.' My three years turned out to be thirteen." Ken's dad was in the air force, so the family "traveled a lot domestically. My whole family wanted to go abroad during some station, but each time my dad would get orders to go to Europe, my mom was too far along in her pregnancy for them to move us. I missed being born in England because if my mom had been a few months less pregnant, they would have gone to England for four years, and I would have been born there. But I always wanted to travel, and my peers on the base had traveled all over the world. I'd hear my school friends all talk about 'We were in Saudi Arabia.' Meanwhile, we were in Oklahoma City."

International Experience

Whether their international experience was personal (like Robin's) or vicarious (like Ken's), it influenced volunteers from all decades to join the Peace Corps. Occasionally, children of Peace Corps volunteers became volunteers themselves. About a quarter of the returned volunteers we interviewed had some individual international experience, travel, or study abroad before their Peace Corps experience.

Lloyd Jones (Colombia 1973–1975) was intrigued by the idea of living overseas because his mother and father had met in the Philippines during World War II. Elaine Collins (Micronesia 1989–1991) described her "aunt, who was in the first Peace Corps group in Brazil. She has two scrapbooks that are about her experience in Brazil and I was always really impressed. She had a letter from President Kennedy thanking her for her service. I think that's where the seed was planted in my head." The older sister of Marianna Colten (Ecuador 1981–1983) married a man from India and moved there, where she lived for five years and had her first child. That inspired Marianna to think that "the Peace Corps is a good way to experience the world."

Another influence cited by the volunteers was immigrant parents and grandparents. Joyce Miller's (Chile 1964–1966) father came from Ukraine and her mother came from Lithuania. "We learned about our own culture, plus my father was very interested in history and had been a geography teacher in Ukraine, so this was just part of our life." Bob Olson (Turkey 1963–1965), who grew up in North Dakota, had a Scottish grandfather and a German grandmother, plus his father's parents were Norwegian. Susan Samuel (Liberia 1964–1967) was the grandchild of Jewish immigrants who came to New York City from Poland. "I'm a grandchild of Lebanese immigrants," explained Joshua Mike (Nevis 2004–2006). "My grandfather and my grandmother, who was born in Mexico, settled in Louisville in the twenties."

Dianne Bazell (Zaire [now Democratic Republic of Congo] 1975–1977) grew up in Chicago as a third-generation immigrant— her father's parents were Lithuanian Jews, and her mother's parents were Dutch. Even before joining the Peace Corps, she saw herself as "a citizen of the world, interested in international things, and understanding 'newcomerhood.'" One of her closest friends in high school was Greek. "We would go to her house and her *yaya* would bake and I would bring back feta cheese to our refrigerator. It would drive my mother crazy." Dianne's experiences with people from other countries expanded when she went to Bowdoin College in Maine. "My roommate was one of the very few African American students there, and within about two weeks she began dating one of three Ethiopian students on campus. So I knew all the Africans, a Zairean, and a couple Nigerians, just because they would either visit our room or I would see them on campus. I wanted to see the world through a set of cultural lenses other than ones that would be very familiar to me. I asked to go to an African country."

Sometimes family members' experiences traveling and living overseas offered motivation and encouragement to future volunteers. Sheila McFarland (Micronesia 1972–1974 and Philippines 1974–1976) was influenced by her grandmother, who was "very much a lady of the world. She went around the world with her dad in 1920. One of her sisters was a missionary in China, so when she went back to China, great-grandfather and grandmother went along. My grandmother always said giving to missions is very important. You've got to think of your fellow man." Sheila and her husband Cecil (also Micronesia 1972–1974 and Philippines 1974–1976) both grew up in and returned to Anderson County, Kentucky, after retirement, following Cecil's career with USAID. They were role models for their daughter Kathleen (Jordan 1999–2001). "I grew up with the stories my parents told me," she said. "In fact, I thought all Peace Corps volunteers did two services in two different countries." As a child, Kathleen lived the expatriate life in Guyana, Guatemala, and Kenya; then she spent two summers in Egypt working at the American embassy while she was attending Transylvania University. However, she credits the Peace Corps with providing her the opportunity to really experience how others live.

Both daughters of Tom and Susan Samuel (Liberia 1965–1967 and 1964–1967) became volunteers—in Turkmenistan and Namibia. One of their daughters then served in Malawi, working in the HIV/AIDS field through the Peace Corps Crisis Corps, now called Peace Corps Response, a short-term opportunity for returned volunteers. Deborah Payne, daughter of Marlene (Malaysia 1967–1969) and

John Payne, who was a Peace Corps physician in Malaysia, served in Uganda from 2007 to 2009. Mark Miller, son of Joyce (Chile 1964–1966) and George Miller (Washington staff, Tonga 1979–1982), served in Congo Brazzaville in 1997.

Other parents who had traveled or lived overseas sometimes set the stage for their children. Abby Gorton's (Jordan 2005–2006) parents had lived in Germany and Korea with the military and thought the Peace Corps sounded interesting. The father of Jules Delambre (Cameroon 1965–1967) spent two years in Venezuela as a welding supervisor, so Jules read everything he could about Venezuela and became interested in Latin America. Visiting her father in Turkey and Europe was important for Cori Hash (Zimbabwe 1999–2000), but her mother was influential, too. "My mom really taught me about giving back and doing something that's important to you, that makes a difference in your life."

Kristen Perry's (Lesotho 1999–2001) parents "were conscious of wanting to help me and my sister be wise about the world." In high school she traveled to Spain with her mother, and "we had an exchange student from Germany who came and lived with us for a year, which was really wonderful. She helped me a lot with my German studies. We also hosted a Japanese exchange student for a summer." Kristen spent a college semester in Oxford, England, too.

Like Kristen, other volunteers in all decades cited individual study or travel abroad as a reason for joining the Peace Corps. John Skeese (Nigeria 1961–1964) had been in the army in Germany and participated in international work camps in Spain and Greece, and Marlene Payne (Malaysia 1967–1969) had spent two years in Norway on a Fulbright scholarship studying social psychology. Later volunteer Rachel Savane (Guinea 1990–1992) attended a folk high school in Denmark and applied for a Fulbright scholarship in Sweden at the same time she applied to the Peace Corps. Twenty-first-century volunteer Ashley Netherton (Senegal 2003–2005) studied in France and Belize and did research in Australia before her Peace Corps tour.

How have such international experiences prepared individuals to consider joining the Peace Corps? Researchers have described the impact of international experience in somewhat different but overlapping ways: (1) intellectual development, development of an international perspective, and personal development, and (2) substantive knowledge, perceptual understanding, personal growth, and interpersonal connections.[12] Returned volunteers with prior international experience illustrate how these outcomes might lead an individual to desire a more extensive and deeper international experience and thus apply to the Peace Corps. For example, in describing his junior year at the University of Exeter in England in 1961–1962, Dan Sprague (Colombia 1963–1965) mentioned both an interest in the world and interpersonal relationships. "It opened my eyes to an international arena that I didn't appreciate or understand very much before. I lived in a dorm with Nigerians and Yugoslavs and a very rich international community, and it really got me interested in the world, so I came back and finished my senior year at Washington and Jefferson and became keenly interested in the Peace Corps." Sarah Payne (The Gambia 1989–1991) studied for twelve weeks in Mexico and then traveled for two weeks in Guatemala, Costa Rica, and Nicaragua. She described learning about other cultures—intellectual development—and also gaining a consciousness of her own perspective and the practice of nonchauvinism—both attributes of perceptual understanding. "I knew that I wanted to be overseas. I loved learning from different cultures. I knew I wanted some type of service component, and Peace Corps was one of the few organizations that didn't have a real religious component to it, because I didn't want to be pushing my religion on other people." Perceptual understanding also encompasses empathy, something Maurice White (Afghanistan 1974–1976) learned during six months in India during his junior year in college. "I was profoundly affected by that trip in many ways, and I thought I wanted to do something to help mankind." Although not raised in the interviews, other aspects of personal growth gained from previous international experience, such as self-confidence and independence, may have encouraged individuals to apply to the Peace Corps. A recent book about intercultural student teaching concludes: "International lived experience sets the stage for developing a consciousness of multiple realities and serves as the stimulus that prompts new learning."[13]

Several interviewees had a rich combination of study, travel, and work abroad before joining the Peace Corps. For instance, Abby Gorton (Jordan 2005–2006) lived in Argentina for three months as a high school student, spent a semester in Chile as an undergraduate, and taught English in China for several years after graduating from college. She later interned at the U.S. consulate in Chennai, India, as part of her master's degree from the University of Kentucky's

Patterson School of Diplomacy. Joshua Mike (Nevis 2004–2006), whose mother was a Spanish teacher, went to Europe twice as a high school student; studied in Mexico and in Segovia, Spain, during his undergraduate years; and taught English in Brazil for six months before his Peace Corps tour. Sara Todd (Armenia 2001–2003) grew up in a biracial family in Milwaukee, Wisconsin, and started going to a German immersion school when she was four years old. "I think that was my first experience with another foreign culture. That's where I became interested in travel, when I was young." Sara's parents traveled in Europe, and her cousins had traveled too, so she grew up hearing their stories. She first studied abroad in Germany during high school and also traveled to Italy and Austria. In college she studied twice more in Germany on a yearlong program and then a summer program. "When I graduated [with a degree in international studies and economics and a minor in German], I decided I loved to travel and wanted to do more, and Peace Corps sounded like a perfect thing to do."

Like Sara's attendance at a German immersion school, international experience sometimes took place in the United States. "Living in Texas, I had interacted with a lot of people from Latin America, had been living around Mexicans all my life, and I felt some affinity," explained Bill Davig (Peru 1965–1967). "I was interested in economic development, so I thought the Peace Corps could be a good opportunity for me." Bill had served in the navy and worked in a bank for three years before going to the University of Houston for a math degree.

Besides his parents' meeting in the Philippines, the International Banana Festival was an early influence on Lloyd Jones (Colombia 1973–1975), who grew up in the small town of Fulton in far western Kentucky. When he was young, the town hosted the Banana Festival, "so we always had an influx of international people, mostly from South America. I can vividly remember the Banana Festival was an integral part of the Alliance for Progress, which came out during the Kennedy years, and I can remember, as a fourteen-year-old, sitting at the Fulton High football stadium right next to Averell Harriman, who was Kennedy's ambassador-at-large at that time. He was right there in Fulton and made several speeches. They even had an international soccer match between Ecuador and Guatemala." After returning from Colombia, Lloyd was the first returned Peace Corps volunteer to attend the Patterson School of Diplomacy at the

University of Kentucky, and he met Harriman again when the latter was a guest speaker at the school.

Four returned volunteers we interviewed were born and began their lives in other countries, so they had special international experiences and backgrounds. Another was born in the United States of Nigerian parents who were graduate students at Ohio University in Athens, Ohio, at the time.

Born in England, Jeff Kell (Dominican Republic and Ecuador 1962–1963) came to the United States when he was nine. His father, a musician, was looking for more opportunities. After Jeff earned an undergraduate degree at the University of Colorado, he went to Australia for a year. When he came back, he recalled, "I wasn't through traveling and got very interested in the world in general. That's when I decided to join the Peace Corps, but then I found out you couldn't join unless you were an American citizen, which I was not. So I set out doing something about that and joined up with the Peace Corps."

Richard Bradshaw (Central African Republic 1977–1979) was born in Tokyo, Japan, of missionary parents who "believed in engaging in activities which were of use to people." He explained:

My father worked in a hospital as a chaplain when I was very young, and I was influenced in part by that. Later we lived in Hiroshima, and often when people came to visit I was asked, or one of my brothers was asked, to take them to the Peace Museum. So from a very young age I had it in mind to become a doctor. I intended to go to medical school, but right at the end of college I got a call from the U.S. Information Agency, and they wanted me to go to Japan to work as a translator at an oceanography exposition in Okinawa. After that I decided to travel, and during that period of travel I became very aware that health problems are essentially social problems. I decided to try to work in public health. I met Peace Corps volunteers in different places, and they seemed to be quite happy with their jobs and doing things that I thought were quite admirable, so I decided to join Peace Corps for that reason.

In 1956, when he was seven, Angel Rubio (Costa Rica 1971–1973) moved with his parents from Cuba to Miami. They were motivated by visits from cousins who told them, "'The streets are paved with gold and your children will do better.' We were probably typical immigrants. We started pretty close to downtown, and then as my parents got better jobs and saved some money, we kept moving north and away from the downtown area toward the cousins and more Americanized neighborhoods. They were very self-conscious that they wanted the kids to really adapt and learn the language and fit in." Angel recalled driving through the streets of San José when he first arrived in Costa Rica and being reminded of "where I had grown up those first seven years in Cuba. And I thought, 'Wow, this is really cool.'" He was the only native speaker of Spanish in his group, but "a Cuban and a Costa Rican talk completely different kinds of Spanish."

Born in the state of Chihuahua in northern Mexico, William Salazar (Guatemala 1972–1973) arrived in Phoenix, Arizona, when he was five. His father had come to do agricultural work with the bracero labor program in the 1950s and would return to Mexico during the winter, but "the way the story goes, my mom just didn't want to be a widow anymore." William followed the crops with his family from southern to northern California, but they always returned to Phoenix after Labor Day. They lived "in a different house in a different neighborhood every year," he recalled, "usually a low-rent house in a white neighborhood because of the schools. My mom really valued education simply because she didn't have the opportunity. What made it possible for my siblings and me to maintain Spanish is that my mom had a functional vocabulary of 150 words in English and my father 40, so we had to translate for them when we'd buy a refrigerator or sign a lease for a house or buy a car. And later on, as I got more interested in really speaking Spanish very well and reading it, my mom would tutor me as far as reading, so I grew up bilingually." William remembered cultural identity being important as he grew up in the 1960s. "That's probably one of the reasons why I'm so interested in culture and cultural diversity and multiculturalism and speaking two languages. And that also led me to volunteer for Peace Corps later on."

Although Oghale Oddo (Jamaica 1994–1996) lived in the United States as a young boy, first in Athens, Ohio, until he was about seven and then in New York City for a year, he returned to Nigeria with his mother for the rest of his education through college.

My mom was a high school teacher. She taught home economics and economics and she became a principal in the Delta region of Nigeria.

And my dad is a university professor in Port Harcourt—he teaches forestry. I first got to know about Peace Corps when I was about ten years old. My dad was still in the United States, doing his PhD at the University of Florida in Gainesville. I came to the United States on vacation, and on my way back to Nigeria I met a Peace Corps volunteer on the plane. This tall white guy was speaking Pidgin English [like a Nigerian] to me. I was just so surprised that he could speak Pidgin because I'd been in the States for three months. At that time I never imagined anyone could understand Pidgin, let alone some other African language. Anyway, I was really fascinated and I asked him where he learned the language. He said he was a Peace Corps volunteer. I can't remember what country he was working in, but he was definitely from West Africa. I thought, "Wow!" When he told me about what he was doing, I thought this was something I would like to do later on in life. You know, when I grow up I want to go back to the United States and become a Peace Corps volunteer. He also taught me to play blackjack on the plane, so I went back to my community and taught my friends, all the ten-year-olds in the neighborhood, how to play blackjack.

PRIOR VOLUNTEER COMMUNITY SERVICE

Occasionally, international experience included community service that prompted individuals to think about the Peace Corps. For instance, Lauren Goodpaster (Malawi 2005–2007) attended Birmingham Southern as a college student and had two service learning experiences abroad—one in Mutambara, Zimbabwe, and one in Calcutta, India. "The villages in Zimbabwe, that's really what got me to fall in love with Africa. We worked with children in the schools, we worked in the hospitals, but it was just really that exchange of human interaction—they were learning about us, and we were learning about them. And it was just such a happy time in my life, it really gave me an energy."

Others, young and old, did volunteer work in the United States that led them to consider the Peace Corps. Elaine Collins (Micronesia 1989–1991) had done a lot of community work with Head Start at the local elementary school. She went to Germany as an exchange student but said, "With the Peace Corps, the big draw was more the idea of helping a community of people, not that it was necessarily international." Participating in a service fraternity in college and working in a soup kitchen prepared Blake Stabler (Russia

2000–2002). He also volunteered at a center for immigrants. "We mainly had people from Somalia at the time, and some older folks from Vietnam who had been in the United States a little longer. I enjoyed working with the people and helping them with their English. I didn't want to go write Internet Web sites and try to sell gifts on gifts.com."

Lettie Heer (Senegal 2001–2003) volunteered with immigrants in Washington, DC, including one girl who was especially memorable:

> I was a mentor for two or three years for a young girl who had been brought over by Catholic Charities. I helped her get into a Catholic high school and realized that time management was very different—I mean, it didn't occur to her to show up on time. I helped her write a life history and learned so much about her life as an Eritrean refugee in the Sudan. Her father was working in Saudi Arabia and was killed over there. Her mom died in childbirth. She lived with her grandparents, and there was no running water, no electricity. Every now and then somebody would hook a television up to a car, and the whole village would come around to watch. So I was hearing all these stories and then watching her transition into an American girl. I just loved [that kind of] work, much more than I did the environmental work [her career]. I could see that there was need. I could feel that I was giving to people, that it was appreciated.

Several Peace Corps volunteers began their service in what is sometimes known as the domestic Peace Corps, VISTA. Older volunteer Peg Dickson (Ukraine 2000–2002) worked with VISTA in Frankfort, Kentucky, focusing on adult education and family literacy. Jenny Howard (Gabon 2000–2002) also served as a literacy volunteer with VISTA, working first in David, Kentucky, and then with the homeless in Phoenix, Arizona. Jenny, who grew up near Fort Knox, Kentucky, remembered her year in the eastern part of her home state as one of the most eye-opening experiences of her life. She was "amazed that there were adults who couldn't read and write and lived in homes where they had dirt floors and no plumbing."

For two of the volunteers we interviewed, their volunteer work in Kentucky was direct preparation for specific Peace Corps jobs. Ron Pelfrey (Ethiopia 1966–1968) joined the Appalachian Volunteers, a group begun on the University of Kentucky campus. "I worked as a math tutor in Wolfe County in a one-room schoolhouse. I went down every Saturday through my junior year to teach math." He later taught math in Ethiopia. Patrick Bell worked with an after-school program at the teen center in the Bluegrass Aspendale housing project in Lexington and went on to do youth work in Costa Rica (1997–1999).

MENTORS AND RETURNED PEACE CORPS VOLUNTEERS

Throughout the five decades, Peace Corps volunteers had mentors. Sometimes these mentors were returned Peace Corps volunteers who were influential in the decision to join.

John Skeese (Nigeria 1961–1964) had just returned from participating in an international work camp in Europe and was considering marrying a woman he had met in Greece. Then he visited a dean at his alma mater, Berea College, who told him, "The Peace Corps is starting. You might be interested in this!" When Phil Dare's (Malaysia 1965–1967) invitation to join the Peace Corps came, he was still working on his master's degree at the University of Kentucky and wasn't sure he should go. "So I told the dean at Midway College, where I was teaching, and then went back to my class. All of a sudden the door to my classroom opened, and he walked in. He'd gone home for lunch and had his paint clothes on. He said, 'Been wrestling with this, thinking it over. You've got to go!' I took him at his word, and we packed up everything. Our first airplane trip was to Hawaii for training in August 1965." Don Stosberg (Malawi 1965–1966), who grew up in Louisville, studied at St. Thomas Seminary for three years of high school and two years of junior college before completing a BA in philosophy and deciding not to become a priest. "There was one thing that happened there that I think is critical to my joining the Peace Corps," he explained. "We had a not very interesting high school teacher. He was boring to most of us, but he would come in and read us the *New Yorker* magazine. We always cheered when he got out the *New Yorker.* He preached against parochialism—get out of your neighborhood, get beyond your boundaries. Even though I didn't like him, that concept was valid and stuck with me." Like Phil, Don's first airplane trip was to training—in New Mexico.

Later volunteers had mentors, too. Ashley Netherton (Senegal 2003–2005) had a professor at Hanover College in Indiana who had been a Peace Corps volunteer in the 1970s between his master's and PhD work. He told her the Peace Corps was a good idea. Gary Griffin (Thailand 2004–2006) was almost fifty when he joined the Peace

Corps. Although he had lived in Germany for a year as a child and had traveled during his three and a half years in the coast guard before going to college, Gary credited two 1960s volunteers for getting him interested in the Peace Corps much later. The adviser for his graduate degree in teacher education (he already had an undergraduate degree in East Asian studies from Indiana University and a law degree from the University of Kentucky) had been a Peace Corps volunteer, and he first learned about the Peace Corps from her in a cross-cultural education class in 1987 at the University of Kentucky. He also had a friend he admired, Paul Winther (India 1961–1963), who called the Peace Corps the single defining event in his life. So why did Gary finally decide to go? He said, "I wanted to do some good. It's something I believe in. I think it is crucial for other countries to see an American, put a face on an American rather than what they hear or read."

Sometimes just meeting a returned Peace Corps volunteer was influential. Eastern Kentucky University (EKU) student Sheila McFarland (Micronesia 1972–1974, Philippines 1974–1976) became interested when she offered a ride to the daughter of the dean of EKU's Business School, who had just returned from a stint with the Peace Corps in Liberia. Tom Boyd (Colombia 1964–1966) was won over by a Peace Corps recruiter who spoke at the Wabash College chapel. He recalled that the recruiter was "wearing a necktie at half mast and a tweed jacket. We're all wearing tweed jackets, but he has on blue jeans and work boots. He's introduced by the dean and gets up and talks about what it's like out in the world. He answered some hostile questions from the professors, that this is sort of a children's crusade, and this young man really held his own. He went over to our coffee shop afterward to meet with anyone, and I followed him over there. By the end of that I had a role model. I was impressed. I thought, by golly, this is something I would like to do independent of anything that has to do with career."

Susan Samuel (Liberia 1964–1967) saw a good-looking man at a bar in San Diego, went over to meet him, and discovered he was a Peace Corps recruiter. He said, "Now you are going to take the test tomorrow, aren't you?" And she said, "Yes, I'll be there." Intrigued by a college course in African civilizations, she had already been thinking about how to get to Africa.

Sara Todd's (Armenia 2001–2003) introduction came in an international careers course that was required for her degree. "Every week they would have a speaker come in [who was involved] in international business or international banking. And they had one come in who had served in the Peace Corps. And I was just really inspired by the talk." Through the Council on Foreign Relations in Oak Park, Illinois, Lettie Heer (Senegal 2001–2003) met a sixty-eight-year-old woman who had been in the Peace Corps. "It had never occurred to me that it was anything other than a young person's game, so I talked with her and thought about it and decided this would be a good time to try." Lettie said, "I had heard of the Peace Corps in 1961, the year I graduated from high school, and I kind of put it in the back of my mind." However, she married before finishing college, had two children, and moved to Kentucky. After she was divorced, she completed a BA at the University of Kentucky, followed by an MA in environmental science. Lettie worked for several corporations and ran her own firm in Louisville doing environmental impact statements. When her children were in college, she moved to Washington, DC, and then to Oak Park, where she met the older returned Peace Corps volunteer who inspired her to join.

Michael Geneve (Mozambique 2003–2005) explained that he had known about the Peace Corps since he was sixteen. He thought about it again when he was a twenty-five-year-old graduate in graphic design with a good job as art director for the Lexington-based *Ace* magazine. "Something wasn't fulfilling my needs. I wasn't sure if it was just one of those crazy ideas that I had about helping people, but I researched it more at this point. They actually had everything online. My friends and family all said I was crazy [except his dad, who travels a lot and said, 'Do that, man!']. 'What are you doing? You've got a really good job and you're on your way up. You have everything you need here. Why do you need to go over there and not have electricity and do this?' I didn't know how to respond. I just told them that I had this void in me, that I needed to see the world and help some people out." Michael also talked with returned volunteers in Lexington, including Tara Loyd (Lesotho 1999–2001). "We did a piece on her in *Ace* magazine, and she told me everything I needed to know about it and really encouraged me. I was really fortunate to meet her."

PRACTICAL IDEALISM

Tara Loyd was herself inspired by a Peace Corps mentor, and she had pragmatic reasons as well as idealistic ones for joining. Her mentor, the director of a camp for people with disabilities in California, where Tara worked during the summers throughout college, had been a volunteer in Paraguay. "She was a real hero of mine," Tara said, "somebody I thought was living her life right. Somehow, I was already interested. I definitely wanted to see her pictures and listen to the tapes she sent home to her mother about her experience. And I felt like I had somebody sort of holding my hand through the very, very long application process." In the fall of her senior year at the University of Virginia, Tara saw investment banks and consulting firms interviewing her friends for $100,000 starting positions. "I didn't get it," she said. "I couldn't even imagine what was happening. The Peace Corps was setting up interviews, and I just thought, I think that's what I want." But Tara was practical, too. Her father was a traveler and a dreamer, and she figured she had lived in thirteen houses while he was getting his medical training before ending up in Lexington, Kentucky. In contrast, her mother was a nester and a homebody. Tara explained that, rather than just "packing up my bags and setting out to see the world by myself, I realized that (probably taking my mother into consideration) I needed to do something a little bit more accountable. The Peace Corps seemed to me a very reliable, accountable organization, medically and politically. I felt like if I were to get into some sort of trouble, they would get me home."

Leigh White's (Bulgaria 2001–2003) rationale for joining was similarly practical and idealistic, and it would resonate with many volunteers from all decades. Leigh felt the need to do something more than get a regular job or go to graduate school right after college. "I knew several people who graduated from Bellarmine [in Louisville] who had gone into the Peace Corps. As well, we had one professor of philosophy at Bellarmine who was in the Peace Corps, and she talked about it frequently in her classes. So it always sounded interesting to me. Plus it meant living abroad, traveling, finding a new language, learning a new culture, all those things. And then there was a part of me that wanted to serve my country in some way. I thought I would be a good 'ambassador of my country,' and at the same time I knew I would be getting a lot of benefit out of it."

Jody Olsen—Peace Corps volunteer in Tunisia, country director in Togo, deputy director of the Peace Corps from 2002 through 2008, and acting director for the first six months of 2009—summed up this practical idealism in an essay written for *Making a Difference: The Peace Corps at Twenty-five*: "I specifically remember wanting to join the Peace Corps long before I could give it a rationale. I wanted to go to another country, live in a new environment, test myself on the unfamiliar terms that I knew I would encounter. I knew I wanted to 'make a difference,' a notion that seems to be a recurring theme among Peace Corps recruits. Who knows where this motivation comes from? In one way or another almost every volunteer has it, combining a fundamental idealism with a practical objective."[14]

Chapter 2

Getting In

I put Pakistan as my first choice on the application because
Hibbing, Minnesota, was 8,000 miles through the globe from
Lahore, Pakistan. And I wanted to get as far away from Hibbing as
I could.
                                        —Bob Olson (Turkey 1963–1965)

It was a time-consuming process and a lot of waiting. I started in
August, filled out an application online, interviewed in Cleveland.
They told me in the interview that I would be nominated. Then
I had to get medical clearance. I was notified of my placement in
March before I graduated. I was offered Niger and accepted.
                                        —Elizabeth Greene (Niger 2003–2005)

Six Volunteers in Five Decades

Martin and Patsy Tracy (Turkey 1965–1967)

Martin remembered that "the application process went smoothly.
We did have to go through a psychologist that we met with, and there
were a lot of questions about whether or not our marriage could sustain living in harsh conditions." Patsy said, "Everything seemed very
routine, except when an aunt of Martin's had been interviewed by
the FBI in California. She was an active member of the John Birch
Society, so we worried that her interview might be the glitch that
might keep us out."

Patsy remembered that her "mother was horrified. My husband
had brought me to rural western Kentucky, which she considered
another planet. And his mother was horrified because she had envi-
sioned maybe having grandchildren sooner. When we decided we

35

would go to Turkey and were determined to do it, people said, 'Well, I guess they're going to do it. We might as well help them.' So then the whole community sort of pitched in to send us off. Our friends gave us a trunk for graduation and gave us things they thought we could use."

Rona Roberts (Philippines 1973–1975)

A recruiter helped Rona and her husband Howell fill out their applications.

> I had a bunch of courses in German but I couldn't speak German, and the recruiter would say, "Put fluent!" I remember the strong sense that we were sort of padding our résumés to some extent. The recruiter also kept saying, "You know both of you must be volunteers." And we're saying, "Well, of course." What he was trying to say was you can't be a tag-along spouse.
>
> In May, a few days before we graduated [she was working on her master's degree in communications, and her husband had just finished his BA at the University of Kentucky], we went to the campus mailbox, and there was a big brown envelope from Peace Corps—one envelope addressed to Howell. And in it was all this exciting information about the Philippines. We had chosen Micronesia as our number one preferred location. They offered the Philippines, and I remember we were standing in the plaza outside King Library and saying, "Where is the Philippines?" So we went into the library and looked at the giant globe, found the Philippines, and said, "It's islands. It will be all right."

In the envelope was a multipage description of the program—supervised agricultural credit. There was also "one badly copied sheet that said 'spouse' at the top. And we just ignored it because we thought it had been inserted by mistake. The recruiter had said we were both going to have jobs, and we presumed we were both being invited into the same program. I had a lot of farming experience, and Howell had raised pigs."

They went to staging in Denver with perhaps sixty or seventy people. "And the whole mode was, 'Do you think you would fit in Peace Corps?' It was basically rule yourself out. They needed people badly. We were long past the era where you had to scale rock faces and survive psychological testing in order to be invited in. We were appalled at some of the people who had come just because they wanted to go to Denver. But in the end thirty people did choose to go [to the Philippines]."

In Denver, Rona learned that she was something called a non-matrixed spouse—a Peace Corps concept that had a short life in the early 1970s. One spouse, usually the man, was accepted because of his skill, and his wife could go along. In Rona's case, both Filipinos and Americans at the staging had assured her that she would get a job, but it became clear that only Howell had been invited to the program. "It was our first introduction to the famous frustrations of Peace Corps bureaucracy." Rona got on the plane not knowing what would happen in the Philippines.

Rebecca Roach (Liberia 1988–1989)

Rebecca completed her degree in elementary education at Morehead State University in December 1987 and left two weeks later for preservice training in Atlanta, Georgia. "I had applied very, very early, and they wanted to send me to the Philippines first. I said no, and I realized it hurt my chances. But I said, 'No, I am meant to work in Africa, and that's where I would be.' So I ended up in Liberia, which was perfect."

Sarah Cross Oddo (Jamaica 1993–1995)

Sarah applied through the campus recruiter at the University of Kentucky. She had several friends who had joined the Peace Corps and terminated their service early, so she was very determined not to do that.

I did the paper application. Since I had French and since in college I was taking African dance classes through Syncopated Inc. and I really, really enjoyed that, I really wanted to go to West Africa. So on my preferences I had put West Africa or the Caribbean. I thought, if I don't go to Africa, then at least the Caribbean will have the African influence. Maybe six months later the first thing the recruiters in Washington offered me was Nicaragua or Panama. I was very discouraged because I didn't want to go to a Spanish-speaking country. So I turned them down and waited, and eventually they offered me Jamaica, which I thought was okay. But in retrospect I sure wish I could speak Spanish now.

Aaron Shraberg (China 2004–2006)

Aaron filled out an online application and wrote essays about why he wanted to join the Peace Corps and what he hoped to gain by joining. He went to campus information sessions and was able to talk with a former volunteer who had just returned.

I met my recruiter at that time, too. Her name was Liz from Chicago, and she was very helpful in answering the questions I had. She knew that I really wanted to go into the Peace Corps. And I interviewed with her on two occasions. The first was a get-to-know-you kind of interview, and we talked about my motivations for joining Peace Corps and what skills I had and what I wanted to do. The second interview was more concentrated on the work itself, what it would be like—I would be an English teacher somewhere overseas—and what I should expect when joining the Peace Corps.

We talked a lot about my personal ability to be flexible, whether or not I'm a patient person, what my personal qualities are, and at the end of the second interview she said she was going to recommend me to go to the next level to be invited into the Peace Corps. At that point I had to get my medical clearance, which was a pretty arduous process. I don't think I had much to worry about—but just getting everything in line, all the paperwork, dotting my *I*'s. All that was probably the most difficult part of the process in the end. And then I got an invitation in the mail. I had to go all the way out to the post office to pick up this special post that needed to be signed for. It said: "Congratulations! You've been invited to join the Peace Corps China program."

Aaron had told his recruiter he had been studying the Chinese language for almost seven years, beginning in high school.

I said I could be a more effective volunteer in China because I could speak the language. She agreed with me but said, "I cannot recommend you for a specific country. That's part of Peace Corps policy." I accepted that reality. The important thing is I wanted to go abroad.

The process took about nine months from start to finish. I probably spent a month or a month and a half deciding whether or not I even wanted to apply. I would go to the library probably four or five times a week, get on the computer, and just look at the Web site. Sometimes I would even open up the application, then realize I had five minutes till class, and I would say, "Okay I'll do it tomorrow." Then one day I just decided, "All right, I've got some time. I'm going to finish this application and press that submit button." And I did. And once I got the ball rolling, it was really exciting and I really set my sights on it.

To apply to the Peace Corps today, an individual can begin the process by logging on to the peacecorps.gov Web site and submitting an application online, as Aaron did. That interested individual might have talked to a friend or a mentor or a recruiter about the Peace Corps or may have seen an ad with the tagline, "Life is calling. How far will you go?"

The Peace Corps Web site provides a lot of valuable information. Besides reading about the mission, programs, and countries, potential applicants can peruse journals of current volunteers and listen to volunteers answer questions such as "Can you stay in touch with family and friends?" and "Do you feel safe?" They can also view picture galleries on topics ranging from housing and lifestyle to teaching and working, search a database of volunteer stories, view a recruitment video, and discover when a Peace Corps recruiter is coming to their area (sometimes the recruiter does an in-person interview, and sometimes a phone interview).

The application asks for educational background, employment history, volunteer activities, and essays on cross-cultural experience and motivation. Three references are requested: from a job supervisor, from a volunteer supervisor, and from a personal acquaintance. After submitting the application, a potential volunteer can check the status of that application online as well. Of course, recommendations (completed online), medical clearance, and background checks are also involved.

In contrast, the 1969 paper application was eleven pages long, with a reference form inside that asked for the names and addresses of at least three employers; at least three professors, advisers, counselors, or teachers; the registrar of the last college or university attended so the Peace Corps could obtain a transcript; the one person who knew the applicant best (could be a relative); and five close personal acquaintances. The applicant had to describe his or her marital status and military status (if male), provide legal information (convictions) and medical information, answer specific education-related questions (including course work and grades), and list teaching and farming experience, foreign travel, sports and hobbies, organizations, primary and additional skills (e.g., auto mechanics, carpentry, child care, cooking, first aid, health or hygiene, masonry, plumbing, sewing, welding), awards, and employment. The final item was a two-page essay: "Tell us why you want to join the Peace Corps. Your motivation for joining is particularly important." The applicant was asked to list three countries and his or her reasons for not wanting to be assigned there, and three countries or areas where the applicant would most like to serve. Foreign language ability was also an item on the application, and applicants were required to take a placement test, given in post offices and on university campuses, to measure language-learning ability.

Testing was an important part of the screening process when the Peace Corps was first organized in 1961. "To become a volunteer, anyone interested had to fulfill the rigorous requirements established by Nicholas Hobbs, the psychologist who became the Peace Corps' first chief of Selection (he had helped develop U.S. Air Force selection methods in World War II). Hobbs decided that applicants should initially take written tests rather than interviews since he felt the latter had little or no predictive efficiency."[1] So besides filling out the comprehensive questionnaire and giving references, early applicants took a six-hour general aptitude and language test and completed a thorough medical exam. Between 1961 and 1963 only one out of five applicants was invited to join, and only one of ten decided to accept. By 1963 Hobbs had changed his mind, and the Peace Corps had simplified the application and reduced the number of psychological tests. It had become apparent that volunteers selected themselves to a great extent, and the tests were not making any difference.[2] Later, interviews became a regular part of the application process.

In terms of actual numbers, the Peace Corps had record numbers of applicants and volunteers in the field in the mid-1960s. By the end of 1962, 32,692 applications had been received and 2,940 volunteers and trainees were in the field. In 1964 a record number—45,653—applied and there were 10,078 in the field. The largest number of volunteers was accepted in 1966—15,556 out of 42,246 applicants. By 1972 the numbers had slumped to 6,894 volunteers in the field from 23,849 applications. In 1982 there were 5,380 in the field and 14,577 applications. Although in 1996 there was an increase in volunteer numbers—6,910—they came from a pool of only 9,187 applicants.[3] In August 2008 the Peace Corps Web site reported there were 8,079 volunteers in the field—the most in thirty-seven years, but far fewer than the goal of 14,000 by 2007 set by President Bush in his 2002 State of the Union address.[4] Applications in 2009 grew 18 percent over the previous year, to 15,000.[5] After the largest single-year dollar increase in its history—$60 million, bringing the total budget to $400 million—the Peace Corps is poised to grow. In January 2010, there were only 7,671 volunteers in seventy-six countries. By September their numbers had increased to 8,655 volunteers in seventy-seven countries.[6]

In comparing these numbers, it is important to remember that the Peace Corps was better known by the public at large in the 1960s, when general enthusiasm, extensive publicity (mostly good), and intensive recruiting netted record numbers of applicants and volunteers.[7] No one asked, as they often did in later decades, "Is there still a Peace Corps?" Indeed, the extensive cover story in the September 1964 *National Geographic* was written by Sargent Shriver himself, with reports from volunteers in Bolivia, Tanganyika, Gabon, Turkey, Sarawak, and Ecuador. In succeeding decades, there were also many more opportunities for people to gain international experience with nongovernmental organizations.

Regardless of when they joined the Peace Corps, volunteers remembered getting in. For some, it was a fairly straightforward process. Kay Roberts (Ecuador 1982–1984) said, "Anyone who can wade through a college education can wade through the application." Over the decades, many of the frustrations were related to the time it took to get in and to get medical clearance—usually months. A third frustration was choice of country. Some volunteers had clear ideas about where they wanted to go. Some got their first choice, but many didn't. Good advice to prospective volunteers over the years was: "Don't be set on one country." Timing, programming needs, and medical issues are all in play.

This chapter continues the story of "getting in" with many more examples. Sometimes the process went smoothly; sometimes not. Persistence could be key, from Dan Sprague's (Colombia 1963–1965) youthful demonstration of push-ups and a handstand to Mimi Gosney's (Slovakia 2000–2002) stubborn insistence on her country choice. Some of the volunteers even suspected that the long process of getting in was itself a test of sorts. Was the applicant patient enough to succeed as a volunteer?

1960s

Memories of getting in during the 1960s focused on country of choice. Only a few volunteers had memories of the early application and tests.

Harold Freeman (Ethiopia 1965–1967) remembered that the application "was probably the longest form I'd ever filled out in my life. There was a fairly detailed language aptitude test which was based on Kurdish or Urdu, something from a part of the world that the test makers assumed the average American college student or other applicant would have no idea about, so no one would have a leg up on anyone else because of previous knowledge. They would give you a language principle or a set of vocabulary words and then ask you questions about them. It was entirely foreign, but I must have passed to some degree anyway."

Joyce Miller (Chile 1964–1966), one of those who applied right after Kennedy's assassination, also remembered the intensive all-day test. She remembered her country of choice as well: "I had requested Nepal and they offered Chile, but I figured it was mountainous, so I would take Chile. I was living in Florida at that time. It was very boring and flat."

Other returned volunteers talked about their countries of choice versus countries of assignment. Nancy Dare (Malaysia 1965–1967) recalled being asked to list three countries, none of which was Malaysia, where she and her husband Phil went. Jules Delambre (Cameroon 1965–1967) put down Peru, Nigeria, and Thailand as his choices. Terry Anderson (Ghana 1965–1967) explained that he did not want to go to South America because some Peace Corps volunteers had just been killed in Colombia. He requested Southeast Asia because he had friends who were agricultural missionaries in Thailand. Invited to Ghana, he knew where the country was because he had been a stamp collector as a child. When the invitation arrived for Bill Sweigart (Liberia 1967–1970) to go to Nigeria in West Africa rather than North Africa, his first choice, he said, "'Oh yeah, fine, sure.' I was in a training program to go to what was soon to become Biafra [the eastern region of Nigeria that broke away and thus began the Nigerian civil war]. So I was to go off and teach math to junior high kids." Because of the war, he was reassigned to Liberia.

Occasionally, volunteers got their choice of region or even country. Tom Boyd (Colombia 1964–1966), who had written a paper on

Colombia in college and taken Spanish, asked for Latin America. Fred Cowan (Ethiopia 1967–1969) had written his senior thesis on the Ethiopia-Somalia conflict.

Then there were medical issues. Dan Sprague (Colombia 1963–1965) related the following story:

> I got a letter in late spring 1963 saying that my application had been accepted for training, and that I got my third choice of places to go, which was South America. As the training would begin in September, I worked that summer. I was visiting some friends and getting ready to say good-bye to people, when I got a telegram in the middle of the night saying that they had reviewed my medical history and saw I had a shoulder that would separate. It was an old high school football injury, and it didn't happen very often, but when it did, it was pretty painful. They thought I was a medical risk, especially because I was going into a group of physical education and health people. Through my father's contacts, he set up an appointment for me at Walter Reed Hospital to have that shoulder x-rayed and examined. I remember sitting out in Lafayette Park in front of the White House near the Peace Corps office. I had met with a stern physician, and he said, "I don't know. This could be a problem. Are you actually using that arm a lot?" I quickly snapped off a few push-ups and then I did a handstand against his wall, and he said, "All right. You go outside." I spent about an hour and a half in that park just wondering what was going to happen and what I would do. I was really very eager to go into the Peace Corps. The doctor called me back in and said, "The most important thing we're impressed with is how much you want to do this, and that will overcome a lot of other things. So you're back in the training program." I had told them I would sign away any liability for the Peace Corps if anything happened to that shoulder while I was there. They agreed to that.

What was it like to get the acceptance letter? The parents of Jim Archambeault (Philippines 1966–1968) didn't know he had applied. He described their reaction:

> Appalled would not be too strong a term. They wanted me to get a job and proceed on with my life as they envisioned it. Finally they accepted it, of course. I remember the day I got the letter from the Peace Corps. My mother was downstairs. I was still in bed. It must have been a Saturday. Anyway, the Peace Corps letter came. And she ran upstairs into my

bedroom, waving it. She was so excited about it. I said, "Well, read it." And she opened it and read it, and I was accepted. And she was just as happy as I was. It was a defining moment in my life. And from then on, everything changed in many, many ways. The letter was actually signed by Sargent Shriver. I still have it. It said I was accepted into training at the University of Hawaii, which was a bonus I didn't even anticipate. And I accepted. I think the letter came in August and we went into training in October.

1970s

From the beginning, the basic requirements for joining the Peace Corps were being at least eighteen years of age—the oldest volunteer to serve was eighty-six—and being a U.S. citizen. A college education was not required. In fact, the Peace Corps Web site clearly states that although "having a four-year college degree by the time you're ready to leave for the Peace Corps will help your chances of acceptance, it isn't absolutely necessary, and for some programs work experience, relevant skills, and/or a community college degree can qualify you."[8]

Though only nineteen and just finishing his freshman year of college, William Salazar (Guatemala 1972–1973) was considered a good candidate because Spanish was his first language and he had done agricultural work. He was part of an experimental advance training program called PREST, "like pre-enlistment, which was really quite a lot of fun because I got a chance to bond with people whom I eventually went to Guatemala with." His age was an issue in another way, though. He recalled, "Some of us were in Denver for a two-day period of interviews and they said, 'We're going to this place and have a couple of drinks.' And I said, 'I'm sorry guys. I can't go with you because I'm not old enough.'"

Being accepted was not a given, and sometimes exerting political pressure or applying a second time with more experience was necessary. Maurice White (Afghanistan 1974–1976), who was living in Vermont, applied in his junior year but didn't hear anything until his senior year, when one of his college classes went to Washington, DC, and visited Senator Aiken's office. "I told him about my Peace Corps application and how I hadn't heard anything. That afternoon someone from his office called Peace Corps, and the very next week I got my letter of acceptance." Sally Spurr (Ecuador 1975–1977) was not accepted when she applied right out of college with a teaching certification in psychology and sociology. So she worked in a mental hospital in Louisville at night, did substitute teaching during the day, and saved money to travel in Europe with a friend. Then she went to Israel and later to Morocco. "All of that was adventure and fun, and I really got the feel for traveling," she said. "After that my goal was to go either to Africa or to South America. I wanted to see how people lived in other continents, what we called the Third World at that time. I ended up going to South America with another female, traveling, backpacking. I met Peace Corps volunteers everywhere. In Ecuador I put my tent up outside Peace Corps people's houses and went in and met the Peace Corps director. In Peru I also hooked up with Peace Corps people and stayed there for six months. I applied as a field enrollee to the Peace Corps, where the country requests you. They knew that I was acculturated and really wanted to be there. I came back to Louisville, and it took nine months to process everything. I went to Ecuador in community development."

The experience of Ann Neelon (Senegal 1978–1979), who joined after college, was more typical. She remembered her interview with the recruiter in Boston. "I talked up the teaching English as a second language connection because I was an English major and associate editor of the paper, and it seemed pretty certain I would get to do that. In those days you had to have all your wisdom teeth out, and I had them all out at once. About five months later I was on my way."

1980s

Volunteers who served in the 1980s also remembered medical issues, country of choice versus country assignment, the long wait, and a few other glitches.

The long process of applying wasn't too overwhelming for Kay Roberts (Ecuador 1982–1984). "I don't remember too much about it, except that when I got to the medical exam, I did not pass because I didn't have enough iron in my blood. They agreed to let me work on that a little bit, so I went home and spent probably about a month eating red meat and beets and broccoli. Then I went back and had another blood test, and my iron level was just fine, and away I went." She had a phone interview, all the pertinent background checks, and got letters of recommendation. She got her first choice of countries, Ecuador.

Andrew Kimbrough (Sri Lanka 1984–1986) had minored in Spanish in college and gone on mission trips to Honduras and Guatemala, so he assumed the Peace Corps would find some place in Central or South America for him, but he was told he could be better used in Thailand, Nepal, or Sri Lanka. "My godfather Ed moved over to Thailand, where he still resides. So I knew where Thailand was, and I knew where Nepal was, but I had no idea where Sri Lanka was. And sure enough, I got posted in Sri Lanka, the one country I couldn't find on a map." Andrew remembered driving from Wake Forest in North Carolina, where he went to college, to Washington, DC, with a friend for an interview. "What I found a bit disconcerting at the time was the long wait once we were accepted conditionally, five or six months before we were asked to report anywhere."

Sarah Payne (The Gambia 1989–1991) also applied while in college. She had a Spanish-language background and wanted to serve in Latin America. Because she knew the application process could be a long one, she bartended for about eight months after college while she waited. She had just decided to give up and move to Kentucky, where her boyfriend was, when she finally heard from the Peace Corps. "About two weeks before I planned to move I got a phone call saying, 'We found a position for you.' It was in The Gambia, and I'm talking on the phone and reaching for my atlas at the same time because I had no idea where The Gambia was."

A 1985 college graduate with a degree in English and creative writing, Glen Payne (Gabon 1989–1992) was working for his family's construction company and studying for a master's degree in linguistics and literature at the University of Akron when he applied to the Peace Corps. Then "I got a letter saying, 'We want you to come to China. We're going to open a program in China. There's going to be extra training. They're going to be extra careful about Beijing's needs.' I'm very excited. I know there is going to be three weeks of training in California. But you'll recall that 1989 is when Tiananmen Square happened. So the plug got pulled in the blink of an eye. They said, 'There's not going to be a program in China, at least not for the near future. So what else do you do?' I'm a builder, right? So I was asked to go to Gabon in West Africa as part of a school construction program. I thought, well, great. I'm equally excited to go to Africa." Glen said, "I think the application process is partly filtering out people who are having trouble keeping their life together." He remembered "some flags getting thrown." One was a DUI when he was twenty. Another was the fact that he was working on a master's degree. "And I said, 'No, no. My life is all together.' So I worked it out with the faculty at the University of Akron to continue my master's work while I was in Africa." In fact, Glen took a thirteenth-century Norse manuscript, a saga of Andrew the apostle written in Icelandic, with him to Gabon to translate into English. "I'm doing this at night with a candle or a kerosene lantern, sitting on a wooden bench with my stub of a pencil. But I got it done and managed to turn it in and get my master's degree."

1990s

Volunteers from the 1990s talked about similar issues related to "getting in," but their descriptions were somewhat fuller than those of earlier volunteers.

Jenifer Payne (Gabon 1990–1992), who met Glen in Gabon and later married him, applied during her senior year in college and was invited to go to Papua New Guinea in June. However, that summer a medical checkup uncovered a problem that had to be corrected and monitored, so the invitation was retracted. After working at a bank for a year and a half—"boring, boring, boring"—she was chosen for Gabon. "When I got my second invitation, I quit my job the next day!" However, Jenifer had second thoughts because she had waited so long. "I thought, are you running to do something different?" Then one night she heard missionaries at her church talking about their projects. "They said, 'Everybody has to find some place to give. You don't have to go to Africa and build wells, but you have to know in your heart what you can do to contribute to society. You may not be the one, but some people have to go because we have so much here, and there are people all over the world who have nothing and need help. You can't look at the person next to you and say that person is going to do it, because that person may not. Unless you do it, you're part of the problem, not the solution.' And it was like they were talking to me. How did they know what I was thinking? So I took that as my divine sign from God to just stop thinking about it and just go."

Africa, "somewhere where French was the official language," was the request of Debra Schweitzer (Mali 1993–1996). "I'd just always known that I wanted to go to Africa, and I had some French in high school and college. I remember that it was a very long application.

You had to write about why you wanted to join the Peace Corps, what kind of experiences you'd had. You had to have references. I just had a phone interview. There's a lot of bureaucracy after the acceptance. You had to go get your shots, get your yellow World Health Organization card, get your background checked. I was invited to go to Mali in small enterprise development."

Getting a letter from her dentist about her wisdom teeth was a requirement for Carolyn Cromer (Morocco 1992–1995), but she almost didn't go to Morocco. "I was offered Morocco in May 1992 and turned it down at first because it wasn't sub-Saharan Africa. I understood I could turn down two countries and still get another invitation, but I was told there was nothing else available and that I could reapply in a year. I said let me think about this over the weekend, and I talked to a recently returned volunteer from Morocco who was a friend of a friend of a friend, and through some soul-searching and talking with other people who had experience with Morocco, I decided it was worth not having to wait another year. It was worth going for."

Brian Arganbright (Slovakia 1991–1994) remembered that although Penn State had a Peace Corps recruiter, he contacted Peace Corps Washington directly. He was asked to consider going to a French-speaking country because he was completing a master's in French and had taught in France. But, he said, "Peace Corps was just starting to go to Eastern Europe, and I really wanted to be a part of that. I wanted a break from French." He was delighted to be assigned to what was then Czechoslovakia and was "just hungry, hungry, hungry for information about the language, the culture, the literature. It was an exciting time, too, because I could put aside all my French stuff and focus on a new country and a new way of life and a new people."

In 1990 Oghale Oddo (Jamaica 1994–1996), who had been born in Ohio of Nigerian parents, returned to the United States after finishing his university degree in Nigeria. He worked for a while as a bank cashier and had a little business selling African cloth, but he wanted to join the Peace Corps. So in 1993 he submitted an application. "It was funny, because at first they were thinking of sending me to a West African country, but I could not pass the medical exam. They said something about my being allergic to chloroquine, so I couldn't go to any of those malaria countries, which was interesting because I had been in Nigeria for almost fourteen years and had malaria every year during that period. But I got called to go to Jamaica. I actually requested Eastern Europe because I did business management in school."

"Desperate to get in the Peace Corps, to get out of Wichita Falls," Ken Wilson (Malawi 1997–1998) said, "I didn't really care where I went, even though they were talking about Latin America at first. I would have gone, but I wanted to see Africa, and thankfully, that's what they offered me right off the bat. I had no idea where Malawi was. At first I thought Maui, Hawaii. So I found an encyclopedia, found Malawi." Ken described the application as "rather grueling. I didn't have a computer, so I used a typewriter. I wanted it so desperately. I felt like I was campaigning for president. I wrote so many personal statements, told my whole life story, working my way through thirteen years to finally get a degree, just how much that had taught me." Like some of the others we interviewed, Ken remembered being concerned about getting medical clearance. "The medical part seemed really difficult. I was very honest. I told them that my back wasn't very good and I'd been to a chiropractor. They never mentioned it at all. But through one of my medical exams it was suggested I might be infertile. So Peace Corps wanted to make sure that I understood I might be infertile and that once I got on the government payroll I wouldn't claim for the government to fix me afterward. But they didn't care about my back. And the first thing I did, within a month of being in my village, was to pull my back out by drawing water at the bore hole."

Tara Loyd (Lesotho 1999–2001) remembered being under the impression that it was pretty hard to get in to the Peace Corps. "They asked me questions like did I have a country of preference, did I have a church I needed to be near, was I worried about leaving my boyfriend. I said, 'You can put me anywhere in the world you want. I don't have a boyfriend I'm going to miss, I don't need to be near a church. I can be sent as far away from here as you can send me.' But really I was pretty anxious about being sent to Africa." Peace Corps Washington called Tara a week before she was supposed to depart and told her that her dental records had expired; she would have to wait until February and go to the Dominican Republic. But she assured the Peace Corps that she could get new dental records in less than a week. "I went to my dentist, begged him to take out my wisdom teeth and everything else that needed to happen. And I was there! I got to the Radisson Hotel in DC, where we did our staging before we departed for Peace Corps training. I wasn't on any of the rosters. I was sure they didn't have a plane ticket for me. But it was just the hotel that had messed up, not the Peace Corps. They did have a plane ticket for me. I remember being homesick and nervous. I guess I thought everybody would be about my age, and it was very interesting to see people in their midcareer or retirement. I shared a room with a woman who was just my mother's age, and she got on the phone crying to say good-bye to her daughter just before I got on the phone crying to say good-bye to my mother." Tara flew to southern Africa with fifteen other volunteers; it was 1999, and her seatmate and fellow new volunteer had never been on a plane before.

"Frustrating" was the word Cori Hash (Zimbabwe 1999–2000) used to describe the application process. "It tried my patience. I really wanted to go to Latin America. My background was in Latin America and I spoke Spanish. It made sense to me. But they didn't have programs that were leaving that time of year that matched my skills. So I said, what about Eastern Europe? Then they found out I had childhood asthma, and I swore, I pleaded, I promised. I don't even carry an inhaler. I had to see tons of doctors who would confirm my asthma was okay, and eventually I got shipped to Zimbabwe, where they must have put people with asthma, because about half the other people there had asthma. When I first got the assignment I didn't know anything about Africa, about Zimbabwe." After being in Zimbabwe only five months, Cori, a community education resource volunteer, was evacuated from her town to the capital, Harare, for several months. Most of the volunteers were then sent home, hoping to return after the election. Ironically, six months later the Peace Corps found something for Cori in El Salvador, working in water sanitation. But she had just gotten a job in the States and declined the opportunity.

2000s

As online communication became more commonplace, the way potential volunteers applied to and got in to the Peace Corps changed substantially. However, the process was still fairly straightforward for some and very frustrating for others. Several volunteers described how their persistence in the application phase eventually paid off. The 2000s was also a decade of increasing numbers of older volunteers with long life histories. Older volunteer Harry Siler (South

Africa 2001–2003) was one case study in persistence. He finally discovered that his application was being held up because he had had a drinking problem at one time. After he was turned down, he called Peace Corps Washington and then wrote a letter saying, "You have made a tremendous error in judging me." He got a call from a counselor who reversed the decision, and he went off to serve in South Africa.

In contrast, the experience of Leigh White (Bulgaria 2001–2003) was fairly typical for someone applying before college graduation. She started in August at the beginning of her senior year. "It was kind of a long process, but I did turn everything around as quickly as I could. I got everything in, and as soon as they sent me the next notice, I turned it in. Then I went and met a recruiter in Lexington to do a personal interview. She said, 'We can let you in, but now it's time for the medical stuff.'" Leigh remembered a dental exam, an eye exam, and getting fingerprinted. "It's kind of a blur now. But I remember in February 2001 I was teaching English as a second language to adult students through the Jefferson County Public School System in Louisville at night as a volunteer, and there was actually a Bulgarian woman in my class. I was so excited because all my students knew I was applying to go into the Peace Corps. And she just looked at me and said, 'Why would you want to go to Bulgaria?' You know, she'd worked so hard to get here. And she didn't understand why an American would be, in her opinion, running away."

For Blake Stabler (Russia 2000–2002), as for Leigh, "the recruiting process was smooth." In the fall of his senior year of college he went to the recruiting office in the federal building in Atlanta and got an application, which he typed on an electric typewriter in the student center. "I had to go downtown one day for an interview, where I was asked that fateful question: 'Do you want to learn French?' And I said, 'No, I didn't like French in high school.' And they said, 'What about Russian?' And I said, 'Russian sounds interesting.'" By midwinter he was through with the medical part. The invitation came in May, with an August departure date.

Jenny Howard (Gabon 2000–2002) remembered the application process as tedious but exciting. "I wrote my soul-searching essay for the Peace Corps—what I could offer—on the island of Maui, where I went with friends for New Year's 2000, when everybody thought the world was going to end. But I felt on top of the world, literally. I had decided this was what I was going to do. I actually applied for my passport in Hawaii, and I thought that was glamorous." She turned down her first invitation to Niger. "I'm just a green person," she explained. "I'm from Kentucky, by golly. I had told the recruiter and put on the application that I'd go anywhere in the world except those five Sahara Desert countries. I'm a little embarrassed now because I know I could have done Niger. At the time, however, I was still a Kentucky girl who had only been to Arizona. So they said, "Okay, we'll give you a choice of Côte d'Ivoire or Gabon.' I did some research and let them know within that week that I would go to Gabon, and that was a good thing, because within a year they had pulled Peace Corps out of Côte d'Ivoire."

Older volunteer Gary Griffin (Thailand 2004–2006) wanted to go to Thailand to see how Buddhists lived day to day, and he got his "top pick." Gary applied in September 2003, and by January 2004 he was in Thailand. "I think it was probably a record for Peace Corps," he said. "Most of the people in my group had been in the process for probably a year, some of them eighteen months." Gary was rare in another way: he went to Thailand by himself, while his wife stayed home. Both of them had to sign documents to the effect that there were no marital problems and there would be no financial problems. Gary's wife came to visit him the following January for a month, and he went home to Eugene, Oregon, for a month the next September. They talked on the phone almost every Sunday.

Older volunteers Peg Dickson (Ukraine 2000–2002) and Mimi Gosney (Slovakia 2000–2002) are case studies of persistence. Both finally got assigned to the countries they requested. Peg remembered the online application as being very frustrating:

I think it took me at least two months to complete it. It was not an easy task. And then I thought, "There, that's done." Well, that's just the beginning. I had to get a transcript from the first college I attended, telephone interviews, medical forms. I was trying to get it all done before my graduation from college. The day before my friends and family were to arrive for my graduation, I was trying to track somebody down to get a signature on a form, and I could not connect with this person. And I just threw up my hands and said, "I can't do it!" After graduation I called Washington and they said, "Well, you really don't need that. Send in what you've got and we will see whether you need anything more." I really wanted to go to the former Soviet Union or Eastern Europe, and during my interview I was given an indication that's where I would probably go.

But they offered me the Philippines, and for a number of reasons I did not accept the Philippines. That group was leaving sooner than I had planned to go, and it just wasn't the part of the world I had thought about going to.

Peg left six weeks later with the last group to Ukraine.

In contrast, Mimi thought the application process went fast. "Most people say it's slow. I got online and asked for a packet. They sent it to me. I filled it out. A fellow called from Chicago and did the oral interview. He said, 'It sounds good to me. We'll get your medical stuff in order, and your invitation will be in the mail.' There was something insane that had to be done, maybe the thyroid test." Mimi wanted very much to go to Slovakia. Her father, a journalist, had been stationed there during World War II when he was captured by the Nazis and executed. She was first assigned to Moldova, but after several phone calls she persuaded the Peace Corps to let her go with the last group to Slovakia. When someone in Washington told her she couldn't go to Slovakia because they didn't offer mammograms there, she told them, "Vienna, Austria, is right across the border."

Sometimes frustration occurred because of the difficulty communicating with Peace Corps Washington. Older volunteer Lettie Heer (Senegal 2001–2003), who had worked in the environmental field for many years, complained, "I was not impressed with the application process or with the fact that it was very difficult to get hold of anybody. We volunteers figured this yearlong deal was their way of getting rid of people. They did not make selections based on what your background was. They were not interested in what I knew and what I didn't know. The associate Peace Corps director for environment in Senegal had never read my résumé. They weren't linking you with a government agency. They were putting you out in a village, and we figured they wanted to see what your stamina was."

Joshua Mike (Nevis 2004–2006) had to complete his application while living and working in Brazil. He had his medical exam there, sent the results to Washington, and received an e-mail saying they were "undecipherable." Joshua replied, "You guys find somebody who can read it. *Carboidratos* are carbohydrates. The numbers are the same." They eventually accepted the exam, and he worked with his recruiter to figure out a program that was starting after his return from Brazil. With his Spanish and Portuguese skills, he wanted Latin America—he got the English-speaking eastern Caribbean.

Miscommunication with Washington was also a problem for

Michael Geneve (Mozambique 2003–2005). He wanted to go to a former Soviet bloc country, but the Peace Corps said, "'No. You're going to teach English and art in Ghana.' I said, 'Okay. I'll take whatever I can get. If you guys say I can do it, let's do it.'" The Peace Corps promised to send him a packet in six weeks, in March 2003, but nothing came. Michael called Washington. "They said, 'Oh, no, we forgot to call you. That program is not going.' I'm basically telling the lady, 'I quit my job, I sold my car, I'm setting somebody up to live in my house. What am I supposed to do now?' And she said, 'Well, I told you you're not supposed to do anything like that until you're ready to go.' I said, 'You told me six weeks. What do I do now?' She said, 'Well, we can put you in for a new location.' I just assumed that they were sending people out every couple months. And she said, 'No, no, no. The program we're going to put you into is Mozambique. And it's not until October 2003.'" So Michael begged for his job back, bought a junky truck for $500, and stayed in town until October.

The results of the National Peace Corps Association's December 2009 survey echoed the concerns of Michael and others. Issues that needed to be addressed included "communication during application and medical screening process" and "increasing speed in moving from application to selection and placement," as well as applicant input and choice on country assignment.[9] The Peace Corps has recognized the need for speed: one goal of its 2009 Performance and Accountability Report was to reduce the response time to applicants from 123 days in 2009 to 80 days by the end of 2011.[10]

Lauren and David Goodpaster (Malawi 2005–2007) also had to wait for an assignment. They were not older volunteers, but they were not just out of college either. Lauren had completed a master's degree in student affairs and development at the University of Kentucky; she then spent a year in admissions at Transylvania University in Lexington, followed by three years at Rollins College in Florida, where she created an office of community engagement. David had worked at the Kentucky Historical Society for three years and taught high school in Florida. Both were almost thirty years old when they applied in spring 2004 and waited more than a year. They left their jobs in summer 2004, got married in August (after dating since college), and expected to leave in September for Africa. They were finally offered Eastern Europe the following February or Malawi the following May, and they chose the latter. David had actually applied to the Peace Corps himself after college graduation, and he remembered saying to Lauren, "'You know, I've always thought about the Peace Corps. What would you say about us going and doing it now?' All the people we talked to thought we were crazy. They just didn't understand it. They would say, 'Lauren's doing great and you're doing all right teaching. You all should go buy a house and start thinking about having kids and buying a new car or whatever newlyweds do. Why in the world are you talking about going and joining the Peace Corps?' This probably lasted a couple months, and I think Lauren realized how much it meant to me, and I knew it was something she would really like to do as well."

The Goodpasters' story illustrates the longevity of the desire to join the Peace Corps, but the story that concludes this chapter is a particularly dramatic illustration of both longevity of desire and persistence.

A Decades-Long Tale about Getting In

Wini Yunker (Ukraine 2000–2002) was born in Nicholasville, Kentucky, in 1934. She graduated from high school in 1951, married, went to Texas, divorced, and moved to Washington, DC, where she worked for a magazine, *Military Engineer*, and acted as a hostess for the USO. Wini's story begins in 1961.

> I always read the paper, the *Washington Post*, every day. And there was this big story about Kennedy starting the Peace Corps. And it just seemed so glamorous to me. I loved to travel. And I thought you get to travel for free. My office was a block from the White House, and the Peace Corps office was in Lafayette Park, so one day on my lunch hour I just trotted over there to join up. I didn't tell anybody. I just thought I'm going to write home and say, "Well, I'm off for Central America tomorrow." My family always thought I was audacious anyway. So they would have just said, "Well, that's Wini."
>
> When I walked in, I remember there was a young man and a young woman there. I said, "I've come to join up." I was so excited. The young man said, "Do you have a degree?" I said, "No," and he said, "Well, we can't use you." So it was just like a two-minute interview, and it was just terrible. I went back to work and I didn't tell anybody about it.
>
> Thirty years later when I was getting a degree I thought, "Wow, I can join the Peace Corps." You didn't hear about the Peace Corps in the

1980s. I thought it was defunct. I called and they said, "Oh, no, Congress funds us. We're still up and running. We can use you. No age limit." But at that time my son was small. I was forty-three when he was born. I just couldn't think about going to the Peace Corps. So then I said, "Well, what if I go when I'm sixty five? I can retire in Peace Corps." The person said, "Well, why don't you get a master's in the meantime?" And my company, God bless them, had an education reimbursement program.

While working full-time as assistant to the president of lock manufacturer Sargent and Greenleaf, Wini had already earned her undergraduate degree in marketing through Spalding University's weekend program; it took her four years. Then for nine years she attended school part-time and completed a master's degree at the Patterson School of Diplomacy and International Commerce at the University of Kentucky. "Finally when I got out it was 1998, so I called the Peace Corps. And the first question was, 'What's your education?' I said, 'Well, I just got a degree in international commerce in May.' So that started the process."

The application was all online and very simplified, about ten pages. The medical application was about fifteen pages, and I really had to outline everything, my sixty-odd years of life. Three references wrote secret letters. I had to send them sealed to the Peace Corps, so I have no idea what they wrote about me. And I had to write an essay about why I wanted to be in the Peace Corps. I had two interviews, but this surprised me—they were both telephonic. Chicago is the nearest office, and the Peace Corps, interested in cost cutting, didn't require personal interviews if you were a certain number of miles away. So the first one was sort of general. I remember one of the questions was what if I went to a Muslim country where I had to wear long skirts. I said, "Well, I like to wear jeans. I wear pants everywhere, even to church, but I guess I could adapt." They arranged another interview about a month later. Each one lasted about an hour. Just questions. So at the end of that one, the interviewer said he's going to recommend me for acceptance.

Wini was then told she would have to have three caps on her teeth replaced.

So I said, "Well, what if I have them pulled instead?" The Peace Corps dentist said, "No, you don't pull healthy teeth." I said, "Well, what if I found a dentist who will? Because I can't spend thousands of dollars." So I kept trying dentists. Finally, I had an appointment with an oral surgeon here in Nicholasville. I had lunch with my friend, and I said, "Should I tell him I've wanted to be in the Peace Corps thirty-nine years and I've waited and I need to do this, it's the only thing holding me back?" And she said, "No, just cry." So when I got in his office, talking with him, he kept saying no, no, no he couldn't pull those. I told him all this story, and finally I just burst into tears. And he said, "I'll do it." So I had the teeth pulled, had an operation on one foot where I had a bunion. I think those were the last hurdles. I started in the spring of '98 and I was accepted in late fall of '99.

Wini left her job with the lock company on January 20, 2000, and left for the Peace Corps on January 31.

Peace Corps said I could go to the Far East and be a teacher or to Africa and be a teacher, but if I went to Eastern Europe, which just opened up in the early nineties, I would be a business volunteer. Well, I sure didn't want to teach because I think it's the hardest profession there is. So I said, "I want to go to Eastern Europe." I'd always wanted to go to Romania because Dracula seemed so romantic and also because Romanian is a Latin language. In Ukraine I had to learn the Cyrillic alphabet, but it was just very exciting. I went to Chicago for staging for two days and then we arrived in Ukraine on February 2. And that was the worst winter of the three I was there.

Wini was assigned to *teach* business in Ukraine.

Chapter 3

Training

Peace Corps training was better for me than college. Culture training—the first place I'd heard of culture shock. A lot of physical training like running and swimming. Language training in Malay about five hours a day. We took a battery of tests, psychologists watched us and interviewed us.
—Nancy Dare (Malaysia 1965–1967)

It's kind of like you're just a baby starting over again and you have to learn everything. You have to learn as much as you can in twelve weeks to be able to take care of yourself in a totally foreign culture and environment and be on your own.
—Debra Schweitzer (Mali 1993–1996)

SIX VOLUNTEERS IN FIVE DECADES

Martin and Patsy Tracy (Turkey 1965–1967)

Martin and Patsy trained for two months at Princeton University and for one month at what was then called Robert College in Istanbul. Martin remembered that the Princeton part oriented the volunteers to Turkish culture, history, politics, and the language and included training in teaching English as a second language. Patsy's memories from Princeton were of "sixteen-hour days, grueling days learning language and culture. And bonding, of course. It was a very large training group, 250. It was exciting and demanding and interesting. We got a huge dose of history, politics, religion, societal change. We felt like, by the time we finished, we knew a lot about Turkey. In fact, we were so arrogant, we actually thought we were competent in the language, until we hit the rural village."

Patsy explained that most of the volunteers were recent college graduates, "what Peace Corps called 'BA generalists,' most probably upper- or middle-class folks who had had very little in terms of service training. Few had experience with other than people like themselves. So I felt a little more privileged that I had more basic skills—what do you do when there's no food or you run into an emergency. There were about fifteen married couples, as I recall. The most unusual person was in her sixties. We all flocked around her because she was very nurturing and a lot of fun and had an incredible philosophy of adventure for life. We all wanted to be as brave as Margaret."

The primary focus in Istanbul was language and culture training, especially what life would be like in the small towns where they would be going. Patsy remembered "field trips to different schools and communities. And we certainly got immersed in food and then immersed in life. And it really did make the transition to the rural village somewhat easier."

Rona Roberts (Philippines 1973–1975)

Rona remembered landing in the Philippines at six in the morning, going through a full day of events, and realizing late that afternoon that she was not a supervised agricultural credit volunteer, just a nonmatrixed spouse without a job.

> I went into the waiting area outside the office of the country director and I just started sobbing. And he walked through and said, "Come into my office." He listened for a few minutes and said, "Oh, we'll take care of this." And I knew he would. He had been a Proctor and Gamble executive. By the point I came to know him, he had been there four years and really understood the country and the Peace Corps situation.
>
> Within a day Howell and I had a specific offer to go to a specific place. Howell would do the agricultural credit, and I would work at a college. And then in another day or two they came back and said there's something more exciting—there's an international development effort starting that's unlike anything else that's ever happened in the world. We had a very long training, sixteen weeks, I think. We had a lot of cross-cultural training and learned the language, Bikol.

Rebecca Roach (Liberia 1988–1989)

Our education and health group had really good training by an outside consultant group in Bomi County, Liberia. They hired another consultant to come in from Arizona and give us some very good motorcycle training. As a result, I can't remember one motorcycle accident in our group. We had a very specific program that was designed by USAID for cultural training. Liberians talked to us about the history of Liberia, proper etiquette, and the reasons why there were certain rules in society and how to understand and follow them. Primary education had a training program for teachers that provided materials which told the teacher exactly what to say and do, and then our job was to go in and make sure the materials were being properly used.

After about two weeks we were sent to Kakata to be trained with the rest of the teachers who were learning this new program. So we sat side by side with other Liberian teachers, all equals learning a new program together. We assimilated very quickly because you have to when you're a minority. We learned Liberian English, and the other folks who stayed together in the little "America Town" in Bomi were way behind us.

Sarah Cross Oddo (Jamaica 1993–1995)

In the beginning it was a lot of learning about the culture, learning about the history of Jamaica, a lot of volunteers talking to us about their experiences. I remember we had a week where maybe a couple different times we went out with just the environmental volunteers, and we would go to different sites around the country. And that was fantastic, really fun. Like we went to the marine lab and went snorkeling. We went to some caves. We saw some banana plantations and farming projects and learned about all the different environmental aspects of the country. We went to a place where all the pirates used to hang out in the 1400s and 1500s, and then they had a massive earthquake and everything went into the sea. I remember motorcycle training was really fun, and we saw a lot of places on the island that we wouldn't have seen otherwise. We got trained by the Jamaican police force.

A lot of people thought, "I can't wait to just get out there and do what we were going to do." But I thought training was great. You just did what you had to do and you went where somebody told you. You didn't have to think about what you were going to eat. It was just very easy. Volunteers would say, "You have to slow down, and you have to take your time to see what's around you." And you know, I really think that people can tell you that as many times as they want to, but you just have to figure it out on your own. You just have to learn it on your own, which I did.

Aaron Shraberg (China 2004–2006)

Aaron flew from Chicago to Beijing and then to Chengdu, the capital of Sichuan province and headquarters of the Peace Corps. His group went through training—"the most rigorous thing I've ever been through"—at the Southwestern University of Science and Technology in a city two hours north. They lived with "families of university professors who were part of the burgeoning middle class of China. Their fathers were the labor heroes of early China, the new China. And their hope was that their sons would go to university. So a lot of the people we stayed with were from that generation. In the morning and at the end of the day and at night we were part of a Chinese community, a larger Chinese community. It was amazing how each volunteer adapted so well to the family and was, in a way, adopted. I still keep in touch with my Chinese family."

Aaron got up with his host parents and had a boiled egg, bread, and soup or rice porridge for breakfast. In the morning they had technical and cross-cultural training—education in China, Chinese society and culture, and cross-cultural issues in the classroom. After lunch they would do four hours on Chinese language.

> That was really tough. I'd already had that fundamental level, and I was put in a class with another student who had lived in China for some time. I learned so much; my ability went up like five or six levels just in those two months because the language training was so excellent. Our teachers were very good, and for them it was exciting to be in that atmosphere, teaching these future teachers. After class we would go home and then it was time with our families. We would maybe go out and play basketball with our brothers or sisters, then have a meal. The whole eating experience was fun because that was your time to practice your Chinese.

Training is one part of the Peace Corps experience that has changed the most across the five decades, and most of that change happened within the first decade. Moving to almost entirely in-country training that utilized more host country nationals was the first change. How the Peace Corps handled the selection of volunteers was a second major change.

In the beginning, Peace Corps director Sargent Shriver "decided upon roughly an eight- to twelve-week intensive training period. From this decision there developed a three-phase pattern for all training programs: eight to ten weeks at a college or university in the United States; two to four weeks field training at one of the Peace Corps' 'outward-bound' camps (located in Puerto Rico, Hawaii, St. Croix and St. Thomas); finally a brief one- to two-week period of in-country training overseas."[1] There were various versions of this pattern, and the Outward Bound type of physical training occurred only in the first few years, and only for some programs. For one thing, as the number of trainees increased, the camps could not handle them all. While it lasted, physical training at the camps and elsewhere was quite demanding because some thought young Americans were soft and had to be tested to ensure they could survive overseas.

The partnership with universities was convenient because their facilities and faculties were available during the summer months; the Peace Corps could use the dormitories and hire area studies experts and psychologists, but faculty members also benefited from the new challenge. When Peace Corps training began, there were eight core components: technical studies, language studies, area studies, international relations and danger of communism, American studies, physical education, medical studies, and a general orientation to the Peace Corps.[2] The international relations component, especially the emphasis on dealing with communists, lasted only a few years. Soon a troika of language, culture, and technical studies related to job assignments emerged as the main focus of training.

By the late 1960s, training was increasingly done in-country. Tom Samuel (Liberia 1965–1967) and his wife Susan (Liberia 1964–1967) worked in subsequent Liberia training programs, and both their daughters joined the Peace Corps when in-country training was the only model. Tom talked about Stateside versus in-country training in his interview. "I think Peace Corps has made a mistake by not having Stateside training because we have lost the ability to create experts in a particular area. I'm convinced that the experts on Liberia remained expert because they were regularly training volunteers. That's one of the key objectives of Peace Corps—to bring back the country to the U.S." Interestingly, in spring 2010 new Peace Corps director Aaron Williams was in discussions with several universities about doing some Stateside technical training, for instance, in teaching English as a second language.

In *Twenty Years of Peace Corps*, Gerald Rice notes that "by 1966 most of training staffs were made up of former volunteers who had already had overseas experience in the countries where new volunteers were being assigned. These returned volunteers were instrumental in gradually changing the emphasis of training programs from physical exercise to cultural sensitivity."[3] Peace Corps administrators who had been volunteers began to argue for in-country training because it was practical rather than theoretical, real experience versus academic lectures.

In 1968 almost half of all Peace Corps trainees did part of their training in their countries of assignment.[4] With the exception of the process called staging—a several-day to weeklong preparation that takes place in the United States—training was gradually moved to the country or at least the region of the world where the volunteer was assigned. In 1967, for instance, the totally in-country training program in Ghana was situated at a teacher training college in the coastal town of Winneba, which the trainees had time to explore. They also spent three weeks in villages, where they taught in schools and lived with families. Field visits were considered particularly important because they could combine technical, language, and cross-cultural training. Training also began to expand beyond a designated length to include continuing education, such as further language lessons.[5]

In this chapter, besides describing their training, volunteers explain their experiences with selection, deselection, and self-selection. In fact, the selection process is one of the most frequently recalled memories among volunteers from the 1960s and occasionally beyond. Although Joseph Blatchford, Peace Corps director from 1969 to 1971, eliminated most psychological evaluation from the selection process, certainly during the early 1960s, "poor performance during training, health problems, psychological instability, or general unsuitability were all potential grounds for 'de-selection'" or removal from the program.[6]

The 1967 *Peace Corps Handbook* and the 1968 *Peace Corps Factbook and Directory* explained that the final selection board used seven criteria to decide whether a trainee became a volunteer: motivation; aptitude to meet the demands of the program; personal qualities, including initiative, determination, friendliness, patience, ability to communicate, and respect for other people regardless of race, religion, nationality, social standing, or political persuasion; physical stamina and emotional stability; competence in the skills required for the assignment; sufficient progress in the new language; and adequate knowledge of both the host country and the United States.[7]

However, ideas about selection were already changing. In 1967 the director of the Peace Corps in Sierra Leone was Joseph Kennedy, a psychologist who also served as the country's assessment officer. He declared that trainees would decide themselves—self-selection—whether to become volunteers after completing in-country training. An agency report on in-country training in 1968 concluded that there began to be agreement that trainees should come to the country believing they were almost volunteers, committed to the Peace Corps, rather than coming with the attitude of seeing whether they liked the country. "Further selection pressures should be minimized, selection boards deemphasized and self-assessment stressed."[8] By 1970 that was happening in Fiji, where Jack was director, as well as in other Peace Corps countries.

David Searles, Peace Corps director in the Philippines from 1971 to 1974 (and later deputy director of the Peace Corps in Washington), described selection during his tenure in the Philippines:

> [Volunteers were sworn in] within two or three days of their arrival in-country. It was important that they know right from the start that they were part of the organization; everything would be done to ensure their success, not to weed them out. It is important to point out that standards remained high even when volunteers were sworn in immediately upon arrival. Those who were obviously not qualified went home. But the vast majority who had the potential to expand into their sometimes larger-than-life new roles did not have to endure the anxieties and distractions of a subjective and flawed evaluation procedure.[9]

One of Searles's volunteers was Rona Roberts, who described the staging experience in chapter 2. She felt the staging process itself discouraged some potential volunteers when they learned what was involved. Peace Corps Philippines also "eliminated the traditional qualifying process for trainees with its formal assessment, psychologists, and review boards."[10]

Still, as late as 1980, Lee Colten (Ecuador 1981) said that staging "felt like we were under psychologists' microscopes. They would follow us around with notebooks, and it was just amazing some of the things they wrote down." The woman who later became his wife, Marianna Colten (Ecuador 1981–1983), explained:

> They interviewed us, and we had to do these role-playing activities, and they observed us and wrote lots of reports on us and tried to decide if we were worthy of the Peace Corps or if we were mentally healthy. The process was very detailed but not very accurate. I remember a guy getting chosen that I felt was mentally ill and shouldn't go. He had admitted to me that he had tried to commit suicide on various occasions. He falsified his forms for Peace Corps selection, and when I went back home I called and said, "You might want to check this guy out a little further." There were other people I thought might have made good volunteers who didn't get selected. We had one girl who was a fluent speaker and had traveled a lot, and she was very interesting. But she took the whole process tongue-in-cheek. When she was asked to role-play, she was sarcastic and fooling around. I think she got deselected because of her attitude.
>
> I remember one of our co–possible volunteers was having a birthday, and that night at dinner we had cupcakes. I took mine to the kitchen and brought it back with a candle on it, and we sang "Happy Birthday" to her. After she blew out the candle, I took my cupcake back because she already had one. Well, in my final evaluation, that was cited as one reason why I might not be selected. At the end of that week there was a decision, and the ones who were chosen had to have their shots. Then we went home and packed and flew to Miami and on to Quito.

Although selection has been a problematic area of training, over the years, the Peace Corps developed a reputation for very strong language and cross-cultural training. In the beginning, the cross-cultural training was specific to the host country. Later, such as in *Culture Matters: The Peace Corps Cross-Cultural Workbook*,[11] the general building blocks of culture (the concept of self, personal versus societal obligations, the concept of time, and locus of control) were described with exercises and stories. Volunteers were also prompted to compare host country views and American views across a number of cultural categories such as attitude toward age, attitude toward formality, and concept of equality.

However, Jonathan Zimmerman, a Peace Corps volunteer

teacher in Nepal in the 1980s, points out in *Innocents Abroad: American Teachers in the American Century* that general acceptance and teaching by the Peace Corps of the traditional anthropological view of culture as a bounded entity seems to set up a choice for volunteer teachers: when faced with a decision whether to use corporal punishment or how to respond to gender discrimination, should they "impose their own culture or capitulate to the local one?" But, Zimmerman contends, "the very terms of this dilemma blinded them to diversity within the cultures they encountered and—especially—to values they might have shared with their hosts."[12]

Although the concept of culture can indeed become a closed trap instead of an open forum, one of the Peace Corps' gifts to teachers in the United States has been its cross-cultural materials adapted for schools and available from the Peace Corps' WorldWise Schools Web site.[13] An example from one of these print resources, addressing a cross-cultural dilemma, concludes this chapter. During their service, Peace Corps volunteers usually discovered that differences did matter and had to be taken into account, but they were often forced to consider whether there are universal values and, if so, what they are—and then what?

Because of the changes in training, this chapter is organized chronologically by decades, beginning with early volunteers' memories of Puerto Rican and Hawaiian camps and university-based training. Later volunteers recall their in-country training; as for Rebecca, Sarah, and Aaron, most of those memories are positive.

1960s

The memories of training for 1960s volunteers ranged from rappelling off dams and castrating pigs to giving themselves injections to usually strong language and cultural training. And they definitely included the psychologists and deselection.

Philip Curd (Guinea 1963–1965) remembered being in Puerto Rico for two weeks before going to the School for International Living in Vermont to study language and African history and culture. The training in Puerto Rico was "physical fitness and pushing yourself past your limits by swimming underwater as long as you could, going out in the ocean and learning survival underwater skills, rock climbing—stuff I had never done before, so it was fun. Taking us out in the countryside and dropping us with a map and some food rations for two days and [then] a four-day trek back to camp." Older volunteer Bill Bridges (East Pakistan [Bangladesh] 1963–1965) remembered Puerto Rico as "a pretty stiff physical program" that only twenty-nine out of forty-two survived to become volunteers. Linda Delk (Honduras 1964–1966) "loved the training. I liked pushing myself physically. I enjoyed the Outward Bound training, climbing the rope ladders, rappelling off dams." Win Speicher (Honduras 1967–1969) trained in Puerto Rico for three months to work with agricultural cooperatives. Besides intensive Spanish language, "we had to raise a sow, have her give birth to the babies, take care of the pigs. And I'm a city slicker from Philadelphia."

Training in Puerto Rico for Jeff Kell (Dominican Republic and Ecuador 1962–1963) was even longer. He spent four months in Puerto Rico, partly in survival training but also in class work at the University of Mayaguez learning conversational Spanish and well drilling. He, too, remembered swimming underwater and being dropped off in the middle of nowhere and having to find his way home. "They had us rappelling off the front of dam faces, which was pretty scary."

Volunteers for some programs in Asia trained in Hilo, Hawaii, on the "big island." Hawaii seemed to be "a good transition from mainland U.S. because we were with cultures very different from anything we had known," as Phil Dare (Malaysia 1965–1967) remembered.

"The first few nights there were eight couples in an abandoned wood-frame school on old cots and no sheets to separate us. We [he and wife Nancy] had been married five years, but some of the couples had planned on this as a honeymoon. It was a beautiful location. On one side were sugarcane fields, then out to the ocean. On the other side it went right up to Mauna Kea, Mauna Loa, and the saddle in between. Incredible sunrises and sunsets, and the people were so incredibly hospitable. We never walked the whole distance into town. People would just pull over, pick you up, and take you to their homes. After several weeks we moved into what had been a hospital in Hilo proper. There was a period when we taught in Hilo schools and stayed in homes, too. And there was a home stay with the manager of a sugarcane operation." Besides language instructors from Malaysia, the Dares listened to lectures on history, economics, and politics by professors from the East-West Center. The trainees also played soccer with the Malaysians and learned a Malaysian game played rather like volleyball but with a bamboo ball and one's feet. "One week they took us down to Waipio Valley. They had duplicated Malay houses so you had a twenty-four-hour alone experience with a little bit of food, some matches, and directions." Phil described getting soaked in a stream and having rats crawl over him as he slept in the grass house. "I thought this was one of those experiences I didn't need and was hoping we wouldn't have this every night while we were overseas."

Another "big island" trainee was Marlene Payne (Malaysia 1967–1969). For her, training took place in "a former boarding school. I think I had sixteen roommates. We had four hours of Malay every day and studied history and culture. And it was a great three months. We had a wonderful cook and we had fresh pineapple every day. In the evenings after lectures she would invite some of us to come down to her home to have tea and continue conversations about going to Malaysia and about Hawaii. She was a Japanese who had married a Filipino." They also went to Waipio Valley.

Although island training was part of the reality as well as the mythology surrounding the Peace Corps, more volunteers trained at universities. Some did both. Kenny Karem (Chile 1966–1968) went to the University of Washington for part of his training and then spent a month in Puerto Rico. He remembered:

> We practiced giving shots just in case we had to give ourselves shots. We practiced on oranges and cabbages and then on each other. I still remember a volunteer practicing on me and the needle bouncing off my arm, and I kept tensing, waiting. Finally I just passed out. I can still remember they took us out to a barn to learn to castrate pigs with razor blades. I just thought it was ridiculous. I'm never going to some Third World farmer with my "nothing" agricultural skills and castrate his pigs. I can still remember the psychiatrist walking around with a grumpy look on his face writing little notes in his black book. I said, "Write my name down, I don't care." Then we had to kill chickens, pluck them, and dip them in hot water. We dwindled down to seventy-seven, and only forty-four actually went. We were constantly called in and asked to evaluate each other in secret. "Who do you admire the most, the least?" They got us to rat on each other.

Once the psychologist asked Kenny what he would do if he got into an argument. He said, "I don't know. I'm sort of a pacifist-type person." The psychologist then asked how he would defend himself, and Kenny explained he usually defended himself with his sense of humor.

Paul Winther (India 1961–1963), a member of the first group to go to India, trained at Ohio State University. He recalled, "The language training wasn't that good; the teachers were graduate students who happened to be at Ohio State. It was very much an experiment. I think we started out with thirty-six and ended up with twenty-four people, all males except for one female married to a volunteer. We were taught by Sikhs from the Punjab, and they cooked for us."

A member of a health group, Katherine Sohn (India 1967–1969) was in an innovative training program that started with cultural and language training the summer before her senior year in college; then during her senior year she took related subjects such as Indian history. The following summer she lived for two weeks in inner-city Milwaukee, then two weeks on a Native American reservation. She went to India and spent another month learning about the public health system there.

Ron Pelfrey (Ethiopia 1966–1968) was part of another special program that included advance training. Between his junior and senior years at the University of Kentucky, where he was majoring in math and chemistry and getting a teaching certificate in math, he participated in a summer of training at UCLA. He then returned to Los Angeles for a week during the Christmas break and for a month the summer after he graduated. He completed his training in Ethiopia by teaching summer school at an agricultural school founded by Oklahoma State. For Ron, training "was a very good experience. I taught in Watts and lived in Watts the summer of the riots. I lived with a family, a mother and I think nine kids. The sixteen-year-old girl had had a baby just before I got there. So that was a unique experience. I taught math there. And then two weeks after we left, the Watts riots started. And the Los Angeles newspapers blamed part of that on us, said the Peace Corps had stirred everybody up about their situation." Ron also had an excellent Amharic teacher who had written the textbook for the Ethiopian language. "We were not allowed to speak in English. When we were in the cafeteria, when we were playing sports, we had to speak strictly in Amharic."

In an article in the September 1964 issue of *National Geographic*, Sargent Shriver explained that "the increase in requests for community development led to establishment of a third Peace Corps camp in northern New Mexico [the others were Camps Crozier and

Radley in Puerto Rico, named after the first two volunteers who lost their lives]. Here, under the supervision of the University of New Mexico, trainees perform valuable fieldwork on Indian reservations and in Spanish-speaking communities. The aridity typifies conditions volunteers encounter in much of the world."[14]

One of the trainees at that camp was Joyce Miller (Chile 1964–1966), who recalled "the mountain treks in the snow, killing chickens and rabbits, digging latrines. We had to go up in the Sandia Mountains quite often because *National Geographic* was doing a big spread on the Peace Corps." There are pictures of women rappelling and killing chickens in the article, but Joyce wasn't one of them. She explained, "I didn't have the right color shirt." She also described the selection process. "After the first month, month and a half, you would go down to your mailbox to see if you had a slip of paper. If something was written on it, you were out. If it was blank, you were in. And you didn't know until you picked up that paper. And then at the end of three months, again you went down to your mailbox to see what was on your slip of paper. I thought that was a very unpleasant way of being told whether you were in or out." Out of forty-four, only twenty-four survived the training. Joyce also remembered that "we had the medical doctor giving us training. The men were taken aside and taught about condoms. Not one word of birth control was mentioned to the women. We were virginal forever and ever."

The following year, Tom Boyd (Colombia 1964–1966) also trained at the University of New Mexico as part of a physical education group being prepared to work in sports programs. Of the fifty trainees, he came in last in the daily two-mile run. In the unit on baseball, he got hit in the eye while trying to catch the ball in left field and still has the scar. But he remembered, "I liked the political science and economics, the history of Colombia. It was like going back to college, but from about seven in the morning until about ten at night. The training for me was a great pleasure." For Tom, "the real fear was the deselection." He recalled, "As soon as we got off the plane, they said, 'Now we hope nobody has burned a lot of bridges back home because you are not in the Peace Corps until August. This is just June. Some of you will quit, and some of you will be deselected, so don't have any parties and don't get all excited, because you know that's going to happen.' Within three weeks we went into a room, and they gave us each an envelope and it said to go to a room. By the time we got back to the dorm that night, the ones who weren't with us in that room had disappeared. Then four weeks later the same wretched thing occurred, and in the meantime, some people had quit." Of the original fifty, eighteen went to Colombia. As a psychology major, Tom found the "shrinks" interesting. "In my case, I thought I was going to have an adventure, so they spent a lot of time with me, asking, 'What do you mean by an adventure?' And when I said an adventure was running early in the morning, I think that was okay. They gave us a personality test, and the guy said, 'So you really think you speak to God? That's what you said on this question.' And I said, 'I don't remember that.' And the next time I was with the shrink he asked, 'What about sex? It says here you went to a men's college.' I think they looked for people who were rigid. They did a good job, because of the eighteen people, only one went home early."

Don Stosberg (Malawi 1965–1966) trained first at the University of New Mexico and remembered it as a "wonderful experience. We did the Outward Bound training. We rappelled off stadium walls and later off the hills of the Pecos Wilderness. We hiked for three days and took all our gear. We learned about Colombian culture and learned Spanish and the politics of Colombia. It was an excellent training program. But then they decided I wouldn't work well in an unstructured situation, probably based on my seminary training. I didn't do well in the fieldwork in Taos. I was assigned to this artist project and didn't go out drinking and hang out with the guys at night, and I think they must have thought I was kind of not a sociable person. They didn't think I was so bad I shouldn't be in the Peace Corps, but they decided I should be in another project." Don switched programs as well as countries—from community development to teaching English. "I went to Syracuse University for my Peace Corps training to go to Malawi. Peace Corps made that decision, basically." Don thought that "most people took what assignment they got in those days. They thought, I'm joining the Peace Corps, I'm going to do what my government wants."

Like many others, Jim Archambeault (Philippines 1966–1968) remembered the evaluations, especially the peer evaluations. For these, each volunteer filled out a written form on all the other volunteers in the group. Jim described the process: "Basically, it was our opinion of a particular volunteer's psychological makeup, whether we thought they were suitable to live and work in the Philippine culture. Then each volunteer would meet with a staff member, and the psychologist would present to the volunteers what their peers had said about them and then discuss with the volunteers their reaction. So that was difficult, because we were basically given the power to decide whether or not a person should go overseas, in our estimation. Some of the trainees saw the writing on the wall and went home on their own before training was actually over with. But some of those that stayed around to the very end of the process were deselected right at the end of training." Jim recalled that of his group of about eighty-five trainees, sixty to sixty-five actually went to the Philippines.

Many volunteers trained in cities such as Atlanta and San Francisco. Terry Anderson (Ghana 1965–1967) trained at Morehouse University in Atlanta. That was "probably done to get us right into a black experience in America," he said. "Some white cab drivers wouldn't take us to that section of town. We had to wait for a black cab driver. We had a professor from South Africa who had written books on Pan-Africanism who gave us the historical context of Africa and colonialism; and Julian Bond's father, who was a historian; and Julian Bond himself, who was in the Student Nonviolent Coordinating Committee. We saw Mohammad Ali at a famous restaurant where we hung out. The guy who trained us physically was an Olympic track coach, and then Ghanaians taught us Ewe, one of Ghana's languages. I remember the teacher trainer was a professor at Emory University, and we taught science in summer school in Atlanta high schools."

Tom and Susan Samuel (Liberia 1965–1967 and 1964–1967) trained at San Francisco University—he in the public administration program, and she, a year earlier, in an education program. Tom remembered "good training." One activity involved being sent out with $20 and seeing what you could learn about Castroville in five days. Tom met the president of the Mexican Americans for Political Action (MAPA) and went out in the field to see artichokes being picked. Then he met the mayor, got his picture in the paper, and spoke before a civic group about the Peace Corps. "I walked away knowing a lot about Castroville and a lot about what it takes to be immersed in a community and really get to know it. I found out the post office is an important place to go because the postmaster has certain ties to the community. Found out it's a political process to become postmaster. Got to know the mayor, MAPA, the volunteer fire folks. I think immersion in another culture is a kind of growth experience you can't replicate." Susan remembered some very strong cultural trainers, including anthropologist Warren d'Azevedo and political scientist Gus Liebnow. She found the training program "great fun and an affirming process for the group to be together and know that we were going to have this great adventure." But she hated the physical part of training, especially camping in a "paper sleeping bag in the Sierra Nevadas, freezing cold, digging pit latrines. I thought it was absolutely absurd, and that's when I said, 'You have to put me in a city. I cannot be in the bush.' I knew what I needed. As a matter of fact, we spent a fair amount of time assessing for ourselves what we needed in terms of placement."

Some programs were so large that several universities hosted training. Harold Freeman (Ethiopia 1965–1967) was one of a group of 100 being trained at UCLA. At the same time, another 100 were training for Ethiopia at the University of Utah. Harold explained that Emperor Haile Selassie "had decided that his country needed to come into the modern age and that the only way to do that was to greatly increase the educational opportunities in the nation. There was no way for the Ethiopians to do that alone because they had only one or two institutions of higher education in the country that could turn out college graduates to be teachers, and the competition for this relatively small number of college graduates was intense. So in order to mushroom the number of teachers, they asked the Peace Corps to provide a whole bunch of us. There were 500 or so at the time I was there." Harold recalled that the Peace Corps training process was "generally devoid of government jargon, except for 'deselection.'" He also remembered interview sessions with psychologists and aptitude and personality tests.

Training a few years later at the University of Utah, Fred Cowan (Ethiopia 1967–1969) told about an incident involving their Ethiopian trainers. "The Ethiopians were at a bar, and they were dancing with some of the white Peace Corps volunteers. Some of the patrons of the bar were very upset about blacks, Ethiopians, dancing with white girls. They got in some kind of a fight, and it became a news story." Fred was a ringleader in a press conference protesting the way the Ethiopians had been treated. His other memories of training included learning Amharic, teaching Native American kids for practice, and living in tents in the Four Corners area. His group had 130 people. Two or three who were caught smoking marijuana were deselected.

Puerto Rico was still a training site in the late 1960s, but according to Bill Miller (Dominican Republic 1968–1970), who trained there, his group was one of the first in which everyone who passed the initial application and screening process was accepted; there was only a self-selection process. "We didn't climb mountains or swim across a three-mile lake," he recalled. "We did sports activities and spent most of our time studying Spanish and the cultural aspects of the Dominican Republic. We did more cerebral training."

Several volunteers described technical as well as cultural training. Judy Lippmann (Morocco 1966–1968) was a member of Morocco 8, a group of laboratory technicians who were supposed to work in hospital labs run by French physicians serving in the military, with the volunteers filling the lab tech slots until enough young Moroccans had been trained to replace them. Their culture and language training began at the University of Texas in Austin; then they moved to the medical branch in Galveston for medical training. Judy learned serology. "I studied French in our three months of training and then learned street Arabic so I could shop and count and greet people." After a week in Rabat, the capital, "we were given our assignments. I was sent to Spanish-speaking Morocco."

A member of a group specifically prepared to vaccinate women against smallpox, Charlene McGrath (Afghanistan 1969–1971) received her technical training at a public health facility in Arizona but also had more Outward Bound–type experiences. "We lived in tents out in the desert for about six weeks, and I loved it. We went on horseback rides and saw all the country. Then we moved to Estes Park, Colorado, right before Thanksgiving, with probably two feet of snow, and stayed there until shortly before Christmas, when we got a break before leaving. We celebrated New Year's Eve of 1969 in Tehran" before flying on to Kabul for in-country training.

1970s

By the 1970s, in-country training was the norm, and self-selection was common. There was also a greater emphasis on providing trained manpower, including specific skills, as part of the New Directions policy promulgated by the new Peace Corps director, Joseph Blatchford.

William Salazar (Guatemala 1972–1973) already had agricultural experience and remembered doing an experiment as part of his in-country training, trying "to find the optimal level of fertilizer for rice and corn and beans in Guatemala. Our job was to figure out how much fertilizer the family would have to use to grow a good crop without spending a lot of money."

Another volunteer with agricultural skills, Cecil McFarland (Micronesia 1972–1974, Philippines 1974–1976) and his wife Sheila were part of the first in-country training program for Micronesia. They had a brief orientation, or staging, in San Jose, California. Then, as Sheila remembered, "All 170 of us loaded up on a Northwest Orient plane that went on strike on the way to Honolulu. They unloaded us there and put us on a Pan Am 747 and sent us on to Guam. From there, we spread out to go to our different districts. We stayed in the capital city of Pohnpei, Kolonia. Half the day was spent in intensive language [training], and we also had a cultural class, making us more culturally sensitive and understanding of the whole culture." Cecil added, "We also spent time living with families. There was no deselection at that time in Peace Corps, but a lot of people self-deselected for various reasons. One individual lasted three days, some lasted two weeks, some lasted until the end of training. We went in with about thirty volunteers—trainees—and five left after training. Thirteen lasted the two years."

A business volunteer, Lloyd Jones (Colombia 1973–1975) remembered flying out of Paducah, Kentucky, to go to Philadelphia for staging:

The staging was four days, and that was where I first met my group of people. There were about 150 people who went into initial training for twelve weeks in Bogota. In Philadelphia they gave us all the medical stuff, and we went through different classes. We met our country director and people who were going to teach us languages. We had a charter flight on Braniff Air to Bogota. The whole plane was just full of these people. It was an open bar, and everybody was having a great time meeting one another. They were from all over the United States. I was the only person from Kentucky and from a rural area. Most of the people were from the Midwest, people I still talk to today. They were from bigger city areas. There were guys from Harvard and from all the Ivy League schools. We actually had a couple Native Americans. For a lot of us, it was the first time we had ever had a passport. I'll never forget when they handed out the passports. I still have mine: it says Floyd R. Jones. So I went through two and a half years with the wrong name.

Each Peace Corps volunteer was assigned to live with a family during training as part of adapting to cultural change. These Colombians would basically rent out a bedroom, and you lived and ate with this family for twelve weeks. Peace Corps said, "You can't go out and get your own apartment because this is part of the training. You've got to live with a Colombian family to understand more about these people," which was a great idea. Some people just said, "I'm not going to do that," and they left. We lost twenty people in the first week. I was very fortunate because I lived with a family that was pretty middle class. They had a family of three or four kids, and I fit right in. I took the kids out and played basketball with them, and I became an older son. And to this day we still exchange letters. They became my Colombian family. But there were other people who were assigned to families that were pretty poor.

Maurice White (Afghanistan 1974–1976) recalled his language and pedagogical training:

Right away we were immersed in language training and teacher training to teach English. I learned Farsi almost all day by the silent method. Students worked together as a group cooperatively to learn the language. The instructor would use a series of prods to prompt us as cues, but we had to figure out the structure and the simple grammar. It's a very controversial method not very much in practice nowadays. The people in charge of our English-language training were from Columbia Teachers College. There was a lot of videotaping and viewing of tapes and a prescribed methodology for the language lessons we had to prepare. It was very, very meticulously planned, and you had to follow the script pretty closely. We were living in Kabul in a dormitory-style situation. After a few months we spent a couple of weekends with volunteers who were established in the country, and then we were sent out to our sites.

Also assigned by the Peace Corps to be an English teacher, Ann Neelon (Senegal 1978–1979) remembered two specific events during training:

After we'd been there a week or so, staying at the John F. Kennedy Lycée, they gave us this list of things we had to go find. And on the way back we were walking through this neighborhood. I was wearing glasses instead of my contacts, and this guy came running out from a market area and belted me across the head, and my glasses went flying and the lenses flew out of the frames. All these people came running up to me, apologizing, saying *"C'est fou, c'est fou,"* and I realized they were saying he's mentally ill. This guy was really nuts, and everybody felt terrible about it. The other thing I remember is that I saw a volume of Leopold Sedar Senghor's poems at a revolving kiosk. The minute I was assigned to Senegal I was thrilled, because I knew he was president of Senegal. He was the only poet who had ever been president. I ended up translating his work when I came back. And my earliest publications were really those translations.

Joan Moore's (Swaziland 1979–1981) group landed in Johannesburg, South Africa, and took a bus to Mbabane, the capital of Swaziland, which is surrounded on three sides by South Africa. They stopped to eat at a restaurant, but the African American volunteer in their group couldn't go in, so none of them did—it was their introduction to apartheid. Their language and cultural training was done by local people, who taught them to always use the right hand to hand things to people, signs of respect, and how to dress. Each volunteer spent a week in a rural village living with a family. Joan's "family had five kids. We had to go get water, go out in the bushes to go to the bathroom, eat different types of food. They didn't speak any English. I really liked it a lot, and they were really good to me, dressing me up in the local clothing for women. It was difficult at times because you were really isolated and the days seemed long." They also learned about the educational system and the structured way they should teach to prepare students for exams. Joan became a middle school science teacher.

The main character in the training memories of Richard Bradshaw (Central African Republic 1977–1979) was Emperor Bokassa, and the main problem was the lack of organization in the Peace Corps program. Richard had completed the public health part of his training at Columbia University with volunteers going to Cameroon. Then he moved on to in-country training:

It consisted of language training, French and Sango, and we continued to have some training in health and to become familiar with different projects that were ongoing in the Central African Republic at the time. The training was not very good. We also stayed in a hotel for a month before training started because the project, undertaken in cooperation with USAID, wasn't ready for us yet. The motorcycles had not come.

When the motorcycles arrived, one of our group got into serious trouble by stopping in front of the palace of Emperor Bokassa and asking an innocent question. The policemen hauled the Peace Corps volunteer into Bokassa, and the emperor crushed the man's glasses with his foot. The volunteer was so scared he was sent home. By the time we got up-country and went through training, and given the context of the times—Bokassa, the fear, the lack of organization, and the fact that some volunteers didn't realize Peace Corps was really what you made of it—of the ten of us, only two stayed: me and the woman who eventually became my wife.

Dianne Bazell (Zaire [Democratic Republic of Congo] 1975–1977) and her group arrived in Zaire after a seventeen-hour Pan Am flight from JFK in New York to Kinshasa. Then they got on a plane for Bukavu: "You could smell red earth. I can still smell African grass. I remember being amazed by the varieties of green there. There were bananas, oil palm trees, so many different kinds of green with a backdrop of this very, very red soil. It was beautiful. More than twenty-five years later, that was the place of the slaughter of the Rwandans; the soldiers were in the houses at the little school where I trained." During training she learned French and how to teach English as a second language, and Zaireans explained their culture. "I remember one particular expedition to Virunga National Park with gorillas. We climbed the volcanic mountain there; it was like climbing a ladder, it was so steep. I remember swimming in Lake Kivu. We were told there were snakes at the bottom of the lake, but if we didn't swim to the bottom, we'd be just fine. I remember hearing that our director had swum across a particular finger of the lake, so by golly, I was going to swim across that too, and I did."

1980s

Although several of the early 1980s volunteers remembered the selection process as vividly as earlier volunteers did, most of them talked more about their language, cultural, and skills training.

Marianna Colten (Ecuador 1981–1983) described her three-month in-country training as very challenging:

I didn't have any foreign language in high school or college. We were placed with native speakers—families—and it was sink or swim. You had to learn to communicate pretty fast. They also taught do's and don'ts of how you should behave and talked about cultural differences. They gave us periodic language tests that we either passed in the end or didn't. And some people were actually deselected after training either because they deselected themselves or decided this wasn't what they wanted, or they just couldn't learn the language or their behavior wasn't up to par. I liked training, but it was very challenging. We had to do these survival weekends, too. One weekend didn't turn out very well because I had an intestinal virus, so I found a small movie theater and sat through *Conan the Barbarian* three times. I stayed there for hours because I was sick.

Lee Colten (Ecuador 1981), who later became Marianna's husband, had positive memories of a weeklong stay in a village during his two months of agricultural extension training in Costa Rica. He also remembered having a breakthrough in learning the language, learning to set up test plots, and learning to "dry beans and beating them until you got the beans out of the husk. It's a real eye-opener for somebody who's not used to depending on growing his own crops to survive. We had a party when we killed our own turkey. Got it [the turkey] drunk beforehand, which is the tradition there. We each got a turn to kill a chicken or a guinea pig. We got to raise our own guinea pigs and feed them."

Another volunteer who trained in Costa Rica was Kay Roberts (Ecuador 1982–1984). Kay had "traveled enough in Latin America to realize that the conditions in Costa Rica were not very similar to those in Ecuador. We had a large training group, about sixty-six people, and I think we lost at least a third of our group. Costa Rica was very developed, had good infrastructure, good education, and when people actually got to Ecuador and were sent to their sites, they decided they were not prepared. Our training was at the Center for Human Potential and was divided into cross-cultural, language, and technical training." Since Kay was already fairly fluent in Spanish, she was placed with a family who "didn't speak a word of English and lived the farthest from the training center, so I had about a three-mile walk every morning." She described the three types of training:

[For language training] we were given assignments, such as go interview three people about [a topic] and come back and tell [the trainers], not just sitting and learning the basic grammar and vocabulary. I think having to go through that very intense language training added a level of stress for a lot of trainees. I remember the language testing. You would sit in a chair, and somebody would sit facing you and talk to you, and somebody else was sitting right behind you scribbling notes. It was a very uncomfortable situation to know the person sitting behind your back could go thumbs up or thumbs down, and you were in or out.

[The cross-cultural training was] so-so, primarily because our trainers were Americans. It was a second culture to them. It was more academic than practical. The technical training was agricultural, since we'd be working with 4-H groups. I remember our first morning of training—at 6 A.M. we were out hoeing a field. They got us into the reality of labor-intensive farming very quickly, and we got a lot of practice talking and making very simple visual aids so we could present basic agricultural information to the people we'd be working with. The technical training was great.

Capp Yess (Fiji 1982–1984) remembered fairly intensive language and cross-cultural training:

We had immersion training where we lived with families for about four weeks and met as a group in part of the day and went to various places and had activities to get know the islands. I stayed with an Indian family and learned Hindi, but I also stayed with a Fijian family for a very short time so I would have a taste of the other culture that is part of Fiji. We went to schools and the Ministry of Education because we were going to be teachers, but we also toured the beer factory and landmarks, just things that might be different from what we were used to. All the while our trainers talked to us about how people who grew up in Fiji would view these things. We were encouraged to go to church, since that was a big part of people's lives, and also to Hindu temples and to mosques. Then we went back to the capital city and were housed at Nausori Teachers College because it was school vacation. We were given some basic teacher training for about six weeks and ran a short summer school that the Peace Corps sponsored to give us some classroom experience.

Math teacher Sarah Payne (The Gambia 1989–1991) attended staging in Chicago. She had an infected eye and had to go to a hospital emergency room, and then was worried she wouldn't get to go, but she did, flying through London to Banjul, The Gambia's capital, with about twelve others also going to teach math. The Gambia took math teachers one year and science teachers the next, so each secondary technical school always had one experienced volunteer and one new one. Sarah remembered the training as being very comprehensive:

> They taught us the know-how to teach. We actually taught summer school for free for local kids and learned about the Gambian education system. We also went to language classes. I started off in Wolof classes because I was going to a place on the north bank of the river. Halfway through training, when I went on my site visit, the experienced volunteer asked me how language was going. And he starts talking to me in a language I don't recognize, and it's Mandinka. So I switched to Mandinka classes. We learned how to try to take care of our nutritional needs with the limited diet. We learned how to take a bucket bath. We learned when a medical situation was serious and you should make your way down-country or when you should just look at your book and figure it out, because I was about eight hours from the capital, and there were no phones.

Bukavu, in eastern Zaire (now Democratic Republic of Congo), was a training center for volunteers assigned to Francophone countries as well as those assigned to Zaire, as Dianne Bazell was in the 1970s. Glen Payne (Gabon 1989–1992) did French language training in Bukavu with six other men in the rural school construction program. "I felt pretty good about my reading and writing French," he said, "but I had never said a word beyond *bon jour* in French. So the immersion was just as much an experience for me as it was for people who had never heard a French word in their whole lives." When they got to Gabon, their training focused on building a school as a demonstration, using hands-on learning.

1990s

Training in the 1990s continued to be done in the host country itself or at least in the region, and it continued to focus on a combination of language, culture, and job preparation. As in the 1980s, volunteers were often placed with host families during their training. Understandably, some of the memories of training by these more recently returned volunteers are more detailed and vivid than those of volunteers who served earlier.

Jenifer Payne (Gabon 1990–1992) also trained in Bukavu, Zaire, along with volunteers going to Burundi and Rwanda. To get to Bukavu, they flew into Bujumbura, Burundi, and then drove through Rwanda, where they saw silverback gorillas. Jenifer explained that the school "was on Lake Kivu, right across from the house of Mobutu, Zaire's dictator. Looking back, we were so blessed to have that experience, because Bukavu was destroyed. It was just flattened. Some of our African instructors were killed. But Zaire was beautiful. The architecture at the school was gorgeous. It looked like a movie. The buildings looked old, and there were all these archways. The rooms we stayed in were tiny as a closet, with a little single cot and a little table." Because of the ethnic violence that erupted in Burundi and Rwanda, the volunteers going there were soon pulled out, and some of the Burundi volunteers transferred to Gabon.

A West African volunteer, Debra Schweitzer (Mali 1993–1996), remembered training as "pretty grueling, because you're just in a state of culture shock." She explained:

The official language of Mali is French, so we had French training. Halfway through we had local language training, for me Bambara. I was in small business development, so we had training about the economy of Mali, types of businesses and small business projects others had done, and what you could hope to do. We also had culture training, learning about the culture of Mali, the people, the history, their beliefs, their way of life. It was morning till evening every day, and even meals were not a break, because even eating was different there. Going to the bathroom was different. There was some food I didn't care for, but the food we had in training was quite good. It was mostly rice and chicken and different kinds of meat. But when you eat in Mali, you have a communal bowl, and everybody sits around it on stools low to the ground. If there is any meat, it gets placed in the middle of the bowl. You eat with your right hand because your left hand is for the toilet, and you just take the meat portion that's in front of you. It's impolite to reach over other people's hands and take something from their area of the bowl. You wash your hands before you eat by pouring water from a big plastic teapot.

We were introduced to the endemic diseases—malaria and guinea worm—and how to treat our water by putting it through a mesh cheesecloth filter and then treating it with either bleach or iodine tablets. You had a little medical kit to take to your site, and you learned how to prick your finger to do a malaria slide. It was scary, because coming from America, you're used to having very minor illnesses. You're not used to dealing with snakes and malaria and guinea worm. Malnutrition didn't really affect us, just intestinal parasites and dysentery.

After a week we all got paired up with a family, two to a family. So in the morning we would get on a bus and go to the training facility, and in the evening we would go back to the village. You would stay with the family overnight to get more exposure to the culture and how you were going to live when you eventually went to your site. You used a latrine. You had a bucket bath. You had a lantern at night or candles. You had a mosquito net on your cot. A significant thing about the family you stayed with was that they got to give you your Malian name. They gave you your first name, and then you took their last name. Mine was Kadidia Kante. Family names in Mali are handed down and associated with specific professions, so I was from a blacksmith family.

Technical training was important for Carolyn Cromer (Morocco 1992–1995) as a member of a health and sanitation group. First she trained in Rabat at a teachers college, where she learned Berber and cross-cultural information; then she went to a coastal town for concentrated technical and language training. "We were doing things like teaching people about treating water so it was potable, building latrines, building wells or treating water in wells, contraceptive education, hand washing, germ transmission routes. We learned how to put a concrete cover on a well and how to build a latrine."

Technical training was also crucial for Robin Sither (Cameroon 1996–2000), who was trained to be an agroforestry extension agent, but language instruction consumed a lot of time, too.

They taught us about various types of interventions to teach farmers—about basic types of soil erosion interventions, contouring, bund building, how to site contours, and various types of species you can use for green manure, or what we called improved fallows, which is using these seasonal legumes to build up the soil. We also learned about their agricultural systems. Ngaoundere was a good microcosm of the country, so you basically saw all different types of agriculture. Ngaoundere is in the central part of the country on the Adamawa Plateau, which separates the rain-forest belt of southern Cameroon from the more arid part in the north, a very beautiful part of the country. It was a very cosmopolitan town, with lots of civil servants and merchants. We were parceled out to host families, but our training was at a training center that we hiked or biked to or took a taxi to. The training consisted, first and foremost, of the French language, because Cameroon is bilingual, with two of ten provinces being English speaking. I think I took French until they gave us our post placements and I knew I was going to be in the English zone. At that point they started teaching me Pidgin English, which has a lot of English but is a language in itself and is even different from Nigerian Pidgin. You learned by living with, communicating with, eating with, going to social functions with your host family, but we also had seminars about cultural issues such as gender and attitude toward death.

Training for Patrick Bell (Costa Rica 1997–1999) was community based and also included a site visit. He was part of a small group of eleven in a program called urban youth development in a country where the Peace Corps was phasing out all its programs except for aid to children. Patrick said:

My training was great in retrospect. We used the community-based training model, where we lived with a host family in a target neighborhood for our program. We lived in a housing settlement in San José that had grown up from poor squatters. There was running water, electricity, and paved roads, but there was a big drug problem in the neighborhood. I lived with an older man and woman whose children were grown. I called them Mama and Papa because they wanted me to, and over the course of the next two years, I would stay with them. And they were the last people I saw before I got on the plane to go home. The first week we were on top of a mountain, and the ambassador and other government officials came. During regular training, half the day consisted of language training in the neighborhood; then we went to the Peace Corps office for classes on working with kids, cross-cultural training, sessions with people in our counterpart agency, National Patron of the Child, and medical sessions. We also had individual training visits to see what it would be like. I went to Limon, a big banana port on the Caribbean side, and stayed in one of the worst neighborhoods in a government project that was supposed to be good. That's the first time I saw a monkey. I walked into the house where I was going to be staying for two nights, and the owner had a monkey sitting on his head. Then we had site visits, a visit to what was going to be your site. I went to San Isidro in southern Costa Rica, about three hours by bus from the capital. You go over 11,000-foot mountains, a beautiful, beautiful, incredible drive. We were doing this in October, which is the rainy season in Costa Rica. It was raining as we went, and it rained the whole time. The town was at least 50,000 people, an agricultural, coffee town. So I got to my host family, and that first night we ordered pizza because it was pouring down rain, and we played Super Nintendo, and I just said, "Okay. I'll give this site a shot!"

In her nine weeks of training, Tara Loyd (Lesotho 1999–2001) was amazed by the "language process," which she called "by far my most positive experience of Peace Corps."

I kept asking questions about when we were going to learn how to conjugate verbs and why we weren't learning anything about the grammatical structure or how to read Sesotho. And they kept saying, "Because it doesn't matter. You're learning to speak and hear this language." Really hands-on language listening and learning and practicing. We had to go into the dining hall and ask for food in Sesotho, or they would pretend they couldn't understand us if we spoke English. We learned a lot, and we learned it fast. There were women in their seventies who said, "I'm never going to learn to speak this language," but they passed their proficiency tests just fine. Peace Corps has been in Lesotho for thirty years, so they know a lot. These teachers knew a lot about Americans, what we've learned about our own language, and what our holdups are in terms of learning Sesotho sounds—sounds that we can't make but you learn to make as a child.

Tara learned about culture, too—that eye contact when a woman approached a man was sexually suggestive and that the dress code for female volunteers was smart business casual—a long ironed skirt over a slip showing no legs, and no Birkenstocks or Tevas.

Cori Hash (Zimbabwe 1999–2000) remembered arriving in-country for training as part of a new project of community education resource volunteers. "They had arranged this wonderful ceremony with singers, dancers, music, a children's choir. I wanted to know whether I could drink the water, where am I going to sleep, can I go to bed. After our introduction to the staff, we began language and cultural instruction. We met current volunteers, and people in the community came to talk about Zimbabwe culture and race issues. The first few days we learned a bit of Shona and Ndebele. Once we got to our main training site, they split us up based on where we were going to be living. I thought the language training was really great. We were broken up into small groups of five or six people with a language instructor, a native speaker." She described her host family, too:

> We were at a Seventh Day Adventist mission in a pretty rural area, and we all lived with families in an adjacent village from October through December. My family lived the farthest from the training site, so I had to walk two miles every day to get there. They lived in a very small, three-room cement block house, and I took up a whole room, which I felt really badly about. They didn't have running water or electricity, but they did have a solar panel hooked up to a car battery that would power little things, and they did have access to a well. They had a separate thatched-roof cooking hut and a latrine and an area to bathe in. The family was just great. They loved to have me sit in the evening and watch TV, and they liked to play games and let me cook. We ate tea with milk and bread for breakfast and *sadza,* made from corn, with stewed vegetables and a very small piece of meat, if they had it, for the evening meal.

Besides language and cultural training, the Zimbabwe volunteers also began to learn about their jobs. Cori recalled, "We were the first ones to be community education resource volunteers, and the idea was for us to start community centers that local schools and communities could use. But really we focused on training teachers and having books and computers and programs they could use. So we got training in library science and teaching and community organization." Cori concluded that "training was probably the hardest time of the whole Peace Corps experience because we spent so much time with the other volunteers. For many, it was their first time away from family and friends, and people got stressed out a lot, but in another way it was really great because I met all these great friends."

2000s

Living with host families became a more usual and even longer part of training in the twenty-first century in all regions of the world, and almost always language and cultural training were critical. Training could be very tough, but selection was a nonissue.

Abby Gorton (Jordan 2005–2006) went to Washington, DC, for staging and then flew to Amman with thirty-one other volunteers planning to work in special education, English instruction, and youth and community development. After a week of introductory sessions, the volunteers were divided up. Abby said:

We were assigned to training villages, with five or six volunteers in each village around Irbid. We each had a language and cultural facilitator who was Jordanian and spoke English really well and was also well educated about customs in the villages. Each volunteer had his or her own host family, but we would come together and have language and cultural classes and then spend evenings visiting other people in the village or with our host families. We had Arabic language class from about 8:00 to noon, then lunch with our host families, then back to class from about 4:00 to 8:00. My group had a really good facilitator, and he made sure we visited one host family's house each night.

My host family was an older couple who had children and grandchildren, a wealthy family who lived in a huge house. My host father was retired military, and he had several fruit trees and two cows. Another volunteer's host family had a car, and her father was a former intelligence guy. My family didn't speak any English at all. They had five children, so it was fun to see them on their first day of school and help them with their English homework. After the first month we had a practicum where we taught English at an unofficial summer camp in our training village. The three female volunteers co-taught; we were observed by Peace Corps staff, as were the boys, who taught in a separate village at a boys' school. One day a week we went into Irbid, the big city, maybe half a million people. Then we did teacher training, group classes on culture, health, security. Security was a big deal.

The Peace Corps teaches you what you need to know right away, like greetings and food and health issues and numbers. They observed us in trial classes with different teachers and paired up those who learned in similar ways with a facilitator who used that style. Our group wanted to learn to write even though we weren't really supposed to, so we copied down things while we were learning the basics. And of course we got a lot of practice with our host families. My host mother and I really connected, and she would know what I wanted before I knew it. In cultural training, visiting was the focus. Most of our cultural training came from visiting families and learning how to eat. We learned that showing the balls of your feet to someone is very rude, and not to turn your back to someone if you're sitting down. As women, we learned how to sit on the bus. Men and women are not allowed to sit on the bus together, so there's kind of a shuffle, a little dance that goes on when there are seats.

When I arrived in my village I felt I could comfortably visit people and not totally screw up. The big difference between China [where Abby had taught for several years] and Jordan was that in China if you mess up, you're a dumb foreigner and it's not a big deal. In Jordan if you mess up, it can affect your reputation and your effectiveness as a volunteer and your safety. People had a great sense of humor, but the dynamic between men and women is different.

For volunteers in Eastern Europe, Russia, and the former Soviet republics, training also focused on living with host families and learning the language. Older volunteer Peg Dickson (Ukraine 2000– 2002) flew to Kiev with forty-seven others and then traveled south on a bus to Cherkasy for training.

That bus ride was memorable because the bus broke down, and it turned out that whenever you took a bus ride it was very unusual when the bus didn't break down. So that was just a forerunner of things to come. Our host families greeted us in Cherkasy, had a welcoming ceremony, and then helped us get our luggage to their apartments and had dinner for us. I was tired; all I wanted to do was go to bed. Training started at 9:00 the next morning. We had three hours of language training and three to four hours of technical training every day. There were three of us who were teacher trainers, so we went in with the university teachers, but they said, "Go and see what you can do, and then you can train the next group," which we did.

Living with a family really did involve us in family life and got us used to how Ukrainians did things, as opposed to how Americans do things. After the first couple days I went into the kitchen to help my host mother, who was a couple years younger than I am, fix dinner. She sat me down with a pan of potatoes—none of them bigger than a large golf ball—and a knife close to twelve inches long. She probably thought I was totally incompetent, but I had never peeled potatoes with a knife that big. The first morning I was presented with a big, thick sausage, like a giant hot dog, and a plate of plain spaghetti for breakfast. It was my introduction to "You aren't in Kansas anymore." We got used to the food and the customs, such as the way people relate to each other. Ukrainians don't smile, and if you walk down the street with a smile on your face, they think you're crazy. Their history has not been nearly so pleasant as ours, so they don't have a lot to smile about. My "mother" was a good mother. She would sit me down every night and help me with my Ukrainian homework and make sure I did it. For the host families, this was a way to make some extra money, and they also wanted their Peace Corps volunteers to be successful.

For her eleven weeks of training, Sara Todd (Armenia 2001–2003) lived with a host family in a village outside the second largest city in Armenia, Gyumri. "Each village had about four or five volunteers, and the language instructor stayed in the village with the volunteers, so there was 24/7 support if we got sick or needed a translator or just someone to talk to. In the morning we would have four hours of language training. We were supposed to have language training in the school, but we were kicked out because the principal of the school did not get a volunteer because the housing situation just wasn't appropriate or wasn't up to Peace Corps standards. So we had language training at one of the host family's houses, which ended up being great because we would have nice little tea breaks." By the end of training, Sara felt confident enough to "do some shopping and have small conversations with neighbors and ask for directions in Armenian. I continued my language training once I got to the site." Sara took a full year of language classes with a private tutor, reimbursed by the Peace Corps, and by the end of her service, she estimated she could understand about 70 percent of the language, and her speaking ability was around 50 percent. She couldn't do a full training session for the business center in Armenian, "but I could probably get by a little bit. And of course, they loved it when you would try to train in Armenian."

Host families and language training were paramount for volunteers serving in African countries as well. Jenny Howard (Gabon 2000–2002) trained in the capital city of Libreville for three months, and the seventeen in her group were sent to live with host families.

I remember it being the most terrifying feeling to go off with this family. They smiled at me. They seemed very nice. They were Fang, but I couldn't even differentiate between the Fang language and French. I was completely overwhelmed. The first week I would go in my room and fall asleep from exhaustion and cry a little bit, just feeling: what have I gotten myself into? But I remember also being amazed by moments that would happen more and more during those three months, when I understood what my family was trying to say or made a connection with my host family sisters or my host family father.

Every weekday we would have French training. It started out kind
of formal with worksheets, and then we were divided into groups by our
level of proficiency. The staff person would take us out in the city, and he
would work on our vocabulary at the market or challenge us to get a taxi
or figure out how much we owed this person. I remember watching him
closely so I wouldn't lose him in a crowd, because I wasn't sure I could
get back to the training center.

Jenny's training also included culture, particularly nuances regarding
gender differences and dress. In environmental education training,
they learned about the ecosystems of Gabon, the government's natural resources agency, and several nongovernmental organizations.

Ashley Netherton (Senegal 2003–2005) left for West Africa the
day the war in Iraq began. After four days of shots and crash courses
in health, language, and culture, the volunteers did what was called
"demystification," a three-day trip to the interior. "We got into air-
conditioned land cruisers and headed out on a nine-hour bumpy
ride to the Tambacounda region, where I ultimately ended up being
stationed. We get out and it's 113 degrees, and it hits you like a ton of
bricks, a dry heat that sort of sucks the moisture out of you. I stayed
with a woman who was also an agroforestry volunteer. We taught
some folks in a local village how to start a tree nursery, and I just
hung out with her." Back at the Thies training center, Ashley lived
with a Bambara family and got training in the Bambara language
and in agroforestry. She recalled "learning about the environment
of Senegal, local trees, low-tech farming techniques, how to grow
things in a very, very dry environment. We also were shown techniques we would be using with our villagers to start tree nurseries.
We learned a little bit about grafting fruit trees. Basically, a lot of the
instruction was showing us how to teach other people to do things
in an environment where they didn't have a lot of tools or resources,
without having to spend money to buy new tools or poly sacks for
tree nurseries or watering cans or fertilizer or pesticides."

Elizabeth Greene (Niger 2003–2005) trained for eleven weeks at
a site about thirty kilometers outside the capital, Niamey.

The first two nights we stayed at the training site, and they taught us
how to use the latrine, how to wash your own clothes, how to set up your
mosquito net. Then we were paired with another trainee and assigned
to host families. The host family had built us our own hut with our own

latrine and shower area. But I think the training center had been in the village for so many years, since the 1960s, that the village had been ruined by Peace Corps. Six months of the year they have Americans there who are ignorant of their culture and language. They've been around Americans too much, and it's hard to get the real experience there. It's funny, because when I helped with training later, I was walking with some trainees in the village, and some kids walked by me and said obscenities in the local language. I just turned around and said, "What did you say?" Half of our training was language. I learned Zarma, others learned Hausa, and the education volunteers learned French. Other sessions covered Islam, how to ride in bush taxis, gender, and then security, safety, and medical sessions. The Nigerian people are great at acting, so they do funny skits about what it's like when you're meeting your host family for the first time. In the technical parts we did basic health care lessons. A lot of it was trying to incorporate local know-how and do things relevant to a villager's life, such as hand washing and making oral rehydration solution for diarrhea.

Elizabeth helped train the following group. She said, "After our group, they decided to shorten the training to eight or nine weeks and took the technical stuff out until the end. They were very adamant about your first three months on site being only for cultural integration and learning language."

Not all the volunteers praised their training. Gary Griffin (Thailand 2004–2006), part of a teacher collaboration and community outreach program in which he was supposed to be teaching teachers, was one critic. "The really sad and unfortunate thing is that we had some incredibly talented [Peace Corps volunteer] teachers, and they were never tapped into. That was a real shortcoming on Peace Corps' part." For Gary, a volunteer who had extended her time of service was the most valuable resource. Another woman who had made a career of doing Peace Corps training was knowledgeable about teaching methodologies but too theoretical, in his view, for people without a teaching background. Gary did praise the language training and the hardworking Thai women teachers, but he was concerned about the differences in pay between Thai and American staff. Gary was also critical of being treated like a child. "I found it almost like a boot camp. A major source of contention for me is that I have a beard, and at the time, I had a long ponytail. One of the non-Thais literally marched me to the barbershop and sat there while I got a haircut." He also had to shave off his beard, which he had had for twenty-five years, in order to be culturally appropriate, although he grew it back when he got to his site. He and other volunteers talked about "this cross-cultural thing" and the belief that it should go both ways. "We're supposed to be making all the adaptations here," he said. "We're Americans, and Americans have beards. You know, they're going to have to accept me. If it's an acceptable thing in America, that's something they need to adjust to. I'm 100 percent in support of being respectful to their culture and their religion. But I also think you have to allow volunteers a part of their own identity."

Like Gary, other volunteers have been arguing for a greater role in their training and in program development as well. In an October 2009 survey of returned and current volunteers and staff, under the category of "volunteer empowerment," volunteer input on programs, training, and site selection was at or near the top.[15]

A CROSS-CULTURAL DILEMMA

As the following chapters entitled "Living" and "The Toughest . . ." will show, one of the major challenges a Peace Corps volunteer faces is living in another country with people who may act and think very differently. Drawing from its long experience in cross-cultural training for volunteers, the Peace Corps' global education division, known as WorldWise Schools, has been sharing its knowledge with teachers and students for many years. Originally a correspondence match program between volunteers and U.S. classrooms, WorldWise Schools now provides an array of curriculum resources, including online lesson plans based on volunteers' writings. One of its print resources designed for middle and secondary school students is *Building Bridges: A Peace Corps Classroom Guide to Cross-Cultural Understanding.* It includes the following story, along with questions asking students to compare Dominican and American perspectives and try to solve the jogger's dilemma. All volunteers experience cross-cultural dilemmas. This is one.

Jogging Alone [from Lesson 9: Resolving a Cross-Cultural Misunderstanding]

When I first arrived in my village in the Dominican Republic, I began to have a problem with my morning jogging routine. I used to jog every day when I was at home in the United States, so when I arrived in my village in the Dominican Republic, I set myself a goal to continue jogging two miles every morning. I really liked the peaceful feeling of jogging alone as the sun came up. But this did not last for long. The people in my village simply couldn't understand why someone would want to run alone. Soon people began to appear at their doorways offering me a cup of coffee; others would invite me to stop in for a visit. Sometimes this would happen four or five times as I tried to continue jogging. They even began sending their children to run behind me, so I wouldn't be lonely. They were unable to understand the American custom of exercising alone. I was faced with a dilemma. I really enjoyed my early morning runs. However, I soon realized that it's considered impolite in Dominican villages not to accept a cup of coffee, or stop and chat, when you pass people who are sitting on their front steps. I didn't want to give up jogging. But at the same time I wanted to show respect for the customs of the Dominican Republic—and not be viewed as odd or strange.[16]

Chapter 4

Living

I had half of a separate one-story home that had a living room and a bedroom and a kitchen. And it had a toilet indoors with a shower over the toilet. So you go in the bathroom and close the door and turn on the shower, and it would go into the toilet and on down the drain. It was really quite elegant.

—Judy Lippmann (Morocco 1966–1968)

I lived within the compound of the family of the assistant of the subprefect, a government official, and by default, they became my host family. I had my own bedroom, but everything else was shared. I would buy a bag of rice, but I ate with them.

—Rachel Savane (Guinea 1990–1992)

Six Volunteers in Five Decades

Martin and Patsy Tracy (Turkey 1965–1967)

For the first year, Martin and Patsy lived above a hardware store in Kirsehir, a town of about 20,000 in Cappadocia, about six hours southeast of Ankara, the capital. Martin described their living quarters: "The apartment had a living room, bedroom, and bathroom (oriental style, just a hole in the ground). There was cold running water. The shower was a jerry-rigged mechanism where you had to put wood underneath and heat the tank up. We heated with a potbelly stove using kindling and coal. We had a nice little balcony, so you could walk out and see the town. Behind our building was a row of ten shoemakers in wooden cubicles. The roads were all dirt, and there were horse-drawn carriages, very few automobiles." Their building was between two mosques, so they heard all the calls to prayer.

After a breakfast of eggs, olives, cheese, crackers, and tea, they walked up the hill to their school, teaching perhaps four classes. Martin remembered, "We would often meet with the faculty in the morning for coffee and chat about the news and weather. About 3:00 we would have coffee again and then come home after the school assembly at the end of the day. We might eat out at one of the local restaurants or eat at home. In the evenings we read a lot. About three months after we arrived, the Peace Corps sent us a trunkful of books. And that was a godsend. It was filled with novels, history, and poetry. So we would spend the evening reading, writing, planning lessons, grading papers. On the weekends we would go out on hikes or go to the old Roman thermal bath in Kirsehir."

Patsy called this, their first assignment, "a plum. This was a prestigious city with a beautiful new high school, a large faculty, and it was very cosmopolitan. It was not difficult to live in this town at all. They had many services, wonderful hot springs. It was affluent by any standard. It was a wonderful market town, wonderful cafés. It had everything you could possibly want. It made the Peace Corps actually too easy. And we knew this would not last."

The second year the Tracys were assigned to Ürgüp, a small village where they taught at a high school and an elementary school and lived on the second floor of a family's home. Patsy explained: "So we lived with a family, literally. We had the upstairs apartment. They had the downstairs apartment. We saw them often. We ate with them sometimes. And they made our presence much more welcomed, because as they accepted us, people who might not have accepted us began to think that we're not threatening, we're not going to do anything to disrupt the community." Their living quarters were larger and the heating system better than in their first assignment, but food was harder to come by. Patsy remembered that cooking was a struggle. "We ate a lot of rice, a lot of cabbage. Fortunately, there was a good village bakery. I think we must have lived on bread. We lost forty pounds each."

Rona Roberts (Philippines 1973–1975)

Rona and her husband rented a downstairs kitchen and the upstairs of a solid, concrete house in Naga City, a crowded agricultural center on Luzon. The house, "which had screens and shutters but no glass in the windows, had been built by a schoolteacher and her husband.

After he died, she lived on her minimal schoolteacher's salary, raised a small child, took her meals next door with her sister, and rented most of her house to a succession of Peace Corps volunteers. We had electricity most of the time, but no running water. There was a well outside that past volunteers had used with no problem. It was within a few feet of a drainage ditch containing raw sewage."

At first, Rona got to her job in a "jeepney." She explained:

A jeepney is a truck with a back that has two bench seats running its length. They are incredibly vividly colored and decorated, every inch. Sometimes even the windshields are narrowed down with decorations of brilliant colors. They don't run on a schedule but in a constant and specific circuit. So when you want a jeepney, you wait at a jeepney place until it comes and fills up with typically fifteen to eighteen people and several animals. The top is covered with packages lashed down and more animals—chickens dangling by their feet and pigs usually. Then young men jump on the running boards of the jeepney and hold on to some kind of railing at the back for dear life. A jeepney stops anytime someone goes "Sss" or "Hara." It's a great form of transportation. Later all the agricultural credit volunteers were invited to buy a small Honda motorcycle, and we did. It wasn't much bigger than a scooter, and we had to bring the motorcycle or the battery inside our house at night or risk having it stolen.

Rebecca Roach (Liberia 1988–1989)

The second year I moved into Bomi and found a house I liked. My mother came to visit me during Christmas break, and I was negotiating the terms of my house. I explained to my mother, "We're not going to talk about the terms of the house right away. This woman's come from Monrovia. She's a very big woman, very wealthy, and she's a big person. So we're going to sit down and we're going to have something to drink. We'll have Cokes, we'll talk about our families, and we are not going to bring up the business of the house until she brings up the business of the house. That's very important. She's the important person; she needs to step forward and take control of the negotiations first, or I'll be seen as just being too big for my britches." I told my mom, we'll just sit quietly, so we did. We sat and we had Cokes and we talked about our families and how hot it had been, and we talked about politics, and finally she said after a long time, probably an hour and a half, "So you want to rent my house?"

And I did. She was a wonderful landlady. She said, "Take all the rent and fix up my house." So I got to redecorate, remodel, do everything to that house. It was fun.

I had four girls who lived with me because they wanted to attend the Catholic school. The only way they could do that was if they moved in with me, because they were from outside the village. I didn't like living by myself. I thought it would be seen as stingy. My first year I hired a cook-housekeeper, but I wasn't a servant kind of person. So I had one female teacher and four girls who lived with me. We all took turns with household chores, and that was seen as culturally acceptable. And there wasn't as much pressure to take on a man.

Sarah Cross Oddo (Jamaica 1993–1995)

Sarah lived in a cottage that had once been the tiny, separate kitchen of a historic great house. "The original owners of the house, the uncle, I believe, invented Pickapeppa Sauce in my little house. You can buy it here [in the United States] in the grocery store. My little house had beautiful antique furniture inside. It had a little kitchen, a little bathroom with this hot water heater on the wall that flamed up in gas, and as the water went through the pipes it would get hot, but you had to put it on a trickle. I had a telephone. I had a beautiful view. The house was tiny, about the size of your dining room, but it was nice. I really liked it."

Aaron Shraberg (China 2004–2006)

Aaron recalled, "Our apartments were very nice, actually, very well furnished, and they gave us a microwave, a stove. We had a kitchen sink, we had a bathroom, bedroom, study, and a living room with a couch and a TV. We had hot water, electricity. Our living circumstances were very, very good, better than other volunteers who lived in the same city. We even had a washer. Some volunteers had no washer and they had to use a squat toilet. We had a Western toilet. Some volunteers didn't have any heating. We had heating during the wintertime, which was good."

The mythic Peace Corps volunteer lives in a mud house in the African bush or in rural Latin America or Asia. The truth is different. Over the five decades, there has always been a variety of living conditions. In the 1960s some volunteers lived in neat bungalows on secondary school campuses in Nigeria or behind mud walls with stoves burning sawdust in the modernizing city of Kabul, Afghanistan. Some twenty-first-century volunteers lived in apartments with telephones in Ukrainian cities, while others lived in mud houses in villages in Niger or Senegal. In all decades, volunteers have lived in towns and cities and isolated villages.

Rather than being organized by decades, this chapter is divided by topics associated with living conditions: homes, host families, a typical day, recreation and travel, and finally, communication and safety and security—the two areas in which the most change has occurred over the Peace Corps' fifty years of existence. We conclude the chapter with Sargent Shriver's views about how a volunteer should live.

HOMES

The Peace Corps' goal was for volunteers to live like the people with whom they worked. The 1961 Peace Corps instructions stated: "Housing and sanitary facilities will be simple but clean and healthy. Except where central dining facilities are provided, housing will include provisions for food preparation. Necessary furnishing may be provided in whole or in part with the house, or the Volunteer may be given additional funds to buy such furnishing on the local market. In all cases, such equipment shall be of local styles and frugal."[1] This was a radical idea, since American diplomats, aid workers, and missionaries typically lived in American compounds, often separated from people in the host country. Diplomats received their mail via special diplomatic pouches. Military people had access to commissaries for food and other items. In contrast, volunteers lived (and still live) on a monthly allowance and existed mostly within the local economy. The difference was and remains a point of pride for most volunteers.

The 1967 *Peace Corps Handbook* offered a further explanation for the simple lifestyle:

The importance of living modestly overseas cannot be over-emphasized. In many places, the thing most remembered about Peace Corps Volunteers is their willingness to give up things they are known to enjoy in order to work for things they profess to believe. In a sense this is the Volunteer's clear-est expression of the spirit of service. . . . The practical value of modest living in the host country is obvious: it avoids artifi-cial social barriers and places Volunteers on a more comfort-able footing with modest means. In many instances it permits them to live physically closer to the people they are work-ing with and helps make them part of the communities being served.[2]

The handbook did acknowledge that there would be considerable variety in living conditions and that living allowances would vary from country to country. The following descriptions are organized by region of the world and document that variety.

Central and Latin America and the Caribbean

Housing for volunteers who served in Central and Latin America and the Caribbean ranged from a little house in a small town to an apartment in a city to a room in a boardinghouse for Joyce Miller (Chile 1964–1966). "There were fifteen of us, all Chileans, except for me, one bathroom, and a few termites. I only had one lightbulb. It was fine. They took care of me. I had a bed and the wonderful Peace Corps book locker. I read every book the first two months. We didn't have a working shower for six months. Once I developed friendships with the local people, they knew if I came to visit them, I'd bring my towel and take a shower."

Gwyn and Angel Rubio (Costa Rica 1971–1973) lived in a little house with big holes in the floor and walls that didn't meet the tin roof. It was very hot. Angel got water installed in the backyard so they could wash pots and pans. They had an outhouse, a little gas canister stove, and no refrigeration. In contrast, Ben Worthington (Costa Rica 1973–1975) lived with a family in a suburb of San José. He also remembered a "gap between the roof and the cinder block. We were at 3,500 feet in elevation, so in the winter it would get pretty cold at night." They had electricity and television and running water, but they did not have hot water, "so I started doing calisthen-ics to get myself ready for my shower."

Sally Spurr (Ecuador 1975–1977) lived in a city in three differ-ent houses, the last one with a refrigerator. "We all had the little stove with a butane tank. In each place we had a good-sized living room and a very small kitchen, at least two bedrooms, one bathroom. And then you would have your *lavanderia,* always on the roof of the building. There were open tanks on the roof to hold water, so you did your laundry up there. There was city water, but the water would run out. And electricity was on a schedule where they would turn off the electricity in different barrios. Sometimes you just had low voltage, and water pressure was the same thing. So you always saved a couple of big pots of water to wash with. If I wanted a shower I went to the casket company, where they had public showers. They used the waste lumber from making caskets to make showers."

Also in Ecuador, Marianna Colten (1981–1983) rented a room from a local nurse and shared her kitchen. In her Ecuadoran village, Kay Roberts (1982–1984) rented two rooms at the community center, a concrete block building with a tin roof and a bucket-flushed toilet but no electricity or running water.

At the very high end of living was Joshua Mike (Nevis 2004–2006), who worked with the Ministry of Youth and Sports. His rent on this tourist island in the Caribbean was $400 a month. His two-bedroom apartment had a large kitchen and living room and came with cable TV, electricity, and water. He remembered, "I could reach out from the hammock on my balcony and pick a guava."

Asia and the Pacific

In Asia and the Pacific, even within the same country, living conditions varied. Sometimes volunteers chose to change those conditions. One recent volunteer even helped build his own house.

Jim Archambeault (Philippines 1966–1968) first lived with a well-off family, where he shared a large room beneath the main house with another volunteer and had the amenities of electricity and running water. After four or five months he moved to a fishing village on the ocean, about three or four miles outside of the provincial capital. He took a bus or jeepney into town for his work in an office. "I wanted a different experience," he said. His wooden house stood on stilts about ten feet off the ground and was attached to another house. "Essentially, I had a bedroom. Outside was a thatched-roof place that had a fifty-gallon tin drum, and I would take my baths there." Jim ate mostly fish and rice. "The fish was fresh, right out of the ocean. It was fabulous."

Pacific island living was fairly basic. Capp Yess (Fiji 1982–1984) taught at a rural secondary school on the island of Vanua Levu. Although there was a lane of houses for faculty, he wasn't offered one, perhaps because he was a single person.

> I lived in a little converted classroom that was in the compound of the elementary school. Behind my "house" were the bathrooms, and for some reason my shower was in the girls' bathroom. So every morning I had to get up and make sure I had taken my shower before the kids started arriving for school. The girls would know I was in there if the door was locked. The problem was that the kids walked to school in plastic sandals, so one of the first things they would do is wash their feet under the taps at the elementary school, and then the water pressure to my shower shut off. I also used the school toilet. The floor was cement with a piece of linoleum for a carpet and bamboo-laced walls and a tin roof.
>
> I had a little entryway, kitchen, sitting room, and bedroom with a bed and a mosquito net. I had a kerosene stove and a little cupboard to keep things in. You put little bowls with kerosene on the feet so ants couldn't crawl into your food cupboard. I didn't have a refrigerator, so every day I walked down to the little store and bought what I needed. I had running water a few hours in the morning and occasionally in the evening for an hour or two. I did not have electricity. We used Coleman-style lamps. I did cook for myself, although the people assumed I couldn't cook and often invited me to their homes. The first week I made lunch for myself, but somehow ants got in my food. Someone must have seen me brushing ants out of my lunch, because from then on someone always brought me lunch.

Cecil and Sheila McFarland (Micronesia 1972–1974, Philippines 1974–1976) described their house on the island of Pohnpei in Micronesia. "We had a two-room concrete block house that was about thirty feet by thirty feet. We had an average of 400 inches of rain a year, so with a fifty-five-gallon drum hooked up to a gutter, you had all the water you would want. The school had built a dam and piped water in." Sheila called the rain her "second rinse cycle." She would leave the laundry, "especially the towels and sheets, [hanging outside] through one extra rain, and that was the rinse." They ate tuna, Mary Kitchen roast beef hash, and Dinty Moore beef stew ordered from San Francisco, supplemented with fish the men caught along with green beans, eggplant, scallions, and corn from the school garden. Kerosene was an important commodity. "We had a little kerosene refrigerator that used about a gallon a week. I could make one tray of ice a day. We had two little kerosene stoves that used a three- to four-inch wick. You could cut slices in the bottom of a cookie tin and rig it up on top of your burners like an oven. The school generator ran from seven to nine at night so students could study, and the rest of the time there was no electricity. We didn't need it. We went to bed early and got up early, and if you needed light, you had kerosene and hurricane lanterns."

A recent volunteer in Asia was determined to live modestly, even in the twenty-first century. Gary Griffin (Thailand 2004–2006) explained, "I actually lived much simpler than I had to. I had this wooden platform bed. Every other volunteer I know had a frame and a mattress, and most of them had air-conditioning. So I made this rather feeble attempt to rough it. Having a fan and a screen was my giving way to luxury. But I had a hard bed and a plastic chair." Gary and the janitor of his school actually built the house Gary lived in. "I have the carpentry skills. So that worked out really well. The house was ten by thirty, the bedroom ten by ten. Then there was a bathroom where you could wash clothes and shower, and toilet facilities. So I had electricity and I had water, but it wasn't really running water. I didn't have a sink or anything. It was gravity fed—running water, but only up to a level of about two feet, so I could fill buckets and use water. I pumped the water from a pond to be stored in clay urns. And then it would last several weeks."

Russia, Eastern Europe, and the Middle East

Housing for volunteers in this region of the world usually consisted of one-room apartments with electricity and plumbing. The first descriptions here are from the 1990s, when the Peace Corps began its programs in Russia and Eastern Europe.

Brian Arganbright (Slovakia 1991–1994) began with a room in a student dormitory. He shared a bathroom with another foreign lecturer and ate at the student cafeteria for the first year. "I had electricity, plumbing, heating in that dorm room." For his second and third years he lived in an apartment in the center of the city—"a nice walk to the university."

In the Penza region in mid-southern Russia, Blake Stabler (Russia 2000–2002) taught in school number 45 and lived in a housing settlement—two clumps of apartment buildings with some wooden houses and little farm plots and jet fuel tankers. He had a room in "a two-bedroom communal apartment owned by two different sets of people, neither of whom were living in it anymore. There were two people [students] in the other room, and I had my own room. There's a specific piece of furniture where you store your boots and coats and hats." The room had a sink and a bathtub, and there was a room with a toilet; he shared the kitchen. Blake said, "They overheat everything. They had one central boiler, so you had one knob to control the heat on your sort of hot water unit by the window."

Peg Dickson (Ukraine 2000–2002) had her own one-room apartment with a living area that included a bed, kitchen, and bathroom. "I was lucky," she said. "It would not be unusual [for Ukrainians] to have three or four people living in one room. It was in the middle of the city, which was convenient because it was right by the trolley, which was what I used to get around to visit different schools. I was basically a country girl at heart, and I had three bars within spitting distance of my apartment. There was a small apartment-sized gas stove you had to light. It had a dial, but anything less than turned all the way up didn't bake anything. I was lucky to have a hot water heater you had to light each time you wanted to use it. I bought toasters twice. The first one worked for three days, the second one for three weeks. In order to use the toaster I had to unplug the refrigerator, so I decided it wasn't worth it."

In another former Soviet republic, Sara Todd (Armenia 2001–2003) described her "small one-bedroom apartment. It was a very similar structure to an American apartment, maybe a little more rough, with exposed wires and faucets that didn't work. I had to heat up my water in a bucket with an electric coil. You plugged the coil into the wall, and you'd have to make sure the coil was in the water before you plugged it in. You didn't want to stick your finger in the water, because you would get a shock. So I had water a couple times a week, and I would fill up buckets, and that would be what I used for a couple of days. I did bucket bathing. My living allowance was $150 a month, and then I received $40 for my apartment."

Leigh White (Bulgaria 2001–2003) also lived in "a very small apartment on the second floor of a typical Eastern bloc apartment building. I had a small bathroom with a shower, a toilet that flushed, and a sink with hot water. There was a small entryway. Then I had the main room where my bed was, and everything was in this main room—my dining table, my TV, everything. I had fifty-something channels with cable: VH1 and MTV and CNN and BBC and the Hallmark Channel, among many other Bulgarian channels and European stations as well. I had a very small kitchen, a little terrace with a stove. I had pretty much everything I was used to having, although it wasn't as nice as what I was used to. I had a telephone. I didn't have a washing machine or a dryer."

In Jordan, volunteers lived in houses. Abby Gorton (Jordan 2005–2006) described a "stand-alone home." The front part was occupied by a newly married couple, and she lived in the back half. "I had a pretty big bedroom with a bed and a rug, and I bought a closet. I had a small, longish living room with lots of windows. I had a kitchen, and Peace Corps gave us a refrigerator and a stove top with gas burners. I had a sink and shower, a Turkish toilet, and a hot water heater. Across the street was a field where onions were grown, and beyond that was another field where Bedouin people set up their tents with their camels and other animals; they worked the fields in the summer and fall. And there were olive trees all around my house."

Africa

Homes in African countries ranged from staff houses on a school compound to mud houses in villages, even in the twenty-first century. One issue mentioned by the interviewees was household help.

In West Africa in the 1960s, John Skeese (Nigeria 1961–1964), Terry Anderson (Ghana 1965–1967), Jules Delambre (Cameroon 1965–1967), and Philip Curd (Guinea 1963–1965) recalled fairly comfortable living situations. John taught at one of the best secondary boarding schools in eastern Nigeria and lived in a bungalow; he had a cook and a steward and belonged to a club where he swam and played pool. Terry shared a bungalow at a top secondary boarding school in Ghana with a teacher from Britain who had a jeep; they also had a steward who did the cooking and house cleaning. Jules taught at a Catholic teachers' training college in the Bamenda Highlands in the Northern Province. He shared a staff house, which was made of mud brick with a concrete floor, whitewashed walls, tin roof, and paperboard ceiling. He had his own room, as well as a sitting room, dining room, and outside kitchen. They also had a houseboy and a cook. "We had a mud brick shower behind the house, which at that altitude, tended to be kind of cold. We had a bucket that you pulled the lever and got a shower, so when we wanted to take a shower, we would have the cook or houseboy heat up a bucket of water and pour it into the shower bucket. Then we pulled the string to shower as the cold air blew in." Philip shared what was called a villa at a fruit research station established by the French when they were the colonial power in Guinea. His house had running water and electricity most of the time. "The water reservoir in the attic would warm up during the day, but we got used to taking cold show-ers. The Peace Corps provided us with a refrigerator and kerosene stove, so we were really living high on the hog. We had a houseboy who would keep the house clean, go to the market, buy food, and cook it for us. We were told we were expected to have houseboys. That supported the local economy, and it was really good because we got to know them and find out about their lives."

Forty years later, Robin Sither's (1996–2000) living conditions in Cameroon were somewhat similar to Jules's. He lived in a house with an outside kitchen and a houseboy, "somebody who wouldn't other-wise have a source of income." Although he had a pit latrine, Robin had running water from an outside spigot and electricity. "If I had wanted to, I could have hooked up a phone. I was outside a major town, where I could get access to the Internet, and there was a supermarket where I could have anything I wanted in terms of Western food." He also had two gardens—one in front and one in back that he called "a sanctuary, a beautiful little tree-canopied area where I planted some grass and had my fire pit. I had parties and sat out there."

Some volunteers were not comfortable having servants. For Bill Sweigart (Liberia 1967–1970), the solution was to hire "kids from school to do work and basically adopt them and cover their school fees. Two volunteers in Ethiopia—Ron Pelfrey (1966–1968) and Fred Cowan (1967–1969)—both supported students who worked for them and also had maids. Ron and his Ethiopian housemates, who were doing national service, supported students who gardened and shopped for them and lived in the one-room quarters in the back of their mud house. "We also had a maid/cook—not unusual for teachers, because teachers were the upper class in Ethiopia. From my perspective," said Ron, "living conditions were good. I had some-body to take care of me and somebody to raise a garden for me." At first, Fred lived in "a pretty nice house that had been built during the Italian occupation—two bedrooms, a nice living room, and a bath and toilet in the house. It had a couple little mud outbuildings where three students lived. They did some errands for me, and in return I provided them money for food. I had electricity and I had a cook. Later I moved to a place over the police station and then to another place, which was a mud building with an outhouse. I was trying to be more like the average guy and hang out with Ethiopians."

Bill Sweigart's living conditions in up-country Liberia in the 1960s were more basic than those of volunteers living on school compounds in Cameroon, Ghana, Guinea, or Nigeria—all former colonies with an expatriate tradition. He had no electricity or running water and had to use an outhouse. But, he said, it was a "very nice dwelling, for Liberian standards. We had a cement floor, and it was plastered and painted inside, with the standard tin roof that during the rainy season was very noisy when the rains pounded on it. We had fifty-five-gallon drums for collecting water off the roof, so we almost always had water, and a well not too far away. There was a small antestructure in the back where we had a fire going for cooking, a two-burner kerosene stove, an oven, and a tin box oven that sat on top of it. I actually learned to bake bread and pineapple upside-down cake."

Teachers in other African countries and in later decades lived in local staff housing but did not always have household help. Dianne Bazell (Zaire [Democratic Republic of Congo] 1975–1977) lived in a row of teachers' houses made of concrete blocks and with metal roofs. "We had cold running water. We boiled our water religiously, all the time, even to brush our teeth. We had a living room, dining room, kitchen, and two bedrooms. We had some industrial school African furniture, a couch and some African chairs that slanted to one another. The kitchen had a concrete sink, a stove, a small refrigerator. Whatever food we got once a week, we would refrigerate. We hired a villager by the name of Placide who did our laundry and cleaned up outside the house, but we did our own cooking. We lived mainly on rice and those cans of mackerel and tomato sauce. We ate lots of spaghetti."

Lauren and David Goodpaster (Malawi 2005–2007) had a four-room brick staff house near the health center where they worked. Built in the early 1990s, it was wired and piped but had no electricity or running water. They decorated their home with furniture made in the village and maps and pictures. David found a big map of Africa with all the African flags. Lauren explained, "We just wanted to make it a welcoming place not just for us but for anyone in the village."

Richard Parker (Côte d'Ivoire 1973–1974, Morocco 1976–1978)

described living in a modern three-bedroom furnished apartment in government-sponsored university housing in Abidjan, the capital of Côte d'Ivoire. "I actually used the air-conditioning the first month," he said, "until I got the electric bill. In some ways my lifestyle improved from the way I'd been living in California. I lived about a kilometer from the Hotel Ivoire, which was an Intercontinental Hotel with a bowling alley, a supermarket, and man-made lagoons where you could rent a boat and go out to the casino and gamble all night long. I didn't do that, but that was what it was like."

What might surprise 1960s volunteers who served in Africa is the number of twenty-first-century volunteers who lived in mud houses. Elizabeth Greene (Niger 2003–2005) lived in a mud house provided by her village. It was "a circular mud hut with a thatch roof. And it had a separate shower and latrine area with a millet fence around it. Inside on my right was a basic wooden table that I covered with a cloth. And I had my water filter and my two-burner stove, and my gas bottle was under the table. And I had three metal trunks—one for my food, one for clothes, and one for odds and ends. These were always placed on cans so critters didn't go under them and hide, like scorpions, crickets, and ants. Most of the year I slept outside, but I had a metal cot that was woven with string and a thin mattress I bought and a mosquito net."

Lettie Heer (Senegal 2001–2003) had her own twelve-foot-square house "made out of mud bricks with a thatch roof top. I think I had been wanting that my whole life." The floor was sand, with a cement top. There were two doors and a window. "I didn't open the window, which had a sheet metal piece on the outside, because it opened onto a road where people traveled from the next village to ours, and the first day I was there, a horse stuck its head in. My bed sat on stacks of mud bricks and was made of saplings put together with baling wire. I bought a three- or four-inch piece of foam that went on top of that. Peace Corps gave us malaria nets. I had a desk built." She put her clothes and food in plastic containers and reed baskets and swept every day to keep the termites out.

HOST FAMILIES

Many volunteers lived with host families during in-country training, but later, in some programs and some countries, host families became the preferred or even required way for volunteers to live.

A wealthy family in her Bambara village took in Ashley Netherton (Senegal 2003–2005).

They had a big compound with small mud brick thatch huts and several cement brick buildings. Peace Corps required that we have our own living space, so they had to build me my own hut under a tree. It was a four-by four-meter mud brick thatch hut with a little fenced-in backyard where I had my latrine and my shower area. I had a little garden the first year, but then I ended up putting my bed out there the second year because it's so unbelievably hot sleeping inside. My parents came to visit me around Christmas, so my [Senegalese] brother built a sort of veranda with logs and thatch for me. Then the next year he built one in the back so I had shade over my outside bed.

In the beginning, I always ate with the family. I got there in June, which is right before the rains and the beginning of what they call the starving time, because almost everyone's food reserves have begun to run out, so there wasn't a lot of food. We pretty much just ate rice for lunch and dinner, occasionally with peanut sauce, and three types of cornmeal-based porridges. After harvest they had squash and more peanuts and millet. They ate fish, and for holidays they would kill a sheep. I'm a vegetarian, so I would go to the market once a week and try to buy vegetables. We were all encouraged to contribute to our families, and I preferred to give them food as my contribution.

Sarah Payne (The Gambia 1989–1991) lived in "a compound that had two rows of houses facing each other. Padja was a local midwife who lived in one house with her granddaughter and great-granddaughter, whose families had gone to France and would occasionally send money. An uncle lived in the house on the end. A student rented the room next to me. A goat used to live in my house, but we kicked out the goat and cleaned up the house because Peace Corps required that you have a cement floor and screens on your windows."

A private roof and access to a well and a bathroom were the amenities for Carolyn Cromer (Morocco 1992–1995), who lived on the second floor of a mud building in a family compound in her village.

I had one room which was maybe twelve feet by fourteen feet with a small closet and two windows, and I had a private roof. Roofs were used quite a bit in Morocco as other rooms. I had access to a well and the bathroom I had built as part of the agreement to live with this family. To get to it, I went down two flights of stairs, out the door, into another door to a whole other courtyard and a whole other building, and through the courtyard. It was a pit latrine with a concrete squat plate that worked great. The family created a bathing room next to it. They could, in fact, create a mini-sauna. They had a way to heat water so that it was steaming. The family I lived with had about twenty-seven people, and I think maybe three of the men might have used the latrine sometimes, but I was definitely the only person consistently using the latrine. Obviously, the idea was that I would also do education about latrines.

Maurice White (Afghanistan 1974–1976) located a host family in Mazar-i-Sharif with the help of a fellow teacher and chose to live in their compound because he was single. "I was very close to the family, and one of the younger boys was in my seventh-grade class. The oldest son in the family was a year younger than me, so he always wanted to be with me and emulate me and learn English through me. The mother in the house was head of nursing at a hospital, and the father was on the verge of retiring from the military. The oldest daughter was a schoolteacher, and her husband was in the Afghan military. All the kids went to school, even the youngest daughters. I spent a lot of time with them. I had someone who worked for me, and when he and his wife had a baby, they lived with me."

Andrew Kimbrough (Sri Lanka 1984–1986) chose to live with a host family in order to experience the culture and learn the language. The household included his landlady, a widow with a son in New Jersey, a daughter in East Germany, and a fourteen-year-old daughter at home; her father; and a housegirl. "The food was excellent," he said. "I had rice and curry every day for the main meal at lunch, and I would eat with the grandfather. They didn't spice it up as much, so I could at least get it down. I had a nice room, a nice window that looked out over the street, a fan, and of course, I had to have a mosquito net made for myself. I had electricity and running water in the house. I could bathe inside in the bathroom. I filled up the tub with water and with a small hand bucket just dumped water over myself—cold water, but you're in the tropics, so it was actually quite refreshing."

A TYPICAL DAY

Even some volunteers who had regular jobs, such as teaching, found it hard to describe a typical day, but most developed some routines. Early to rise and early to bed was the rule for many volunteers.

Education

Teacher Cecil McFarland (Micronesia 1972–1974, Philippines 1974–1976) got up at sunrise in Micronesia. "Classes started at 7:30. We would teach usually three classes in the morning. I would teach two agriculture classes and then another math or English class. At lunchtime all the teachers ate together—rice, perhaps with fish, perhaps fresh tuna. Afternoons we would go to the farm and manage the student labor to both teach and earn funds for the school. We raised chickens and sold the eggs, and we raised pigs and vegetables like cabbage and peanuts to sell on the marketplace. Students got to go back about 5:00 or 5:30, and we would head back to the house, have a supper of rice and Dinty Moore beef stew, and play board games with our neighbors. At 9:00 the lights would go out, and we would go to bed."

Capp Yess (Fiji 1982–1984) woke up early, cooked breakfast, had a shower, and got ready for school. "I walked up to the high school, which was about a block from my house, often with students. I taught chemistry for six of the eight thirty-five-minute periods. At the end of the day and during the middle, we had chores. We teachers would oversee cleaning bathrooms, sweeping floors, cutting grass. Sometimes teachers would stay to grade papers for a while after school. If it was soccer season, I would go play with other people in the village. Then I would eat supper and do my dishes. The headmaster, my neighbor, would come over with his little bowl of *yagona* [a tranquilizing, non-alcoholic drink made from the dried roots of the pepper plant]. He'd have some, share it with me, and we'd chat about the day. He might bring his son or two with him. Then I'd grade papers and go to bed."

After bathing and shaving, Andrew Kimbrough (Sri Lanka 1984–1986) began his day with a cup of coffee.

My landlady brewed the coffee from beans she would roast herself—a great way to start the day. I would dress for work—no jeans, a nice pair of pants, button-down shirt—go into the dining room, and have breakfast of what looked like small pancakes. I asked my landlady if she wouldn't mind frying or scrambling an egg every once in a while. Then I'd walk to my school two or three blocks away. We would have a large meeting with everybody. and basically we'd get into our routine. We would teach our four classes, and we'd be done by 1:30 or so.

After eating with Grandfather, by then, it'd be hot as the dickens outside. Everybody would go take a nap. Then I'd get up and start on my lesson plan for the next day. All my lesson planning had to be done that afternoon and that evening. I'd just turn the fan on and point it at me as I sat there at the desk. Everything was written out by hand. Late in the afternoon my landlady and her daughter and the housegirl would watch Indian movies. Then right before dinner I would go out and try to meet neighbors, visit folks. Then I'd go back and have a dinner of leftovers, and I'd be in bed fairly early.

Resource teacher Kristen Perry (Lesotho 1999–2001) was awakened by roosters. "I didn't necessarily bathe every day," she said, "especially in the winter, when it was cold. But when I did take a bath, I would have to heat up my water. We used big basins, and I would sort of crouch over the basin and wash my hair and my body. I boiled water in the evening." She alternated between schools—one in her village, and one a five-mile walk away. She visited classes, had lunch at school with the teachers, and spent time talking to them. She recalled:

It was a very leisurely lifestyle. I might come back to school for the English club. I loved Tuesdays and Thursdays when the church choir practiced; I liked to go listen. If I was in my village that week, I would sometimes take a walk or go hiking in the afternoon. I would start cooking dinner fairly early because it would get dark, especially in winter. For the evenings I had a very set ritual that sort of kept me sane, I think. I'd try to eat dinner at a certain time when there was a program on the radio that I liked to listen to and be done by 6:30 when the classical music came on. I would usually write in my journal or write letters home and then maybe do a crossword puzzle. I did a lot of crossword puzzles. I was usually in bed by about 8:00 or 8:30 because it's dark and there's nothing else to do. I had my little kerosene lamp. I would usually read for about an hour or so. I kept a list of all the books I read, something like 115, 120.

Community Development and Agriculture

Community development volunteer Kay Roberts (Ecuador 1982–1984) began her day early too, at 6:00 A.M.

A lot of times I helped some friends milk the cows in the morning—by hand, of course. Breakfast was usually coffee and bananas, sometimes eggs, and then we would work with school kids. We'd have our English classes or work on the school garden or visit folks. We'd wander up to the one little store in town and chitchat. Although lunch is typically the biggest meal, if I was cooking for myself, I didn't eat a huge plate of rice with soup. Early afternoon I went to the river to wash, because it was a way to cool off, or I sat in my hammock and read. Two afternoons a week I worked at the health clinic. We had a light supper. It was often rice, tuna, eggs, carrots, bananas, pineapple. We made quite a lot of bread. Then early to bed. It's pitch dark at 6:30 on the equator. There was no electricity, so I read by candlelight or flashlight or lantern and was usually in bed by 9:00.

Extension agent Oghale Oddo (Jamaica 1994–1996) got up at 5:00 or 5:30, depending on how far he had to ride his bicycle or walk to get to one of the farms. He met farmers between 6:00 and 10:00, four or five farmers every morning. Then he would return to his house, wash up, and go to one of the two primary schools where he taught from 1:00 to 2:00. When he had a break, he said, "I would go down to one of the farmer's places, sit with him or them, and just talk till about 5:00 or 6:00 in the evening. If I was not sitting with the men I was playing soccer. Sometimes I taught after-school classes, math with a group of high school students from maybe 7:00 to 8:00, three or four days a week. If it was harvest season I didn't meet a lot of farmers, but during planting or preplanting I did a lot of work. Other times I traveled up to Kingston to see people at the Hillside Agriculture Project and get some seedlings for the farmers or talk to them about some issues the farmers were having and get advice on what to do."

Agroforestry volunteer Ashley Netherton (Senegal 2003–2005) also got up with the sun. "When you sleep outside, it's hard not to, and the chickens and donkeys get going about then, too. I would make tea in my hut for myself, perhaps read, and then go over to my family's house. If we had training planned, we would go early to another village. If we didn't have anything planned, there was a lot of hanging out with the family. After harvest we'd sit on the concrete floor and crack peanuts for hours and hours on end. People would rest in the afternoon and then get up and start preparing dinner. Some of the girls would pound corn or millet or grind and roast peanuts. I played with the kids and went on walks in the woods and went to see the sunset on the river. I went to the market once a week on my bike, seventeen kilometers one way, and saw my Forest Service counterpart, too."

Recreation and Travel

Ashley described a "lot of hanging out with the family," and that was true for other volunteers as well. Recreation often meant hanging out with friends and colleagues. Volunteers also read a lot, played sports, occasionally went to movies, and sometimes used their thirty days of vacation to travel inside and outside their host countries.

Harold Freeman (Ethiopia 1965–1967) remembered that "daily life was recreation, to a great extent." He enjoyed interacting with people, for instance, trying out his language skills in bargaining to get the "brother-in-law" price. As William Salazar (Guatemala 1972–1973) said, "What people do for recreation is you talk to each other. People really want to know what you're thinking and what you're like and your experiences." Glen Payne (Gabon 1989–1992) concurred. "We talked because there wasn't anything else to do. It's almost like a new skill you learn again. Wow, people are really interesting!—if you talk to them at length. With other volunteers, you raged about things you didn't understand, had humility about things you thought you were right on and turned out to be wrong on. And lots of mutual wishing: 'Gosh, I wish I had a glass of cold milk. I haven't seen a glass of cold milk in a year, and I'm thirsty for it.' Or a new shirt. Something that didn't smell like diesel fuel and dust and manioc."

One of the best things she learned was "to slow down," Sarah Payne (The Gambia 1989–1991) remembered. "In the U.S. you always want to be doing something or be entertained. I could just sit and have tea, three rounds of brewing this green tea, or we would have coffee. People would tell jokes, and I might understand a fifth of what I heard. Life was about living; it was about gathering your food; it was about being with family. And that was appealing."

Audrey Horrall (Zambia 2000–2002) would "hang out" with her neighbors. "They had a fire every evening, and they would just sit around and talk before everybody went to bed. I read a lot of books and magazines and wrote letters. I would listen to BBC. I was never more informed than when I was in Peace Corps because I listened to the news every morning and every evening." Sometimes Audrey went to a falls in the river near her village. "You could go swimming there, lounge around on the rocks, and read a book. The guesthouse there had cold drinks if the electricity was on."

"Once you got to know the kids," Phil and Nancy Dare (Malaysia 1965–1967) explained, "they would take you across and upriver, where there was a little stream that fed in and a waterfall that was fun to ride into a deep pool underneath. You'd go swimming up there. You could walk out to the longhouses; there was one not too far away. You could just spend time learning about their culture."

Sheila McFarland (Micronesia 1972–1974, Philippines 1974–1976) described borrowing an outrigger boat with a little motor that a neighbor had built and going out to one of the atolls one Saturday a month to swim. "Girls had to swim in skirts. It didn't matter that you were topless or whatever, but your thighs had to be covered. So I had a skirt just for swimming."

Twenty-first-century volunteer Elizabeth Greene (Niger 2003–2005) reported, "We had libraries in the transit houses across the country. You read books and left them for somebody else. I tried to pick up embroidery. The women who could afford to would buy yarn and material to embroider cloths to carry the babies on their backs. One of my friends in the village taught me how to do that."

Recreation for Gwyn and Angel Rubio (Costa Rica 1971–1973) also included reading and riding their motorcycle to go see a movie. Gwyn remembered getting "books in San José and then taking them back to the Peace Corps office and exchanging them. So that's what I did, read, mostly by kerosene lantern." According to Angel, "It wasn't uncommon for us to jump on the motorcycle a couple times a week when it was dark already and drive all the way to San Isidro, sometimes in the rain, to go to a movie or go out to a restaurant. After the bridge washed out, you had to go across this swinging bridge on a motorcycle." Later volunteer Patrick Bell (Costa Rica 1997–1999), who was in the capital of San José, said, "We would go to Cinemark and get popcorn, and before the movie we were in the food court, which had McDonald's and Burger King."

Bill Miller (Dominican Republic 1968–1970) remembered "going down to the plaza. They had a movie house, a theater, and a little orchestra that would come out and play for the people. One of the first songs they played was 'My Old Kentucky Home.'" Maurice White (Afghanistan 1974–1976) always "had visitors. People would smoke, we'd drink tea, and talk. On weekends I really enjoyed going to the Hindi movies. It was ironic, because the Hindi movies showed all the things you couldn't really do in Afghan life. The actors and actresses were all Hindu, and the audience was strictly Muslim. The stories would go on for three hours, complete fantasies."

Marianna Colten (Ecuador 1981–1983) had been a volleyball player in college, but in Ecuador, "volleyball was more the men's sport. They played three-on-three instead of what I was used to. So I played volleyball with people, I walked, I learned how to knit from some of the ladies in town. Sometimes I would go down to the plaza and watch TV. We only had electricity for about four hours in the evening."

In Fiji, the village soccer team included Capp Yess (1982–1984).

I started out playing barefoot, like a lot of them, until I had an opportunity to buy shoes. They wanted me to play because I was a novelty. They enjoyed the fact that they had a big white guy playing on their team. I might have been lousy, but I was bigger than most of them, so they had to watch out that I didn't kick them or push them down. I never did score. A typical Thursday night activity was going to the Hindu temple, where they would sing songs out of one of the sacred texts. We would play instruments—the harmonium, cymbals, and other percussion instruments—and then we would have the religious blessing and a couple of sweets and go home. On weekends I was often invited to an event by one of my students' families, sometimes for a wedding. Usually the men were in charge of cooking, so I would help. Occasionally students and I or neighbors and I would go to the beach to catch tiny little crabs called *puka*, and we would bring them back and cook them up to eat with our beer.

Sometimes sports activities were related to schools. Terry Anderson (Ghana 1965–1967) "organized a small boys' soccer league; I had a mark on my classroom doorsill set at five feet three inches, and you had be to under that to play." Teachers at his school in Ghana were often asked to be patrons or advisers for various student societies. He was the patron of the Volunteer Work Camp Association. "We'd do social projects in the villages. The work camps were coed, and the students really liked this because I was in a boys' school. The camps were set up through a social agency. It was like a rural development organization, and villagers would put their money together to buy enough cement to put up a blockhouse that would be used as a washhouse. We would provide the labor and make the bricks. We got fed by the village and maybe would sleep in the school. I was also the swimming coach. There was a good beach outside of town that we could get to with the school lorry. We also had a Junior Investigators Club, which was set up for field trips, so we went to the Akosombo Dam and to the museum in Accra."

A proud achievement for Ron Pelfrey (Ethiopia 1966–1968) was going to the YMCA in Addis Ababa and getting $700 to start a YMCA in his town. He and his students bought Ping-Pong tables and soccer equipment and basketballs and organized teams. "We had a mixed faculty-student YMCA soccer team that played against the other smaller communities around us. I was a goalie, because I didn't have the foot skills, but I did have the hand skills from playing baseball. We played every weekend. Then I taught them how to play Ping-Pong. And I was the referee and coach for basketball." For his own recreation, Ron hiked in the countryside. "There was a volcanic crater almost a day's walk south of us. So we walked there a couple of times each year. You'd walk up to the crest and look down inside this volcano. It was just gorgeous. It was a capped volcano with a lake inside of it. But it had been dormant for quite a while because there was a village and a rain forest inside. I've traveled all over the world since then, but that volcano is probably the most beautiful sight I've seen anywhere."

Another Ethiopian volunteer, Fred Cowan (1967–1969), also hiked in the mountains. "Sometimes we'd ride donkeys. That was the first time I realized that donkeys were so much more sure-footed than horses going over mountains. I went to a couple wedding celebrations. I also went with some Peace Corps volunteers down to the Red Sea and went swimming. We went to the famous place called Laileba, where they have rock churches built in the eleventh or twelfth century, which is a tourist attraction."

Talking about traveling in her host country made Judy Lippmann (Morocco 1966–1968) nostalgic.

The countryside was just heaven. There were mountains with snow, and in a few hours you could go from the Atlas Mountains down to the Atlantic Ocean. It's just a beautiful country. Fields and fields of red poppies and sunflowers. And riding the bus was fascinating. The goats and hens would all get on top of the bus and get strapped down, a little netting over them. And all the people would get in the bus. The back of the bus was for women and kids. There were no seats. You just got in, and there were blankets spread around. You'd sit down on the floor, and they'd all take their picnics out. Kids were laughing and playing, and moms were nursing their babies and feeding each other and the other kids. Coming back from town it would be pitch-dark outside, and there were these two little headlights of this bus in the middle of nowhere. And all of a sudden somebody would holler out, and the bus would stop. A whole family would descend from the bus, get their animals from the top, and just walk out into a field of pitch-darkness.

Possibilities for recreation changed over the decades. Jules Delambre (Cameroon 1965–1967) described socializing with the teaching staff in town. They would go down the hill to one of the two off-license bars. He explained: "An off-license bar had a license to sell beer, but you couldn't drink on the premises. You were allowed to go into the proprietor's home to drink, so each bar had a bedroom off the bar with plenty of chairs and a bed. We drank Cameroon beer and Star from Nigeria and Heinekens for prestige. Most of the time you ended with an orange squash soft drink or a champagne soft drink. You were not drinking to get drunk; you were just drinking for good companionship. The people in the bars tended to be men, but I got to be good friends with a veterinary assistant about three miles down the road, and he and I would go to the bar there and drink with some of the daughters of the local Fulani chief, who, as was the custom, had returned to their mother's compound to stay with their babies until they were weaned."

Thirty years later, Robin Sither (Cameroon 1996–2000) had many more choices for recreation. "All the volunteers in Northwest Province pooled our money and rented a very nice house in the provincial capital, Bamenda, which is a beautiful city. So whenever we came in, we'd have a place to sleep and get a shower, and then we'd go out. I went to the city of Douala, the commercial center. There you've got everything under the sun—really nice hotels, French food, great grilled fish, and good markets. Or I would travel around the country, visiting volunteers or visiting the game park in the north, where you could see giraffes, lions, and elephants. There were rain forest treks and various mountains to climb. Every year Guinness sponsors a race to the top of this mountain, and almost every volunteer climbs Mount Cameroon. When you reach the peak, if you are lucky, you can see Nigeria and Equatorial Guinea. That view is just insanely gorgeous over the ocean."

COMMUNICATION

One of the major differences between the experiences of early and later volunteers was communication home. In the 1960s, letters were the major means of communicating between volunteers and their families. Oghale Oddo (Jamaica 1994–1996), who was country director in Fiji from 2005 through January 2008, explained the current situation: "Right now, volunteers in some of the remotest corners of Fiji can send a text message back to their parents, or parents can send their children text messages, and people get the news immediately. I had an occasion where a volunteer's house was flooded. She called her parents in the United States, her parents called the Peace Corps office in Washington, DC, and then Washington called the Peace Corps office in-country to say, 'Hey, do you know this girl's house is flooded?' It just got flooded two hours ago. But when we were volunteers just fifteen or twenty years ago, you talked to your neighbors in your community, and they would come in and help you, and then you probably got in touch with Peace Corps."

In a 2008 interview, Peace Corps director Ron Tschetter was asked what had changed the most from the time he was a volunteer in the 1960s. More than forty years later, he estimated that 75 to 80 percent of volunteers had cell phones, and most had access to the Internet in regional towns. He described that change as 90 percent positive and 10 percent negative.

> The positive, of course, is that it does keep them in touch with home and they are sharing their experiences, sometimes daily, at least weekly, and that's a good thing. It's fulfilling the third goal [teaching folks at home about the experience]. It also gives them protection from a safety and security standpoint. On the other hand, our directors will tell me volunteers don't stay or get quite as connected to their communities because they have this enhanced communication now. So if they have a really bad day—and we've all had them as Peace Corps volunteers—they call home which is sometimes the worst thing they can do. Volunteers need to learn to work out their problems in their own communities. So that is the negative side of it, and I know our directors and training people try to make them aware of it. You can't control that, of course, but I think finding your own way makes a difference in your service.[3]

Marlene Payne (Malaysia 1967–1969) remembered, "It was hard not being in instant communication with my family. There was no phone, except maybe at a hotel, and the only time I called home was when we had riots and I wanted to assure my family that I was fine." She, like many other volunteers, wrote letters, and her mother saved them. Nancy Dare (Malaysia 1965–1967) said there were no telephones on Sarawak, "so you were out of contact with them [parents]. Being a grandmother now, I have a little different point of view. When you're young you have no fear and don't even think about it."

For Sheila and Cecil McFarland (Micronesia 1972–1974 and Philippines 1974–1976), mail came to Micronesia through the U.S. postal system, since Pohnpei was a U.S. territory. Sheila said, "Mother would write me on Sunday night, and I would have letters by Friday or Saturday." One Christmas, Sheila and Cecil walked over the mountain to see a priest who was a ham radio operator, "so we actually got to call home. It piped through to [someone in] San Diego, who hooked up with a shortwave guy in Denver. It seemed like it was three connections, so you can imagine all these guys flipping switches. That was very much appreciated by our family." In contrast, their daughter Kathleen (Jordan 1999–2001) had e-mail access. "I used to send e-mails to my parents about once a week, so communication wasn't a problem. There was a phone at my school, and sometimes my friends and I would communicate that way."

Sarah Payne (The Gambia 1989–1991) called her boyfriend and her family from Banjul, the capital, every six to eight weeks. "You would go to the local phone company, and there would be this little phone booth. That's where I learned about country codes. We would probably talk for thirty minutes. To this day, no one has told me how much those phone calls cost, so that means they were a lot of money. My mother was a nurse, and she would say, 'Oh, it was worth it!' But I know it caused a financial strain."

For volunteers in the 2000s, e-mail and cell phone contact was fairly common. "Thank goodness for e-mail," Peg Dickson (Ukraine 2000–2002) said. "I'm not sure how I would have survived, or if I would have survived as well, because I made time at least once a week to do e-mail." She sent e-mail from an Internet café at the cost of $1 per hour. Sara Todd (Armenia 2001–2003) e-mailed her family almost daily and talked to them on the phone on major holidays and once every other month. Leigh White (Bulgaria 2001–2003) rarely used the telephone because it was very expensive, but she did use one of the four or five Internet cafés in her small town almost every day. "It was very inexpensive, about fifty cents an hour. You know, sometimes the connections weren't very fast, but it was still a great way to check up on news and just stay in contact with people. It was much cheaper than writing letters, too. I mailed birthday cards and cards for the holidays, and I did write to my grandmother at least once a week, and she wrote me tons of letters too, because we're very sentimental and romantic about not losing letter writing to e-mail."

Lauren and David Goodpaster (Malawi 2005–2007) had a cell phone but no electricity to charge it, so they set up a time once or twice a month on Sundays to turn on the phone. "Occasionally we wouldn't have a battery. You know, it was like, 'Oh hey guys. Sorry!' And it would hang up." Lauren explained, "When we did get into town we were able to e-mail. We had this e-mail Listserv of 200 people, and I would write journal stories pages long and hope that people would be interested." In neighboring Mozambique, Michael Geneve (2003–2005) used a prepaid phone card to call his family and then let them call him back, and he did a lot of text messaging. E-mail access was three and a half hours away, and although he sent e-mail descriptions of his Peace Corps experience back to the magazine he had worked for in Lexington, at one time he didn't use his e-mail for about eight months. Returned volunteer Gwenyth Lee (Cameroon 2004–2006) also had a cell phone, and there were a few wealthy people in her village with cell phones, too. However, "in Bamenda [the closest town], everybody had a cell phone. My village was too small, but it had good coverage because of elevation, so I could get phone calls from my parents, and I could send text messages. They tried to call every week, and they probably got through half the time. So I probably talked to them once or twice a month. It was good."

Blogs are yet another communication possibility for twenty-first-century volunteers—with the explicit disclaimer that they do not represent the views of the Peace Corps. For example, on his blog, Hunter Dreidame (Guinea 2008–2010) wrote about his experiences as a new Peace Corps volunteer in a Thanksgiving 2008 piece entitled "Now I Can Help." It was featured on the front page of the *Lexington Herald-Leader*.[4]

SAFETY AND SECURITY

In 2010 the Peace Corps Web site stated: "Safety and security are our highest priority."[5] An online essay described the volunteer safety support system and the expectation that volunteers will adopt culturally appropriate lifestyles and build relationships. There were also paragraphs on ongoing training and emergency communications.

Vehicular Accidents

Even though safety and security were not mentioned in the 1961 personnel policies, such concerns have always been present. In the 1960s vehicular accidents were a particular concern. Jules Delambre (Cameroon 1965–1967) remembered a group of volunteers who took a Peace Corps jeep to Bamenda. "They assumed there was a little bit more edge on the road than there was, and the jeep turned over and rolled about sixty feet. Luckily, although they got banged up a little bit, no one was really hurt. I'm sure the jeep wasn't going very fast at the time. They were trying to make a little room for a lorry that was coming downhill as they were going up." Jules concluded that his two years in Cameroon "might have been safer than two years here [in the United States]." However, between 1961 and 2003, eighty-nine volunteers died in motor vehicle accidents.[6] Although Jules bought a Honda motorcycle and put about 5,000 miles on it, motorcycles were eventually banned in most countries.

Bicycle safety continues to be a concern. Gary Griffin (Thailand 2004–2006) was especially worried about the number of bicycle wrecks among his group, so he incorporated bicycle safety in the safety manual he wrote as a member of the volunteer advisory committee. Chapter 7 includes stories about serious motorcycle and bicycle accidents.

Civil Strife

In all decades, the most dramatic safety and security issues were related to civil strife. Coups occurred in the 1960s in Sierra Leone and Ghana, and from 1967 to 1970 there was a civil war in Nigeria. Volunteers stayed through several successive coups in Sierra Leone in 1967, although there were evacuation plans in place at the time. The Peace Corps did leave Sierra Leone during its civil war in the

1990s, and it left Liberia during its civil war that began in late 1989. The Peace Corps has returned to both countries. The Peace Corps did not leave Ghana during the 1966 coup; in fact, it remained in that first Peace Corps country throughout all five decades. Terry Anderson (Ghana 1965–1967) remembered there was never any question about Americans staying during the coup that overthrew President Kwame Nkrumah. "If you were recognized as an American, you were as safe as if you were in a small town in America, but you might be asked if you were American, and if you said, 'No, I'm Russian,' then you'd be in trouble. I got challenged a couple times walking down the street. 'Where are you from?' they asked. And I would say, 'America,' and they would say, 'Good.' Actually, it was a fairly peaceful coup. We were told not to travel during that time, but of course, Peace Corps volunteers did. They snuck into Accra and saw the Nkrumah statue torn down." Peace Corps also stayed in the Dominican Republic in 1965 when "the Johnson administration sent in Marines to abort attempts to overthrow a military regime and reinstall exiled President Juan Bosch."[7] In July 1967 the Peace Corps evacuated volunteers from eastern Nigeria, which broke away as Biafra to start the Nigerian civil war, although volunteers stationed elsewhere in the federation completed their tours over the next several years.

The cold war and competition between the United States and the USSR affected volunteers in Asia. Although the first group of Peace Corps volunteers in India met Prime Minister Nehru twice, Paul Winther (India 1961–1963) recalled that India was leaning toward the Soviet bloc at the time, and "we were suspicious in the eyes of many people." Sargent Shriver, believing that the Peace Corps could help the United States win the cold war, was delighted when President Sukarno invited the Peace Corps to work in Indonesia.[8] However, Bob Leupold (Indonesia and Thailand 1963–1965) remembered the "tremendous anti-American feeling" in Indonesia. He transferred to Thailand when the Peace Corps shut down the Indonesian program because it could not guarantee the volunteers' safety. Bob recalled, "No American movies were allowed to be shown in Surabaya. They had groups of people going around and slashing the dresses of girls who wore Western-style dresses, and they were cutting the hair off of women who had Western-style hairdos." Bob was asked to show a film at a local sports college but was prevented from doing so by the students and the military. The film, which began with Rafer Johnson carrying the American flag into the Olympic stadium, was considered propaganda, and a local newspaper declared, "Bob Leupold, CIA agent, disguised as a Peace Corps volunteer, attempted to subvert the revolutionary students of Indonesia last night."

In Latin America, Joyce Miller (Chile 1964–1966) said, "I was there for Allende's first attempt at election. We were told if anything happened to stay where we were because we would be protected. My part of Chile was heavily communist because of the copper mines. I had several friends that were communists. I'd be at activities where they would sing the *Internationale,* and several times my name appeared in the communist newspaper as being a spy, but everybody took that with good humor, saying, 'Oh, you're a spy again.' Before the election we were called back to Santiago to be briefed on what to do or not to do." The policy was that embassy personnel should not ask volunteers for information. Joyce said, "The consul general did not ask us our opinion on how we thought our areas would go. I knew, but no one ever asked me."

Dan Sprague (Colombia 1963–1965) recalled that the "university was a hotbed of anti-Americanism, and there were a number of demonstrations. You had to be careful being near those situations. You could get spit at, people would throw things at you. So if you were in those situations you better have some Colombians with you who would protect you. It got violent at times." Lloyd Jones was in Colombia ten years later (1973–1975) when they held the first open election since 1948. The Peace Corps brought volunteers "out of the countryside because they were afraid that somebody might get kidnapped or hurt." Nearly everybody he met had been affected by the civil war, losing a brother, a father, or knowing somebody who was killed.

Also assigned to a university, Sally Spurr (Ecuador 1975–1977) was kicked out during her second year. "So they built classrooms on the farm, and students started coming up there from the university and ultimately called for the ouster of the Peace Corps brigade, which we all thought was very funny, since there was only one of me. We had been so quiet they didn't even know we were there. Because at that time everybody said you were *Corpos de Paz,* 'Oh, *un espia de la CIA.*' This was post 1973, when Allende was assassinated [in Chile] and everything was very leftist. The [university] administration was very apologetic."

Back on the African continent, Dianne Bazell (Zaire [Democratic Republic of Congo] 1975–1977) remembered the Angola war going on during her first year and then fighting in the north of Zaire in 1976. "You heard stories about the national army pillaging villages and raping women. There were always soldiers at roadblocks. That was part of life. They would just aim their machine guns at the windshield. They would expect a bribe, and I would say, 'I'm not going to do that.' If I had been an African woman, I would have been killed or raped at least. So there was a boundary that not only my international status but also my skin color gave me among Africans. It's not a pleasant topic, but that was the reality." Dianne knew it was difficult for African American volunteers, who were expected to be African because of their appearance; both African American volunteers she knew went home early. Dianne recalled, "One afternoon our regional rep came in from Lubumbashi with his Land Rover and said, 'Be ready to pack up. I'm going up north to get the people from Kolwezi, and I want you packed in two hours to get out.' They were afraid the main highway was going to be cut off. They evacuated us to Lubumbashi, and then things cooled off. We got taken back to our posts and finished off the school year." The Peace Corps left Zaire soon after Dianne completed her tour.

Civil strife was also an issue in Sri Lanka. Like Dianne, Andrew Kimbrough (1984–1986) might not have been in danger himself, although in retrospect, he felt the Peace Corps should not have placed him in Batticaloa, where he was teaching. "I'm pretty sure the Tamil Tigers came to the house and looked through my things while I was teaching. One of my students just asked me point-blank, 'Are you with the CIA?' I'd be woken up at night because I'd hear bombs go off in the distance, and then I'd hear the next day that a police station in a smaller village had been attacked. Batticaloa is an island in the middle of a lagoon, so there are bridges coming in one side and a bridge going south from the other. There was an army base out on the beach, and they had helicopters coming in and out. I understand that when young people were picked up, they were held out there." Andrew described one day when an army jeep was blown up, and the Sinhalese soldiers picked up the first young boys they could find. Another time, he went to the police chief to speak for a female student who had been picked up. "She's this eighteen-year-old girl with a cherubic face. Anyway, they let her go about an hour later."

Because of a spate of bombings, Andrew wasn't permitted to go back to his site for a while. He stayed in the capital, Colombo, for a month and worked on teaching materials and taught for several weeks for a friend on the south coast. Then he returned to Batticaloa to prepare students for their big exam, but the trouble was not over. "A week before, the government had asked all our students to come into the school on a Sunday, claiming they didn't have anybody properly registered. This was the sort of discrimination the Sinhalese used against the Tamils. I spent the day visiting friends in the convent and the boys' orphanage south of town. As I was riding my bike over the bridge, the traffic was backed up. When I got to the other side of the bridge, I saw an army jeep overturned on the side of the road and Sinhalese soldiers running from house to house. What they called the Tigers had blown up that jeep, and now the soldiers were rounding up guys. I went home, but as I was eating lunch, one of my students came to the door and said two of our older male students— both of them married, and one had kids—had been arrested and were being held at the army base." Andrew went to the commander of the base, who claimed to know nothing. "This is what they do. They take the best of a community, and of course, that weakens the community. These two guys disappeared, so they were killed at some point that day, and their bodies were never found. The entire school was depressed and sad, and they were looking at exams coming up. I went to visit the families, and they were in tears." Andrew called the Peace Corps director, but he could do nothing. Andrew was told to pack his things and go back to Colombo. He was offered another site, but he said, "I can't stay in this country."

Safety in the Twenty-first Century

Safety has become such a concern that every program now has a security officer, and volunteers are also involved. The Peace Corps provides annual reports of volunteer safety, with details on sexual assaults, physical assaults, property crimes, threats, and deaths. "Crimes against volunteers, with minor fluctuations, have remained steady over the last ten years."[9]

Peg Dickson (Ukraine 2000–2002) remembered "very stringent rules." She explained: "You had to notify them if you were going to be away overnight. They wanted to know where you were. You didn't always have to let Peace Corps know, but you had to let somebody you worked with know, so that if Peace Corps needed to get in touch with you and they couldn't reach you, they could reach somebody who knew where you were. You let them know when you were going to be gone on vacation so they wouldn't try to contact you. I did see Peace Corps put [its security plan] into action. We had a volunteer missing, and they put out an all-points bulletin for that person through two or three countries until they found him."

In the same Ukraine group, Wini Yunker had a telephone, "but a lot of Peace Corps volunteers didn't. Two of my friends who were stationed down in Crimea didn't have one, and one night they were attacked outside their apartment and beaten, and they had to walk half a mile to a telephone. So that's one thing I helped change when I was on the Peace Corps Security Council." Each volunteer had a small alarm. Wini kept hers on a cord on her wrist. "We were advised not to be out alone after dark. And the safety expert said when you pull that alarm—it sounded like a police car—run, because they're only going to be scared for a moment." In contrast, Elizabeth Greene (Niger 2003–2005) remembered that although they had security people, "Niger was a very safe country, so there wasn't a lot we had to worry about."

In some countries, volunteers were part of a security system. Aaron Shraberg (China 2004–2006) was safety and security subwarden for twenty volunteers in his province, which meant he had a cell phone that he checked three times daily. His job was to be the contact between the volunteers and Peace Corps headquarters in China, the embassy, and Washington.

Sometimes the Peace Corps evacuated volunteers to the capital, and sometime volunteers were sent home. Cori Hash's (Zimbabwe 1999–2000) Peace Corps tour was a short one. The Peace Corps "got really concerned about our safety because of the violence toward white people and against educators. Most of us worked with the education system, and we were all white with the exception of a few volunteers. In my small town, a bus had been set on fire maybe a hundred feet from my house and from my center, although no one was hurt. This happened on the weekend, when I was in the capital. There was a lot of stuff going on in my region, so they asked all of us to stay in the capital until things calmed down. It just got worse and worse, and more volunteers were pulled in. Finally, they had everyone in the capital just hanging out, and we were there for almost two months waiting for things to improve." The Peace Corps eventually decided to send most of the volunteers home until after the election on the constitution, hoping they could come back later.

Jordan was another country where security was a big issue. Oghale Oddo (Jamaica 1994–1996) was associate Peace Corps director in Jordan on September 11, 2001, and he said, "We got to all of our volunteers within ninety minutes [of the 9/11 attacks]." Summing up the issue of safety and security in the twenty-first century, Oddo, who subsequently served as associate director in Swaziland and director in Fiji, said: "It's not just the Peace Corps that has changed; it's America that has changed. Society expects us, expects the government, expects institutions like the Peace Corps to be accountable. I've had volunteers say to me, 'If I did not want that safety, I would have gone off to China to teach English on my own, just taken my backpack. But I joined the Peace Corps, and I expect to be safe.'"

Volunteers have died in service. Harold Freeman (Ethiopia 1965–1967) described the shock of being notified of the death of his roommate, killed by a crocodile in a river in southwestern Ethiopia. Larry Radley and David Crozier were the first volunteers to lose their lives, in an airplane accident in Colombia in 1962.[10] According to the Peace Corps Memorial Project, 274 volunteers have died since 1961,[11] and they have been honored with a service at Arlington Cemetery during Peace Corps reunions.

Living According to Sarge

The first director of the Peace Corps, Sargent Shriver, had strong ideas about volunteer living, evident in a letter he wrote to his brother-in-law, President John F. Kennedy, in December 1961: "Volunteers are expected to live simply and unostentatiously. We believe it will make their work more productive and effective. They have a twenty-four-hour-a-day job. They receive little or no pay and accept substantial hazards to their health and even to their safety. . . . The Peace Corps is not just a job. There are no 9:00 to 5:00 days in our operation."[12]

Sarge connected living to serving. And he affirmed this passionately when he spoke to returned volunteers at the abbreviated fortieth Peace Corps anniversary ceremony held near the steps of the Lincoln Memorial the week after September 11, 2001. "Serve, serve, serve," he said.

Chapter 5

The Toughest . . .

You had to build new friends, and that took a while. You really had to be self-reliant, get interested in the culture and people, and not stay in your bungalow.

—Terry Anderson (Ghana 1965–1967)

You have to have a lot of patience, because things just do not get done there like they get done here. I think that was one of the hardest things, because when you're dealing with life and death or something that you think might truly matter, it gets frustrating when things don't get done.

—David Goodpaster (Malawi 2005–2007)

SIX VOLUNTEERS IN FIVE DECADES

Martin and Patsy Tracy (Turkey 1965–1967)

"Patsy lived pretty much in a separate world," Martin said. "When we walked out into town, she would wear a coat and scarf and walk behind me a couple of steps. One of the wonderful traditions in small towns in Turkey is that in the evening everybody strolls. Two husbands are holding hands, walking along, and then two wives in back are holding hands and walking along, just chatting about the day's events. That's what we did with our friends. I spent time with men in coffeehouses, where we would talk about politics, sports, and local events."

Patsy remembered: "Of course it was very difficult for me to walk three steps behind, address female relationships, the whole thing. I had to work at it very hard. In town it was assumed that you would have a jacket or a coat on and a scarf, and pants were not permitted.

And there were times when it would be inappropriate for me to ask a merchant a certain question—it would be something that should go through Martin. So I had to slowly learn the roles. I assumed the cultural role in order to be more effective." Patsy discovered that while Martin was invited to join the men on special occasions, the stay-at-home women eventually invited her into their circle. "Women turned out to be much more powerful than we had anticipated. When it came to deciding things for the family and the allocation of money and education of the children, women had the major say. So I had an entrée into the private world, the world of fun and dancing and sewing and women's work, but I discovered that it was a powerful position, not a weak position." Patsy also explained that birth control and family planning were big topics that "women talked about with women, men with men. Women would ask behind closed doors, 'How do you control not having children? That's very important to us, how to not have children.'"

At the time Martin and Patsy were volunteers, one out of five volunteers was married. A 1967 Peace Corps brochure entitled "Two's Company" quoted a veteran staff member, who declared, the "ideal Peace Corps Volunteer is a married couple . . . if they are happily married." The brochure gave the number of couples who had served to date as 2,910, and 145 first children had been born overseas to serving couples. The brochure asserted: "The one bonus each of these couples enjoys is the companionship that provides a great psychological boost in unfamiliar surroundings. They can enjoy the teamwork and collaboration in their work that few married persons ever experience at home."[1]

Patsy Tracy echoed that: "You had a sounding board. You didn't have to go public with everything. In the privacy of your own long walks, you could say, 'These are the difficulties we've faced so far. How are we going to handle them?' Or if somebody actually had a good day, then it was great to be around someone who was up and positive for that moment, and that would see us through the next week. The other thing is, you can laugh a lot more because you've got somebody to joke with who understands your sense of humor."

Rona Roberts (Philippines 1973–1975)

For Rona, "the hardest thing to get used to was the absence of privacy. There was no sense of leaving other people their personal space, especially among kids. So we were constantly surrounded by and trailed by people talking to us or talking about us or looking in our windows at night. The spring after we got there, on Good Friday we took our motorcycle and went up into a forest, and there was no one there, just parrots in the trees and a stream, a tropical paradise. We said, 'Oh, this is what we thought the Philippines was going to be like.' But instead, the Philippines was an experience of people, this crowdedness."

Rebecca Roach (Liberia 1988–1989)

Rebecca said, "I don't remember feeling culture shock. It just felt like from the time I got there I was always meant to be there. A lot of people from my group said they just absolutely loved being in Liberia. I think because we didn't learn a second language and because Liberia was colonized by the United States and because I am from a southern culture, there was so much already familiar to me. Sitting and eating together out of the same pot, putting relationships first just was really comfortable."

Sarah Cross Oddo (Jamaica 1993–1995)

Sarah was one of several female volunteers who mentioned sexual harassment as a difficult issue to deal with. "We found that if you dealt with it humorously it was easiest. So we would have guys on the bus who would say, 'I like you, I want to go out with you, I want to marry you.' And we got to the point where we learned from other volunteers to say, 'I don't like you.' If you're nice, it just prolongs it and makes it awful. So I remember specifically one time this guy said, 'I like you and I want to go out with you,' and I said, 'Well, I don't like you.' And he said, 'Why don't you like me?' I said, 'Well, you're kind of short and you have a gap in your teeth and I'm just not interested.' And he just started laughing, and after that we were able to have a normal conversation on the whole bus ride, and he didn't pester me anymore."

Aaron Shraberg (China 2004–2006)

Aaron explained that he was prepared "to meet the communication and cultural barriers because of the training and because I grew up

Jewish in Kentucky, in a place where there aren't many Jews, in an environment where there was a need to reconcile your culture with the mainstream culture. I think that taught me how to balance well and how to be able to work well in a multicultural environment." And yet Aaron reflected:

> They would tell us, "You're responsible for your own experience," and I personally believe attitude determines outcome. You try to maintain your sense of humor, but sometimes you're in a vulnerable position and somebody yells at you inappropriately or calls you a foreigner, and you just don't want to be a foreigner that day. You want to be someone who's walking through a crowd anonymously. And it seemed like sometimes when you get to that point where you're finally accepted, something happens and you feel really foreign. You feel really like an outsider, and sometimes that could be frustrating. Going out on the street, maybe people don't like you if you start speaking Chinese and you use all the perfect tones and you sound better than the news report on CCTV, Chinese TV. They still don't really understand what you're saying because all they see is this foreigner, this person talking Chinese who maybe shouldn't know how to speak their language. You have to realize that you aren't Chinese. You don't live there. You're not a native. You weren't born there. This is a very common awareness in China among people who are non-Chinese. You are reminded daily. Some people like to integrate more, maybe make an effort to learn the language, pick up some cultural habits like calligraphy writing or shadow puppet making or something like that, and you try to find things that will gain you more and more acceptance. I would say that just being an outsider, always referred to as *lao wei*, or "old outsider," can sometimes be frustrating.

A favorite description of Peace Corps service comes from one of its ad campaigns: "the toughest job you'll ever love." Jenifer Payne (Gabon 1990–1992) remembered seeing the commercial as a high school senior. "It showed some scenes from an African village. It was just like an epiphany. I saw that and I thought, I'm going to do that!" But, true to the ad, being a volunteer could indeed be tough.

So what was toughest? Across the decades, many volunteers found cross-cultural male-female expectations and relationships particularly daunting. Volunteers also cited the lack of privacy (recall the dilemma of the volunteer who wanted to jog alone in chapter 3), lack of structure, slower pace, language, isolation and loneliness, health issues, and food. We begin with a description of culture shock and conclude with Paul Winther's (India 1961–1963) explanation of how he got through "the toughest" to the "job you'll ever love," which is the topic of the following chapter.

CULTURE SHOCK

Bill Sweigart (Liberia 1967–1970) remembered the very moment when he made the necessary adjustment. "I was standing in a cafeteria line at the University of Liberia [during training]. It was lunchtime, and I was early, with about three or four other people. It was time to serve the food, which was all out there, the piles of rice; it was all set. And there were people just talking and looking around, and I was just beside myself, thinking, 'Well, what are they doing? Why isn't somebody . . . ?' And this was internal. But there was this moment when I realized—an epiphany—I realized where my head was and that I was never going to survive under these circumstances. Is this the way you're going to be for the next X number of years? I thought, no. You're not in Kansas anymore, or whatever metaphor we want to use. After that it was fine."

For Lauren Goodpaster (Malawi 2005–2007), culture shock hit on the first night of training in the small village of Mkonkera. She remembered:

> That first night I almost didn't make it. Of course it was freezing [June is winter in Malawi], and I hate the cold weather—one reason I wanted to go to Africa, though not the main reason. Dedza is the mountainous region, so we were very high up in elevation. You know, you're on the mud floor, and I literally put all the socks I had brought with me on my hands and feet. I had on skirts with my hiking trousers. I was still freezing. That first night, for some reason, we only had one small twin mattress. So David and I were on this tiny twin mattress on the mud floor, and we tried to tuck our mosquito net in, and we woke up in the middle of the night and felt these things all over us. There were these tiny, tiny little ants that just really are so small they can get through the mosquito net. And I guess they didn't spray enough, and there were thousands and thousands of ants, just all over us, all in our stuff. So I was like, "This is it, David, we're going home. I can't do this! I can't do it!" But of course, I'm thankful I did. The next day I called Aida, our Malawian training mom, and she brought the dust that you put on the floor. We survived. It wasn't that big of a deal.

Lauren was suffering from what the 1990s *Peace Corps Cross-Cultural Workbook* called "initial country and culture shock," experienced in the first few weeks in-country. The workbook described the characteristics as follows: "Wider exposure to country and culture means more realistic and more mixed reactions; enthusiasm is tempered with frustration; feelings of vulnerability and dependence are common; homesickness is frequent; nothing is routine; limited language ability undermines confidence; and close bonds are formed with other trainees."[2] Other arrival stories like Lauren's appear in chapter 7. With the passage of time, it probably becomes easier to say, as Lauren did, "It wasn't that big of a deal."

According to the workbook, volunteers' initial shock and then adjustment are followed by further culture shock and further adjustment. The further culture shock happens during the first few months after training, during the settling-in period. "You experience post-training withdrawal symptoms; you're adjusting to being on your own in country; it's your first experience taking care of yourself in country; you're having your first encounters with the work-related aspects of culture, with initial surprises and frustrations; you miss daily contact with Americans and host country nationals who understand you and your version of the local language; and you're surprised at still having culture shock (you thought you adjusted during pre-service training)."[3]

Rachel Savane (Guinea 1990–1992) called the adjustment "like being born—you have to learn everything." She remembered, "Often I would find myself in situations where something is happening I have no idea about, but I'm here, I'm a part of it, or I ignore it and I'm not a part of it. But I don't understand what's going on, who's saying what, what it means, what's implied, and what's going to happen afterward. So when those situations happened—which were often—in my head I would say, 'Think of this as if you're watching a movie.' So I would pull myself out of it and think in objective terms and be entertained and get what I could, and what I didn't understand I just didn't. That was my way of coping."

Like Rebecca Roach (Liberia 1988–1989), quoted earlier, some volunteers found it fairly easy to acclimate. One of eleven children in a North Dakota farming family, Bob Olson (Turkey 1963–1965) did not have much trouble adapting either. Bob remembered that his Peace Corps representative used him as an example of a volunteer whose standard of living rose when he came to Turkey. "While middle-class kids were talking about how difficult it was to go get water and heat it up to take a bath, it was an easy thing to me to heat water over a wood stove and take a bath."

A few volunteers "went native." Carolyn Cromer (Morocco 1992–1995) said, "I don't remember having a hard time adjusting. I was very open to learning about their culture and being a part of their culture. I was guilty of experiencing that pendulum swing when you're more native than the natives are. I almost got a tattoo on my forehead, and now I'm glad I didn't. I didn't miss Americans much. In fact, I was one of the people who tried to be at my site as much as possible." In contrast, Caroyl Reid (Philippines 1964–1966) remembered learning "how to walk a line between participating in their customs and at the same time reaching a point where it went beyond something that I felt I could do." She said there was a question about individuals who went "native," and "it just wasn't quite acceptable."

Oghale Oddo (Jamaica 1994–1996) had a different experience from other volunteers. Having grown up in Nigeria, he had seen the ups and downs of development, so "I came into Jamaica with that expectation." His attitude was, "Oh, well, this is what it is. And okay, let's see how we can make things work. Of course, until I opened my mouth, people thought I was Jamaican. They refused to call me an American. 'You have an American passport, but you are Nigerian, you are African.'"

Although volunteers often felt they were fairly well prepared "to be open to new experiences," as Susan Samuel (Liberia 1964–1967) said, and "to understand there would be times we would be uncomfortable," they couldn't be totally prepared. Her husband Tom pointed out that in Liberia they weren't prepared to see past the similarities between U.S. and Liberian politics and society and recognize the real differences. They didn't see what would happen later in Liberia because of the huge gulf between the Americo-Liberians, or Congo People, and the indigenous people, or Country People, as vividly described in Helene Cooper's 2008 memoir *The House at Sugar Beach*.[4]

MALE-FEMALE EXPECTATIONS AND RELATIONSHIPS

Cross-cultural differences in male-female expectations and relationships were most difficult for women, although they also affected men. In many societies in which volunteers worked, male and female spheres were much more separate than in the United States, as Martin and Patsy Tracy found in Turkey, and some volunteers experienced sexual harassment, as Sarah Oddo did in Jamaica.

Debra Schweitzer (Mali 1993–1996) understood that women's and men's roles were very strictly defined, but "they would banter and have a good time." She found that "being a white person, from another country and culture, they viewed me as a man because I was supposed to be this person with knowledge. I don't really think the woman part had any bearing because I wasn't one of them. I could cross a lot of different barriers. I ate with the men and I ate with the women, too." Being a woman in the role of agricultural adviser was not an issue for Audrey Horrall (Zambia 2000–2002) either. "I never received any outright, 'You can't do this, you're a woman.'" Twenty out of twenty-six in her group were women, and her predecessor had been a woman. Still, "it was something that you definitely had to be sensitive to because you really wanted the participation of the whole family and the whole village." It was important to avoid the "perception that you're just going off with farmer guy—you really wanted to include everyone, especially the wives of the farmers." She also had to be sensitive to how people might perceive her behavior— something "I might think of as perfectly normal" but could be seen differently by "someone who really had no idea who I was and what I was here for."

Gwenyth Lee (Cameroon 2004–2006) felt she was treated with a lot of respect and recognized that the father of the family compound to which her house was connected was a "big man, an important person in the community who could resolve problems. The family in that compound took good care of me." Gwenyth also knew that she "wasn't treated like an African woman." However, the issue of male attitudes toward women became more difficult for her as time went on. "At first, the whole thing was so foreign to me that I didn't identify with it personally. I was just watching what was going on. They [men] were throwing bottle caps at that woman as she walked down the street. It was like I was watching television. By the end [of my tour], I took it much more personally. To men in the village I would say something like, 'You shouldn't sleep with young girls in your school.' They'd say, 'You're just a little woman.' I'd go crazy, and that, of course, just made it worse, because they said, 'Yes, she is a funny little woman.'"

"It was really ridiculously hard," Ann Neelon (Senegal 1978–1979) remembered. She taught in a school where all the other teachers and most of the students were men. "The school director had gotten a lot of the girls pregnant. A couple of the guys would grab my breasts in front of students, and no matter what I told them, they would think it was funny. I was kind of an overprotected twenty-three-year-old, I think. Now I would be able to handle that."

Kristen Perry (Lesotho 1999–2001) said, "There was a lot of sexism and a lot of sexual harassment. When I came home, I told my mom I may never ever get another marriage proposal in my life, and I think that's fine. They would come running down the street after me. 'I love you, I love you.' My personal favorite was this guy who came running down the street saying, 'Hey, Momma, nice, nice, I love you, I wanna marry you.' And he's never seen me before. Men would come up to me and tell me they wanted to sleep with me and understand what the white woman tastes like. That was really hard for me." Kristen and the other volunteers spent a lot of time trying to process the different ways Americans and Basotho think.

> The worldview and perspective were very different. But I could really tell over time how I had changed. I could understand why it made sense to them. The example I like to give is the bride price, which at first I thought was awful. The feminist in me was like, you can't pay for women. But after having conversations with lots of people, I got it, I understood why it made sense. It's the same thing as a prenuptial agreement. People I talked to said people use it like a wedding shower. They use this money to buy gifts for the family that they'll need to set up their homes. It's like insurance: if the husband treats his wife badly, her parents can say, "I'm sorry, give us back our daughter, and we'll give you back the money." I understood it, but I still wouldn't want it. I think I moved past the culture shock to sort of acceptance and understanding. There were still things I was not okay with, like the harassment. I tried to ignore it as much as I could, and with some of the guys I would have fun, just try to turn it into a joke.

Occasionally, volunteers would move because of sexual harassment. Elizabeth Greene (Niger 2003–2005) became friends with the chief in her first village in Niger because he was "interested in asking me questions about America, so it was a more stimulating conversation than someone laughing at me learning to pound with a mortar and pestle or trying to learn the language. So I kind of bonded with him, but he mistook that. Men see women for only one thing, and I learned that the hard way. He was very persistent even after I said, 'This is not okay, I don't want you to ask me that again.'" The country director talked to the chief of her chief and then gave Elizabeth the option of staying or moving, so she moved to a second village. "I loved my second village, and it was because I had learned a lot more language and I could really chat with people."

It was somewhat easier for married women. Lauren and David Goodpaster (Malawi 2005–2007) attended their local Central Church of Africa Presbyterian in Malawi. Lauren recalled, "There were a couple times during our two years that they called us up to the front of the church for one reason or another. And they would always turn to David to talk, but David didn't know the language as well, so I would just step right up there and start talking in Chichewa. At first there were these shocked looks on people. David was supportive because he wanted to show them that I was his wife and we confer on everything."

In Latin America, Sally Spurr (Ecuador 1975–1977) found the "sexism and gender stuff was pretty amazing. I made a lot of good friends, mostly men, because I was in a male-dominated profession [agriculture], and it was hard to make women friends. All the guys would say they couldn't get dates because no self-respecting family would let their daughter go out with a Peace Corps volunteer, an American guy. They'd all seen those American movies." But for women in the Peace Corps, it was the opposite. "We always laughed about how the [American] guys couldn't get a date, and they [Ecuadoran men] were after us like crazy." Sally learned from an experience she had at a party soon after arriving in Ambato. "This guy kept asking me to dance. He was darling, and I was having a great time talking to him." Later she found out his wife was in the kitchen. "I had no idea."

Gwyn Rubio (Costa Rica 1971–1973) remembered that "the roles for women were quite different. They were meant to stay at home and take care of the children. There were things women weren't allowed to do, and I broke some of the rules." One day, one of her husband's coworkers came to the house to visit. "Angel was not there, so I went out and spoke to him on the porch, and that was a no-no." She also danced with some of her husband's friends at a Christmas party. Afterward, some of the locals came by the house and called her a whore.

However, Joyce Miller (Chile 1964–1966) said, "No one ever hassled me. I never had any problems. It was this certain protection, the men from the shop would make sure I was okay." Joyce thought that because she was the only Peace Corps volunteer in town at the beginning of her tour, she was "adopted. Everyone made sure that I was taken care of. If I needed to buy a pair of shoes, somebody would say, 'Okay, let's go find some shoes.' With women advisers it would be tea. With my workers, it would be going to their homes and having dinner. It was just being nice." Joyce also recalled, "My friends decided that the only way I could learn Spanish was to have a Chilean boyfriend. So this group of students and professors had a party and lined up all the eligible bachelors in town and said, 'Which one do you want?'"

Of the volunteers we interviewed, the two female volunteers who served in Jordan had the most difficult time. Abby Gorton (Jordan 2005–2006) wore shirts with sleeves down to her wrists and pants past her ankles, though not the head covering *hijab*. For volunteers in Jordan, male-female relations were "the main cultural issue we had to get our minds around. The guys were not invited to homes because male members of the household didn't want their daughters and wives exposed to strange men. Women got invited to people's homes to visit women and children, but they couldn't go outside for a walk. There were a couple of times when I would say to my friend Hollah, 'I've got to get outside because it's so beautiful and I have not walked.' Because a lot of the social time consisted of sitting around and drinking really sugary tea and eating." In terms of interacting with men, "I was very much like a sister to my host family in training and to the twin sixteen-year-old boys and the oldest son. But in public, we didn't acknowledge each other. There was a very clear line. The brothers in my landlord's family at my site did talk to me on the street because they spoke English and were excited to try it. However, I would see my neighbor's husband on the bus, and there was no nod." Abby resigned from the Peace Corps after five months in her village, partly because of sexual harassment.

Almost four decades earlier, Judy Lippmann (Morocco 1966–1968) had been a volunteer in another Muslim country. She remembered, "People thought we were prostitutes. Young women weren't on their own in an Arab culture." She didn't realize it at first, but someone told her, "They think you're a whore." Looking back, Judy wondered about "our injection into other cultures. We knew to dress way more modestly. This was the mid-1960s and miniskirts. But to intentionally go into another country that had a different position for young women? It was a blast of new awareness and confusion. Maybe that is the best way. I mean, do we just see each other as we are? But having a chance to get to know each other is, I think, the best thing of all."

Also serving in a Muslim but not an Arab country, Charlene McGrath (Afghanistan 1969–1971) knew it was hard for Afghans to understand her all-female group of volunteers traveling around the country with Afghan men to provide vaccinations to women. "At first they thought we were prostitutes, because women just did not go out and about with men. We did try to dress as close to what Afghan women wore as possible—long baggy pants, then a long dress below the knee, and sometimes a scarf on your head. So the Afghan women would look at you and ask if you were a woman and if you had milk— they wanted help with breast-feeding. They wanted to know if you were married, had children, what did your mother think about you being here. They had lots of questions about sex, birth control. The women welcomed us by kissing our hands. It was wonderful being made to feel so welcome by strangers."

On a small, remote island in Micronesia, Elaine Collins (1989–1991) remembered thinking that the customs there were wrong—at first. Then she decided to become a Micronesian woman in terms of culture. She learned that "breasts were okay, but knees and thighs were not. And if my 'brother' was sitting down eating a meal, I couldn't stand up or walk around where he was sitting, so sometimes women were sort of crawling on their knees. At first this seemed ridiculous, but it was a way to be really careful about a woman not arousing a brother or a male cousin. Also, if you're having your menstrual cycle, you do not prepare food. I followed those things, feeling it would be disrespectful not to. I spent all my time with women. I never went to the men's house. I did all the things women did. I loved the women on the island. They were hysterical. I laughed for two years straight, and I didn't feel I needed to go outside of that."

Lack of Privacy

Privacy is a strongly held American value, and volunteers often felt as though they were living in a fishbowl. At the beginning of this chapter, Rona described the lack of privacy in the Philippines, something with which other volunteers also grappled. Debra Schweitzer (Mali 1993–1996) concluded, "The most difficult adjustment was lack of privacy, because we're very used to being able to go into the house and just close the door and be alone. But in Mali, if you're alone, something is wrong with you. There's always somebody at your house. You're always with somebody or visiting somebody."

It was "hard to adjust to being so popular," Sara Todd (Armenia 2001–2003) remembered. "Everyone wanted to talk with the American, and everyone wanted me to come over, all the time. Privacy really wasn't understood. Why would you want to live alone? Why would you not want to come over every night and hang out with us?"

Kay Roberts (Ecuador 1982–1984) explained, "The most difficult part of adjustment was being scrutinized in everything you did. I remember being just appalled that people would go through our trash. They were interested in what gringos threw away. It felt invasive. There was really no privacy in terms of conversations. Everything was open air. My walls didn't even go all the way up to the ceiling. There were always people around."

For Capp Yess (Fiji 1982–1984), the lack of privacy began when his host family took him to his room and brought in his suitcase. "I thought, now they'll all leave me alone for a little while. But everyone from the father to the mother to the smallest child watched me unpack every single thing from my suitcase and helped me put it all someplace."

Lack of Structure and Slow Pace

Because Americans value getting things done—when we meet a new person we ask, "What do you do?" not "Who are you?"—and also because some volunteers' jobs were fairly nebulous, volunteers were sometimes frustrated by what they perceived to be a lack of structure. As a 1963 report on the Peace Corps in the Philippines stated: "The psychic underpinnings of the puritanical American which have seeped into the volunteer—whether he knows it or not—are outraged in day-to-day life."[5]

William Salazar (Guatemala 1972–1973) finally realized that "life really, really slowed down when it took a whole day to talk to farmers. Maybe I just talked to one farmer in one day, but it was a major achievement." Kay Roberts (Ecuador 1982–1984) recalled that she liked working in the clinic in Ecuador because it was structured; at the end of the day, she could quantify what she had done. "You had vaccinated so many children against childhood disease. Yet there were an awful lot of hours in a day. How do you fill up your time and make a difference?" Elizabeth Greene (Niger 2003–2005) also remembered the lack of structure. "I was so desperate at the beginning, I would schedule which days I would sweep which part of my dirt yard. I was sweeping with a sort of whisk broom that you bend down to use. They have a skilled way of doing it." Elizabeth had a routine: "Most of the time I would spend a couple hours in the morning walking around the village just chatting with people, go home for lunch, relax a little in the heat of the day, and then about 4:00 or 5:00 go back out for a couple hours and just wander around and talk with people. I would eat dinner with the family of my chief."

Ken Wilson (Malawi 1997–1998) explained his adjustment to the lack of structure: "Once I got to my village, no one had a watch except me. You might make a meeting time with the village chief, and you might be the only one there because everyone else had something else that became more important. You would organize a village chiefs' meeting and you'd show up for maybe two weeks in a row, and no one would be there but you because 'It's time to do our planting' or 'I'm sorry, someone came by for tea.' If you were on your way out the door and someone showed up, you forgot why you were leaving. You immediately became a host and offered that person tea and sat down with them and visited, because that was so highly valued. Americans like myself were like 'but, but, but.' It was very hard. It became quite refreshing afterward [to realize], 'Wow, they value people, not time.'"

Gary Griffin (Thailand 2004–2006) talked about "the frustrations of trying to get things accomplished. And work ethics aren't the same. Western expectations want to get things moving. [For Thais] if it happens today or tomorrow or next week, that's fine, so adjusting to that [was hard]. Almost all of us said that the physical hardships were nothing relative to the frustrations and misunderstandings."

"The pace was different," Joshua Mike (Nevis 2004–2006) said. "Living in the Caribbean just totally slowed me down. I'm cool now. In fact, I drive so slow. I talk fast, but I drive slow." However, Joshua found it a challenge to get people to share his enthusiasm and to take him seriously. Sometimes he felt as though he had too much energy.

In the film *Once in Afghanistan*, Kristina Engstrom, Peace

Corps training director for the smallpox vaccination program in Afghanistan beginning in 1968, reported receiving this advice from an Afghan: "Teach them how to wait."[6] Similar advice comes from mountain climber Greg Mortenson, who returned to the village in Pakistan that had saved his life, intending to build a school. He discovered that the village wanted to build a bridge first. In his bestselling book *Three Cups of Tea*, he shares a lesson that resonates with Peace Corps volunteers: "We Americans think you have to accomplish everything quickly. We're the country of thirty-minute power lunches and two-minute football drills. Our leaders thought their 'shock and awe' campaign could end the war in Iraq before it even started. Haji Ali taught me to share three cups of tea, to slow down and make building relationships as important as building projects. He taught me that I had more to learn from the people I work with than I could ever hope to teach them."[7]

LANGUAGE

Language acquisition is a centerpiece of Peace Corps training, and as William Salazar (Guatemala 1972–1973) noted, it is "a gateway to accomplishing your goals as a volunteer." However, learning to speak a language well can be tough. Bill Miller (Dominican Republic 1968–1970) found communicating a real challenge. "Even though I'd taken four years of Spanish and took intensive Spanish [during training] in Puerto Rico, when you get there and start talking to Dominicans, it's a totally different world. You think, 'Are we all speaking Spanish?' The accent is the same, but sometimes the words are different. They speak very fast and use all types of slang."

Tom Boyd (Colombia 1964–1966) also identified language as a major problem. "I like to talk a lot," he said, "so I was talking, and nobody's figuring out what I'm saying." Bill Davig (Peru 1965–1967) had difficulty "just communicating and understanding what other people were communicating." It took about six months before he could "communicate pretty well." Marianna Colten (Ecuador 1981–1983) wished she had had more language training. "When I first got to my site," she said, "people thought I wasn't that intelligent. Even though my comprehension was really good, my verbal skills were not. I was so frustrated because it's like, 'These people think I'm stupid, but I'm not.' The kids were the ones who were very patient with me, teaching me the language."

Richard Parker (Côte d'Ivoire 1973–1974, Morocco 1976–1978) was the only Peace Corps volunteer who didn't speak French in Côte d'Ivoire because he had come as an electronics specialist on an individual placement without previous training. He said, "French sounded to me like the rain on the roof. It was absolutely incomprehensible. I couldn't tell where one word started and another stopped. It made me feel very stupid. But the Peace Corps arranged an Ivorian tutor for me. He came to my apartment every afternoon for three hours. He worked me and worked me and worked me, and after a month I discovered I was making sense out of this language. I was understanding what people were saying, and I could take care of my basic needs."

Volunteers sometimes had to deal with more than one foreign language. Although she learned Malay during training in Hawaii, Marlene Payne (Malaysia 1967–1969) had the challenge of teaching psychology to Malay, Chinese, Indian, and Eurasian students at a two-year teachers' training college. "I was teaching in English, and I was supposed to teach in Malay for the twenty Malay students, but they hadn't yet coined the [psychology] words for Malay. There was a dilemma of trying to speak as much Malay as I could, because the students spoke no English at all." Marlene lived in a Chinese part of town, so she took regular Chinese lessons as well.

Stories related to language mistakes are a Peace Corps volunteer staple. Blake Stabler (Russia 2000–2002) told several from his first year in Russia. Once when he was teaching older students, a group of third-graders who were already out of class started banging on the window. He thought he said, "Go away please," but he actually said, "Come here." They were ready to play. His worst word confusion happened on a teachers' field trip. "I always got the words for *church* and *circus* confused because, depending on how you do the endings and how it's used, they sound the same to me, though Russians claim they don't. There's a holiday called Teachers' Day, and the students bring flowers and cookies and jam for the teachers. Then the students leave and the teachers all go on a field trip. I thought we were going to the circus, so I was very excited. The Penza region has a very nice circus in the provincial capital. It's one of the best—they train so many acrobats for Cirque du Soleil every year. It's a really fun thing to do and, I thought, the perfect thing to do on Teachers' Day." But as it turned out, their field trip was a visit to a monastery.

ISOLATION AND LONELINESS

One of the problems with slowly developing language skills was the isolation that came with it. Even volunteers who knew the language couldn't always escape the loneliness. Sarah Payne (The Gambia 1989–1991) found herself in a very different situation from that of the ordinary Muslim woman of her age, who was already a wife (whether number one, two, or three) and had three to five kids. She could talk to young girls, but "their lives were going to end up being very different, so you didn't always have the bonds."

Isolation was also one of the challenges for Cecil and Sheila McFarland (Micronesia 1972–1974 and Philippines 1974–1976). On their island in Micronesia, they were "an hour and a half boat ride from the nearest town." And, as Cecil explained, "You could only take the boat ride when it was high tide. Once you got to town, the airplane came three times a week. One of the flights would go to Kwajalein to Majuro and on to Honolulu or to Chuuk and then on to Guam. You were still a long ways from anywhere. So isolation was one of the more challenging things. I think we were lucky we went as a couple."

"I think we were warned about loneliness and culture shock," Dianne Bazell (Zaire [Democratic Republic of Congo] 1975–1977) said, but "I don't know that anyone was fully prepared for the extent and depth of the loneliness, even if you had other Americans around, and I had one. But I was on my own a lot." Don Stosberg (Malawi 1965–1966) also mentioned the loneliness. "I had left the [Catholic] seminary because I wanted to date, and there weren't a lot of people for me to have social interaction with."

HEALTH

Although Marlene Payne (Malaysia 1967–1969) said, "I was probably the healthiest I've ever been in my life," volunteer health has always been a major concern of the Peace Corps. In the 1960s each Peace Corps country had at least one public health service doctor serving as a Peace Corps staff physician. In fact, Marlene later married one of those doctors—John Payne, whom she had originally met as a freshman at Berea College when both were undergraduates.

John, who had just finished his internship after medical school at the University of Kentucky, fulfilled his military obligation—there was a doctor draft at the time—by becoming a Peace Corps physician from 1967 to 1969. He saw himself as "halfway between staff and volunteer, trying to keep a lid on kids doing drugs and other lifestyle things." After about a month's orientation in Washington, DC, focused on language, culture, and tropical medicine, he was assigned to Borneo in Malaysia. He described a day's work:

> You'd take a little airline that went up and down the coast and fly up to a town at the mouth of a river. And then you'd get on a launch, some kind of a boat going upstream, and go to some town where the volunteers were teaching. You'd talk to the headmaster and ask if any of the volunteers were going crazy or had any big problems. Then you'd go meet with the volunteers in their homes and give them injections. This was before they had a hepatitis vaccine, and they had a program to prevent hepatitis A by giving this huge dose of gamma globulin every six months—that's hard on your butt. I carried these bottles of gamma globulin around with some ice, and I'd have to give everybody a shot and treat whatever. Afterward I'd go down to the market and have some beers, some good Chinese food, and talk to the guys and say, "You need to hide your illegal motorbikes." At that time, people could only have motorbikes with certain job descriptions. Anyway, I'd tell them hide your motorbikes and send your local girlfriends back up the river to their villages, and hide your marijuana because the boss is coming on Thursday.
>
> Most of the volunteers were pretty healthy, and there wasn't too much to do medically, but you had to be ready for the serious problems if they had to go back to the States for evacuations. I made three trips back to the States myself [accompanying patients]. I was about halfway through my two-year experience when I got married to my first wife; she was a nurse, and she had three or four trips back. The worst one I had was a pretty good-sized dude who had a psychotic break way upriver someplace. He was hallucinating [and speaking] in some tribal language that nobody else even knew. I brought back one girl who had gotten pregnant the first time she ever had sex and was suicidal, and I brought back another woman to Honolulu who was married but had a complicated delivery.

As far back as the 1960s, the Peace Corps also used host country doctors; later, some were hired directly by the Peace Corps. For example, the Peace Corps doctor in Fiji in 1970 was Fiji Chinese; he went on to specialize in neurosurgery and worked at the Mayo Clinic in the United States. In their interviews, volunteers were generally very positive about their U.S. government health care. Angel Rubio (Costa Rica 1971–1973), for instance, remembered receiving good health care and seeing the Peace Corps physician on a regular basis. In the 1960s volunteers were admonished to "exercise your own common sense in matters of health. No doctor can prevent illness or disease if you ignore the need to boil water or fail to observe other health precautions."[8] The Peace Corps Web site in 2010 stated, "In every country in which Volunteers serve, the Peace Corps maintains a medical unit staffed by one or more medical providers. They inform Volunteers about local health issues and provide them with the basic medical supplies and vaccinations they need to stay healthy. If a Volunteer becomes ill and cannot be treated properly in the country of service, the Peace Corps will transport the Volunteer to an appropriate facility in a nearby country or to the U.S."[9] Several returned volunteers from recent decades mentioned that the Peace Corps provided a book entitled *Where There Is No Doctor* and a medical kit for those in isolated places. Occasionally, a volunteer described a positive experience with traditional medicine. Elaine Collins (Micronesia 1989–1991) said, "I had poked my eye, so it had a blood vessel that was really red. This woman chewed leaves and blew through a papaya stem right onto my eyeball, and it cleared right up. I really trusted these people and I really felt cared for by them. They were using these things on me like I was their daughter or their sister."

Still, some volunteers told stories involving medical issues that constituted one of the toughest parts of their tours. Robin Sither (Cameroon 1996–2000) had malaria after his second year and before extending for a third year. Ann Neelon (Senegal 1978–1979) went home for an appendectomy during her second year and didn't return. Other volunteers described dengue fever, worms, dysentery, and lice.

Rabies could also be a health issue, and shots were required if it was suspected. That was what happened to Michael Geneve (Mozambique 2003–2005), who liked to run four or five times a week, often with kids, on the half-mile cement landing strip in his town. One day while he was running a dog bit his leg, and he had to go down to the capital, Maputo, and get rabies shots. After he returned to his village and resumed running, "You know what? That same dog, the same day of the week, the same location, he bit me again. Actually," he said, "the owner of the dog was one of my students' fathers, and he came over to apologize." The owner killed the dog, so Michael called the Peace Corps medical officer, and she told him to cut off the dog's head and bring it down to Maputo, twelve hours south on the bus. They observed Michael for ten days. "I didn't have rabies, thank goodness. So that's the story on the dog. I still have a really good scar." Michael also got malaria in July 2005 and had health problems during his last six months, so instead of going to Brazil on his way home, as he had planned, he came straight home.

Sometimes illness added to a volunteer's other woes. For Lee Colten (Ecuador 1981), being sick with a fever every other day during his first month at his site, plus homesickness and being shoved to the ground by a drunk villager during a party, combined to make him say, "I think I'm hanging it up." The Peace Corps said, "If you feel that way, we'll send you home." He had been in Ecuador three months.

Perhaps the most dramatic health story we heard was told by Ken Wilson (Malawi 1997–1998), who woke up in "dire pain on October 8, 1997." He had been in his village for three months. Luckily for him, that same day his Malawian supervisor was scheduled to visit the village, a seven-hour trip from Lilongwe by Land Rover, to see how he was assimilating. Ken continued the story:

> I had a 101 temperature. I was delirious, sweating, I don't even remember her being there. She thought I had malaria. She threw me in the back of her Land Rover. It took us an hour to get to the next town that had a phone, where she was able to call Peace Corps and say, "I have Ken Wilson and I think he has malaria." Eight hours later we arrived in Lilongwe. It turned out to be my appendix. I remember I was terrified. Once the doctor diagnosed it, Peace Corps went into full emergency mode. Within an hour I was on a plane headed to Johannesburg. And I remember the doctor in the emergency room in Johannesburg saying, "You should be dead. I cannot believe you're here." I remember being wheeled off to the operating room. I told the physician's assistant from Peace Corps who went with me, "Don't tell my family. What can they do?" So I went to sleep before the operation thinking I might never wake up. But I woke up a couple of hours later with no appendix and twenty-one staples in my stomach.

That wasn't the end of Ken's medical problems. Because his appendectomy had suppressed his immune system, he caught "everything."

First, "I got dengue fever, which prevented me from going to Zanzibar with my friend. Then I got dysentery. Then I started getting migraine headaches for the first time." Ken was sent back to South Africa and learned "it was a parasite that had been with me for so long it gave me toxemia. They gave me a colonoscopy, cleaned out all my flora and fauna, as they called it, basically just flushed out my intestines and put me back together. They wanted to send me home, but I said, 'I left my village. They think I'm dead. I have to go back. I've got to say good-bye. I just can't disappear." He went back to his village to tell them what was happening. "We had very quick closure, some picture taking, a lot of crying. Then I was carted away in a truck back to Lilongwe, put on a plane, and sent home. I was 117 pounds, and I went over there being 150."

FOOD SOMETIMES, BUT SOMETIMES NOT

Sarah Payne (The Gambia 1989–1991) recalled talking to a friend who was going to Senegal, who asked her, "What do I need to do to get ready?" Sarah said, "I told her about a shortwave radio and then I said to soak it up when you get there and recognize that the worst days are the worst days and it's uphill from there. You know," she concluded, "you can't really prepare yourself. You just have to be open to trying new food and expect to get sick, but then expect to get better." However, it took Sarah a while to learn to like the food—she remembered adding sugar and powdered milk to her rice every night at first, and she didn't always eat what was put before her. Once she was visiting the home village of one of her students, and the chief had a party for her. "He brought us this bowl of rice with sauce, on top of which they had very ceremoniously placed a chicken head with its feet crossed through the head. My student asked Peter, my host brother, and me if we wanted to eat it. We knew it would be offensive if we didn't, but I couldn't imagine putting this chicken skull in my mouth. We said, 'Would you like it?' And he said, 'I'd love to eat it.' So he saved us." Sarah also remembered her food fantasies: pink lemonade with crushed ice, double-stuffed Oreo cookies, and pizza. At Christmas break during her second year, she went to Dakar in Senegal and ate hamburgers. "They had fried eggs on them, but we ate them anyway."

Growing up in rural Kentucky, Cecil McFarland (Micronesia 1972–1974, Philippines 1974–1976) had eaten corn, green beans, mashed potatoes, roast beef, and chicken. But, he said, "I don't think I had ever eaten rice in my life, except as a dessert pudding. I hadn't eaten any kind of ocean fish. And the islanders loved turkey tails, shipped in from somewhere. But the most interesting thing we ate there was dog. My wife and I walked over the mountains to another village, where they were having a little festival. We each had a banana leaf, and as you walked down the line you got your yam, fish, and rice out of baskets. The last basket was all closed up, and when I got to it, they opened it up, and there was this burnt-to-a-crisp dog. Looking back on it, it was a test. It got real quiet, and they handed me a knife. I reached down and whacked off a leg, put it on my banana leaf, and walked off. It didn't taste like chicken. After that I always said, 'I never met a dog I didn't like.'"

Michael Geneve (Mozambique 2003–2005) described arriving in his village and going to the director's house for a welcome meal.

This woman comes out of the house holding a pot and pops it right in front of me. There's a lid on it, and they tell me that I need to help myself. I was the guest. So I lift the top of the pot, and it's a goat head looking right at me. I compose myself. All right. I can just eat some of this head here, but I have no idea what I'm doing. So I ask them, "What is the best part?" And they tell me it's the brains. I ask, "Well, how do I do that?" And they say, "Pick it up and then take that knife, the really blunt knife, and crack the skull open to get to the brains." I'm thinking, "Oh, God, the goat's looking at me." The skull popped open pretty easily. Then I got the brains and cut some out and put it on my plate. And it was the most disgusting thing I've ever eaten in my life. I thought for sure I was going to throw up, but I kept it down. And it's really funny, because now I love goat brain and goat tongue and goat cheek and everything like that. That first experience, maybe it was the way they prepared it. I have no idea, but they were all laughing at me.

Jenny Howard (Gabon 2000–2002) bought herself a large mortar and pestle and learned to cook local dishes. However, she was an American and a vegetarian, and her host family liked to tease her. Once they prepared a meal and asked her to look in the pot. "So there was a cat's head, perfectly cooked golden brown, one of the cats that had been running around the neighborhood. And why not eat it? It's an animal. It's meat. They knew I would be appalled and wouldn't eat it, but they just had to share it with me. They loved it! And everybody in the neighborhood laughed for an hour. Another time they took me to the freezer that the neighbors shared to see my reaction to what appeared to me to be a man's hand with a black leather glove on it. It was a gorilla hand! They thought it was hilarious."

"The food was interesting because sometimes you didn't know what it was. Other times, you knew what it was, but you didn't want to eat it," Ruth Boone (Philippines 1962–1964) explained. "We got there in November, and our host family tried to make us feel welcome. Not having a turkey for Thanksgiving, they cooked a goose. It's customary to cook it with the head still on, so you sit down to eat this thing with its feathery head lying there. It was also the custom to cook fish with the head on, and the honored guest gets the eyeballs. You're always the honored guest, so you always get the eyeballs. It's a treat. I don't ever remember eating an eyeball. I did get used to seeing the head."

In Slovakia, Mimi Gosney (2000–2002) enjoyed the national dish of potato dumplings with cheese and bacon crumbs, as well as poppy seed cakes. However, she wasn't enthusiastic about the custom of buying a live carp on Christmas Eve, putting it in the bathtub, and then killing it on Christmas Day and eating it.

Of course, Peace Corps volunteers also had to learn *how* to eat in a different culture and how to drink things that might be familiar yet different or even very different. Ann Neelon (Senegal 1978–1979) remembered learning to eat with her hands. "People literally burn their hands the first time they try it. I was one of the last ones in our group to try." In many cultures, one also had to remember to eat only with the right hand. Beverages could be a challenge, too. Charlene McGrath (Afghanistan 1969–1971) described the tea served in clear glasses. "They would fill the glass about halfway with sugar and then pour about two inches of tea on top of that. It was literally like drinking cough syrup. The first couple glasses were devastatingly sweet. Then as you added more tea, the sugar wore down a bit, and it was manageable. In northern Afghanistan, in the Uzbek and Turkmen area, they drank mostly green tea, which I had never had before." Donald Nims (Fiji 1968–1970) described drinking *yagona* from a half coconut shell that is dipped in a big wooden bowl—the *tanoa*—and passed from person to person. It tastes a little like dishwater and is drunk in one gulp.

The food stories in this chapter should not obscure the fact that many volunteers in all decades loved the food—or at least some of it—in their Peace Corps countries. Almost all gatherings of returned Peace Corps volunteers include host country food, and Friends of Fiji gatherings always include the ceremonial sharing of *yagona*.

Judy Lippmann (Morocco 1966–1968) remembered that "the fresh vegetables and pomegranates and fruits were just wonderful, and lots of lamb and fresh butter. When I was in Tétouan, one of the highlights of the lunch hour was going to the bakery and getting a hot loaf of bread. There's nothing better in the world than a can of sardines and this hot bread and butter. The coffee was wonderful, and the yogurt was fabulous." Richard Parker (Côte d'Ivoire 1973–1974, Morocco 1976–1978) "liked the African cooking very much, especially the peanut sauce. I would go to the market, buy hamburger, and make hamburgers on French bread with avocado. Those were great burgers, fresh off a cow." Michael Geneve (Mozambique 2003–2005) talked about "fruit galore. Bananas all year long, really cheap. Mangoes, avocados, lemons, oranges, tangerines, grapefruit, sometimes apples from South Africa. I was about a half hour away from the beach. You'd have to be in the right spot in the village to see the ladies with fish, and those went quick. A variety of fish really cheap and really, really good."

Sally Spurr (Ecuador 1975–1977) was a vegetarian when she arrived in Ecuador, but she soon realized, "You just couldn't be a vegetarian. You couldn't refuse to eat the meat people gave you, because when anyone gave you meat, it was huge. You were the guest of honor. Guinea pig was the favorite dish of the Indians, and they fixed it with potatoes and peanut sauce. The market was wonderful. You could buy any kind of vegetable or fruit because we were so close to both the jungle and the coast. So you had fresh pineapple, fresh avocado, fresh tomatoes."

Kristen Perry (Lesotho 1999–2001) had a unique experience because her village was "a UNESCO solar village trial site." Kristen described the solar oven in her backyard: "It's a big metal box that has a glass lid and it's painted black inside. It swivels so you can have it follow the sun. Basically, it just heats up with the sun's rays. It takes a lot longer to do things. I would put a loaf of bread in the oven in the morning to bake, and I would come home in the afternoon and I would have fresh-baked bread, and it wouldn't burn. You could cook rice in it, though pies were a little bit hard because there was so much liquid in them. But cakes and cookies I would make in the solar oven."

After his interview, Phil Dare (Malaysia 1965–1967) gave us a booklet of essays he wrote following a return trip to Sarawak thirty years after his Peace Corps tour. Many volunteers would agree with him when he writes:

[There is a] direct link between memory and food. Many of our fondest and most vivid memories are of occasions when friends or family ate together, not just holidays, but simple meals in people's homes. . . . There were the memories of non-stop eating and laughing and enjoying each other as we visited homes of our friends for Chinese New Year or Hari Raya [a Malay/Muslim celebration at the end of Ramadan]. There was the memory of my waving a live chicken over many dishes of food for the *miring* ceremony [including chanting a prayer to bless the spirits] in Banggau and Ando's longhouse, and then the full can of the treasured hill padi [upland rice] they gave us to bring home. There were many happy hours sipping *ai limaus* (limeades) in Tony Wong's coffee shop and visiting with his family. Memories are still so vivid of street hawkers cooking *satay* and noodles in the night, of the spicy delights of India Street in Kuching, of the hours in the open markets in Sibu and in Kuching with Peace Corps friends, of the refreshing *ice kachang* we delighted in [in] the little kiosk in the museum gardens in Kuching. Then there were the farewell dinners in Kapit when sadly we said our goodbyes to Kapit. Memories of festive times and warm friends were jostled awake by food. I never smell those spices without thinking of those happy years in Sarawak.[10]

Getting through "the Toughest" to the "Job You'll Ever Love"

In the Peace Corps commercial, what followed "the toughest" was "job you'll ever love." Paul Winther (India 1961–1963) explained how that eventually happened for him. "I can remember getting off the plane in Calcutta. It was very, very cold, and Calcutta doesn't usually get cold. We saw poverty-stricken people who had died. It was the first time I had seen dead people in the streets. And the smells and the filth and the dirt—the difference was incredible. The different languages. It was tough. And the food was different. We got used to it after a while. The second year I did something I thought was going to contribute to the welfare of the people, and my whole attitude changed. I didn't see a lot of dirt, and I began to love the food."

Chapter 6

... Job You'll Ever Love

I visited the majority of the thirty-three high schools in our city of 250,000, working with the English teachers to help them develop their skills. Part of my job was to develop a resource center. Their style was totally different than ours, so it didn't take me too long to realize that I wasn't there to teach them how to teach. I was there to introduce some new ideas, to provide them with resources, to help in any way I could.

—Peg Dickson (Ukraine 2000–2002)

SIX VOLUNTEERS IN FIVE DECADES

Martin and Patsy Tracy (Turkey 1965–1967)

Martin and Patsy had three successive teaching jobs in three different places in Turkey. For the first ten months, they taught English in the public high school and offered courses in the evening to interested people in the community in Kirsehir. Martin remembered:

> The classrooms were not well equipped. They were often very cold in the wintertime, and in the summers very hot. All the male students had to have a Western-style jacket, often frayed, torn, patched. The girls had to have a standard dress. The students were remarkably receptive, interested, but we were confronted with the things all Turkish teachers were confronted with: widespread cheating, and they liked to talk in class, so you had to be creative about ways to keep their energies focused on lessons. We taught them a lot of songs. We had oral examinations at the end of the semester, and the principal would sit in on those. When a student was struggling, the principal would often tell us whether or not that student was a pass—he had been in the class long

155

enough and it was time to pass him, regardless of his skill level. You didn't fight them about that. But there were some very good, sharp, bright kids.

The following summer they taught advanced English at Middle Eastern Technical University in Ankara, and during their second year they taught in the elementary and secondary schools in the village of Ürgüp.

Rona Roberts (Philippines 1973–1975)

My work life was divided into two separate years, but both revolved around the Bikol River Basin Development Project. It operated on an American principle, which was that you would be there from eight to five. That was terribly hard for me to work a full, long day every day, day after day, with no semester end, because I had been a student all my life until then. I worked in a crumbly little building with desks back to back, ten of us. There was one typewriter in our building. You had to plead and get in line if you wanted something typed.

My job in my first year was on a crew that was all Filipinos except me, and the job was to develop a grant proposal to USAID for a barefoot doctor program. Barefoot doctor programs were popular in China around then. A person who lives in a village gets trained in a set of basic medical and hygiene skills and then practices those on behalf of the village. Seventy-five percent of the population in the river basin lived more than a day's walk from any town, so the idea was that we would have people walk in from the remote locations to one of the thirty-five or thirty-six towns in the river basin. They could get clean gauze and birth control pills and even drugs, if there were any. So we visited every town, and we talked to the rural health people. They had no supplies and usually one thermometer. The people who worked in the health clinics had good training; there just wasn't a good infrastructure of support. Well, we brought all that [information] back and made the proposal. I ended up being the writer, which was a great role. I wrote it up, and they edited and fixed and changed it. We didn't get a cent. USAID said: "It's not our priority to fund social projects this year."

So I got a new job: to be on a team to visit the same communities and set up a local planning council that would feed us its needs. But I learned when we went back three years later that USAID's priorities had changed. They had dusted off the barefoot doctor program, and USAID had put more than a million dollars into it.

Rebecca Roach (Liberia 1988–1989)

Twice a year we brought new teachers in to train them how to use specific primary education materials, and the second year we taught them how to branch off and be more creative using the materials. I had a very good job description, unlike some of the other Peace Corps volunteers. The Ministry of Education identified the schools I needed to visit, but I would show up at one of the schools, and no one would be there. And you can't call ahead; no one had a telephone. I quickly learned that you don't go anywhere during the rainy season until afternoon, because often I would be sitting in a leaking school with chickens and goats. My first year was spent just getting to know teachers, getting to know principals, building those relationships, and then my second year I moved over to another town. The nun who was going to be the principal of the new Catholic elementary school had to go home, so it was a very good opportunity for me to get experience as a principal. I decided to begin to work my way out of a job by training principals to supervise their own teachers in the program. So I was twenty-four years old, I had never been a principal before, and here I was trying to advise these principals my second year on how to supervise. I was working with principals, trying to train them so I would work my way out of my job.

I would wake up in the morning and walk over to my school. We would say the pledge and sing the anthem, classes would start, and I would go from classroom to classroom and check on my teachers. Then I would get on my bicycle sometimes and go out and visit the schools where I was working with teachers. Every two weeks, the Catholic mission would lend me two of their jeeps, and their drivers would pick up all the principals at the schools I was supervising. They would meet me at my school, St. Mugaga's Catholic School. The school cook would make us all lunch, and then the principals and I would sit down and talk about the burning issues in their schools—teachers trying to get their students to pay bribes for good grades, or the ministry locating teachers in unfamiliar towns where they didn't know people—and we would brainstorm possible solutions.

Sarah Cross Oddo (Jamaica 1993–1995)

Sarah was initially assigned to a group called Friends of the Sea in Runaway Bay, but she was later transferred to the fifth largest town, Mandeville, in the southern part of the island, to work with Jamaica

Junior Naturalists. Of the first assignment, Sarah said, "Now that I think back, it was actually perfect, and I kind of wish I'd stayed there. I thought I didn't have anything to do, and I thought I didn't know what I was doing, but it was actually one of the best parts of my Peace Corps experience."

Her second assignment was a more structured, nine-to-five job.

> I was supposed to be preparing materials for teachers to use in the schools for environmental education, as well as going out and doing environmental education projects myself. We had a huge mass of old magazines like *Ranger Rick,* and I would go through those magazines and look for projects I could adapt for Jamaica. For example, we had one of the world's largest swallow-tailed butterflies in the Blue Mountains in Jamaica. One of the projects showed how to make this little kite. So I adapted it by drawing the design of the butterfly, making it the actual size of the butterfly. I did a natural history of the butterfly and made it something teachers could use in a classroom. I made up sustainable fishing project games. We had a magazine called *Crocodile News,* and I finished a big issue about eutrophication, where too many nutrients wash into the ocean and the algae covers up the coral.

She also organized an environmental song contest for the country. "There were just amazing songs the kids came up with, so we picked the top three or four and went to the schools and filmed them. The idea was to make music videos that would be played on TV."

Aaron Shraberg (China 2004–2006)

Aaron was assigned to the Lanzhou University of Science and Technology in the capital of Gansu province. Lanzhou, in northwestern China near Mongolia, was a city of 3 million people, 30 percent of them Muslim. Aaron remembered his first day with a class of fifty freshman English majors in September 2004.

> The minute I walked through the classroom door they all erupted in applause and cheered. They were so excited for me to be there, and they had a big sign that said, "Welcome Aaron" or "Welcome to our school foreign teacher Aaron." I was really nervous. I just remembered one thing: I need to speak loudly. So I introduced myself and told them where I was from. And I spent that whole class just telling them about me and having

them ask questions about me. And I remember at the end of the first class, I walked out and the monitor made a comment in Chinese, and they all started laughing. I have no idea what was so funny, but they grew to like me, and I had those students for a couple semesters.

The classroom itself was very long. It was hard to reach across the classroom with your voice. There was a chalkboard, a desk, and a lot of chairs. And it was a cement floor. There was no heating in the classroom, so it was a little chilly. The lights worked that day, but some days they didn't.

So after that first day I got an idea of what I could prepare for the classes and what I could bring to the class. I had them write down things they might want to learn about America. I began to draw up some lessons after I got an idea of their level of English in that first class. I really just wanted to be prepared—overprepared, if need be—for the classes. I was new at teaching at that time, so I had a lot of questions, and I ran into some problems with planning and with classroom management. I had to learn how to be a good teacher, how to be a good classroom manager, how to get the students interested in what I was talking about. Whether I liked it or not, I felt like I was an emissary from this country. And they really looked up to me. They wanted to know about me. They wanted to know why Americans did this, why Americans did that, and they brought me their ideas about our country and our culture. Many times, whatever I said they took very seriously. I looked into their eyes, and they were all so young and very impressionable. I'm sure a teacher here gets the same sense, but it was just really clear to me that I was in a very important position.

Martin, Patsy, and Aaron represent the large numbers of volunteers who were teachers over five the decades. Although each of them taught English, many other volunteers taught math and science. Rebecca and Sarah were also in education programs, although more specialized ones responding to new host country needs—resource teachers and environmental education. Community development, which Rona participated in, was often less straightforward. In the 1960s it was mainly a Latin American job; later it was tied to other specific needs, such as health.

Underlying this chapter's title is the question: what is an appropriate job for a Peace Corps volunteer? That question leads to a consideration of the Peace Corps' goals. The kind of work volunteers should do has been contested almost from the beginning of the

Peace Corps, at least partly because some have seen one or another of its three goals as more important than the others. The Peace Corps Act, passed by Congress on September 22, 1961, enumerates those goals:

1. To help the people of interested countries in meeting their needs for trained manpower;
2. To help promote a better understanding of the American people on the part of the people served;
3. To help promote a better understanding of other peoples on the part of the American people.[1]

This chapter first explains the Peace Corps' job philosophy over the decades and highlights some volunteers' views about jobs. Volunteers then describe their specific jobs under the categories of education, community development, agriculture, health and health education, and other jobs, including business and school construction. After descriptions of some of the secondary projects individual volunteers found meaningful, the chapter concludes with the story of a unique Peace Corps job in Slovakia.

PEACE CORPS' JOB PHILOSOPHY OVER FIVE DECADES

Those who see the first purpose—trained women and men—as most important believe that the Peace Corps, especially in the twenty-first century, should recruit "the best of recent graduates—as the top professional schools do—and only those older people whose skills and personal characteristics are a solid fit for the needs of the host country"[2] Others put more emphasis on the second and third goals of international, cross-cultural understanding. Senator Chris Dodd, who served as a volunteer in the Dominican Republic, answered the Robert Strauss column in the *New York Times*, quoted above, the following day. "Every American of good will we send abroad is another chance to make America known to a world that often fears and suspects us. And every American who returns from that service is a gift: a citizen who strengthens us with firsthand knowledge of the world."[3]

Indeed, the Peace Corps has had different emphases over the years. For example, the 1960s was an era of young BA generalists, but not exclusively (architects in Tunisia, for instance), and in the early and mid-1970s, more skilled volunteers—even, for a very brief time, skilled men with families—were recruited, but again, not exclusively. In 1967 Peace Corps director Jack Vaughn stated his faith in the liberal arts major, writing:

> This category of American does the best job because of his age and background, at an unparalleled peak of energy, curiosity, flexibility and optimism. It has also been found that much of the work that needs to be done in the villages of developing nations does not require the services of skilled technicians; "experts" often feel frustrated or wasted at the grass roots level. An English major, on the other hand, who is trained to converse in a local language and can master one useful skill (poultry raising, basic construction, the organization of a credit cooperative), can supply a good deal of stimulus at the first stage of development.[4]

The Peace Corps began with "one broad precondition for any project: it should meet the 'felt needs' of the host country and be wanted by the local people. Volunteers were at the service of their host government, not the United States. As Shriver put it: 'The volunteers go to work with people, not to employ them, use them, or advise them. They do what the country they go to wants them to do, not what we think is best.'"[5] So from the beginning, Peace Corps staff worked closely with host country officials to match that country's needs with available Peace Corps volunteers' skills and experience. The Peace Corps asked where volunteers fit into the country's own development plans. It did not come with its own plans and experts. Sometimes volunteers worked directly with in-country agencies, as Rona and Sarah did, and teachers worked in schools and universities. In the early 1960s, however, there was often mutual disdain between other U.S. governmental offices abroad and the Peace Corps, which cherished its independence. Secretary of State Dean Rusk called for a policy of friendly disassociation, stating to ambassadors: "The Peace Corps is not an instrument *of* foreign policy because to make it so would rob it of its contribution *to* foreign policy."[6] In later decades some Peace Corps volunteers worked closely with USAID; in 1983 there was an interagency effort that sparked cooperative USAID–Peace Corps initiatives in sixty countries,[7] and small project assistance grants were mentioned by a number of the volunteers we interviewed.

Many host countries asked for help in the areas of education and agriculture in the 1960s. They wished to expand and upgrade their educational systems, so Peace Corps BA generalists often served as temporary replacements for host country teachers the government had sent elsewhere for advanced teacher training, or Peace Corps teachers were used to expand the number of schools available to students. In Sierra Leone the Ministry of Agriculture wanted to introduce swamp rice cultivation as an alternative to upland rice and to improve village poultry production, so volunteers with some level of agricultural experience, but not trained specialists, were assigned to chiefdom areas to assist. Normally, when planning its programs, Peace Corps staff visited schools, villages, and offices prior to assignments to ensure that the jobs were real and that the volunteers were really needed and wanted.

Volunteers were usually expected to have host country counterparts with whom they worked, often with similar jobs, and perhaps with complementary skills. It was hoped that the volunteers and their host country counterparts could have collegial relationships, learning from each other as well as learning together. A Mali Peace Corps volunteer begins a rare memoir of a host country counterpart this way: "I was almost always with Monique. She was not only the village's midwife and sole health care worker, but she was also my assigned host. At twenty-four, she was only two years my senior, but I was in awe of her knowledge and ability."[8] See chapter 8 for our interviewees' descriptions of their counterparts.

As the 1970s began, Peace Corps director Joseph Blatchford initiated "New Directions," especially recruiting more older and highly skilled volunteers to meet priority needs of developing countries and using host country nationals on the overseas staff.[9] Looking back, business volunteer Lloyd Jones (Colombia 1973–1975) said, "I was very fortunate to be in the Peace Corps when it was a technical assistance time. I was a successful Peace Corps volunteer because the model created no controversy, created no waves, but created a lot of opportunity for a lot of small business people who became very successful."

One example of New Directions in action came from our own experience in Fiji when Jack was director. The Peace Corps' 1971 country plan explained how volunteer assignments would fit into Fiji's own five-year development plan (1971–1976). In 1970, 100 of the 150 volunteers were primary and secondary school teachers; six volunteers taught at the university, three worked in curriculum development, one in teacher training, one in preschool, and two with crippled children; one was a librarian. Other job assignments included fifteen in cooperatives, five in forestry, four in fisheries, four with youth clubs, two in marketing, one in rural development, and one geologist. The next year, primary school teachers were phased out and replaced by junior and senior secondary school math/science and English/social studies teachers. Peace Corps Fiji also responded to very specific government requests and assigned three civil engineers to public works in rural development, a forty-seven-year-old California fruit grower to run a cooperative, a forty-nine-year-old chicken geneticist to do agricultural statistics, and a thirty-eight-year-old physics PhD from MIT with a family to teach at the University of the South Pacific. The binational staff included a Fiji Chinese doctor, a Fijian bookkeeper, and several Fijian and Indian language and cultural instructors to train new volunteers. Peace Corps Fiji also sent a proposal to Washington suggesting that responsibility for programming and volunteer support be transferred to the Fiji government. It was not accepted.[10]

Richard Parker (Côte d'Ivoire 1973–1974, Morocco 1976–1978) provides an example of a volunteer filling a specific country request. Bored with his job in California, encouraged by a friend, and wanting to travel, Richard applied to the Peace Corps without a college degree but with electronics skills. His placement in Côte d'Ivoire was an individual one, like those in Fiji. "They just needed somebody with electronics skills at the university to take care of their language labs, their closed-circuit TV systems, and the microteaching lab. That was the job. They needed a technician."

Including families in the Peace Corps was the policy briefly in the early 1970s. The Philippines, under director David Searles, had twelve to fifteen families with a combined total of as many as twenty children.[11] Malaysia in 1972 was home to twenty volunteer families, including fifty-seven children, and a congressional team's report was complimentary about the program.[12] The New Directions vocabulary, which included terms such as *institution building, multiplier effect, appropriate technology, binationalism,* and *host country contribution,* also used the term *nonmatrixed spouse,* Rona Roberts's designation before Searles found her a job.[13] Likewise, Sheila McFarland (Micronesia 1972–1974, Philippines 1974–1976) went to the Philippines as a nonmatrixed spouse, and the McFarlands' first child was born there.

By 1980, there was a new emphasis—"Basic Human Needs"—which echoed a change in thinking throughout the world of development agencies. Although almost half the volunteers continued to be assigned to education programs, some overseas projects were redirected toward health, nutrition, and water supply; food production; economic development and income generation; energy and conservation; and community services and housing. In 1978 an amendment to the Peace Corps Act had recognized the role of women in developing countries, especially in economic production and family support, and the Peace Corps added concern for poor rural women to its programming.[14]

In the late 1980s, as the cold war ended, the Peace Corps entered former Soviet bloc countries and later even Russia. It was a major and controversial change. Some returned volunteers were concerned that directing resources to what had been the so-called Second World of communism would mean fewer resources for the so-called Third World.[15] However, by the early 1990s, Poland had the largest Peace Corps program in the world, and in 1992, 100 business volunteers departed for Russia.[16] Blake Stabler (Russia 2000–2002) explained that the Peace Corps began with its headquarters in western Russia in a "backwards former industrial area" with a business development program. By the time Blake arrived, the office had moved to Moscow, at the insistence of the central government, and the focus was on English as a foreign language and business English. However, almost all volunteers still did some business development, as Blake did, or worked on projects involving youth groups or orphanages. Some of Blake's group didn't get visas for their second year, and the following group got only six-month visas, so the Peace Corps phased out of Russia in 2003.

As the twenty-first century began, new job areas opened up in HIV/AIDS prevention and information technology, although educational programs remained the largest job category. With Mexican American Gaddi Vasquez as director, the Peace Corps entered Mexico for the first time, where highly experienced volunteers, all having master's degrees in areas such as civil engineering, worked with the Environmental and Natural Resources Ministry and the National Council for Science and Technology. In 2007 director Ron Tschetter initiated the 50+ campaign to recruit more midcareer and older volunteers. In 2008 a Brookings Institution paper called on the Peace Corps to tap baby boomers as well as first- and second-generation immigrants.[17]

In February 2010, 35 percent of volunteers worldwide were in education programs; 22 percent in health and HIV/AIDS; 15 percent in business, information, and communication technology; 14 percent in environment; 5 percent in youth and community development; 5 percent in agriculture, and 4 percent in other programs. A new category entitled "food security" was listed under jobs to which about 40 percent of the volunteers working in health, environment, and agriculture contributed.[18]

Dealing with the reality that 85 percent of volunteers are recent college graduates, a June 2010 report under new director Aaron Williams stated that the Peace Corps should "embrace generalist volunteers, recruit them recognizing the competition for their services, and provide them with training and comprehensive support."[19] The example offered would be familiar to past volunteers: a water systems volunteer trained by the Peace Corps and assigned to a host country partner and counterpart who is encouraged to start an English club in the community as a secondary project.[20]

DIVERSE VIEWS OF THE JOB

From the beginning, there has been tension between general community development and relationship building as a job and technical assistance as a job. Kenny Karem (Chile 1966–1968) did both in successive years. He was assigned first to the Indian Affairs Department in a little town of 200 Mapuche Indians. "There was no job," he said.

> I got attached to a little rural school and started teaching physical education and English classes. Then I got involved in community development projects, everything from building a little community bus shelter to putting river gravel on the roads. I raised rabbits and tried to get people to raise rabbits to put meat in their diet. I did some garden projects. I tried to plant different grasses and teach the farmers about grasses. I was sort of a point person to try to talk farmers into planting pines. Pines down there grow twice as fast as they do in Kentucky. The second year I transferred to the south and was given a specific job with the Ministry of Agriculture vaccinating cattle against hoof-and-mouth disease. I trained farmers on recognizing diseases and how to prevent the spread of infection. I had a truck and went out with a vet. This is the classic Peace Corps argument: community development versus a job. Even though the first year of my Peace Corps assignment was far more

frustrating because it wasn't structured, I was part of the community. I got to know so many people, and they got to know me. The other was just a straightforward technical assistance job.

Audrey Horrall (Zambia 2000–2002), who worked with fish ponds as an agricultural volunteer, cast her vote in favor of specific technical assistance projects. She said she had written on her Peace Corps "close of service" survey that the "type of projects that seem to be most successful were ones that had a really specific objective, like agroforestry, or not just [developing] fisheries but [doing] things to help people in the really poor rural areas make a better living—things that promote sustainability and help people improve their standard of living in basic ways, like programs to promote better health care for children."

In *Twenty Years of Peace Corps*, Gerald Rice states: "Peace Corps is not solely a development agency nor solely an organization devoted to promoting international friendship and understanding. It is both."[21] Searles, from his perspective as both a country director in the Philippines and a Washington staffer, made it clear in his analysis of the 1969–1976 Peace Corps that a debate between goals is time wasted and that a balance is needed.[22] Still, tension persists between Peace Corps' first goal of providing trained personnel and the second in-country goal of learning about the community and letting the community learn about you.

Cori Hash (Zimbabwe 1999–2000), who was a community education resource volunteer, remembered that her Peace Corps director told her, "'Your job is not to go out and build X. Your job is to go in for the first year, sit by the well, and get to know people in your community and what the needs are and what you'll do from there. Your job is not to go in and say this is what needs to be done and this is how it needs to be done.' At times I thought she was crazy, but once I got back to the U.S., that was an important part of the experience." Cori concluded, "In my mind, the skills set is just a bunch of hooey. You're going as a cultural ambassador, and your ability to get to know a community is what's important. What kind of skills you have may not necessarily be what you need to survive and do well in your job in the Peace Corps."

Most of the volunteers we interviewed seemed to see their Peace Corps experience fairly holistically, not dependent only on performing a job or providing "trained manpower." Nevertheless, each volunteer had to go to his or her site either with a job or with the job of creating a job. Besides *being* somewhere, they needed to *do* something.[23] As Tom Scanlon wrote in his book about being a member of the first group in Chile in 1961, "The most important challenge of Peace Corps is not *conocering* (getting to know about) Chile, or perfecting your Spanish, but performing a job."[24]

Paul Winther (India 1961–1963) realized that his group, the first to go to India, was an experiment.

> They made a lot of mistakes, and they learned from the mistakes. I was supposed to be a dairy expert, but when we got over there, the volunteers chose me to be their group leader, and I was a liaison person with Washington the first year because there was no permanent staff member yet. The Indian administrators didn't know why we were there. All the jobs we went there for were nonexistent, so we made our own jobs. Some of the volunteers started the poultry industry in northern India. Another volunteer and I—he was supposed to be advising small businesses—decided to start a small industry on our own. We picked a refugee colony that had a lot of under- or unemployed men and said, "We're going to start a small business and teach these people how to become entrepreneurs with a product." We made educational wooden toys using only locally obtained hand tools. We used our own meager Peace Corps allowances to start this business called Lion Toys. Steve did the marketing, and I handled the men and procuring supplies. It was going really well, but then we had to leave.

Another early 1960s volunteer, Philip Curd (Guinea 1963–1965), had been told that part of the Peace Corps vision was for the volunteers "to figure things out. Go to this fruit research station and find something to do. I had to figure out, with the resources and the equipment I had, what I could do, whether or not I could do the analysis, and what particular analysis to use to get the results I wanted."

Occasionally, the Peace Corps simply didn't do a good job of programming. Judy Lippmann (Morocco 1966–1968) ended up in Spanish-speaking Morocco after spending three months learning French; then she discovered the first week she was there that she was redundant. A Spanish woman had been doing serology in the lab for about twenty years and didn't need her. "Evidently, the termination reports of the group ahead of us had not been processed before our group was recruited, because I learned that the position was not supposed to be refilled. And around the country, other volunteers were placed in positions where they weren't needed, so many folks went home. Peace Corps Rabat, which was our headquarters, was saying, 'Just wait, just wait, we're trying to reshuffle everybody.' So some people waited and some people didn't." Judy didn't want to go home, so first she cleaned drawers and washed glassware in the lab where she had been assigned, then she tried unsuccessfully to offer her services at the little clinic in town. She eventually proposed a project in dental hygiene, which was her own Stateside training, and returned to Rabat. After contacting the Ministry of Health, Crest, the World Health Organization, and her own dental hygiene school back in the States and doing a pilot project in a little village, she found out that people from Denmark were coming to do oral health care in the schools, so her idea was a nonstarter. Toward the end of her first year, Judy spent a month in a chemistry lab in Agadir taking over for someone who was on vacation. She spent her second year replacing a volunteer in Marrakech doing food hygiene and pregnancy tests at a hospital and carrying on for another volunteer teaching English at a school for the blind. She loved being in Morocco but felt that none of her jobs was really satisfying or valued in the country.

The experience of Jeff Kell (Dominican Republic and Ecuador 1962–1963) provides another example of poor planning. He was trained as a well driller, but "it turned out the Dominican Republic didn't need any well drillers. There were already plenty of well drillers, and not only that, they were out of work. Some USAID official had noticed that there were a lot of defunct banana and sisal plantations and thought all that was needed were a few wells. He went back to Washington and talked to Peace Corps but never checked with the government down there." Jeff and the other volunteers did join some Dominican well drillers, and "we actually got to drill a well and got to know the Dominicans. So it was educational for us but really wasn't too useful for them." After the coup in the Dominican Republic, Jeff and others went to Ecuador and helped build schools there.

Another volunteer in the Dominican Republic, Frank Gemendin (1968–1969), was unhappy with his experience.

I tried to apply what I knew about agriculture, having grown up farming, and I had a degree in agricultural economics at that point. It [the project] was a dismal failure because it just wasn't adapted to what they wanted. They had a system that worked, and it worked very well for what they were doing, growing enough food to eat on their small parcel of land. There was a great effort to organize people and get them to buy a tractor. They'd been fine with oxen or mules, or they'd have somebody come in who had a tractor, or they'd use hoes. So they were going to go in debt for this tractor. There we were just 120 miles from the U.S., and instead of buying a John Deere or a Ford, they were buying tractors out of Italy, I think because the director of the Agriculture Institute's brother-in-law was the guy selling them. Then the story came out that all the tractors were coming with an extra engine because the original engine had cracked blocks. They wanted me to front this to people. And finally I just refused.

Much more recently, Gary Griffin (Thailand 2004–2006) was frustrated working in a program requested by the Ministry of Education. "The idea was that we would work with teachers to help them learn new teaching methodologies, and [we would] do that by teaching English and just being an example. Despite everything the Peace Corps did to let them know what the project was about, they [the Thai teachers] really didn't buy into the project. What they bought into was getting a free English teacher." Gary wanted the program to work, so he refused to teach unless the Thai teacher was in the room. He ended up teaching fourth, fifth, and sixth grades at two schools and also teaching at a high school.

Sometimes when volunteers changed jobs they found greater satisfaction. Bill Davig (Peru 1965–1967) taught algebra and introductory calculus at the University of Huanuco for a semester, until students in the Communist Party began a strike. "They threw a few firebombs and it got a little violent, so they shut down the university. So I started looking for something else to do." Bill ended up working with other volunteers for a community development agency in road building and school building. He helped with the school plans and taught English to local people. Bill Miller (Dominican Republic 1968–1970) went in the other direction—first working on building projects for the Office for Community Development and then finding greater satisfaction as a teacher. "They had started a school project in El Rancho," he recalled, "and I coordinated the project, hiring local carpenters and masons. USAID provided the money to build the school." He was supposed to work on a road project the second year, but instead he found a job teaching social research at a school of social work in Santiago and supervising students who had field placements with different agencies. Win Speicher (Honduras 1967–1969) was initially placed in the second largest city in the country to work with a small committee of well-to-do women who wanted to bring the Girl Scouts to Honduras, but she created another job—training young women at a child-care facility for the children of market women.

Tara Loyd (Lesotho 1999–2001) eventually created her own job, too. She said, "I didn't go to Peace Corps to do this, but I landed in the middle of a very important part of history. A tragic time! I'm watching this happen. And I can't not do something." She worked as a special education volunteer her first year, but when one of the teachers at her school died, Tara realized it was going to be difficult to train teachers to work with children with special needs when the teachers were dying of AIDS. Peace Corps training had been about how not to get infected with HIV themselves; it had not prepared the volunteers to go out to villages where their colleagues were dying.

Six months after Tara arrived in Lesotho, she went with a young Basotho woman from the local Red Cross to the first HIV awareness workshop the Peace Corps hosted. There, several volunteers from Zambia talked about how to incorporate decision making, saying no, and respecting oneself into life skills education. They also suggested how HIV training could be incorporated into regular projects. Tara quickly became interested in HIV awareness. She and her friend went to the district secretary in Teyateyaneng, the headquarters of Berea district. He became a crucial supporter and offered his help. He understood why people were dying and told Tara they needed to talk to the chiefs. He had influence, according to Tara, because "he could say, 'It's mandatory that you come on February 1 to a weeklong HIV/AIDS workshop.' So he sat with us and we looked at the calendar and picked a time—not during planting season or circumcision school—and I approached the Peace Corps for funding." Tara got a grant to host a series of five workshops, each for 100 chiefs. They got help from people doing HIV work in the capital city, translated all the worksheets into Sesotho, and asked people from various organizations to present the material. Local women catered the weeklong event. At the end of the week, participants were reimbursed for mileage, encouraging them to come on time and stay for the whole workshop. Condoms were provided, and the chiefs were told how they could have the National Drug Association deliver condoms to their communities. The chiefs then had to make action plans for their communities, and Tara and her counterpart were invited to present follow-up awareness days in some of the villages, where they gave out AIDS ribbons and condoms, organized skits, and painted murals. At one point, Tara had 9,000 condoms in her bedroom!

Tara explained, "I did none of the training myself because I'm young, I'm a woman, and I'm a foreigner. We did as much asking of older men to come and speak as we could, but we also had at least one local woman present at the sessions, once people got more comfortable with the subject matter. Our workshops were a success. We had different measures for that, but we certainly had a lot more openness as the week went on about how comfortable they were with HIV in general and saying it was happening. Because it's a really important thing that when a chief buries a person, he doesn't say, 'One more person lost to tuberculosis,' but says, 'One more person lost to HIV.'" After its success in the Berea district, the Peace Corps decided to reproduce the project countrywide. Tara said, "I became sort of the first HIV/AIDS educator the Peace Corps ever really recognized. We wrote an application, by hand on legal paper, for grant money to the Bill Gates Foundation, and we were granted enough money to reproduce the chiefs' workshop around the whole country. The intention was that once the chiefs were trained, then we'd go on to different leaders in the community and different groups particularly at risk." By the end of Tara's service, HIV/AIDS was something all the volunteers were working on, and the Peace Corps began to invite health education volunteers to Lesotho and other affected countries in Africa.

The experiences described by these volunteers demonstrate the challenges of finding and doing a rewarding job—rewarding for people in the host country, and rewarding for the volunteer. Most Peace Corps jobs involved two of the three criteria that Malcolm Gladwell identifies as making work meaningful: autonomy and complexity.[25] However, fulfilling the third criterion—the relationship between effort and reward in doing creative work—was sometimes a challenge because Americans are "doing" people, and many volunteers were in "being" cultures.

EDUCATION

At the beginning, "teaching was the natural Peace Corps program, from both the host countries' and the agency's standpoints."[26]

Especially in African countries that were achieving political independence, governments wanted to expand access to education, and teachers were in short supply. "For the Peace Corps, teaching was the optimal Volunteer assignment. It provided a relatively structured environment, was well suited to young college graduates, had a direct people-to-people impact, and it allowed the agency to get off to a dramatically fast start. By 1963 nearly four thousand volunteers were in education, accounting for nearly 60% of all volunteers. The percentage of education volunteers in each region was 80% for Africa, 61% for North Africa/Near East/Asia and Pacific, and 22% for Latin America."[27] The annual report for 1968 showed that the percentage of education volunteers worldwide was 48.4 percent.[28] As noted earlier, in 2010 it was 35 percent.

English Teachers

"Teaching English as a second language is very, very important," new Peace Corps director Aaron Williams said in 2009.[29] It has been and continues to be a mainstay job in many countries. The renewed Indonesia program began with thirty English teachers in March 2010.

Like Martin and Patsy Tracy, Bob Olson (1963–1965) taught English as a second language in Turkey—one year at a high school, and one year at a middle school. He remembered that not knowing Turkish well when he arrived was a problem. "I walked into class. There were almost sixty students in the class, three at each desk— the boys on one side, and the girls on the other. Of course, in Turkey when you come into a classroom, all the students stand up. So the Turkish teacher introduced me and left. And the children just kept standing, and I didn't know the word for 'sit down.' I went home and studied like hell to memorize 'get up' and 'sit down.' I taught by the direct method, so I would say, 'Repeat after me,' and all sixty kids would say 'Sit down,' and it would ring through the corridor. The Turkish teachers complained that my students were shouting, but it was a problem to get them to speak in a moderate tone of voice because they were so enthusiastic."

Nancy Dare (Malaysia 1965–1967) taught English to children in the upper primary grades and also supervised a small school upriver once a month. She was particularly excited about the class of blind children in the school who were beginning to be mainstreamed. Her husband Phil taught English and geography in secondary school. He remembered thinking, "How am I going to teach Shakespeare? But they just plowed right into English, butchering it to pieces, and they weren't hesitant or shy about trying their English out. They loved Shakespeare. There were some complications trying to teach things in context. I saw some of those Cambridge overseas exams, and one of the essay questions was to write an essay on your feelings and emotions on the first day of snow. We were two degrees north of the equator! Or [write an essay on] thoughts that come to mind while sitting at a railroad station, but there are no trains in Sarawak anywhere. So you just have say, 'Well, think of it like a boat. You're waiting at the river. Or the monsoon season's going to start.' You translate for them." Phil had grown up in Missouri on the Mississippi River, so for their English exams he assigned a kind of Mark Twain's *Life on the Mississippi*, but life on their river, the Rejang.

In Afghanistan, Maurice White (1974–1976) taught seventh- and twelfth-grade English as a second language at a boys' school. He liked the respect accorded teachers. Even though he had seventy students in a class, "there were really no major behavior problems. I had some problems because I wasn't really savvy to all the distinctions in social classes and ethnic groups. So if someone failed a test or didn't do homework, they got what they deserved. But in that culture, if someone fails a test and his father happens to be important, that person passes the test." Maurice was proud of starting a library at the school with books he got from the Asia Foundation.

Volunteers taught English in African countries that had once been Belgian, French, and Portuguese colonies. Dianne Bazell (Zaire [Democratic Republic of Congo] 1975–1977) was a teacher in Katanga province in southern Zaire at a Catholic boarding school for girls run by Ursuline sisters. The school, which had been founded as a memorial to the copper mine owner's wife, attracted politicians' children and girls from well-to-do families who wanted their daughters to have a good education, possibly go on to university, and marry well. Dianne taught English, music, and geography. "One of the things I did was subscribe to *Ebony*. They were very interested in *le noir Americaine*, black American women, so we'd use pictures and photographs and look at hair and dresses and English texts. For the homeroom I would do lots of other things with them. We would go on walks on weekends. We'd go to some place they called the desert and pick mangoes. That was always a treat for them and for me. I always said to them I was learning so much more than they were."

French was also the colonial language of Senegal, where Ann Neelon (1978–1979) taught English as a second language from 8:00 to noon and then again from 3:00 until 6:00.

I taught first-year and second-year students. The African teachers were thrilled that Peace Corps people took the lower years, because they wanted the highest. Because I didn't know anything about teaching, I think the job was really helpful to me. Of course, I had to rethink my own language. How do you describe whatever in French if you don't know how to say the tense in English? Having to work with the structure of language helped me a lot in future years. I'd bring these figurines in and set up a dialogue, and that was the beginning of every lesson. I also gave out a lot of articles and copies of *Time,* which we got for free. They were a prized item. I particularly remember the afternoon stretch because it was so hot, and the sweat was pouring out of these students, three or four on a bench, fifty or sixty in a class. There were peanut shells all over the floor. Most of my students were men, and one class had nine people with the name Mamadou. I had a couple of students who had had polio.

Portuguese was the colonial language in Mozambique, where Michael Geneve (2003–2005) taught English to six different eighth-grade classes, fifty-five students to a class. The Peace Corps had instructed him to use only English, which worked for the first week when the students were learning "How are you?" but when he got into grammar, he needed to use Portuguese. "I would use Portuguese in my class a little bit, but anytime I made the slightest mistake, those kids would laugh so hard at me, just because the rest of their teachers were so strict about getting Portuguese exactly right. When I said something in the masculine tense instead of the feminine, they would laugh their heads off. I told them, 'Hey, I just started to learn Portuguese when you guys started to learn English. So you've got to give me some leeway here.' They gave me a really hard time." Michael explained the classroom situation: "Only two of the classrooms had desks. The rest of my four classes, the kids were on the ground. Most of the classrooms had chalkboards. The classrooms were made of reeds and a zinc metal roof, which made it hotter inside the classrooms than outside. The rooms were connected, so you could hear all the other teachers, and you couldn't be too loud. I was trying to do really fun things like singing songs. I'd say the toughest thing for me was learning how to discipline the kids, but eventually they figured out that I'd send them out of the classroom if they didn't do their homework. I really enjoyed teaching, and the kids started showing improvement quickly."

Teaching English was a popular Peace Corps request in Eastern European countries, too. Brian Arganbright (Slovakia 1991–1994) was assigned to the philosophy faculty of a university. "My main responsibility was to teach what they called practical English. It was basically conversation classes, and I was given a lot of freedom to do what I wanted, as long as the students got to practice their English. My main task was to prepare them for the oral exam that lasted from twenty to thirty-five minutes. The grade was based on their performance in that. I found that to be cruel." Brian also organized a weekly screening of an American or English movie and taught an English course in other schools in the area. He particularly enjoyed visiting a Roma (gypsy) school on a regular basis.

Leigh White (Bulgaria 2001–2003) taught English in a primary school according to requirements devised by the Ministry of Education: three hours a week for first graders, four hours for second graders, and five hours for third and fourth graders. She also taught English once a week to adults at the school, and she held three very small classes for different levels in her apartment. "There were people who were interested in talking to me, so it was really a good time and very social. I had planned lessons, but usually we digressed and spent a lot of time just chatting or talking about customs. So it was a lot of cultural exchange, too, in those classes at my apartment, but all very fun. Sometimes we'd meet at cafés or outside if the weather was really nice."

Math and Science Teachers

Math and science teachers were requested mostly by former British colonies in Africa and by Liberia. John Skeese (Nigeria 1961–1964), who taught physics and mathematics at a Catholic secondary school, was one of the earliest education volunteers. "Some of the kids I had were equivalent to our seniors in high school, pretty sharp kids, upper form and some at the lower form (junior high). We did our labs. The tests would be sent from England. I didn't have any discipline problems because if they were talking, I would just stop talking and not go on. One of the kids would turn to the other one and say, 'Shut up!'" In Ghana, Terry Anderson (1965–1967) taught in Cape

Coast, at the oldest boys' school in West Africa, and remembered it
as a wonderful experience. "You didn't have to spend much time on
discipline because, although there were some cutups and kids you
had to pay attention to, education was really important in Ghanaian
society. We were in a boarding school where the tuition was free, but
books and board had to be paid for by family members. Students had
a lot of pressure to finish school, and they studied all the time. I was
a housemaster in the dormitories. I'd go around making sure their
lights were out, but the kids would have flashlights and try to study
under their blankets at night." Terry taught biology and chemistry
and stayed an additional two years under a program called Teachers
for West Africa.

Cameroon was a combination of British and French colonies.
Jules Delambre (1965–1967) taught math and Gwenyth Lee (2004–
2006) taught chemistry, both in western English-speaking Cameroon. Jules was assigned to a grade three Catholic teacher training
college. That meant his students were in the equivalent of seventh, eighth, and ninth grades. Some had been teaching elementary school for many years with only an elementary education, and
the government was phasing them out, so the students were motivated to learn. "I had two days a week of algebra with every student. I think I was successful in conveying the concepts of algebra
and getting them started in using those concepts." He also cataloged
books in the library. About forty years later, Gwenyth taught chemistry in a village secondary school. She had sixty students in some of
her classes and about thirty in the upper grades. The age range varied a lot because students would sometimes miss a year if they ran
out of money. She had one twenty-seven-year-old student. Gwenyth
noted, "Another thing that was different was the kids would have
machetes sitting on their desks on manual labor day because they
were all going to go out and cut the grass." She had some discipline
problems, but because the village was small, she knew most of the
parents and could get in touch with them if necessary. She used the
syllabus in the Cameroon textbook to give the students notes on the
board, which they copied. Most students did not have textbooks. "I
got people to send me books with titles like *Five Experiments You
Can Do with Cotton Balls and Aluminum Foil.*"

Bill Sweigart (Liberia 1967–1970) taught junior high school in
up-country Kolahun. "School started at 7:30, and I taught six classes,
three each in math and science. When I think about it now, I'm

nearly overwhelmed imagining that I could do that many lessons. The next year a student teacher was supposed to show up from Kakata to teach the first-grade class, and the person was delayed. I said, 'I'll do it until the teacher shows up.' So I taught in the junior high from 7:30 to about 1:30 and then in the afternoon, for three or three and a half hours, I taught a first-grade class with forty-two students. When you're twenty-two you think you can do anything!" Bill remembered his only discipline problem: "During a factoring lesson, this one student was yakking, and finally I stopped and said something like, 'I can't continue if you keep talking like this. You're disturbing the class.' And he looked at me, and before I could say anything else, two guys got up and said to him, 'Get out!' Two other students in the room threw him out! This guy came to me and begged me, 'I'll never be out of line again.' That was my one discipline problem in three years in Liberia."

An editor at the *Louisville Courier Journal* when we interviewed him, Harold Freeman (Ethiopia 1965–1967) declared that his Peace Corps job teaching math and science "was the most interesting assignment I've had in my working life." He explained:

I was supposed to be an "experiment" teacher, working with all twelve sections of seventh graders. My job was to do things like when we moved on to sound [as a topic], I would take in rubber bands of various thicknesses and lengths. You hold them between your fingers and pluck them, and you get different pitches. If you stretch them more tightly, the pitch goes up. They all knew that "sound was the vibrations of molecules in the air as transmitted to the eardrum," or some such sentence. So what does vibration mean? Put your hand on your throat as you talk. Or I've got a lower voice than you, so put your hand on my voice box as I speak, and you'll feel a different thing. One day I finished one of my sessions where, instead of standing up and droning on about a camera being a device for making a record, which they had to copy down slowly and laboriously, I had done something that had helped them learn, and they'd all gathered around me on the floor. One little boy followed me out to the empty room that served as a teachers' lounge. He said, "Mr. Freeman, if you have some free time, could we do some more of that?" You know, that's about the highest compliment you can get as a teacher.

Also in Ethiopia, Ron Pelfrey (1966–1968) taught ninth- and tenth-grade math and trained his fellow teachers, all on contract from India, in the newly adopted Entebbe math, which had been developed in Uganda and was based on the American new math system. "I taught the math teachers to teach modern math, and I was also appointed by the headmaster [to serve] on the discipline committee and the scheduling committee. So that was very unique, somebody straight out of college having that kind of a broad range of experience that certainly paid dividends later on." Ron described his classes and his students: "The smallest class was forty-five. They were pretty well packed in. It was different in the high school there. Rather than the students changing classes, the teachers changed classes. So we'd go from 10A to 10B, 10C. You never had any discipline problems. Nor did you have any problem with motivation. They already had left their homes. They wanted to learn. And they rented a house and took care of themselves, washed their own clothes, bought their own food, cooked their own food. They were very dedicated. They wanted an education. They were just open vessels."

Across the world, Capp Yess (Fiji 1982–1984) taught at a secondary school that drew students, mostly Indians, from the northern part of the island of Vanua Levu. Posted at the school because it was starting a form-seven curriculum, a year beyond the traditional high school, Capp taught chemistry and math to this class. He remembered taking his students outside one day and telling them that he was going to demonstrate a "really cool reaction. I took a small piece of sodium metal and threw it in a coffee can with some water in it. It sputtered around for a little while and then it kind of blew up. I was pretty proud of myself and said, 'That was pretty neat, wasn't it?' Then, just as we were going back in, one of my students said, 'Sir, the principal's sugarcane field is on fire!' And I looked over the ditch, and sure enough, I had started my principal's sugarcane field on fire. So my whole class ran down, and then other classes saw us down there trying to put out this fire. Pretty soon the entire school was down in this sugarcane field stomping on the ground and using pieces of cardboard and other things to try to put out this fire. We got it out, thank goodness, but I never did that experiment again."

Some Peace Corps teachers had difficult experiences. Jenifer Payne (Gabon 1990–1992) taught seventh- and eighth-grade math classes of fifty students who had no books. She thought, "Oh, these African children are going to be so grateful. And it was totally different. The discipline problems were terrible. In every class there were a couple of real bad ones, a couple of real good ones, and the rest didn't really want to go to school, but they didn't want to work either, so they would try to stay in school. One 'kid' was twenty-five years old and had been through almost every school in the country. He finally ended up at our school. He was just contrary and loud and even physically aggressive at times. I've had them all beating on the desks so you couldn't talk or anything. And at those times I would just take my books and go home." She quoted her principal, who said, "'I know you want to help them, but there's too many kids. And only a few kids are going to get to do anything educational, go to college. If you have kids that are disrupting the class and you can't teach, get rid of them. You really have to concentrate on the ones that have a chance of getting out.'" Jenifer did have some good experiences with individual students, and her second year was better than the first. She concluded, "I would go through it all again. It was just not what I expected."

Environmental Education

Environmental education became a Peace Corps job category in the 1990s. Earlier, Sarah Cross Oddo (Jamaica 1993–1995) described how she prepared environmental education materials.

In Gabon, Jenny Howard (2000–2002) figured out that working in the eight elementary schools in her town was the way to accomplish environmental education. She found teachers who would "allow me to come into their classrooms two days a week. One day we would be in the classroom, talking about gardening and plants and related concepts, and later in the week I'd come back and we'd go into the schoolyard and create a garden. That allowed me to build on the ideas the agriculture volunteer who preceded me had taught, concepts such as ecology, biodiversity, interdependence. I tried to get them to think about 'What does your tropical forest area here on the equator have to do with other ecosystems around the world?'" Jenny also worked with "high school groups as time went on, and we had some eco clubs that would go into the villages and take informal surveys, asking questions such as: What does a plastic bag in your environment mean? What does the logging behind your village mean? We did some World Environment Day fairs and got the public involved. Looking back on it now, it is the strangest thing in the world to be from the richest, most wasteful country in the world trying to educate central Africans about the destruction we are adding to their environment."

Resource Teachers and Teacher Trainers

Some Peace Corps programs used volunteers more as resource persons, supervisors, or teacher trainers. Marianna Colten (Ecuador 1981–1983) was supposed to work with children with special needs.

> But this was a small school, and they didn't really have a program for special needs. They were hoping we would identify special-needs kids and then start a program. The problem was that a lot of those kids were kept at home because of the cultural stigma. I identified some in the schools who had learning disabilities and went around and talked to teachers. On weekends I went to homes and worked with some kids who just lived too far away from the school. But after a year I felt I wouldn't be leaving anything behind, so I talked to parents and said we should start a kindergarten so we can identify and start working with these kids, learning gross motor and then fine motor skills. We were told we couldn't start a kindergarten, and the parents said, "Yes, we can." And I said, "Yes, we can." So during the summer months when school was out, the parents and I got together and organized. The children had to bring their own chairs, and the parents made tables and uniforms. The school director came back and saw the kindergarten, so he went to the Ministry of Education and told them what we were doing. The Ministry came out and said, "Yes, we can give you a teacher." So we got a teacher, and the kindergarten is still there.

Sri Lanka wanted to reintroduce the English language in the elementary schools, so it requested volunteers to train students aged eighteen to thirty-five to become English teachers. One of those volunteers was Andrew Kimbrough (1984–1986), who taught English in a Department of Education Language Instruction Center. Two volunteers were posted to each province to teach an intensive year-long English program. Andrew recalled:

> Some of the students were just coming out of high school, with no career path charted for them. I remember having a couple of housewives who didn't have jobs. Some of the fellows did have jobs, but they were making a career move. They thought this was going to be good for the résumé.

So they came at it from lots of different angles. We organized them in three classes with colors—red, green, and blue, I think it was. I was the homeroom teacher for the green group, and I asked them to come up with another name. They came up with Emerald, which I thought was kind of clever. We would teach the four language skills: reading, writing, speaking, and listening. There were four teachers—two Tamils, two Americans—and we would trade off teaching a different skill every other week. We would pick a theme, like history or evolution, to get a vocabulary base, but then we would build grammar and speaking and listening exercises around the particular topic, banking on our one month of intensive training. The groups would shuffle between one teacher and another and get their four classes every day—a five-hour class day—plus some time on Saturday. About halfway through that first year we had another twenty or thirty Muslim students from farther south in the province join us. So we had Muslims and Hindus and Catholics.

"Primary resource teacher" was Kristen Perry's title in Lesotho (1999–2001). "I had two primary schools," she said, "first grade through seventh grade. I would visit these schools and do teacher training because the teachers did not have much training, if any. Some of them didn't even have a high school degree. I would do demonstration lessons. I would observe their classes and give them feedback and suggestions, help them develop materials. The things that were most successful were their ideas. One of the teachers wanted to paint the alphabet on the wall so the kids could have that as a reference. I was thinking we could paint the letters up high, but the teacher said no, let's paint them low so the kids can come and trace them. Then they had the idea to do the capital and lowercase letters in different colors. I started a little school library, and we got a little mini-grant to get some books and bookshelves. I had an after-school English club."

Physical Education and Youth Development

Tom Boyd (Colombia 1964–1966) began his assignment by leading sports classes at several orphanages and a women's prison; then he led sports camps around the country in schools and orphanages. Assigned to an urban youth development program, Patrick Bell (Costa Rica 1997–1999) worked out a daily routine: After having lunch with young workers, he went to the orphanage to help the kids with their homework and take them to the park. He also taught English at the neighborhood elementary school; he taught chess and, after he got a grant, guitar as well.

Joshua Mike (Nevis 2004–2006) was assigned to the Ministry of Youth and Sports in Community Affairs. As a tennis player and a competitive swimmer, Joshua used those skills to teach both sports. Then he developed a proposal to do small business and entrepreneurship education with young people. He became the island coordinator for Young Americans Business Trust, which is affiliated with the Organization of American States. Joshua organized regional trainers' workshops that focused on putting theories of business into practice.

COMMUNITY DEVELOPMENT

Community development has meant many things, from working with a cooperative or a regional development organization to working with young people or with a health program—with the goal of injecting some sense of community. Although Latin America had more community development volunteers than any other part of the world, especially in the 1960s, our examples come from all regions. There is no longer a separate category entitled community development on the Peace Corps Web site.

After being trained in community development and rural education, Joyce Miller (Chile 1964–1966) was sent to the northern desert to work in production cooperatives because of her graduate work toward a master's of business administration. "They figured I could handle whatever was there," she said. For the first year Joyce was the only volunteer in Antofagasta, a town of 120,000 that was a seaport for the copper mines. "It originally belonged to Bolivia, and the Bolivians still want it back. Up until a few years ago, they never had recorded rainfall." Joyce worked with a group of men to help them turn a sheet metal workshop into an official production cooperative. "We had the monopoly on wastepaper baskets. We provided wheelbarrows for the country and made ship hatches. I worked with the worker-priest who was head of the building co-op and with a group of upper-class Chilean women who believed it was their social duty to work with these people. I also worked with the mothers' center, where we set up a child-care center. I was trying to set up a bookkeeping system, trying to develop business, trying to get contacts and then set up an apprentice program. I didn't touch the money. We had an accountant who did all the money handling. We were always very careful never to get involved with money. When my tour was up, they asked me to stay on because they figured I was the only one they could trust to do money. But I said no."

Angel Rubio (Costa Rica 1971–1973) had a specific job assignment in two small rural towns south on the Pan-American highway toward Panama with a new agency called DINADECO. He explained: "Legislation was passed that said every year they would set aside 2 percent of all the tax revenue for the staff and its programs and for grants to designated community development associations. It was very typical development work. You were supposed to see if they had plans. Had they thought them through? Did they have approval by the majority of the people that were representatives to the association? Did they have the money to be successful? All those sorts of things now seem second nature to me after being in this work, but back then, I was more of an observer. I was supposed to show leadership, but I was more like, 'Wow, how do we do this?'" After a year they placed a DINADECO agent in San Isidro who had a jeep and a secretary. "All of a sudden, I wasn't out there by myself. Javier and I would get together and plan. He had maybe twelve associations, and I was responsible for two. I would go with him when he traveled to the other ten and help with presentations and get ideas about what other people were doing." In his second year, Angel worked with a farmers' cooperative to plan a building that would serve as a storage area and a school, raising a little money in the States to match some USAID money. He extended his tour for a third year and became part of the central office of DINADECO, where he worked on a promotional campaign, using his mass communications background from college. "We actually did some pretty progressive things like radio shows."

In Ecuador, Kay Roberts's (1982–1984) job description included organizing 4-H clubs in her community and surrounding ones, primarily doing agricultural projects. "They had already started a pineapple project," she said, "and we did some family gardens. We did some calf projects and raised corn, but it was a tough time to do agriculture because it was the year of El Nino, which meant very heavy rains. That year it rained more than since they began measuring rain. So the agriculture wasn't particularly successful; the seeds washed away or rotted, and the cattle had hoof problems. I worked at the little health clinic, administratively. I also did nutrition and first-aid courses and taught a little bit of English and did a little 4-H organizing, teaching them to keep records and figure out if they had made a profit from their products."

Occasionally, other regions of the world also had community development programs, often paired with some other program area. For example, Rachel Savane (Guinea 1990–1992) worked in a community development and public health program. She remembered the reality was to "find something to do. I saw quickly that in my village of Bangouya the nurse was charging exorbitant amounts for medicine. I got funding through the American embassy to complete construction of the health center, so they had a little pharmacy and more staff. I was the organizer, contracting people to finish the roof, build furniture, make doors, and build a wall around it."

In a community development project in Micronesia, volunteers were trained in teaching English as a second language, which was their initial role in their villages. Elaine Collins (1989–1991) taught English at the school on her island, working with eighth graders ranging in age from twelve to sixteen. Then in her second year she completed a sanitation project on the island with a grant the community wrote to get money for water-seal toilets.

AGRICULTURE

Agriculture programs were usually more narrowly focused than community development and included agroforestry. Such programs were present in almost all regions.

In Guatemala, William Salazar (1972–1973) and his fellow volunteers were able to duplicate their training experiment with fertilizer, but because of the oil embargo, "we couldn't afford fertilizer for the trials. So our project was really a wash. Peace Corps didn't know what to do, so we traveled around the country for a while until they figured it out. Some of my friends left, but I really liked being in Guatemala. So we turned around and worked with co-ops. We did a lot of classes at the elementary school. We did a lot of classes with local economists. We went around on motorcycles and soil tested the whole area, which the Department of Agriculture really loved because now they had a database. We also did a lot of composting and taught people how to do that."

Sally Spurr (Ecuador 1975–1977) began training in community

development but asked to switch to the horticultural research program. "This project was administered through the Ministry of Agriculture and through the universities and technical colleges. We would grow similar crops and see how they adapted to each of the regions. So some people were doing mountain crops, high-altitude crops, and some people were doing rain forest crops. We were more or less in the altiplano, high altitude. My project was on peas, and my Peace Corps coworker worked on onions. My goal was to get clean strains of peas so you could actually buy the one you knew was going to grow well at this altitude. Every three months I would start another group of twenty-four pea patches in different locations." Sally described her coworkers—Lucy, the other Peace Corps volunteer; Roberto and Ermel; and the Indian workers. "Roberto Marinovich was the head of the farm and did things like drive the tractor around and talk to everybody. And Ermel did whatever Roberto told him. They were the more directly Spanish and white guys. They dressed in good-looking pants and never got themselves dirty. Lucy and I had overalls, straw hats, and work boots. We were out in the fields doing the labor with the Indian *peones*. In Ecuador at that time the Indians were very oppressed and were called 'little boy' all the time, so they never assumed to make friends with us, but we hung out together at the farm. The women would bring the food up to the men in three-tiered enameled dishes. And they'd have their babies." Sally explained what she learned. "It was always interesting to me, because we were all speaking Spanish from a second language point of view. And I learned a lot about indigenous agriculture and growing techniques." For example, she learned how to dig into an irrigation ditch to make the water flow in a circuitous path. "You had to bank the rows so that it would hold the water long enough for the crops to get enough water, so the water couldn't flow too fast or too slow. And of course these *peones* were artists at that. They knew exactly what they were doing."

Agricultural extension agent Oghale Oddo (Jamaica 1994–1996) began his tour by volunteering to teach math and English at the two primary schools in the area. After four or five months of getting to know the students and their parents, "I started walking up to the farmers and talking about what they needed, what they were thinking of doing with their crops, how best to plant, or what they needed from the government. There were several government agencies that dealt with subsistence farmers who planted cocoa and coffee and peppers. So I became somewhat of a liaison between the farmers in the rural area and the government ministries, and I went to the Hillside Agriculture Project people. That was actually the core of our agri-program in Jamaica. I started making that connection and bringing people to give presentations to the farmers, talking about erosion, types of crops or types of seeds, the best seeds to plant depending on the type of soil. By the end, we had gotten together a group of about ninety farmers, and we started exporting peppers." With a coworker, Oghale also started a youth development program that included leadership training and a chess club.

A number of volunteers worked in forestry. In Costa Rica, while some in his group worked for the Ministry of Forestry, forester Ben Worthington (1973–1975) and two others were assigned to the Instituto Costarricense de Electridad, a kind of Tennessee Valley Authority, with offices on the fifteenth floor of a building in downtown San José. Ben mapped the reservoir so they could look at problems in the watersheds. He also researched the water hyacinth and how to get rid of it in the reservoir.

Several volunteers worked in agroforestry in West African countries. Ashley Netherton (Senegal 2003–2005) worked with her host brother on a windbreak project. "We talked to the people who were farming the land where we wanted to put the windbreak and explained the benefits—how it would help prevent fires in the village because the wind could just blow a cooking fire up under a roof, and how it would protect the crops from the wind during the rainy season. We had three line windbreaks of cashew, eucalyptus, and mesquite. I was a little conflicted because these trees are not native to their environment, but it was the recommended method at the time. Eucalyptus trees require a lot of water, but they are tall and make a good windbreak tree. We didn't put eucalyptus trees near the banana plantation because bananas require so much water. We also planted mangoes and some citrus trees and guava trees from the Forest Service." In her second year Ashley did some environmental education and health work. Since her host brother was also a nurse's aide, they both worked with the local nurse, vaccinating children and weighing babies and charting their growth.

In Cameroon, Robin Sither (1996–2000) "met regularly with these social groups that got together once a week or once a month. Everyone pooled their money and gave it to one person so they could perhaps start a small business. I had some demonstrations, and I

Kentucky Returned Peace Corps Volunteers gathered at the state capitol in 1991, with first Peace Corps director Sargent Shriver in the middle.

Martin and Patsy Tracy (Turkey 1965–1967) as volunteers (in the back row, wearing glasses) with friends in Turkey. Günaydın Günaydın (see chapter 7) is in the middle of the front row.

Martin and Patsy Tracy in 2009.

Rona Roberts (Philippines 1973–1975) as a volunteer, acting as sponsor at the baptism of a baby belonging to a Filipino friend.

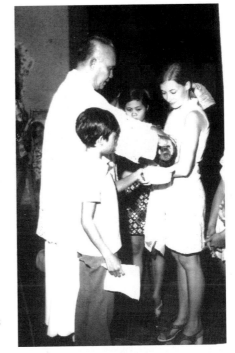

(below) Rona in 2009 using her community development skills to work with Charles Boland in planning a 2040 Visioning process for Lexington.

Rebecca Roach (Liberia 1988–1989) with her husband Randy Barrette and children in 2010.

Sarah Cross Oddo (Jamaica 1993–1995) with husband Oghale Oddo (Jamaica 1994–1996) and their sons Uzezi, Kai, and Seneca in Fiji in 2007, during Oghale's tenure as Peace Corps director there.

Aaron Shraberg (China 2004–2006) at the White Pagoda in Lanzhou, Gansu province, in 2005.

Philip Curd (Guinea 1963–1965) exploring Mount Gan and looking down on the city of Kindia. Dr. Curd was honored with the prestigious Sargent Shriver Award for Distinguished Humanitarian Service in 1992 for his work in health care services in rural eastern Kentucky.

Susan and Tom Samuel (Liberia 1964–1967, 1965–1967) being married in Buchanan, Liberia, on April 16, 1966, by Monsignor Juwle, the first Liberian ordained a Catholic priest and a bishop. *(below)* The Samuels greet their guests after the wedding.

Cecil and Sheila McFarland (Micronesia 1972–1974, Philippines 1974–1976) on the day they were sworn in as Peace Corps volunteers in Pohnpei, Kolonia, Micronesia.

Kay Roberts (Ecuador 1982–1984) bathing in the river at her Peace Corps site, Flor del Valle.

Andrew Kimbrough (Sri Lanka 1984–1986) with students at the Department of Education Language Instruction Center at St. Michael's College in Batticaloa.

Harry Siler's host parents Herbert (*second from left*) and Martha Mageza with two community members and some of the 33,000 books sent to Ponani School by the International Book Project of Lexington, Kentucky, in July 2010.

Harry Siler (South Africa 2001–2003) carrying books to a primary school in Mahlaba Cross, Limpopo province, where he was the resource teacher.

Jenifer and Glen Payne (Gabon 1990–1992, 1989–1992), at the end of the middle row, with Peace Corps trainees and a Gabonese work crew building a school in Moungali.

David Goodpaster (Malawi 2005–2007) on his porch with dog Snoop and friends Edward, Aaroni, and Chisomo. Edward helped the Goodpasters make a garden, and they helped send him to secondary school.

Lauren Goodpaster (Malawi 2005–2007) walking home with Memory. Memory and her parents were members of the People Living with HIV/AIDS Support Group that Lauren and David advised.

Deborah Payne (Uganda 2007–2009) demonstrating hand washing to schoolchildren and at her farewell party surrounded by friends from the Katosi Women Development Trust, with whom she worked as a public health officer.

Jack Wilson (Liberia 1962–1964) refereeing a basketball game between B. W. Harris school from Monrovia and Suehn Industrial Academy. He coached the Suehn team to a national championship, even though the school's court had only a dirt floor.

Angene and Jack Wilson in front of Strong Hall. They lived on the second floor. The first floor housed a clinic, a library, and a classroom.

Angene and Jack in January 2010 at the wedding of Bibi Roberts Jr., the son of friends they met in Liberia in 1962.

would do some hands-on stuff, such as how to build an A-frame level so you could site a contour across a slope. Or how to build a nursery or plant seedlings or how to incorporate green manure into your field. Most of the people I worked with who were successful were men who owned their own land, women who were married to men who owned the land they worked, or people with substantial means, enough to purchase a farm—they cared enough to think about a permanent farming system."

Fish farming was another project area under agriculture. In Zambia, Audrey Horrall (2000–2002) helped farmers build and maintain small-scale fish ponds to provide additional family income. She explained:

There was a specific design for these ponds, developed for a specific kind of fish. We were growing tilapia, a fish that reaches maturity at six months, so you could harvest two cycles per year. These ponds were designed to be drained completely at harvest. So you've got the mature fish that have grown about as big as they're going to get, and you've got a bunch of little fingerlings. You harvest all the big fish and all the fingerlings and keep a couple hundred of the fingerlings to restock your pond for the next cycle. We had regular meetings of all the fish farmers so they could share their stories and help each other. I had about fifteen established farmers, and I went into another area and started about ten more. These ponds weren't completed by the time I left because it takes anywhere from six months to a year to build these ponds. It's a lot of work because it's all done by hand.

To get the fish to grow to a maximum size and be a good yield, make a good profit, and provide a decent meal, they needed to be fed every day some chopped-up leaves or termites. There were termite mounds everywhere, so you could pluck one off the ground, smash it to pieces, and throw it in the pond, and the fish would go crazy. Another component of management was to maintain compost fences inside the pond, where you would put different kinds of green manure and maybe animal manure, anything to get a plankton bloom going, because a large part of the tilapia's diet is plankton. Maintaining an algae bloom in a pond actually takes a lot of work to scavenge for the green leaf material.

I wanted to make sure that everybody was on the right track, so I would try to have meetings with the farmers and their families. I would have workshops on composting and the different types of things you could feed your fish, and just stop by about once a week and see how it was going. And I always tried to participate in all the harvests and help them sell their fish, sometimes just going door to door to different villages.

Health and Health Education

Health and health education have always been important Peace Corps programs, and in recent years, HIV/AIDS education became part of the assignment for many volunteers.

Part of an all-female group whose mission was to vaccinate women against smallpox, Charlene McGrath (Afghanistan 1969–1971) described their special program. "We were identified with the Ministry of Health, and two Peace Corps girls would go with six or seven young men who were under the supervision of an older man, who might have had a ninth-grade education. They would bundle us into Land Rovers and drop us off in various rural areas for a month or six weeks or two months. We did a lot of outbreak containment work, because there was still active smallpox in Afghanistan. We did some epidemiological work, too. We used Russian freeze-dried vaccines and bifurcated needles, and we had several Russian doctors working with us. A bifurcated needle looks like a devil's pitchfork, except it has only two prongs. You get a drop of vaccine between the prongs, and then you rub it on the person's arm and stick them at least twenty times, and they are vaccinated."

The other health volunteers we interviewed did their work in African countries. Richard Bradshaw (Central African Republic 1977–1979) was a special case. He had been trained for a public health program but developed his own job when all the other trainees went home following the troubles described in chapter 3. Richard explained: "My idea from the beginning was to learn as well as teach. So one of the first things I did was to organize classes in health in my backyard. A group of young people started attending the class, and I would tell about illnesses and the causes. And then they would tell me what they thought and how they treated the disease. I took quite seriously that we were supposed to study the situation first instead of just launching programs." Later, when Richard returned to Central African Republic as associate Peace Corps director, he got money from USAID for a project in which people were given shots to overcome iodine deficiency.

Health and sanitation was the program assignment for Carolyn Cromer (Morocco 1992–1995).

I had a very discernible job. My official site was all forty-eight villages served by a small health clinic near the market. This was up in the mountains. Two nurses worked there. They had almost no equipment. They had some needles, some syringes, some immunizations, some prescription medicine, one type of antibiotic, a pink pill they handed out like candy, and some contraceptives. My role was as a liaison between the people and the two nurses and the health clinic, so my job was to be out in the villages supplementing their work through health education and contraceptive education. I ended up carrying [birth control] pills with me—not condoms, because men there don't use condoms. What ended up working best for me was a lot of one-on-one work primarily with women. I had wells and cisterns that I treated with chlorine bleach, and I tried to hit those once a month in the six or eight villages that were about a one-and-a-half- to two-hour walking distance from the village where I lived. I might spend the day in one village and go to all the wells or cisterns and talk to the villagers about treating their water with chlorine and why it was a good idea and about typhoid. Then we would measure the water together and treat it with chlorine bleach, which they had on hand to wash clothes. It wasn't high tech at all, and the idea was that they would get in the habit of treating their water. The water treatment program was only mildly successful. I think they did it because they liked me.

Carolyn also went out to the villages to distribute a shipment of vitamins from UNICEF that she got at the Peace Corps office in Rabat.

I would take these vitamins, put them in a backpack, head down a river valley, and be gone for three or four days just walking through villages. [I would] enter a village, hang out until someone invited me for a meal or for tea and then invited me to stay the night. I would go to kitchens and sit with the women and get a feel for how many kids they had in the family, how healthy the kids were, how healthy the women were. Were the women using contraceptives? I approached contraceptive use from the angle of spacing kids. I talked about giving their bodies a rest, letting their babies get healthy before they had another child. Teaching people about contraceptive use was probably my most successful program because there was an interest in not having so many mouths to feed, especially since immunizations had come to Morocco in the mid-1980s and kids weren't dying as much. They didn't need to have as many kids in order to ensure a survival rate. You no longer needed to have fifteen kids for eight to live. Most people were very receptive, and in over three years, I had the door shut in my face only once, and that was in a very remote area.

Carolyn also went on health campaigns several times a year with the nurses—by vehicle, by mule, or on foot—to do immunizations and talk to women about IUDs.

In Niger, Elizabeth Greene (2003–2005) was called a community health agent.

A typical day was going around to houses to help parents with a sick child make the oral rehydration solution or encourage them to go to the clinic six kilometers away. At first I walked or rode my bike there several times a week, getting to know them, building up trust with them, helping with prenatal consultations. The doctor there was just a great guy and was really invested in helping his community. So we talked about things we could do, and he said we really needed to do midwife training. He wanted to find midwives from each of the twenty-nine villages in a thirty-kilometer radius and bring them in to train. So we started working on that, the process of getting the proposal in, getting money, meeting with staff. One day we borrowed a car and driver from a hospital forty kilometers away and went into the bush and had a village meeting with delegates from each of the twenty-nine villages. We told them what we wanted to do [and asked them] to pick a woman and get money for their community contribution. It worked out well.

Lauren and David Goodpaster (Malawi 2005–2007) were health education volunteers—Lauren working with the health center and the orphan care center, and David teaching in the schools. Lauren helped with registration and paperwork at the clinic. "I saw myself as a cheerleader because the health surveillance assistants didn't get a lot of support, and I would make them posters and signs." She taught health (washing hands and body parts) at the orphan care center's preschool two mornings a week, but a lot of her work "was just trying to teach the director how to sustain an organization through fund-raising, learning how to create and write a proposal for a grant, introducing him to big organizations in Lilongwe [the capital] such as UNICEF or even the local government, trying to point out resources, creating a local committee of parents and community members, making sure he informed all the chiefs. My main work was helping him stand on his own two feet."

OTHER JOBS

Business was a particularly active program area in the 1990s, especially in Eastern Europe and the former Soviet Union. However, other countries had business programs too, and much earlier. Currently, business jobs are related to information and communication technology. School construction was another specific program requested by a few countries.

Business

Lloyd Jones (Colombia 1973–1975) was part of a fairly early small business assistance program. "Peace Corps had just signed a deal with a government organization that was basically an entrepreneurial development program. We were going to be assigned to these offices scattered throughout Colombia as technical assistance consultants to small and medium-sized businesses. What a great job for a kid coming out of college with an undergraduate degree in business. To say, 'How can I help you? I'm here to help you design a marketing program or help you lay out a production line or help you figure out how to do your taxes or how to do your books and accounting and finance.'" The volunteers were told not to tell people how to run their businesses but to say, "Tell me where I can help you." Lloyd worked on coffee plantations and in all types of small and medium-sized manufacturers making dolls, chairs, desks, and food packaging. "It was all about, 'How do I get my costs under control? Show me how I can do these things or help me set up these systems.'"

Sara Todd (Armenia 2001–2003) described her assignment "to a business center in Goris, in southern Armenia, [that had been] established to provide business training and consultation to the nonprofits and businesses in Goris. So my job was to assist with training and grant writing, and they did a couple of business trade shows. Through the business center I was connected to some other nonprofits, where I did secondary projects—a sports center and a couple of health organizations." Sara also taught economics at a private university. She remembered celebrating when the business center bought a new copy machine. "They were very excited about this purchase. We had to go and celebrate the copy machine. So we went to a little restaurant, ordered a bottle of vodka, and had lunch at 10:00 in the morning. We toasted that business is improving, we have a new copy machine, we can do more work."

School Construction

As a volunteer in Gabon working with the Rural Schools Construction Program, Glen Payne (1989–1992) built schools in small, remote villages. Glen's description of his job illustrates the tension between providing technical assistance and building relationships, but it also illustrates the necessity of both goals and, for him, the primacy of the second. In addition, Glen's experience provides evidence of the value of a third year for Peace Corps volunteers in terms of training others and making an impact.

As Glen explained, the Gabon government provided the teacher, and the Peace Corps volunteer would build the school and a house where the teacher could live. Glen described how hard it was to get that school built. "You might spend a long time convincing your co-villagers what you were up to, considering all the obstacles. You might spend a while just trying to be friends. You had a lot to learn just to get by day to day as far as washing, eating, keeping clean." They used the villagers' methods for building the house. "We made the mud brick by digging a hole, locating certain clay soils, wetting the soil with water, doing lots of stomping and sort of kneading the mud, and then packing it into wooden molds. It was great fun. We could work with the women of the village, the kids, men. [We had] lots of volunteer labor to help make the mud bricks for the teacher's house. It was a good time." For building the school, they paid workers in the village on a monthly basis. "One of the incentives on our side was to train them so they could go into a professional firm, maybe up in the capital, and say, 'I have experience in building.' We did have success with that. We had two or three Gabonese men who came out of the villages and learned enough after a couple of years that they were given their own job sites."

Glen decided to extend his service for a third year and become a trainer. "One of my most important jobs was going to a village many months in advance. If I knew there was a batch of new construction volunteers coming in June, in December or January I'd already be in that village sort of planting seeds, hanging out with the villagers, drinking palm wine with them, gently making friends. It was important to let them build a consensus around the idea." Glen would supply the materials, and the village would provide the labor—some of it volunteer and some of it paid. "It was important that they work together to select a site, figure out where to get sand and gravel." Glen shared his experience with the new volunteers, telling them:

This school is not a complicated building. If you can't build this school in eleven days in the United States, I'm going to fire you, but here, if you can get one done in two years, we're going to raise a toast to you. Because here you cannot order materials to be sent to you. You cannot push people around. It needs to be their school. You're there to transfer as much knowledge—construction skills, job supervision, all those things—as you can, hopefully to a targeted one or two who seem like good soil to till in that way. You're going to have to go stand in the river and make a mountain of sand. You might have to break rocks to make gravel. You're going to have to build a mold to make mud brick. You're going to have to design the house—working with them. You're going to have to build it, and when it rains and knocks your walls down, you're going to have to rebuild. It's in your best interest to be yourself, be as honest as you can, and build respect. You're going to need to eat like them, learn what they do, trust their judgment. You don't have to be the expert on what's good water, which piece of meat is rotten, because they already are. You take their lead on all those things, and then you provide the leadership on things that aren't easy for them to get, like job training, how to use a water level. Spend ten weeks on that, if you need to. We don't need this school. It's not about productivity. If it was about building schools, we would just fly materials in, fly guys in with generators. Crank them out. But that's not what it's about. It's about learning, having fun, building relationships.

He concluded: "And we built great relationships, volunteers did."

SECONDARY PROJECTS

The Peace Corps expected volunteers, especially teachers during school vacations, to do secondary projects as well as their assigned jobs. Sometimes those were what volunteers found most satisfying.

Phil Dare (Malaysia 1965–1967) explained, "In the holidays when the breaks came, you were supposed to find a project unless you were taking your own annual vacation." Once Phil and his colleagues spent a week stomping around in a wet rice paddy planting rice to demonstrate swamp rice as opposed to the hill rice people usually grew. Another time they built steps up from the river to the school and leveled off an area for a volleyball court. One big project was collecting sand and gravel and moving concrete for a basketball court. Phil remembered, "We were completely covered in cement stuff, which was very impressive to the townspeople. They all said, 'Oh, you look like a coolie!' They were very impressed that we had gotten the sand and gravel by boat and hauled it all up."

In Fiji, Capp Yess (1982–1984) worked with five other teachers from his group to invent a problem-solving summer school in Labasa, the big town on his island, and they persuaded the Peace Corps to donate a classroom full of computers. They wrote the curriculum and had to have a lottery because so many students wanted to attend. He remembered, "That was a great project. We really had a good time."

Sarah Payne (The Gambia 1989–1991) taught math at a secondary technical school, but she was most proud of a woodworking project. She had noticed the woodworking teacher drawing pictures of tools on the blackboard and the students drawing those pictures in their notebooks. "I remember looking at pictures about wearing safety goggles for electrical things and thinking, this doesn't relate. So we got funding to buy raw materials and hand tools, and the first class of students made furniture for the school, sold that to incoming students, and then used that money to buy more raw materials."

In Russia, English teacher Blake Stabler (2000–2002) found his future career interest in international economics through his secondary project—helping in a computer lab that was open to the public after school and attracted a lot of entrepreneurial types. "I got interested in agriculture," Blake explained, because it "was a way out of really depressing rural or semirural poverty. People were making food products because everyone buys food. And they might be selling it in different ways. I wanted to see people in my village engaged with something and not sitting around the stairwells and smoking, especially the men."

Kristen Perry (Lesotho 1999–2001) became involved in HIV/ AIDS education as a secondary project, as did many other volunteers in African countries by the late 1990s. "We had a clinic in the village, and there was a nurse at this clinic who was just an amazing woman and was so motivated. She knew what was up, and we worked together to train a group of girls at the secondary school to be peer educators. These girls went around giving little workshops about HIV/AIDS care and prevention. That ended up being the most meaningful part of my experience."

Michael Geneve (Mozambique 2003–2005) was also involved in HIV/AIDS education. He started an English board the first year at his school where the students could display their songs, poems, short stories, and drawings. The second year he taught a drawing class that incorporated HIV/AIDS education. "I always used it in my lesson plans, and I got a lot of pamphlets and information. These kids were essentially doing graphic design. I taught them how to draw a face one day, and the next day I would say, 'Okay, what do you want to be in your future?' And one might say, 'I want to be a doctor.' And I'd say, 'I want you to draw a face with a doctor and a stethoscope.' Now they were talking about their future. And if you want to grow up and be a doctor, you need to prevent yourself from getting HIV." Michael then got funding from a nongovernmental organization for a program called Escola Sans HIV—"school without HIV." He also organized a women's empowerment group with a female teacher and a Catholic sister who taught girls to crochet and to "start talking, have a voice. All these side projects are accomplishments I'm really, really proud of."

A Unique Job, A Unique Story

Mimi Gosney (Slovakia 2000–2002) went to her Peace Corps director after her first year of teaching English in Galanta and said, "I really think you're sort of wasting me here. If you would move me into central Slovakia, I could probably do more." Mimi explained her connection to Slovakia.

My dad had gone into Slovakia during World War II as a journalist. When the Slovak national uprising came, the Office of Strategic Services (OSS, which became the CIA) wanted to help, as they had with the partisans in Yugoslavia. My dad wanted to cover it, and the Americans said, "No, you can't do this. We're just getting this set up. We can't let a journalist go," so the first Americans went in to identify where our planes could land.

When the second group went in to take supplies and bring out downed American fliers, my dad went. I think eighteen fliers came out at that time. Dad stayed with the OSS group and the partisans. He was going to interview several people, and then he planned to go out with the next group of fliers. Unfortunately, the Nazis bombed the airfield, and these guys were stuck.

Then the Nazis started moving into central Slovakia, and the uprising really started to fall apart, so the fliers and the OSS, including my dad, all headed into the mountains. First they went to a little town called Donavaly, and then they followed the ridge of the Tatra Mountains, trying to stay away from the Nazis and get to an American or a Russian line or at least stay hidden until the war was over. This was October 1944. They were captured in the mountains above a little Slovak village called Polomka the day after Christmas with an English group, and they were taken to Mauthausen concentration camp in Austria and executed in January. Nobody talked about it for years because the United States classified the information. And after the communists came in, it was not good for Slovaks to be associated with Americans or English. But once communism fell, some people started talking about it, and that little OSS group became folk heroes because they were trying to help and lost their lives. So there's this museum called the Museum of the National Slovak Uprising that is in Banska Bystrica, and part of it is dedicated to these fighters and to my dad. They have this memorial out front that's got an eternal flame, and once a year they have services. The first time I went there was two years before I joined the Peace Corps, and I laid a wreath. The local people took me to the village, so I'd already made that tie, and that's what I was trying to say to the Peace Corps director. I know this history.

So Mimi moved to Banska Bystrica, where she had two assignments. "Part of my assignment was at the Museum of the National Slovak Uprising. I had a little office there. I also worked with a group that was trying to do some business development in small communities. We'd go into the villages and meet the people. I taught English to some women in the village, too. At the museum I did a lot of translating, wrote a grant, and was able to get basic tape recordings. I taped the tour of the museum in English so that English-speaking people would know what they were seeing. The Slovaks were invited to take one of the barracks at Auschwitz and make a display, so I fine-tuned the English translation for that project."

Mimi was also able to help some of the surviving airmen find the spots where their planes had crashed.

We took John to the crash site. He had been in a fighter on one side of a bomber, and his friend was in the other one. Both of them crashed; John lived, and his friend went in the swamp. While we were there, the local people, visiting Americans, and I did a memorial to John's friend. Then, of course, John had to meet everyone he was connected with. He had landed on a roof. His plane was already on fire when he bailed out, so he was badly burned. The villagers took him to a local hospital. Later they had two people take him to a Jewish bunker in the hills because the Nazis were coming to raid the hospital. After that they took John to a little village, where he lived with a family for a month. Eventually, when our Allied forces came through, he got his freedom. He was never captured.

We took another man to his crash site—I'll cry when I tell this—and a fellow came up to him and said, "I remember when your plane fell out of the sky. My father was plowing that field. My father was burned to death." And the American said, "I am so sorry." And the Slovak man said, "No, you all were angels of mercy. Things like that happened, but you were trying to help us. It's important to me that you know that I buried your crew, because no one knew if the Nazis would get them."

The fliers needed closure, you know, and it was just a wonderful thing to do, and then my time ran out. I'm sure I would have extended and stayed, but we had to leave. Peace Corps closed the program in Slovakia.

Chapter 7

Telling Stories

I have a good transportation story. We were on a bus pretty close to Dakar. But one of the tires broke. So they fixed the tire, we went a few more miles, and another tire went, and they had no spare. So we all had to lean to one side. We somehow made the next two miles. God knows what it did to the rim of the tire, but it was kind of fun, you know.

—Ann Neelon (Senegal 1978–1979)

SIX VOLUNTEERS IN FIVE DECADES

Martin and Patsy Tracy (Turkey 1965–1967)

Martin told the following story:

In Kırsehir, there was a man we met from our evening class, and he had an unusual name, Günaydın Günaydın, which means "good morning, good morning." He was in charge of ensuring that the local towns had ample supplies of freshwater. And he would take us out on some of his trips to the villages because he knew we were interested in small-town life and communities. He took us to one village that had been there for maybe a thousand years. And all that time they had never had a ready water supply. There was water a mile and a half away from the village. It had never been a problem because the women would go and get the water. And, very typically Turkish, they would say, "Well, if God had meant for the village to have water, they would have had water." And you don't mess with God.

Günaydın and the Turkish government had different ideas. They said, "This is silly. It would be very easy to run a pipe from the water supply to

199

the village, and the women don't have to make this trek." Well, the village had not been consulted. They were just told, "That's what you're going to have." And the villagers said, "No, we're not going to do that. It's not going to happen here." The government insisted and brought in armed troops and at gunpoint forced the villagers to build the pipeline. Of course, the troops couldn't stay forever, and as soon as the troops were gone, so was the pipeline.

That lesson has stuck with me all these many years: that if you don't get the community involved in the decision-making process, where they take ownership, it's not sustainable.

Rona Roberts (Philippines 1973–1975)

A couple days after Christmas, after we arrived in Naga City in November, Peace Corps got a telegram to another Peace Corps person in our part of the country, and that person came to see us and said, "You need to go home. Your father-in-law [Howell's father] is sick." So they told us to pack a small bag each and go to the airport. The first day the plane didn't come. When it did come, Howell went out to talk to the pilot, and they let us get on this plane. It was a DC-3 without seats, but they rigged up something. It was carrying iced shrimp in these huge square aluminum tins that filled the cargo space. It didn't have a pressurized cabin, but we weren't going to go very high. Since a DC-3 flies with its back a lot lower than its front, all the shrimp water from the shrimp containers rushed toward us. But we were ecstatic. We were on the plane.

Once we were in Manila, the Peace Corps took care of everything. They got us tickets, and we flew home. My father-in-law was gravely ill but had gotten better while we were en route. By the time we got home, they knew he would live. The interesting thing about coming home after having been in the Philippines for five months was I was never homesick again. I thought, everybody here is okay. I saw my family, too. We went back, and from then on, I was completely and totally in the Philippines.

Rebecca Roach (Liberia 1988–1989)

For breakfast we ate cassava and fish gravy, sometimes Quaker oatmeal, sometimes toast, sometimes shortbread. I had a neighbor who made the best shortbread in a pot outside over an open fire. I gained so much weight, which is so culturally appropriate. I remember my mother was coming to visit me for Christmas, and all my girlfriends had come up to my house for coffee. We'd sit around and just talk if I wasn't tutoring that evening. I remember one of them saying, "Your mother is going to be so pleased to see you. You're getting so fat."

Sarah Cross Oddo (Jamaica 1993–1995)

Oghale [later Sarah's husband] came a year later than me. He had a very different experience than me because he's a black man. He was listened to a lot more by the locals because he was a man and he was black, and also because he was from Africa. People found him very fascinating because there's sort of the whole back-to-Africa theme going through Jamaica.

Jamaica is quite a rough place, and when you get on public transportation, people will pick your pocket and try and steal from you. We had different ways of coping with that, like if you would feel somebody sticking their hand in your pocket. So sometimes I would just grab their hand and hold their hand on the bus just to say, "I know you're there and you're not going to get anything." But I remember one time being in a very busy bus park, and somebody had his hand in my backpack trying to get something out. I turned around and grabbed the hand and held it up and started yelling "Thief!" Well, the thief didn't realize it because my husband—or my boyfriend at the time—just blended into the crowd, but I wasn't alone. So of course he was right behind me and my boyfriend grabbed him on the shirt collar and in a very menacing voice said, "Why are you touching my wife? What are you doing?" I'll never forget the look in the guy's eyes; his eyes just became big as saucers.

Aaron Shraberg (China 2004–2006)

My [host family] grandpa during training was a beer drinker, so every night we would share a cold beer. And he would have one waiting for me. We would chat, and if he didn't understand what I was saying, he would just continue smiling at me. And I was excited about talking to him, and every now and then he'd say, "Yisi?" which means, "What does that mean?" It was just the way he said it, this old, wise Chinese man. One day I said, "Grandpa, how old are you?" It's not impolite to ask an old man how old he is in China. People who are older are generally revered.

And he stood up and said, "I am 152 years old." And I said, "What? 152 years old?" And he almost died laughing. I had actually asked him, "How tall are you?" and he had answered, "I am 152 centimeters tall." So I misinterpreted, but it was something we laughed about for the next three weeks, until I left. Every night Grandpa would say, "Yunlong, I'm still 152 years old." That was just something that stuck with us. Being at home was great. They would serve fruit and watch TV and play poker and just very much be a family. My grandpa knew some good card tricks, too.

There is a row of white rocking chairs on the concrete porch in front of the lodge at Camp Andrew Jackson in eastern Kentucky, where returned Peace Corps volunteers often get together for a weekend in August or September. The folks who sit in those chairs, from 1960s volunteers to those who have recently returned, often tell stories. Some volunteers have actually fantasized about an old folks home for Peace Corps volunteers, with many comfortable rocking chairs on a porch. Maybe there would also be a big stone fireplace inside for wintertime storytelling. Kentucky returned volunteers tell stories at other gatherings, too, such as the monthly meals at various ethnic restaurants in Lexington and in Louisville. We devote a chapter to telling stories because that's what Peace Corps volunteers do when they return—they tell stories. We cannot vouch for the historical accuracy of the following stories. They may have grown in the telling, and their meaning to the volunteer may have changed over the years. We include stories about arriving in-country and arriving on-site. We include traveling stories and stories about famous people, about important events, and about animals. Several stories (like Martin's, told at the beginning of this chapter) demonstrate what volunteers learned, what might be called host country wisdom. The final stories are about feeling included. Some of these stories are happy; a few are sad. Some are hard to categorize. In any case, they were memorable and meaningful to the Peace Corps volunteers who told them.

ARRIVAL STORIES

Arrival stories are special because the volunteer sees, smells, tastes, and hears with an intensity that is often lost once the place becomes familiar.

When Ken Wilson (Malawi 1997–1998) left Texas:

It was a rainy, cold April day. I was scared to death, I was terrified, but also euphoric about my whole adventure. I'd never had a passport before. I'd never been to Washington, DC, before. And it was just amazing. I kept thinking, Charlie Brown's going to the Peace Corps. They'll never believe this. I'd never flown transatlantic before. I was so excited I talked to the girl next to me the entire way. I didn't sleep. We landed at 6:00 A.M. in Amsterdam. Suddenly I was exhausted. Everyone's bounding off the plane, going into town to see everything for our big layover, and I was in a coma. I don't remember anything except the Van Gogh Museum. Then we went overnight on an eleven-hour flight to Johannesburg. Then Johannesburg to Malawi. We were supposed to go to Lilongwe [the political capital], but there was a civil service strike the hour we were supposed to be arriving. So midflight we get the announcement from our pilot about the strike, which meant that the emergency vehicles could not be at the airport, so we were diverted to Blantyre [the commercial capital]. That freaked everybody out, because the Peace Corps volunteers and the country director—all with their big signs—were waiting for us in Lilongwe, and we were five hours away in Blantyre. Well, we landed. And I thought, my God, I'm in Africa! I'm actually in Africa! There was this little tiny ramshackle corrugated metal hangar. Big palm trees, banana trees. It was a million degrees. I thought we must be a mile from the sun. We waited in line. That's when we discovered the Malawi tradition of stamping everything a million times. Our passports were stamped until I'm sure they were bruised.

So we got in, and we'd been told that we should always have water, toilet paper, a camera, and a book with us. So as soon as we got in the country, I was dying to go to the bathroom. I found the closest one I could find, which was outdoors. No toilet paper. I thought, step one, I've already failed. I don't have toilet paper. The tourists got a bus immediately—a real fancy, air-conditioned bus—and they were whisked off. About two hours later this coughing, exploding diesel engine with black smoke, this giant metal thing lurching down the street, showed up for us. On the side was painted an advertisement for something called tomato oil, which I guessed was maybe ketchup in Malawi. So we all loaded up on that. We were thrilled when [we saw] the first Malawian lady with a pot on her head. All thirty of us cheered. It was like little children spotting a mud hut, a village, a little kid, cameras flashing. Our driver was probably just thinking we were insane. We got to Lilongwe about midnight. Of course, by then, all the thrill of our arrival had died down by our awaiting party, and they said, "Okay, welcome to Malawi. Go to your room. Eat something. We'll see you tomorrow." And the next day we were carted to the National Resource Center, and that's where we'd be in training for the next eleven weeks.

For Leigh White (Bulgaria 2001–2003), arrival in-country was a mixture of shock and happy excitement. She remembered flying into the capital city, Sofia.

Everyone was apprehensive, excited, exhausted from layovers in all these airports across Western Europe. So it was great to finally arrive. As we're landing on the strip, you see these terrible large block apartment buildings everywhere. It's just not very pretty around the airport. It was just like, oh my God, am I really going to spend the next two years of my life here? So there was a little of that. Then there was just the logistical stuff of getting all your baggage. They had this huge truck outside the front of the airport, and they were throwing all fifty-four people's luggage into the back of it. We had overnight bags with us we were to take until the main part of our luggage was delivered to us. And we all got on this double-decker bus. I remember there were currently serving volunteers there to greet us. We arrived in June. It was cherry season in Bulgaria. So they had these huge bags of cherries, and they were feeding us these fresh cherries. They were so delicious. Then the Bulgarian staff from the Peace Corps got on, and they were giving us all this information. It was just so much information. All I wanted to do was sleep. So probably the first three days were the hardest there. But we were well received. We went to a hotel where we all stayed together, which was kind of out in the middle of nowhere, near the town where we were going to do training, and we spent the first two days there. They had this huge meal prepared for us the first night, and performers—traditional singers and dancers—put on a show for us. And it was so wonderful. They were so full of hospitality. And at that point, you just knew it was going to be a good fit.

Soon after arriving in-country, volunteers were often sent out to their host families or out to the countryside. Michael Geneve (Mozambique 2003–2005) told about walking for an hour with his host father, Orlando, from the training center outside Maputo, the capital, to the cement block house he would call home for the next ten weeks.

There were other houses in that community that were made of mud and reeds, but we all stayed in a cement house for security purposes. We were the sixth group to go there, and each of the previous groups stayed with pretty much those same families. So every time they get somebody out of the Peace Corps, they get a little bit of cash and fix up their house.

I'm seeing all these people go into their houses. And it's really hot. It's four, five o'clock and still really hot. The sun's going down, and this is when I know it's going to be a really hot experience in Mozambique. But I was up for it. And we walk all the way and finally we get to our house, and I see my family. My father was a teacher and made pretty good money, but the mother owned all these different stores and actually made a lot of money, and all of her family would come and borrow money from her. They invited me into their house. The mother and father actually moved out of the big room of the house for me to live there. They had a TV in their house and they insisted that they put it in my room, and I had no idea how to say to them that I didn't want the TV. We finally get the mosquito net rigged up. Then I have to go to the bathroom. How do I say that? I got my dictionary. "*Bano*. Where's the *bano*?"

They took Michael out to a little reed house with a cloth flap in front and a lock. "That was the latrine. They locked it with chicken wire, so I would have to ask them every time. Inside is this triangular shaft that comes up about two and a half feet. I just assume that everybody sits on that thing. There's this cardboard over the top of it. And I lift the cardboard off, and these cockroaches start flowing out like it's a volcano. I kind of perch over the top. I don't want to sit on it. And my whole family was watching me behind the flap. I'm like, I can't do this. So I just held it the whole night."

Glen Payne (1989–1992) remembered arriving in Libreville, the capital of Gabon:

I got in the back of an overloaded pickup with a couple other volunteers and lots of Gabonese going hundreds of kilometers to a village, where I landed with a volunteer named Brian to spend four or five days with him in the quiet of a Gabonese village. It was a shocker. You're a new volunteer, and you're with the guy who's been there a year and a half. They seem like the oldest, roughest cowboys, right? And you're as green as they come. I'm looking at what Brian is wearing. I'm looking at his house. I'm looking at the village. I'm looking at the way he interacts with the Gabonese. I'm looking at his job site. And I'm particularly looking at what he's eating and drinking. And I'm thinking, I'll never make it. I don't know what he's putting in his mouth, but it doesn't look like something

I'm ever going to put in my mouth. Well, it turns out to be something that I miss very badly right now. I got my first drink of palm wine from Brian, and I thought it was the most disgusting thing I had ever ingested. It's an acquired taste. It tastes like suntan lotion mixed with dandelion leaves. It's bitter and sweet and very strong, speckled over on top with whatever detritus is from the trees—leaf chunks and bugs. But brother, I would give anything for a bottle of it right now.

Sometimes the volunteer's trip to his or her assigned site was a little scary. Tom Samuel (Liberia 1965–1967) recalled his flight from the capital of Monrovia to Buchanan, a town down the Atlantic coast where he was assigned to work as a public administrator.

I got a taxi and went out to the private airport. There were wings and engines and propellers, but no whole airplane that I could see. Finally we came to a whole airplane, but there were parts lying all around, which did not lead to great confidence that this was a good idea. But the taxi driver said, "This is where you belong," and dropped off me and my luggage. So I walked into this little shack, and a European guy sitting there says, "You're going to Buchanan today, right?" I said, "Yeah, I hope so." He said, "Get your stuff. Let's go. And don't step on this wing or the tail section." So we're going down the runway full blast, and he puts on the brakes. "No gas," he says. So we go back and get gas and take off, and we're going down the coast and he says, "Did you ever see sea turtles?" And I said, "No." And suddenly we're on the water looking at sea turtles. And we go inland a ways so he can show me a wrecked plane. And I say, "Can we get back to the coast, please?" By this time, I have my imprint on the little handle in front of me on this plane. We get to Buchanan, and he flies over the town a couple times and then lands on a grass strip. He says, "Okay, they'll be out to pick you up." I say, "Who is they?" because there is nobody, nothing there. Finally somebody did come to pick me up, and it was Susan, whom I married a year later.

Kay Roberts (Ecuador 1982–1984) was dropped off on the main road and walked two kilometers to a fairly large river. There, she put her backpack and sleeping bag on an apparatus called a *tatabita*, a slab of wood strung on a cable, and was cranked across the river into her community. "There were wonderful people there who knew I would be arriving sometime, and they helped me settle in. Somebody invited me to their home to eat, and then folks started helping me find a place to stay and gather up the basic necessities of life, such as cooking pots for the stove. They taught me how to wash my clothes in the river."

Sometimes the site was not what the volunteer had hoped for or imagined. Joan Moore (Swaziland 1979–1981) was assigned to be a middle school science teacher in an asbestos mining town on Swaziland's border with South Africa in the high mountainous belt. She remembered:

I had certain ideas of what Peace Corps would be like. And this was nothing that I ever imagined. The ride in was beautiful. It was mountains, all these trees, really very pretty. Then we get into this town. First, there's a golf course; then you see these multicolored cement brick block houses wall to wall covering the hillside. There were huge piles of asbestos. So they drove me to this house next to the single miners' quarters that were even smaller cement houses much closer together and had these gutters that later you realized all the rats would run through them. I was going to be living with three Swazi women and three kids. Across from the house was a big soccer field, and next to that a miners' clubhouse, and then a market and the mining police headquarters. The house had electricity and a woodstove. I had my own bedroom with a linoleum floor. I remember when the Peace Corps staff and van left me, I just bawled. I never anticipated being in a mining town. I had imagined I'd be out in the country in a hut and it would be beautiful.

Several volunteers got their wish to be assigned to remote sites. Carolyn Cromer (Morocco 1992–1995) "lived in the village of Amejgag, near the town of El Kelaa M'Gouna in the province of Ouarzazate. And to find it from Rabat, the capital, you would go to Marrakech and over the High Atlas Mountains to Ouarzazate, which is about a ten-hour bus ride, and then take a grand taxi three hours east on the road that runs between Agadir and Er Rachidia to M'Gouna, which is where I picked up my mail. That was the nearest health clinic with any kind of facilities. Then I would get on—when I first arrived in 1992 it could be a large truck that hauled animals or supplies or a van, either in the van or on top—and ride three hours straight up into the High Atlas Mountains, where I would get off in the village of Alamdoun and then walk thirty minutes east to Amejgag."

Among the volunteers we interviewed, the prize for the arrival story describing the longest journey goes to Elaine Collins, who served in Micronesia (1989–1991). She arrived at her outer island of Satawal after ten days on a Japanese-donated freighter with a big wooden deck. One by one the other seven volunteers were dropped off at their islands. Elaine was the last. "I got off the ship in this really precarious way onto a little power boat, because the ship couldn't really pull up to the island. And I remember coming onto the beach and I saw 150 kids. I remember thinking, are there any adults on this island? The kids took me into the village, and I met my family and sort of stood there. My 'mother' took me to the other side of the island, where there were freshwater pools you could bathe in. She gave me a *lava lava*, the cloth you wear around your waist, and a belt to hold it up. And she took my shirt, and from that day on, I didn't wear a shirt. It was taboo for men or women to wear shirts on the island."

Traveling Stories

Traveling stories are favorites. Here are stories about motorcycles, a bicycle, a truck, an outrigger canoe, and climbing a mountain.

John Skeese (Nigeria 1961–1964) can tell stories for hours and is the legendary subject of a story that first appeared in the *Amaka Gazette*, the online journal of Christ the King College Onitsha Alumni Association in America. He believes he was "the first Peace Corps volunteer to have a motorcycle. I still have it out in the back right now [in Berea, Kentucky]—a 1960 Honda 250. I brought it back with me, but that was after Peace Corps because I didn't go home right away. The principal of the school [in Onitsha] bought it in his name because Peace Corps didn't say you couldn't have it, but they didn't say yes. And I thought if I asked they might say no. There were so many things I wanted to do and I needed a form of transportation, so I paid him for it and finally got it in my name. I think when I got done I had covered about 30,000 miles on my motorcycle in Africa."

Once John took a "French girl up to the Jos Plateau. We had stopped at a friend's in the afternoon and had something to eat. It was getting late in the day, and we probably should have stayed with him, but we thought we'd go on. We were on gravel roads for a while and finally a dirt road. It started raining, and the road became just slick as anything, and it's kind of round at the top, so you could slide off. So all of a sudden the motorcycle just slides out from under us, and it was pitch-black. We get the motorcycle stood up, and we're sitting there wondering what are we going to do now. It's late at night, no place to stay, so we had an orange and started eating it. All of a sudden a guy who speaks some English comes down the road and asks us, 'What are you doing?' He was from the village right there and home for the holidays for a visit, and he said, 'Why don't you stay in my village tonight?' And we did."

Another motorcycle story with a happy ending was told by Bill Miller (Dominican Republic 1968–1970). One weekend Bill decided to go to the beach at Puerto Plata with a friend.

> We got on our motorcycles and took off, and we're riding along on this two-lane road with sugarcane fields on both sides, except for this very small airstrip with a couple single-engine Cessnas. Traffic was way down the road. I wasn't paying much attention, just looking at those planes, and all of a sudden I heard my friend who was on another motorcycle yell, "Look out!" This guy—that when I had looked the last time was way down the road—had just stopped his truck in the middle of the road to check something. I never had a chance. I was right on him. My friend swerved around him, and I ran my motorcycle right into the back of this guy's truck. It was a little truck, so I grabbed on the handlebars and just held on for dear life. The motorcycle and I started going up over the top of the truck, but luckily, with the weight, it didn't quite get up there and came crashing back down, with the whole front end of my motorcycle jammed in his truck. I said, "I'll pay for your truck damage." I didn't want to turn this in to Peace Corps because they'd take our motorcycles away. I'd already had one accident. So we load the motorcycle into the back of his truck, drive into town, and find this little repair shop. I said, "Can you fix this motorcycle and truck?" and he says, "Yea." So we said, "Okay, we'll come back on Sunday and pick it up," and we got on the other motorcycle and drove off to the beach.

Motorcycle stories didn't always end so well. Richard Parker (Côte d'Ivoire 1973–1974, Morocco 1976–1978) began his story this way: "Some mysterious things happen in Africa."

> I had a dream where I was riding my motorcycle around the auto route in Abidjan at night and came upon some sort of an accident. I saw a group of people by the side of the road and I stopped, got off my motorcycle,

and saw that they were gathered around someone who was injured on the ground. After a few seconds, I turned and got back on my motorcycle. And as I got on the motorcycle, I looked down and saw my left arm covered with blood, and I woke up. I thought, that was such a vivid dream, it's anxiety. It's African traffic anxiety. Motorcycles are dangerous enough anyway. I think it was two nights later I was traveling on my motorcycle and I had an accident and severely damaged my left arm— compound bone sticking out, blood all over. There was no such thing as an orthopedic surgeon in Ivory Coast, and the Peace Corps doctor would not have let me go into the hospital there. The policy was to evacuate to either the army hospital in Frankfurt, Germany, or back to Washington.

So I went to Washington with my arm in a sling and a bottle of codeine tablets. I took a bus out to George Washington University Hospital and walked into the emergency room, my fingers swollen up like sausages by that time—tremendous swelling, and my hand was dislocated and wrapped around the wrong direction. I walked in and said, "I brought you this from Africa." They took x-rays and said my wrist looked like Grape Nuts. It had been destroyed, fragmented, so I had to have surgery to reconstruct my wrist.

Richard was discharged from the Peace Corps, flew back to San Diego, and had follow-up medical care and physical therapy. "It was total coverage. I got top-quality care, every penny paid for, including follow-up, with the Department of Labor sending me a check every month to live on." He finally recovered from his motorcycle accident, studied French for five months at the Sorbonne in Paris with some of his rehabilitation money, and was able to rejoin the Peace Corps for a second tour in another part of French-speaking Africa in 1976—in Morocco, where Peace Corps volunteers were not permitted to have motorcycles.

Another traveling story that did not end happily was told by Rachel Savane (Guinea 1990–1992), who rode a bicycle to avoid the dangers of bush taxis.

When I wanted to go to town, that was forty kilometers, I rode my bike—or started to. I was on my third trip, leaving Kindia, coming back to Bangouya. Leaving the town of Kindia, I'm going down a big hill on a dirt road too fast. I hit a rut and a rock, and away I go off the bike. I dust myself off. I do some adjustments on the bike. I'm scraped up, but not a problem. So I'm reprimanding myself, saying, "Stop it, Rachel, you've got all day to get there." So I stopped and ate my breakfast—which was French bread and Gatorade, which we had in pouches.

I got on my way leisurely, and I get to about the halfway point. I'm in the foothills of the mountains, so there are some hills to deal with, but somewhere in the middle of this trek is a good five, six kilometers of nice, flat, easy, easy riding. I'm on that portion of the road and just passing through a village, where I didn't see anyone because now it's midmorning and everyone's out to the fields. I just passed the last house and splat! I'm eating dirt, and I don't know what happened because it was the easiest part of the road. There was no obstacle like the first time I had fallen. My two pineapples I had strapped to my handlebars were smashed. I was taking them back for my special treat. So I'm there crying with my face literally in the dirt. The little voice is saying, "Get yourself together, Rachel, you're in the middle of a road. You know bush taxis come." I lift my head, listen. I'm picking myself up. Okay, my leg is bloody. I mean, I know this is bad, this is much worse than the first time. I'm crying. I'm trying to get myself up and off the road. I'm limping, my leg hurts, my arm is bloody. I get myself off to the side. I walk back to the last house I passed, knock on the door, and of course no one is home.

I'm sitting there just crying. I don't know what to do because I'm really in the middle of my journey. I'm thinking, I just need some water to clean myself up. Lo and behold, I see a guy coming out of the field onto the road. What is he carrying in his hand? A watering can, but unfortunately, it was empty. I say to him in Sousou (my Sousou wasn't very good), but I can say, "*N'bara*" and make the gesture because I didn't know "to fall." All I knew how to say was "I just." And he said, "*I bara bira.*" I said, "*Iyo n'bara bira,*"—yes, I've just fallen and I need water to clean myself up. So he goes to probably a stream and gets water and comes back to me, and I'm cleaning myself up. Now more people are starting to arrive. As I'm cleaning myself up, I look down and there's a big glob of "guts" sticking out of my leg. Of course, it's men who are approaching me first. I said, "I need a woman to look at this so she can tell them this is serious, we need to get this girl wherever she wants to go." Which would have been back to Kindia and eventually Conakry, where I would get medical help. The culture was in my way—I had to walk through the village to the chief's house, because that's where I had to wait. I walk through the village and there's more and more people because now it's big news: bloody white woman on her bike—or off her bike.

We're waiting for the next vehicle to pass going toward Kindia that I could get a ride with. They had me sitting on a nice chair back in the shade, trying to make me comfortable. They send two young guys out to the road to flag down the jeep that's coming. The jeep is just zooming past because they don't have room for two guy passengers—no way. So I hop up and scream, "Wait! Wait! It's not them! It's for me." I got them to stop, and of course it was somebody I knew, and they squeezed me in as the twenty-first person in the jeep. That ride was terrible because I was in the back. I got to eat all the dust and be in the bumpiest position, and the leg hurt. Not fun at all, and pretty bloody. The nurse from the health center in Bangouya happened to be on his motorcycle heading the same way with another nurse on the back of the motorcycle. So they were staying with the jeep, watching out for me.

So, after a long ride to Kindia, I get out and I am negotiating a taxi to get to Conakry. I didn't like doing that either on this day—again, the culture was in my way. The guy was trying to charge me five times more than it should be. And I can't think straight to do that haggling properly. We stopped by the Belgians' house in Kindia—they were in my village sometimes, and I would visit them often in Kindia—and they kindly called ahead to Peace Corps. The taxi ride to Conakry was convenient for one of the nurses on the motorcycle because she was going home to Conakry to visit, so she got a free ride with me, who was paying too much for it. And on this ride, too, the culture was in my way because we had to stop for a military guy who was flagging down traffic. Then we had to go to the nurse's mom's house, which was off the road—bumpy, bumpy, bumpy—so I could say hi to her mom. She did actually stay with me and accompanied me to the Peace Corps office or the embassy, I can't remember. The Peace Corps nurse was expecting me and had already contacted a French doctor who was going to see me as soon as I got there. The doctor cleaned it up and I was pretty lucky because it was really high up there and very close to the artery. If it had been half an inch over, I was a goner.

I don't want to use the term *voodoo*, but I think somebody did it to me. People kept telling me: "Don't ride your bike, don't ride your bike. You have no business riding your bike through here all by yourself. Not allowed." So I didn't do it anymore.

Bob Olson (Turkey 1963–1965) told the truck story.

I traveled out to the east of Turkey to what is today the Armenian border and the border with Azerbaijan. I wanted to see Mount Ararat. I didn't know that in 1963 the United States had Jupiter missiles and nuclear armed missiles in eastern Turkey, or that part of the subsequent deal with Russia after the Cuban missile crisis was that the U.S. would remove these missiles. It was a highly militarized area. I remember they had a lot of searchlights along the border. I came to the town, and I was by myself. By that time I could speak Turkish pretty well for a foreigner. I remember I went into the hotel room and about fifteen minutes later, because the hotels had to report to the Turkish secret police, a Turkish secret policeman called me down and said, "Who are you and how do you know Turkish?" So he grilled me, and we chatted for a couple hours.

[The next morning] I needed transportation to go over the road about 3,000 or 4,000 feet up Mount Ararat. I saw this truck, and it was full of watermelons. I said, "Can I get a ride?" And they said, "Yeah, get in the back." Later the driver of truck stopped and said, "We need something to eat." So we stopped on this bridge. I have pictures of this. They said, "We have some potatoes, but we need some fish." They had some dynamite in the truck, so we stood on the bridge and threw dynamite in the water to stun the fish, and then they gave a thirteen- or fourteen-year-old boy the equivalent of a nickel or dime to jump in the water and get the fish out. I thought that was extraordinary. There were also beehive houses made out of cow dung near the bridge. And I remember that was extraordinary, too. As we went on it got dark, and I pounded on the roof and said, "I'm really cold." I just had a light blue shirt that my tailor friend had made me, no heavy clothes. It was August, but it was getting very cold on this plateau. So finally they stopped the truck and said, "Get up here." I sat between them, and as we're going along, I said, "I heard there are Kurds around here." And the driver said, "I'm a Kurd!" And the guy on the other side of me said, "I'm a Kurd. Everybody here is Kurdish." And that's when I learned that there really were Kurds.

A more exotic mode of transportation was outrigger canoe, and Elaine Collins (Micronesia 1989–1991) finally got her wish to travel on one. "I kept bothering my host father that I wanted to ride on an outrigger canoe because they had these beautiful canoes they built by hand. So the second summer, my father comes to me one day and says, 'I got you a ride on a canoe.' Someone was taking a canoe out to one of our garden islands two days away, and we would get lots of breadfruit and bring it back. It was amazing, because the navigator was looking at the stars, and that's how we got there. They look at the birds and the waves and the way they move. We spent several days collecting and preserving food. We fished and brought back a lot of smoked fish. It was incredible that they would take the risk of taking me. And for me, it was a trust thing. I didn't even take my life jacket."

Finally, several volunteers told about climbing Africa's highest mountain, Mount Kilimanjaro in Tanzania. One was Harold Freeman (Ethiopia 1965–1967), who called it "by far the hardest physical undertaking I've ever done," including army basic training and serving in Vietnam.

> We had a guide, and we hired porters and rented boots and jackets and heavyweight coats, and they provided food for us. All I carried was my camera. The porters are carrying forty pounds and wearing flip-flops and not having any trouble with their footing. The rest of us are being careful and grabbing a tree or a vine or using a hiking stick. You'd climb 500 or 1,000 feet of elevation and have a fifteen-minute break. The porters sit down, put their forty pounds down, and sing in harmony. They're the ones doing all the work, and they've got enough breath to sing. So you can see you wouldn't want to get into a marathon race with these folks. We started at 4,500 feet, spent the first night at 9,000, the next one at 12,000, and the third one at 16,000. By this time, you're well above the tree line. You spent the night in a hut that had shelves and sleeping bags.
>
> They had told us that in order to get the spectacular view of the sunrise from the summit over an adjoining mountain, we needed to be up there before sunrise. I remember getting up at 2:00. They fed us a little breakfast, and we made our visits to what was called the coldest outhouse on this planet. So we started off. By the time I had taken maybe fifteen or twenty steps, I felt like all my capillaries were wired to 220. We were just gasping for breath. Our guides were carrying a lantern and a thermos of tea, and they were looking back at us as we were slowly going on. And I'm thinking, "We've got 3,000 more feet of this to go. This is not possible." I think my probably stupid male, twenty-three-year-old pride was saying, "This girl's in front of me. If she can make this, I can make this." That was probably the only thing that got me up there. And we did get up there, indeed, before the sunrise, which was indeed spectacular.

FAMOUS PEOPLE STORIES

This section includes stories about Sargent Shriver, the first director of the Peace Corps; the reverence felt for President John F. Kennedy in African countries; and personal encounters with Haile

Selassie, emperor of Ethiopia; William V. S. Tubman, president of Liberia; and President Bill Clinton.

Bob Olson (Turkey 1963–1965) described meeting Sargent Shriver. "My colleague and I were visited by Sargent Shriver, who was head of the Peace Corps at that time and married to the sister of Robert and John F. Kennedy. So he came and stayed the entire day and made a pretty big hit because he shot basketballs with the kids. I was somewhat surprised when, two months later, one of my family sent me clippings from the *Minneapolis Star and Tribune*. It was two whole pages of Sargent Shriver meeting with this Peace Corps volunteer from Minnesota—me! In retrospect, I realized he probably visited quite a few volunteers around the world, and the Peace Corps press office sent articles to all the respective newspapers to make good public relations. I was one of the happy recipients of that."

Like other volunteers in Africa in the 1960s, Jules Delambre (Cameroon 1965–1967) discovered that President Kennedy was greatly admired in his host country. "As I was traveling south of Yaounde, I noticed two houses—mud brick houses with wash white (they called it wash white, not whitewash) on the outside. Each one had a photograph painted on the side. The first was of President Amadou Ahidjo of Cameroon. The second house had a picture of John Kennedy, and that impressed me. Kennedy was quite revered in Cameroon. The closest I ever got into a confrontation with anybody was when I was chatting with the Cameroonian manager of an Indian general store. We ended up talking about Kennedy, and out of the clear blue sky he said he was convinced it [the assassination] was a conspiracy, and if he thought I was part of it, he would kill me. Now, I didn't feel he thought I was part of it, but I was kind of taken aback by such a strong statement 250 miles from the capital and the coast, in a small town."

For Fred Cowan (Ethiopia 1967–1969), it was a thrill to meet Emperor Haile Selassie.

After an incident of rioting, including rock throwing, the school had shut down, and we teachers somehow got word that we were all going to have an audience with the emperor in Addis Ababa over Christmas vacation. We went to the emperor's palace, and he spoke to us in Amharic and it was translated, but I could understand some of what he said in Amharic. Haile Selassie was maybe five feet six inches tall and in his seventies.

He said, "Now I want you to go back to teaching. You must not tremble. We are going to take care of things. You take care of the teaching; we'll take care of the security." So we said okay and went back after spring break, and the army was there in military trucks and helmets, all U.S.-supplied gear. Finally the students calmed down. But it was interesting, because Haile Selassie had been in power since 1930, which is incredible when you think about it. And he was educating these students. But as they became more educated, they became more radical, and they finally forced his overthrow in 1974. There was some question in my mind at that time whether we in the Peace Corps were really doing anything to advance the cause of Ethiopia or whether we were just propping up a dictatorship.

Bill Sweigart (Liberia 1967–1970) was arrested for treason and sedition and, as a result, met President Tubman. "It happened that some of the local executives, the county commissioner, and certainly the paramount chiefs and the local chiefs in the area received their mail sometimes through the Peace Corps mail system. One Friday I pick up the mail, and there was a letter for Tomba Taylor, care of Peace Corps. So I walk over to his place and give him his letter. It turns out this piece of mail has seditious material from somebody at that moment in 1968, I suppose, beginning a political opposition to President Tubman. I didn't know any of this." On Saturday, Bill was at his house, and "in comes this screaming vehicle with Roosevelt Tubman, one of Tubman's illegitimate sons who was a security officer, and he's arresting me. Tomba Taylor's nervous about this piece of mail and this antigovernment information. So he goes to the commissioner, who says, 'Where did you get this piece of mail?' [He answers,] 'Well, the Peace Corps volunteer brought it to me.' I had no involvement in this other than carrying that piece of mail from the Peace Corps truck, unopened, to the person it was addressed to. Yet because of the literalness of everything in the culture, I was implicated. The security officer took it as an opportunity to do his protective and official thing and took me to Voinjama, a neighboring town, for several days." Bill then went back to Kolahun to teach, but his troubles were not over.

Since Tubman was having one of his executive councils in Voinjama at about this time, it was decided I had to appear and explain myself. Tubman used to go around the country and do these executive councils, where he would sit in a huge hall, just like a paramount chief, and he would listen to palavers. That's why he was so brilliant. He knew exactly what to do in running that country. He would sit there, and anybody could get up with any grievance at all, and he would listen and pass judgment. So I went back to Voinjama in a suit at the end of the week. I was lined up to go into the hall. They had lights and cameras on, and there was Tubman sitting at this table with this giant cigar. There was a Lebanese merchant in front of me who had just spoken, and Tubman is saying, "Take this man! Hold him without bail." And at that moment I realized that I better pay attention, that this was not to be laughed at or taken lightly. So I testified, and later I learned that the Peace Corps had a plane on the landing strip in Voinjama with my passport, anticipating that they might have to spirit me out of the country. Somebody had explained to Tubman what was going on, however, that the Peace Corps and I were not implicated, but I had to speak at the council, explain what happened, and Tubman had to say it was clear this Peace Corps man is not involved, the Peace Corps is not involved, in this political opposition to him.

Meeting President Clinton was a highlight for Wini Yunker (Ukraine 2000–2002).

I had to be sixty-five and go 5,000 miles away from home to meet a U.S. president. Clinton came there in June after I went there in February. And he gave a speech in a huge square in Kiev. There were just hundreds of thousands of people there. Peace Corps always took care to give us access to things like that, so there were probably about sixty volunteers there. We were all lined up on a fence that was at the perimeter of the open space where he was speaking. Somebody told him that we were there, that those were volunteers on that fence. So he came along the fence, shaking hands with each of us. I had in mind to say to him, "God bless you, Mr. President." But when he got to me and took my hand, my voice was frozen. I couldn't say anything. I was speechless. So he passed on. But I noticed way down at the end of the volunteers there was this space with nobody in it. So I snuck around and went down there. So this time when he came to me, I said, "God bless you, Mr. President." Well, Clinton is so smart. He looked at me and took my hand and said, "Nice to see you again."

IMPORTANT EVENT STORIES

Events in their Peace Corps countries and at home in the United States affected volunteers. Here volunteers describe riots in

Malaysia, the division of Czechoslovakia, and Victory Day in Ukraine. The final story is told by a volunteer in Lesotho who was at her site on September 11, 2001. In the postscript we describe what it was like to be in Liberia during the Cuban missile crisis and President Kennedy's assassination.

Marlene Payne (Malaysia 1967–1969) recalled the riots in Malaysia in May 1969. "The elections didn't turn out like the Muslims wanted them to. They sort of upset the balance. When the British left, they left the political power with the Malays. The Chinese and Indians had the economic power, and that got upset in the election. So there were riots, and many people were killed, mostly Chinese and Indians. The government had an order to shoot anybody who was out after curfew. You couldn't go to the market or anyplace. My roommate and I went and helped the Red Cross in refugee centers. They used the National Stadium as a collecting place for people to bring their families to be safe, and we packed lots of dried fish and oil for the people to use in improvised cooking situations until they could get resettled in their villages. Houses were burned, people were being killed, families were being shot if they were out after curfew. It was a very trying time."

Brian Arganbright (Slovakia 1991–1994) experienced the separation of Czechoslovakia.

The country split in 1993, and it was really exciting to see how they were actually going to implement that. It was a very complicated issue because before that, the government did everything they could so the two countries would mix. Soldiers from the Czech Republic were sent to Slovakia for their military service; Slovaks were sent to the Czech Republic, hoping they would take root in the other part of the country. But it was amazing to see how civil the discussions were and how reasonably students reacted to this decision to separate. It was also very, very sad, and it happened on January 1. I was at a friend's house, and everyone was watching the evening news. Czechoslovak news was broadcast twice, I guess, in Czech and then once in Slovak. And I just remember them signing off—"This is our last broadcast." At the same time, there was war in Yugoslavia and the bloody separation of those republics. I was just so grateful to experience the separation done peacefully.

Peg Dickson (2000–2002) described May 9, a huge holiday in Ukraine called Victory Day.

It's the end of World War II for the Ukrainians and the Soviet Union, the victory in Europe. On my first Victory Day in Ukraine, I went with one of the teachers. There was a parade with Soviet flags flying because, of course, they fought under the Soviet flag. The parade ended up at the eternal flame in the city, which was a memorial to World War II veterans and victims, and everyone laid flowers on the flame until it was just mounded. There was a military ceremony, and at the end of that we went back to her apartment for a meal together. She and her husband lived with her father-in-law, who had been a colonel in the Soviet army at the end of World War II. He was in his nineties when I met him, and he had on his full Soviet military uniform for Victory Day. I have a picture of him. And through my friend, who interpreted, because he didn't speak any English and I couldn't understand all of his Russian, he told me about Victory Day. The Soviet troops couldn't celebrate until they knew that Stalin had gotten word of the German defeat and acceptance of that. So they celebrated on May 9. He also told how when they got to Berlin and met the American troops, the American troops shared their canned meat with the Soviet troops. That was the first meat they had had during the war. An American officer loaned him his Chevrolet to drive from Berlin back to Khmelnytski to pick up his wife and daughter, because he was stationed in Berlin for a year. And I was at the table with his daughter who had ridden in that American Chevrolet.

The terrorist attack of September 11, 2001, was, of course, a seminal event for all volunteers serving overseas. Kristen Perry (Lesotho 1999–2001) remembered where she was when 9/11 happened.

I had been working on painting maps on some of the classroom walls so that the older kids would have those for their geography lessons. And I would take my little shortwave radio with me and listen to the radio. This happened at like 8:30 in the morning here [in the United States], but it was the middle of the afternoon there. I was listening to my favorite South African program, and they broke in with the news about the first tower had been hit and then the second tower. And I kept thinking, this is a joke. It's like Orson Welles and *The War of the Worlds*. I [then thought], oh my God, this is real. But I stayed in the school and kept painting because I just couldn't stop. I kept painting and painting and painting. And I was getting more and more upset, and finally I went home to my house, and other people in the village had heard about this because they all had radios. My counterpart came over to check on me, and I was just sort of sitting petrified on my bed with this radio in my hands listening, and it was awful. But everyone was so concerned in my village. My counterpart wanted me to come stay in her home with her. I said, "No, I appreciate it, but I think I'd rather be by myself for this."

[Finally, toward the end of the week,] I went into town to be around some of the other volunteers, who had all gotten together immediately at this hotel that had TV and had seen it all. It was just an awful thing to be away when that was happening and to not know what was going on. But then, on the other hand, it was also such a different perspective having lived in another country while that was happening and having seen the rest of the world's reactions to how we reacted. We screwed up and sort of squandered the world's goodwill really, really quickly. As soon as we started bombing Afghanistan, my counterpart Tabitha came stomping down the road and came into my house [and asked], "How soon until your country gets a new president?" It was really interesting to experience that from far away. It was awful in some ways, because you felt so isolated and so lonely. But on the other hand, I saw how much people cared about us. How not everybody in the world hated Americans.

ANIMAL STORIES

Here are three animal stories, two about elephants and one about either an ape or an old man, depending on whether an American or a Gabonese is telling the story.

In her third year, Debra Schweitzer (Mali 1993–1996) was in the northern part of the country doing an elephant project.

I wanted to go out and see these elephants. The chief of the village gave me the name of another guy in the village who could be my guide. I had a motorcycle, so we went together. He spoke a little bit of Bambara, but not much, and I didn't speak Fulfulde very well, so we had to do the hand-signal thing, and we were planning on spending the night. Of course, you get stuck in the dunes, so he's off the motorcycle, running, and I'm just trying to barrel along without wiping out, and he's pointing me in whatever direction, and all of a sudden in front of me, I see this caravan of camels coming from the north, and they have big slabs of salt strapped to either side of their backs. Today there are still salt mines in northern Mali, and salt used to be as valuable as gold. The camels would carry the salt down from the salt mines to be sold and passed down through the country. Nowadays they've got giant trucks because the camel caravans take so long. This caravan was almost like a mirage. I felt like I had been transported back a thousand years. The whole trip was just surreal. [Later we came upon] a small encampment of people, and they gave us water. You always treat your guests as more important than anything. Eventually we came to the acacia forest where the elephants were. I ended up seeing a baby and an adult elephant through the thick spiny trees, but you can't really go in there, and you don't want to scare them. It was an amazing day.

Glen Payne (Gabon 1989–1992) witnessed an elephant slaughter.

An elephant was killed in a legal way, out from my village. I was in my house one night by myself, asleep. At two or three o'clock in the morning, I hear, "Boom, boom, boom, boom." I hear lots of knocking on the door. "Mr. Clem, Mr. Clem!" They never could say "Glen." "Mr. Clem, come on! They've killed an elephant!" So I open my door and wander out groggily. Everybody in the village is awake. There's lots and lots of lanterns and candles, and kids are running, ladies are running, everybody's heading off in one direction. I got dressed, and off I went. They're leading me. We walked and walked for several hours to this place where the elephant had been shot because it was getting too close or who knows why. I don't really know. But what this represented for the village was lots and lots of good meat. Just like that. So everybody's arming themselves with these big banana leaves that they're going to wrap up chunks of elephant in and pack them back to the village. They worked on that elephant all day long. Nothing was wasted. There was no piece of that elephant that was left on the ground by the middle of the next day when they were finished. There were dozens and dozens of people all over it, cutting it up and packaging it. I ate some of it, just like everybody else. And it was incredibly good.

Glen's wife, Jenifer Payne (Gabon 1990–1992), also told a story. "I was walking down a straight dirt road and saw a big ape of some kind. I was terrified, so I just stopped and stood perfectly still. He was pretty far away, but not so far that I couldn't tell what it was and watch him. He crossed the road and walked around a little bit, and then he went back up one side of the road where our houses and the beach and the peanut fields were. The other side was the center of the island, and it was just bush, thick bush." Jenifer continued walking to her Gabonese friend's house to eat fish and drink beer. "I was pretty shook up, but it was awesome. I was excited. So I told her about it, and she said, 'It was probably one of the papas [older men].' I said, 'No, it wasn't a papa. It was an animal, an ape, some kind of big monkey.' And she said, 'Probably not. It was probably just one of the papas.' And I said, 'I don't understand what you're talking about.' She said, 'Well, when they're old like that, and they have work to do, they turn themselves into gorillas and go off into the forest, and they can do their work, because gorillas are strong and papas are not. They're too old. He probably just forgot to turn back into himself when he came into town. And then when he realized you saw him, he went back so he could change back into himself. You'll probably see him walking down the road in a little while.' Then she said, 'I'll go get your drink and be back in a minute.'"

Host Country Wisdom Stories

William Salazar (Guatemala 1972–1973) explained, "We were trying to get farmers to plant differently, and one of the ways was to have more spacing between the rows and between the plants, and we wanted them to plant two seeds instead of three. So one of the farmers said, 'Why do you plant two seeds?' and I was explaining to him that three seeds take a lot of nutrients and you're wasting those nutrients on three seeds where if you would just use the nutrients for two seeds, you would get a better stalk and bigger corn and probably healthier corn that would withstand any insects or any fungus. He said, 'Well, we plant three seeds for these reasons: one is for the birds, one is for God, and the other one is for us.'"

Other volunteers also learned from their hosts—about their roles, about hospitality, and about another culture's logic. Phil Dare (Malaysia 1965–1967) remembered that the "first day we got to our town, this townsperson who spoke very good English met us and was showing us around and quizzing us about different things. He said, 'Tell me, why are you here? Why would you leave your home, all the modern conveniences, and come out here to Borneo?' And about the time I started opening my mouth, he said, 'But don't say to help us.' I have no idea what I said because I know I was having to regroup really fast. But I have thought about that so many times. They've really been out there for generations and have managed to do quite well when you think about it. At that time, only the West thought they were living in poverty. It really did frame the way we went about doing things. Most Peace Corps people had so much more to learn than we had to give."

Capp Yess (Fiji 1982–1984) described how a friend learned about Fijian hospitality.

I wanted her to see this well-known tourist destination island. So we got on the bus and traveled through Labasa and Savusavu to a little place with a dock on the ocean in the bay to meet this boat. And I found out the boat had left. It would leave again the next morning. There was no one to call and no phone. My friend said, "What are we going to do? There's nothing here." And I said, "Come with me. Let's go have a cup of tea in the store." And she said, "Don't you think we should try to find a place where there's a hotel or something." I said, "I think we should have a cup of tea." So we went to this little store, we sat down, and we had a cup of tea. You could tell people were noticing us, these two visitors. After about a half hour, while we were having a cup of tea, a young man came up and introduced himself as the nephew of the ferry driver, and he said the ferry had already gone. I said I knew that, and I said we're going to catch the ferry tomorrow, and he said, "Well, would you like to come to my house and spend the night so you don't have to travel anywhere, and then we can bring you back here tomorrow in time to catch the ferry?" And I said, "Thank you, that's very nice of you." My friend just looked at me and said, "You knew that was going to happen, didn't you?" And I said, "Yes," because I knew there was no way those people were going to let us stay there all night with nowhere to go. That would never happen in Fiji.

In addition to his motorcycle story in Côte d'Ivoire, Richard Parker (Côte d'Ivoire 1973–1974, Morocco 1976–1978) described a happy holiday during his second Peace Corps tour when he visited the Glaoui palace in Telouet in the High Atlas Mountains.

The Glaoui became very famous, almost like kingmakers in Morocco. Under the French protectorate they gained a lot of power, and the French worked with them to actually choose a substitute sultan for the capital in Marrakech. But when independence came, the Glaoui, as collaborators with the French, lost power and went into exile. They built the most fabulous palace in Morocco. They took decades. The best artisans in Morocco came to help build this thing. Now it's abandoned, decaying. But it's a kind of national relic, so we decided we wanted to see the old Glaoui palace. So we took buses, finally got up there, and walked out to the village. And it was too late to tour the palace, I think. It was getting late in the day, and we had to stay somewhere, but there were no hotels. Well, what happened was that the government caretaker of the palace found us a place to put our sleeping bags down on the palace grounds, like an old room adjacent to the palace, a partly open type of thing. A family brought us a big load of hay to put under our sleeping bags. The word had gotten around the village, "We've got some *nasranis* [foreigners] visiting up here." Another family brought us firewood to build a fire for ourselves. And the caretaker's wife cooked extra *tagine,* which is a fabulous Moroccan dish. Lamb *tagine.* You have to taste it to appreciate it. And the whole time we were there, we were treated to this unbelievable hospitality. We were total strangers. We were foreigners. This is the way they treated us. And I remember that evening sitting there, eating the *tagine,* watching the ancient walls of the palace flickering in the light from our campfire, and the stars coming out. And this sense of absolutely timeless peace settling over me.

Gwenyth Lee (Cameroon 2004–2006) also told a story about host country wisdom. In the village of Mundum, where she lived, there was no chief. She explained:

He had died, and there was a big fight over who was going to be the next chief between the village and the royal family. Finally they announced a new chief. I was really excited, and we were all going to see him stoned. Everybody in the village picks up a little stone and throws it at the guy, and that's what gives him his power. So I'd heard all about this. You hiked down the main road until it ended, and then you continued hiking about eight kilometers into the bush to get to the old palace (there was a new palace, too). It was about a thousand-meter elevation difference. I was wearing this really heavy outfit, my fanciest African outfit. I got there, and everybody's drinking, getting really excited, and having a really good time. And I just got suddenly really, really, really sick, so sick I couldn't stand up anymore. I was curled in a little ball and I thought I was going to die. Luckily, one of my friends was building a house where the palace was, and he said, "You can go in my house. It isn't finished yet, but I have a little bedroom set up where I'm sleeping while I work on the house." So they got me to it. I thought I'm going to die in the middle of nowhere. I was sick for two hours, and then all of a sudden I was absolutely fine again. My neighbors came, and we walked back out. They said, "We're done. The chief has been stoned, and you just missed the whole thing. The jujus came and they danced, and you missed it." Everybody was whispering that it was bad magic, juju. "You weren't supposed to be there because it was a special event for only the Mundum people." There's an official ceremony to be made a Mundum person, and I'd never undergone that ceremony because there had never been a chief, and the chief was the only one who was allowed to do the ceremony. Because there was no chief, I wasn't official. And since I wasn't official, I wasn't supposed to be there. So I'd been made sick so that I would not witness the ceremony. I prefer to believe that. I think that's a better story than that I had heatstroke, which is logical.

BEING INCLUDED STORIES

The last stories are a segue to chapter 8. Volunteers describe how they knew they had adjusted in another culture and how they moved from being outsiders to feeling included.

Dianne Bazell (Zaire [Democratic Republic of Congo] 1975–1977) was invited to a New Year's Eve party at a neighbor's house during her second year. The house was "down the row of houses with these metal roofs that I loved to hear the rain in the rainy season pounding on. In the midafternoon there was the howling of a goat being slaughtered, freshly in their yard, for the guests. We got there and were treated royally. We had this goat meat, of course, and all the trimmings. We sat around with one of the few products made in Zaire—beer, Simba beer and Tembo beer. And I remember at some point during that evening it suddenly occurred to me that I was the only woman in the room, the only white person in the room, and the only English-speaking person in the room. Once you remember that you've forgotten that, you remember it again. Even though it was very important to know who you were and how you were being perceived, it was also very liberating to lose that sense of all those demographic categories and just be there. And I thought—I've adjusted."

Joshua Mike (Nevis 2004–2006) described his participation in Carnival. "We were the HIV prevention troop in Carnival, sponsored by the Ministry of Youth and Sports. We dressed up in costume and marched halfway across town and into the night with a big trailer of boom boxes on the back of this flatbed truck. We just danced in the street for hours. That's what Carnival was—a cultural celebration for two weeks. They have concerts. They bring in artists from Jamaica, from Trinidad; all the popular Caribbean bands are there. All the local bands are performing. They have calypso contests. They have a Mr. Cool show, the Queen pageant, local food festivals. So we got to participate, which was fantastic, because we didn't feel like we were outsiders."

Sarah Payne's (The Gambia, 1989–1991) story was about "the first time I saw a baby that had just been born. My host mother was a midwife, and I had been hanging out with the two girls on their front porch because their language skills and ability to talk about things were right where I was. All these women had been coming and going out of Haji's house—she had been to Mecca, so she was Haji. All of a sudden they said, 'Kati [my local name], come here.' So I went back there, and there was this beautiful little baby that they were washing with a gourd and fresh water. This woman had just given birth in the backyard. I had never heard a thing. Everyone was so excited and they were so hopeful, and this little baby was healthy and doing okay. And then this woman who had not had the benefit of any medication, who had no shoes, walked home to her family to present this baby. And all the women and I and Haji walked back with her to present the baby. And to be included in that was a good moment."

Chapter 8

Friends Can Become Family

I ran into some people that have become family. That wasn't part of my plan, but I came to know them and love them.
—Harry Siler (South Africa 2001–2003)

When people have little to do and are together a lot and probably like-minded to begin with, or they wouldn't be in the Peace Corps, the probability is probably pretty high they could end up getting married—and that's what we did.
—Tom Samuel (Liberia 1965–1967)

Six Volunteers in Five Decades

Martin and Patsy Tracy (Turkey 1965–1967)

Martin talked about a friend in Kırsehir: "We offered English courses in the evening to people in the community, and that allowed us to meet some very interesting folks. One individual that I remember particularly was a lawyer—a very, very large man, especially for central Turkey—who took us under his wing and had picnics for us out at his nice, spacious home. He owned some land and he had sheep, and he introduced us to other people and made it possible for me to interact with locals at the clubhouse, where people would play back-gammon and chess."

Rona Roberts (Philippines 1973–1975)

I had two main mentors. One of them sat right behind me at the River Basin office. He was a fifty-five-year-old man named Pedro Arbiso, and he was simply brilliant. He knew how everything worked in the

227

Philippines. He was not a Bikolano, but he had learned Bikol. He actually spoke five languages, as did a lot of people in the Philippines. What he did for me was to teach me the culture so I could avoid big errors, or help me understand where I had made errors, help me be a good team player, particularly my second year. He would say, "Today we are going to Catanduanes. Now the mayor of Catanduanes is a landowner, and we're in a land reform era." The boss of Mr. Arbiso was my other mentor. Salvador Pejo had two jobs. He was deputy director of the Bikol River Basin Project—a huge plum—and he was also the regional minister for agrarian reform, which meant they were supposedly a part of martial law, taking large estates and dividing and giving or selling land at reasonable rates to others. We were underlings of Pejo going to the mayor, and on the other hand, Pejo was trying to take the mayor's land. [Mr. Arbiso would say,] "Okay, here's what you want to say. Here's how you approach this person." Sometimes you didn't go to the mayor first. Mr. Arbiso knew the communities and how to make things work fluidly. He would also tell me in certain places: "Don't mention family planning" or "Don't mention health" or "Here, you want to play up this piece of what we are doing" or "Talk a great deal about the saltwater intrusion barrier," which was not something I was even involved with, but another part of the project. He was a very good cultural coach and guide. It was like being an apprentice in a way; he gave me custom-tailored advice about how to succeed.

Rebecca Roach (Liberia 1988–1989)

Rebecca recalled, "I had a very good friend named Hannah Sirleaf who lived close by, and I would sit out in her kitchen with our friends. We'd sit around the fire and gossip and talk. She was such a happy person."

Sarah Cross Oddo (Jamaica 1993–1995)

Sarah said, "I had one female friend in the first town I lived in. Her name is Jackie Roots, a Rasta. She kind of chided me for crying about being harassed on the bus and said, 'Come on! You're a Jamaican, mon! You've got to get tough!' She sort of taught me how to stand up for myself. After that, when people harassed me I would fight back and get in a verbal argument. I didn't want people to think I was this nice little tourist girl that they could push around. So I stood up for myself."

Aaron Shraberg (China 2004–2006)

I grew rather close to one of my students. His surname was Huang. I called him Tom. We still keep in touch to this day. He was a real standout in one of my classes, and one day he came up to me in class and said, "Let's go play tennis tomorrow." And we arranged a time and we met. He was very open. He wanted to discuss issues about modern China. His English was very good, and he was curious what I thought about why some Chinese college students commit suicide or where China is going as a developing country. And we ended up talking in English and Chinese, and I decided he could become my Chinese teacher, because we seemed to have good rapport. The semester ended, but he kept on tutoring me in Chinese.

Then the next semester ended and the summertime was quickly approaching, and I was going to leave China in about three weeks. He wanted to take us out for some Chinese barbecue. He ordered sheep's kidney, and I ordered just regular meat. He said, "Do you want any kidney?" and he touched where his kidneys might be. And I said, "Yeah, that's right, Tom. Very good. That's a kidney." And he said, "You taught me the word for kidney. You know, Aaron, one day in class we were doing a lesson on the human body, and you were teaching us about organs and you taught us the heart and the liver and the intestine and the kidney. We asked you, 'Aaron, is this the kidney?' And you said, 'Yes, that's kidney. Great job!'" And he said, "You praised us that day. You told us that we were doing good. And later that night in the dorm, everyone said, 'Aaron is a great teacher because he gives us confidence. He gives us compliments. He makes us feel good about ourselves.'" He's just telling this to me so eloquently and I was like, "Wow, okay, thank you, Tom." So I took a bite of kidney—wasn't so bad. I decided I needed to try some kidney. That was a moment for me toward the end of my service.

When Peace Corps volunteers tell stories, they are usually people centered. During their service, they took time to get to know people, learned from them, and learned to care about them. So friendships are basic to the Peace Corps ethos. Those friends might be people from the host country—sometimes peers, as for Martin, Rebecca, and Sarah; sometimes a mentor, as for Rona; sometimes a student, as for Aaron.

Among the host country people the volunteers lived and worked with, there seemed to be, as Philip Curd (Guinea 1963–1965) remembered, "a sense of kinship, a lack of any ulterior motive or commercial advantage or political agenda. We were dealing with these people as one human to another." For Ann Neelon (Senegal 1978–1979), her special host country people were "Rose Diouf and Mame Diaga. They were like my father and mother or sister and brother for the whole time I was there. I remember the two of them in my kitchen going back and forth making fun of each other because he was Islamic and she was Christian. He was making fun of her because of her belief in evolution—*comme singe*, 'like a monkey.' And his daughter came and gave us a chicken when we were ready to leave, and we didn't know what to do with it. He had to help us cut it open and pluck it and cook it. That's what I remember, and that's what I bring back that someone who just studied it [culture] in a classroom doesn't have. You don't have those human connections."

Volunteers who served together also formed special bonds, sometimes developed first during their intensive training and then through common in-country experiences. Sally Spurr (Ecuador 1975–1977) explained, "A lot of the volunteers that I served with, we still keep up with each other, and there's a group of us that gets together every year or two." Kathleen McFarland (Jordan 1999–2001) said her two best friends in the Peace Corps are "still my best friends now, and we talk usually at least once a week. I couldn't have gotten through the Peace Corps without them. They were such an incredible support to me." She lived with one of those friends in New York City after she returned.

Some country groups have regular reunions, and many countries have "Friends of" groups, but even volunteers who have never met before seem to be able to start a conversation fairly easily. Tom Boyd (Colombia 1964–1966) recalled attending a Camp Andrew Jackson weekend of the Kentucky returned volunteers group in the early 1990s and getting up early to do tai chi. "When I get finished, I look over and somebody has sat up in the back of a pickup truck and is watching me. It's a young returned volunteer who came in during the night and decided he would sleep under a tarp in the back of his truck. So we share a cup of coffee, and he's asking me about tai chi and I'm asking him about sleeping in the back of the pickup truck. You know, we're just a bunch of different people."

Sometimes the conversation at the monthly Peace Corps get-togethers at an ethnic restaurant starts simply with, "So where were you in the Peace Corps?" And a volunteer who was in Malawi in the 1960s finds that the couple sitting across the table from him has just returned from a two-year tour in Malawi. Or a volunteer from Nicaragua who recently moved to central Kentucky answers a question about the Sandinistas—"Yes, I lived in a Sandinista village, and Daniel Ortega visited once"—and goes on to describe a scholarship program he set up for students there. Kay Roberts (Ecuador 1982–1984) discovered that she had an immediate connection with a complete stranger who had also served in the Peace Corps. "You automatically know that that person shares some of your same thoughts and feelings about doing their part to make the world a better place. When I count the people I most enjoy working with, and when I count the people I most enjoy spending time with, I find there are a good number of returned Peace Corps volunteers in that group."

In the larger sense of the word *family*, then, friends—both people from the host country (called host country nationals in Peace Corps jargon) and other volunteers—became family. And sometimes volunteers married each other, and sometimes volunteers married host country nationals. In this chapter, the story of a long-term Afghan-American friendship is followed by descriptions of host country friends, mentors, counterparts, and finally mates. The chapter concludes with the rest of the story about Tom and Susan Samuel's wedding in Liberia.

An Afghan Friendship

Charlene McGrath (Afghanistan 1969–1971) told this story at a Kentucky Returned Peace Corps Volunteers gathering in February 2009.

In 1970 I met Mohammad Alam Beluch. My fiancé Mike was a Peace Corps English teacher stationed in Kang, a small village near the Iranian and Afghan border. There he met Alam, who was several years older and from a prominent family. Mike moved to Kabul in 1970, and Alam, who was attending Kabul University at the time, was a frequent guest at his home. I was there quite often and enjoyed drinking coffee and talking with Alam. In fact, when Mike went on home leave for a month, because he was extending for a year, Alam would come over for a cup of coffee and a visit. He did not want me to be sad because I was alone. When the Russians invaded Afghanistan, he moved his family to Zabul, Iran, and from time to time he would send us items made by his family and ask us to market them for him. Of course, we kept them and sent Alam money. We lost track of Alam probably in the early 1990s. Then in early 2005 I received an e-mail from Alam's nephew, who had worked as a translator for American troops in Afghanistan, asking if I was the Charlene Keeling from North Carolina who had nicknamed her mother "Grey Mouse." He told me that Alam was living in Kabul with his family and wondered how Mike and I were doing and if we had children. I e-mailed back, saying that Mike was deceased and that we had two daughters, and the elder was getting married soon. In the fall of 2005, after my daughter's wedding in June, I moved to northern Kentucky. I had sold my home in Jackson and returned to close on the house. I drove on to Hazard to see friends I had worked with there and was very surprised to see a package waiting for me. I opened the box and immediately burst into tears. Alam had sent from Afghanistan a wedding dress for my daughter made of white silk covered with gold embroidery. He had sent a two-piece lovely dark green silk outfit for my younger daughter, and he sent me just a glorious mother-of-the-bride dress made of white and pink silk with lots of gold embroidery. I was just overwhelmed. I had not spoken to Alam since I left Afghanistan in 1971, and yet he treated me like a family member. Mike was his brother, his good friend, and Alam wanted to be sure his friend's wife and children had wedding clothes. I was so touched. That act of generosity just meant so much to me and my family, and it typifies the way Afghans are. They give you everything they have, whether they have a little or a lot. They are so open-hearted and welcoming.

Host Country Friends

Often a person with whom the volunteer lived became a special friend. That was true for Harry Siler (South Africa 2001–2003).

My host father was in his late eighties when I arrived. He was the Indhuna subchief of this region. Herbert Mageza had been born to this royal position. He had run away from his father, the Indhuna, as a young man, and he spent some forty years in Johannesburg as the principal assistant—it's hard to say it, but as the head "boy"—to a white man who owned many businesses. So my host father, Herbert, became the chauffeur and the person who could go into any of these businesses as the representative of his employer and direct people. He was a very well educated man relatively. Alan Paton, who wrote *Cry the Beloved Country,* was one of my host father's teachers back in the forties, when it was illegal for black people to know things, to go to school above whatever level. Alan Paton and a Catholic father would offer evening classes somewhere. It was illegal to be out after curfew for black people, but they worked at elevating themselves. Being at my host father's table to eat for two years, I heard about the Germans bombing Johannesburg, I heard about the collusion between the Afrikaners and the Nazis and about the problems between the English and the Afrikaners, or about what life had been like. It was very, very rich. My host father was the counselor, police chief, everything rolled into one, and people would come to see him all day long with issues. The first day I was there we walked for two to three hours all through his village. I was introduced and seen, and I learned later that he was telling his village, "This guy is with me, don't hurt him, respect him, this is my guy." So I was never challenged in any way at all.

For Ashley Netherton (Senegal 2003–2005), friendship also had a family connection. She was given the Bambara name Sajo Kata, after the mother of the family, who had died some years before. There was also a little girl in her family named Sajo, so she had a namesake and an instant connection. Her family had four brothers, with all their wives and children, and the father was still living too. One brother in her immediate family was her counterpart in her agroforestry work. "His wife early on was really skeptical. I think she thought I had come to marry her husband, because in Muslim society a man can have up to four wives, and he only had one. I made it clear we only worked together. She ended up being my best friend." At first, Ashley thought she "would never make friends with any of the women, because hardly any of them had any education, and I thought, what are we ever going to have in common? I didn't have any children, and their physical work was very foreign to me. They took care of kids, washed laundry, cooked, pounded, and farmed. The women are truly incredible because they work constantly, and I know they are tired, but they just go on. I ended up just hanging out with some of the women while they were taking care of their babies or sitting by the pot stirring something for dinner. We would have discussions about potentially sensitive issues, like how they felt about their husbands having four wives. You hear from the men they [the wives] are like sisters, but they are not. Also their views on their husbands wanting as many kids as they could have because it's prestigious to have large families. One of my best friends is about thirty-two, and she's had eight births, five living children. She just turned to me and said, 'I'm tired.' They're strong women. I have a lot of respect for them, and I feel for their situation."

Zoya Rodionova hosted Wini Yunker (Ukraine 2000–2002) in her home, was a teacher at her school, and became her best friend. "She knew everything. She was forty-eight, so she'd been around. She'd lived under communism. In fact, her husband had been an officer in the Communist Party. But the minute the country went independent in 1991 and the new president said, 'Ukrainian is our language, not Russian,' Zoya's father, who had been in the KGB and the Communist Party and was a colonel, told his family, 'We're speaking Ukrainian from this moment on.' All my friends felt that way." Later Zoya helped Wini organize a Christmas party for children in a local orphanage, and after Wini left Ukraine, Zoya was the point person as Wini and her friends continued to send money. "The things she does with that money for those orphans is just amazing."

Andrew Kimbrough (Sri Lanka 1984–1986) talked fondly about Grandfather, who slept in the garage of the house where he lived.

He had a little desk, and when I would get back from school he'd be there, wearing something like a little tank T-shirt and a sarong around his waist. He'd see me coming and he'd say, "Andrew! How are you today? Good. How's things? So, are you hungry?" We both loved my landlady's cooking, so we couldn't wait to get in there and have some rice and curry. But he'd invariably say, "So, what do you say we have a little?" What he meant was that we'd have a shot of arrack, the local liquor. So he'd pull out a bottle, and it would have a twist-off cap, but nonetheless he'd turn it over and smack the bottom of the bottle to force the cork. He'd pour out two shots, and we'd sit and chat about the weather or what have you. He was a retired surveyor, and every once in a while when there was a land dispute, a property dispute, he would be called to court to testify that his signature was actually indeed on the document, and he was very proud of that. So we would have our drink and then go in and have a meal together.

For Joan Moore (Swaziland, 1979–1981), a friendship led to her future career. First she became friends with Bennett, a South African Xhosa man, and then with Make ("mother") Nzima, the woman who had brought him up and now lived in Swaziland.

We would go visit her, and she was probably in her forties or fifties. She would deliver babies in the room next to this house where she stayed, and that was what got me interested in later becoming a nurse practitioner. I stayed there a few nights, and she would wake me up in the middle of the night and let me come in and be in on these births, which was totally an amazing experience. These women, when they were getting close to delivery, would come and stay there in this small house, and when they were ready to deliver, she was there. Some of them would come at night. She would deliver three babies a night by herself, and they would sleep on clean garbage bags that covered a bed. She'd have a pail for the afterbirth, and she would wrap the baby in newspaper when it was first born to clean it up and get all the stuff off of it. She was this amazingly strong African woman.

The town was very divided, and she had been really immersed in apartheid. One time we went to the grocery store, and I tried to carry the groceries for her because she was an older woman. She wouldn't let me; she would say, "If the mine owners see you carry the groceries, they'll give me trouble." Throughout my time in Swaziland, I had some really close friends who had left South Africa, and they would talk to me a lot about their experiences. A huge part of my Peace Corps experience was knowing and understanding about South Africa.

Robin Sither (Cameroon 1996–2000) described a Cameroonian friend who developed AIDS.

He used to be a motorcycle trainer for the Peace Corps, a great guy, very worldly. His father was well educated, and he was educated in Britain and actually grew up for a spell in Germany and France. He could speak German fluently, he could speak French fluently, and English, too— great guy, and just great to spend time with him. He was very Western in his outlook, but also very Cameroonian, so it was a good balance. He was also very physically imposing, very charismatic, and of course, people like that tend to draw women, and he enjoyed his pleasures in that respect, and it caught up with him. He was actually at my post when he started developing symptoms. I never suspected HIV until I visited the hospital, where I happened to know some of the nurses, and they confided in me that it was HIV. His mother was still receiving a pension from the government, and he had a sister who was pretty well off, so they took him to the capital with the aim of getting him to France for treatment, but by then he was so ill there was no way any airline could take him on a flight. He was the last person I saw before I left Cameroon. And to see him, this very robust, strong guy on the ropes, where the fat had drained out of his face. He was completely emaciated, couldn't walk. To see him in that state was not a good way to end my Peace Corps experience.

When we interviewed Michael Geneve (Mozambique 2003–2005), he had just called his best buddy, Justino, in Mozambique "to see how things were going. He is a mechanic, and I met him on the side of the road one time. We hit it off right away and hung out all the time. He actually bought a little baby goat when we met, and every time he'd come over to my house or we'd go to a local bar and it would turn nighttime, he would say, 'Oh no, my goat!' because he had put the goat somewhere, and we would go and find this goat in the dark and then tie it back up. For my going-away present he gave me the goat for us to eat at my going-away party. That was very cool. He's just really similar to me. We're pretty focused people, pretty silly. I helped him get a job at the hotel that Peace Corps volunteers stay in down in Maputo. The last week I was there, I was staying at that hotel for all the stuff to finish Peace Corps, and I showed him how to use the Internet, and so we send e-mails back and forth."

Sometimes the host country friend turns out to be someone unexpected. Blake Stabler (Russia 2000–2002) developed his most meaningful relationship with the school security guard.

Her job was to sit there with all the keys in case something went wrong. So she would sit in this sort of cage unit in front of the school where you would hang your coat during the school day. We would talk and work on my Russian. Margarita has really been a victim of the dissolution of the Soviet Union. She was an engineer, and she had been to a university in Petersburg and gone off to central Asia and spent her entire adult life and raised her three daughters there. Unfortunately, her husband was dead and her daughters had gotten jobs—one in Ukraine, one over by Japan, and one in Kazakhstan. She was living in Uzbekistan at the time and was told, "You're a Russian. You have to leave." There was actually a building for Russians who had to move back from the other republics. And the vice principal at the school had the same situation. She had lived on an island that Russia gave back to Japan. Yes, Margarita Mikhailev, the woman who kept the keys for the afternoon/night shift, was probably my closest friend. She understood being a foreigner from her experience in central Asia and having to learn a language, which was helpful as a tutor. And we just got along well. We both liked to eat, liked to cook, and have a good time.

Counterparts and Mentors

Counterparts can be crucial for volunteers' work and well-being. For instance, in Guatemala, William Salazar (1972–1973) worked with agronomists, "and for the most part, they were fun to work with. Then there was a group called junior agronomists, who were the equivalent of associate degree people here in the States. They were more our age, so we could relate to them. We did a lot of things with them, and we shared resources. I taught English classes with the junior agronomists in the area, got invited to dinner, and drank beer with them. That was a lot of fun simply because Spanish was my first language and I could communicate very easily. That was kind of neat that they were all male, so there weren't any reservations as far as where you stood. You just became instant friends."

The official counterpart for Kristen Perry (Lesotho 1999–2001) was the principal of the primary school.

She was sort of like the unspoken chief of the village. She was not officially the chief, but she was the chair of the church board, the chair of the secondary school board, the director of the church choir, and on the board of the clinic, too. I mean, she just did everything. And she was well educated. She had gone to the teacher training college. She had her certification. She was this grandmotherly woman, and she was very, very well respected and very, very large. She just welcomed me into her family. As soon as Peace Corps drove up with me, she came up and gave me this huge bear hug to welcome me, which was sort of unusual in that culture. She had a daughter about my age who was in school in South Africa and would come back and visit, and we were sort of like sisters, and her grandkids would come over and play at my house. I felt very much like I had been taken in as part of her family, and I would go over to her house almost every day just to say hi. And sometimes she would invite me over for a meal, and we would have these wonderful conversations in a sort of hybrid of English and Sesotho. It just kind of flowed together, and we just had a lot of mutual respect for each other. She had worked with Peace Corps volunteers before, so I didn't have to break her in to Americans, but she never judged me compared to others, so we had a wonderful relationship.

David Goodpaster (2005–2007) had several close counterparts in Malawi, but "the one who got the most done and had the best relationship with me as well was Geoffrey Sinjani. He was twenty-one years old. He just had so much enthusiasm. He was so intelligent. He was kind of like a little brother, and it was great. To this day, I miss him, and I'll probably miss him for the rest of my life. We e-mail every now and then. He's back in secondary school because he has to finish up two classes before going to university. He's very much into the environment. That was his passion, and he helped me a lot on the health issues. I taught him a lot about health issues, and he would help me with translations. He and I created a class together. We went around and promoted what was called the bridge model, a program created by USAID as part of the HIV/AIDS initiative. We went around to thirty-five or forty secondary schools and taught this class."

The Ecuadoran counterpart for Kay Roberts (1982–1984) was Nestor, who was the equivalent of a county extension agent in the Ministry of Agriculture. "He was one of the people who helped organize the 4-H clubs, and he also had some property in my community, so I had pretty frequent interaction with him. He was a very interesting guy, an anti-U.S., very left-wing socialist who, although Peace Corps was a U.S. government–sponsored program, recognized individual volunteers were there to work with the people of Ecuador on the needs the country had expressed. He had a great working relationship with Peace Corps volunteers, even though he may not have agreed with our government's policies at the time. We were mining the harbors in Nicaragua, so it was kind of an iffy time to be a U.S. citizen in a Latin American country because there were very strong feelings about that."

PEACE CORPS VOLUNTEER FRIENDS

"My relationships with other Peace Corps volunteers are unbreakable, as close as when people say 'my army buddies,'" explained Glen Payne (Gabon 1989–1992). His group has a reunion every three or four years. "It's been in Philadelphia, it's been in Cleveland, New Mexico, various places around the country. We stay in e-mail touch. We stay in phone touch. It's nice to know that there's a network of folks across the country where I know that I can go to any one of their homes and flop there on my way through. And they can, too. That's one of the wonderful things about Peace Corps."

Audrey Horrall (Zambia 2000–2002) also made some close

friends in the Peace Corps. She described their get-togethers in Zambia—thirty volunteers from the northwestern province gathering every three months at the Peace Corps house in Solwezi, having parties, going out to bars, planning vacations together—to Lake Malawi, Dar es Salaam, and Zanzibar and a camping and canoeing trip down the Zambezi on the way to Namibia. "For some reason," she said, many of them "have settled in the Baltimore-DC area, so I've been there twice to visit that whole crew. And it's always just like we saw each other yesterday. We're instantly right back on track with each other. We really, really bonded. And I definitely believe that they'll be lifelong friends. Whenever we hear about someone else somewhere, it's always interesting to share the news."

Linda, who was assigned to a Catholic mission village outside Lilongwe, was the closest Peace Corps friend of Ken Wilson (Malawi 1997–1998).

I would travel to see her, or she would come up and see me. And of all the bizarre things that I learned to do in Peace Corps, she taught me how to quilt. She was a quilter and she'd always quilted. And all this fabric, all these *chitenjes* walking around. She goes, "This [fabric] is beautiful, Ken, we should make a piecework quilt for you so that you'll have this forever." And I thought, you know, Linda, I've got enough problems without someone calling me a quilter. And she goes, "Oh, just try it." So we did something called appliqué on a ten-by-ten square. It was in the shape of Africa from a piece of beautiful fabric. And I did it. I poked myself and bled everywhere, and I finally managed, after hours, to appliqué this one silhouette of Africa on a ten-by-ten square. And I thought, if I do thirty-five more of these, I can have a queen-sized quilt, and I'll have it forever. I became obsessed with it. So I made thirty-six squares, all from different fabric. And it was interesting, because each square ended up telling a story. My favorite T-shirt that I had brought with me had eventually just shredded off of me because it had been washed on a rock—so what survived of it I cut up in the shape of Africa and put it in my quilt. We did a Habitat for Humanity build, and in the place where we were staying was some little resource center, and the curtain was just a piece of fabric about four feet longer than the window. So, I felt kind of bad, but I cut it in a straight line, I cut some of that out and put that in my quilt. So all the fabric, except my T-shirt that shredded, came from Africa. After I did my thirty-six squares, Linda took it to the tailor in her village, and he did the most amazing job of putting it all together and making this huge queen-sized quilt top that I later took back to America with me, and my sister-in-law, who is from a family of quilters, had her cousin hand-quilt it for me. And it's on the bed right now, and it's probably what I would grab if my house caught fire.

About seven years after his Peace Corps tour, Ken went back to Malawi with his friend Linda, who was serving in Crisis Corps (later called Peace Corps Response) in Zambia.

Dan Graham, a fellow teacher in agriculture, was such a good friend of Sheila and Cecil McFarland (Micronesia 1972–1974, Philippines 1974–1976) that they named their son born in the Philippines for him. Dan would come over after work in the afternoon, and as Cecil recalled, "He and I developed a passion for playing board games like Stratego and checkers and spent hours and hours at these games. He's living in North Carolina. I just saw Graham about two months ago. So we keep up with him thirty-four years later."

MARRIAGE

As Tom Samuel notes in this chapter's epigraph, the likelihood of volunteers getting married is good because they share the same values, even if they serve in different countries and meet later, as Ann Neelon (Senegal 1978–1979) and her husband Richard Parker (Côte d'Ivoire 1973–1974, Morocco 1976–1978) did. Volunteers also met and married host country nationals.

Lee Colten (Ecuador 1981) told us how his love story began. He met his future wife Marianna (Ecuador 1981–1983) at the end of Peace Corps staging in the United States.

I remember noticing Marianna—very short hair, very attractive woman. She had cropped all her hair off, a really tomboyish haircut. I remember thinking that she was very attractive, but she's out of my league, so I never felt really comfortable approaching her and introducing myself. And we weren't in the same groups. Toward the end of the week, I'm worn out and I'm going to go for a walk by myself. I'm leaving the grounds of the hotel, and here she comes back with a group of other people. They'd just finished a walk. We're passing each other, and she peels off from the group, puts her arm around me, and says, "I want to get to know you." I'm thinking, okay, this is good. So we go for a walk. We head out across this cemetery in Harpers Ferry through the woods to the other side, where there's an unofficial overlook. So we're sitting on this rock overlooking this cliff, right where the two rivers come together—spectacular view and the sunset and everything. Sort of very romantic, as it turns out. So we end up talking and just sitting there, and time slips away. Before we know it, it's probably five hours later. Somebody comes looking for us and says, "Hey, you guys going to do your thing in the play?" I was supposed to play my guitar and do some music. Anyway, we connected there.

A month intervened between staging and flying out for training. Lee was going to train in agricultural extension in Costa Rica before going to Ecuador, and Marianna was going to train in special education in Ecuador. During that month, Marianna sent Lee some sheet music she wanted him to learn. He called to thank her and got the impression she didn't want to talk to him, but she wrote him several letters. He arranged to see her for twenty-four hours in Miami before their planes left. Lee remembered: "I have two months of training in Costa Rica, and she's doing her training in Ecuador. I got a letter almost every day. This lady was incredible in terms of her letter writing. I'm thinking, I hardly know this woman. We've spent a week at Harpers Ferry and a day in Florida, and I'm getting all these letters." Lee didn't see Marianna when he got to Ecuador, and he left the Peace Corps and went home after three months. Marianna continued to write him a letter every day for the next year and a half. She said, "He was like my diary." Since he had two weeks of vacation time from teaching environmental education in Tennessee, Lee decided to visit Marianna in Cuenca, Ecuador, the Christmas before she would return to the United States. "So I get down there, and lo and behold, we're having a good time. We're sitting on a rock in the middle of the river visiting. We're making these little strings out of clover. And I made one for a ring and put it on her finger. She says, 'So what do you want to do? We need to do something fun while you're here.' And I say, 'Well, why don't we get married?' She says, 'Well, I was wondering when you were going to ask me.'" Lee concluded, "We would see some of our Peace Corps volunteer friends after that, and they would say, 'You're still married? We can't believe it worked, because you guys didn't even know each other.' So it was pretty remarkable that it worked, but you get to know a lot about people with a lot of long letters and a lot of phone calls."

Jenifer and Glen Payne (Gabon 1990–1992, Gabon 1989–1992) got married about nine months after they came home. Jenifer explained, "We had been friends really the whole time we were there, *just* friends until the very end. And then we came back, and a lot of your selection process is done for you." Jenifer said she learned a lot about Glen by knowing him in Gabon. Glen's innovative idea for training new Peace Corps volunteers was to ask another experienced volunteer to come out and cook. He said, "We need for the guys to have one recognizable meal during the day that's not palm oil or manioc or armadillo meat, things they're not used to. The first cook I had was Jenifer, who is now my wife. We knew each other already as friends, but we got closer while we were working there together. We were friends until it got close to time to leave for good, and I thought, man, I'm really going to miss her, and it turns out she was thinking the same thing. And it's worked out great."

Gwyn Rubio (Costa Rica 1971–1973) initially wanted to go to Africa, but she decided after her boyfriend Angel had been in Costa Rica for six months that she wanted to be near him. Gwyn said that the Peace Corps wanted them to get married—it wouldn't be good for them to live together—and she remembered that the director also said, "'We have not had one woman volunteer make it outside the capital city. We don't think your marriage will make it, and you'll be gone in six months.'" Angel Rubio (Costa Rica 1971–1973) described their wedding in San José. "It was a civil ceremony. I had some of my Tico [Costa Rican] friends and some of my Peace Corps volunteer friends as sort of seconds. The story we've told for years is that because Gwyn's language skills and nerves were not great, there came a point where I nudged her and she said, '*Sí*.'" Laughing, Angel said, "That one 'yes' ruined the rest of her life."

Rachel Savane (Guinea 1990–1992) met the man who would become her husband in August 1992, just four months before the end of her tour.

My girlfriend up the road from my village had been dating another teacher at her school, and she said, "We're all going to get together and go out dancing." I went dancing a lot with Belgians, Americans, and Guineans. On that outing I met this Guinean man that I couldn't take my eyes off. So it was love at first sight, and I was spending all my time with him and hardly going back to my village. In November we almost got married there, but I hadn't even told my family or anyone that I really liked this guy. So we just changed our plans and tried to get him a visitor's visa so he could come to the States with me. I'm in the whirlwind of great love, but then I got more practical. I extended my Peace Corps time a month and applied for a position with USAID. I got a short-term contract as a logistics person for a group of potential investors. My boyfriend got his visitor's visa and left for America. My contract was through in April, so I lived with his mom and his sisters in Conakry. I went home via England, where my sister's family was living, and babysat for them in London for a couple weeks, and they paid the rest of my ticket home. Arriving in New York, I thought, "Is it me, or is it my passport?" because he actually had the desire to come to America before he met me. But there he was at the airport, so all was well. We eventually got married and have three children, so all is good.

Leigh White (Bulgaria 2001–2003) saw her husband-to-be in her assigned town the first week she was there, and they were married in December 2002 in Bulgaria. "That changed everything, because there were newspaper articles written about our marriage. And I'd turned into what they call a Chirpan—that's the town where I was— daughter-in-law. If you married someone from another town, you would become a daughter-in-law to that other town. So I became instantly one of them. They already said, 'Your Bulgarian's so great. You're like a Bulgarian.' And then I married one, so it went even further to support their belief that I was half Bulgarian." Leigh and Nikolai announced their marriage when her grandparents, brother, and great-aunt came to visit in summer 2002 and had an official dinner with his family.

Leigh explained that it was not easy to marry a foreigner, "but it was even harder after September 11 when you're serving as a Peace Corps volunteer. You have to jump through a lot of hoops. First, I had to get it cleared with the Peace Corps office in Sofia. I had to go to them and say, 'I want to marry this guy.' My country director said, 'That's fine. I need you to write it up for me.' So I had to say that I wasn't going to ask to move, because they didn't want to have to replace me and find another site for me. They also wanted to know that I wasn't going to ask for any more living allowance to support him and basically to say it wasn't going to interrupt my service at all. Then the Peace Corps did a background check on Nikolai through the local embassy as well as the FBI." Next, Leigh "had to go to the consulate and swear I'd never been married before and sign this paperwork. Then I had to go to my local town. And the guy at the consulate said, 'Good luck, because a lot of people, especially in small towns in Bulgaria, aren't going to recognize this document that I'm giving you. But don't worry, because even if they won't let you get married there, you can always come back to the capital to get married.' Well, that was going to be a pain. His whole family wanted to be there, and we didn't want to have to transport the whole party hours away to the capital." Luckily for Leigh, "everybody in the local government building in the municipality who had to approve the wedding just loved me. And it worked out really well."

As a male volunteer, Capp Yess (Fiji 1982–1984) remembered that the Indian families in his community saw him as a potential "catch." "I was invited to a lot of homes where at least one of the daughters was prominently displayed and usually serving us things. And occasionally I was just asked flat out if I was interested in their daughter or not. I figured out later one of the ways to get out of it was to say that because I'm American, we would have to arrange dating before marriage, and since that was never something the fathers could even consider, we just politely agreed that marriage was probably not a good thing, given my background and their background." At the end of Capp's service, he was asked to stay on in Suva, the capital, and work on several training contracts. He socialized with the other volunteers and met some of their friends—one of them a single Indian woman who, uncharacteristically, lived in an apartment by herself and worked for the Ministry of Aviation and Transport in downtown Suva. Capp recalled, "We started jogging in the morning and going to the Olympic pool in the evenings together, and she enjoyed doing those things that I enjoyed. All of a sudden, we were going out to dinner together, and we had about a nine-month romance. Then I left Fiji to travel through Southeast Asia. Traveling alone for six weeks, I had a lot of time to think, and one of the things I thought about was calling her and proposing. So I called from Bangkok and proposed to her over the phone, and she accepted."

Capp then returned to the United States, spoke to her family, and arranged a date for the marriage. "My mother and I went from Minnesota to Fiji for a week. I was married and came back to Minnesota without my wife, and she attended to her affairs and quit her job and arranged for the immigration papers. Luckily, some of my friends working at Peace Corps knew embassy people, so they were able to help her. On December 22, 1985, she flew from Fiji to Minnesota, and we started our lives together." Capp described the civil wedding and two receptions in Fiji. "We were married in the parliament building by a Fijian justice of the peace whose name I will ever remember—Illiasoni Tabuatamata. We had a small reception in the hotel where my mother and a friend of our family were staying, and then that evening we went to my wife's brother's home in a suburb of the capital city and had a reception that involved some of the rituals of a Hindu wedding but was sort of Hindu wedding lite."

THE REST OF THE SAMUELS' STORY

In the previous chapter, Tom Samuel (Liberia 1965–1967) described arriving by plane in Buchanan and being met by his future wife, Susan (Liberia 1964–1967). Tom visited friends in Monrovia several times after his arrival in August on Liberia's Atlantic coast. In October he invited those friends to Buchanan for Liberian Thanksgiving, the first weekend of November. However, he needed someone to cook the turkey. Susan continues their story:

> He took me to the movies one night and asked if I would cook. I said sure, so that was his first Thanksgiving with me. I was away during the school holidays around Christmas and visited a friend. I told her, "This guy is going to ask me to marry him. Should I do it?" I didn't really come to any conclusion, but I got off the airplane in Buchanan, and that night he proposed down on one knee. Such a sweetie! We got married April 16 and had 125 people at our wedding at the Catholic church. The audience was probably 60 percent Peace Corps and 40 percent Liberians, all the people I taught with. My bridesmaids were all from the Peace Corps group. I was a little bit late getting to the church, and the shoeshine boy came by and saw all these people sitting there in the church and thought it was a great opportunity. I weighed about ninety-five pounds and had a little short white linen dress that someone made for me with a beautiful white lace overtop that buttoned down the back with those little teensy buttons and long sleeves—but all lace, so it was cool and comfortable. My headpiece looked like a donut with some veil coming off of it. The wedding rings didn't come. One of my professors at San Diego State who was a jeweler had made them out of ivory and silver. So the night before we got married, I went down to the local market and bought some plastic earrings that were bendable. We just coiled them around. He got one and I got the other. Father Patrick Juele blessed two sets [the San Diego ones came later] and asked if there would be any more. Our cake was a

gift from the people who owned the bar in town, but it had come by road 100 miles from a bakery in Monrovia, and some of the chocolate had dripped in the heat, looking like chocolate icicles. We had champagne and wedding cake—$100 for the whole thing. Then I extended for an extra year.

Chapter 9

Coming Home

Coming back to the U.S., I was rather appalled by how much we have here. It was hard for me to find that happy medium—to live in the culture where I grew up and was going to continue to live and not feel totally guilty about the things we were able to enjoy, and also to share the wealth through service and through contributions.

—Kay Roberts (Ecuador 1982–1984)

SIX VOLUNTEERS IN FIVE DECADES

Martin and Patsy Tracy (Turkey 1965–1967)

Patsy described their trip home: "We took our airline tickets and cashed them in. Since we'd lost forty pounds, we made a plan to visit every country in Europe and eat our way home so that by the time we got home, our parents would recognize us. So we took off through the Balkans and Vienna and Paris. And we ate. We spent all our money having fun because we knew when we came home we'd be back to being poor. We'd be graduate students."

Martin described what happened next: "We knew we were coming back to something positive that would energize us and something we hoped we could really get involved in. Patsy got a scholarship, and I had the GI bill, so we chose the University of Illinois to get master's degrees—she in social work, and I got mine in political science. But it was a very difficult adjustment for us. Just the shock of what America has—the opulence, the consumerism, the access to so many things that are unnecessary—as opposed to Turkey, where we were living on a much more frugal basis. Knowing you can live frugally and be quite content and happy and have a productive life,

247

coming back to the United States was just so overwhelming. You walk into a grocery store, and it's just really shocking to have all these choices. The lifestyle of American society and wealth were difficult to readjust to. But we've managed over the years to get used to it again."

Rona Roberts (Philippines 1973–1975)

Rona remembered:

> It was terrible. I didn't want to come home. I wanted to stay. I had a job offer from the River Basin Project to stay, and Howell had a job offer from USAID. So for the last six months we were debating what to do. He wanted to go to law school, and he wanted to farm. I wanted to do international development, though I had gone over there with the LSAT completed and I was going to law school when we came home. I became unsure; he became sure. I didn't want to come back, but I finally agreed. We got back in December. I was sick and I was homesick for the Philippines. I felt I had made a terrible decision. It was Kentucky, and it was cold and miserable. The things that jump out are the enormous amounts of consumption. It's so obvious when you've been in a place where, if people ever open a can of food—which would be very, very rare—but if they do, every part of the can is put to good use. We weren't in Kentucky two hours before we stopped at some kind of dairy mart and bought a milkshake and sat there looking at the paper and plastic container and straw and wondered how we could clean it and ship it to the Philippines. Once we went back to the Philippines several years later, for a month, and I finally stopped dreaming about it, crying, being depressed. I said, "Okay, the Philippines is going on without me."

Rebecca Roach (Liberia 1988–1989)

Rebecca came home from Liberia in December 1989, just before Charles Taylor and his men entered Liberia and the country's nightmare of nearly fifteen years of civil war began. "I was heartbroken because I was planning to be a nun. I had made arrangements to go back [after getting a master's degree], and the nuns I worked with were murdered shortly after in Liberia."

"My worst culture shock was coming back," Rebecca said. "Reentry was much harder than arrival. Everything changes in the United

States so fast that I came back to a country I didn't even know. I remember being so overwhelmed. I remember standing in a supermarket just totally overwhelmed by how many types of cereal you can buy. Or being in a mall and being in a sea of white people. Everything was so unnaturally clean, and everything seemed so artificial. It was just very weird."

Two weeks after her return from Liberia, Rebecca started graduate school at Ohio University in Athens, Ohio, studying international development. "I remember being so confused by time. I showed up at a class in natural resource development, and I had completely missed the class. Time had just gotten away from me. I showed up as the professor was walking out, and I remember saying, 'I'm so sorry. I totally lost track of time.' I know he thought I was just a little airhead, but then I said the magic words: 'I just got back from Africa, and I'm still on Africa time.' He said, 'I go to Kenya all the time for research.' And we became great friends after that because it clicked that you're on Africa time still."

Sarah Cross Oddo (Jamaica 1993–1995)

Sarah came straight back to the United States, but her boyfriend Oghale had another year in Jamaica.

I had already been accepted and was ready to go to graduate school. So I got out in July, and school started in August. I went to the School of Public and Environmental Affairs at Indiana University and did a master's of environmental science. It took two years. During my spring break that first year I went to visit Oghale. When he finished his service he got a job as a trainer for the next group of volunteers, so we both went to Kingston, and I did an internship at an environmental consulting firm for a couple months. There's a lot of aluminum mining there, and there was a retaining pond with a lot of sludge that looked like a nasty red soup. We were doing a project to see if there were any leaks in that pond and at what rate it was leaking. It was really interesting and also gave me a different view of what Jamaica was like. I was among more peers. I had Jamaican female friends and male friends that weren't necessarily hitting on me. Then we went back [to the States] and Oghale started in the same school and studied finance and international studies in international development. We got married after I finished school and he still had a year and a half left. I had a job with an environmental consulting firm in Lexington, so we lived in different cities while we were first married. Once he finished school, he got a job with Peace Corps as an APCD [associate director].

Over the years, Sarah has had some typical reverse culture shock experiences. For instance, she remembered coming back to Lexington in the middle of her Peace Corps service in Jamaica.

They had just opened a Wal-Mart on Richmond Road, and I had never been to a Wal-Mart before. It was a twenty-four-hour Wal-Mart, and I went with my friend at midnight. We were just wandering the aisles, feeling so overwhelmed because there was just so much stuff. And it still happens to me. Just a few weeks ago [after returning from Fiji, where her husband was Peace Corps country director] I went to the grocery store with my mom and said, "Look at this whole aisle of pet food!" The number of choices is just amazing. Usually now I adapt a little bit quicker, but I remember once coming back from Swaziland—no, Jordan—and I wanted to buy a shower curtain while I was here. It took me a month before I could buy a shower curtain. There were so many choices, so I just kept looking. It takes me a while before I'm able to shop, and each time I'm less into the consumerism of America than I was before. Each time I take a further step away from it.

Aaron Shraberg (China 2004–2006)

Aaron returned home via Europe with his girlfriend, whom he met in the Peace Corps. First they flew to Paris.

That was culture shock. I mean, that was shock—I don't know if you call it culture shock. But the architecture was different, the air was different, the people were different, everything was different. And it was exciting to be in that new environment. We traveled around Europe for a month and a half. I had to change my routine, change the language I spoke, and just the way I did things. Everything seemed so much easier because there were a lot more English speakers. I looked like some of the people there. When I was in Italy they thought I was Italian. When I was in France they thought I was French. So you know, "Bon jour monsieur!" "No, I'm sorry, I'm American." In some ways I felt like being in Europe I was able to acclimate to living in a different environment and a Western environment, too, something that was non-Chinese. It gave me the opportunity to get to know Western civilization, like Greece, Italy. After being in China and seeing everything Chinese, I was suddenly in the cradle of all these great Western artifacts and sites. I was able to adjust and decompress from my Chinese experience in those few months.

Being at home at first was so stimulating. Everything was really new and delicious and wonderful. And it was great to see my family again. I missed home. Having been abroad, I gained a real appreciation for my own space, my own culture, my own country. That's something that I initially was given a big dose of very quickly. So I felt it was like an element of debauchery to be home in America, the land of the free, where Coca-Cola runs like water, Snickers bars are to be found at every supermarket, and Cheetos grow on trees. It was great being home experiencing all those very physical things and just being in America amongst Americans. And I still do feel like this is home for me, particularly Kentucky and Lexington. I'll always have a home here and really, really appreciate that—being home.

Supermarket shock is probably most common for returning volunteers. For one thing, the prices of those tropical fruits volunteers may have bought in Ecuador or the Philippines for pennies are amazing. Even more confounding are the myriad choices of ketchup and cereals and detergents and the rows of cat and dog food. Even a plastic milkshake cup and a straw can seem extravagant. There are other differences, too, like the way time is perceived, as Rebecca described. Sometimes travel on the way home, as for Aaron, or travel back to the host country in a few years, as for Rona, helps. Sometimes volunteers begin graduate school almost immediately, as Sarah and Rebecca did, and that offers an opportunity to dive into another new opportunity.

A 2004 article entitled "The Toughest Job You'll Ever Leave" described the readjustment of University of Wisconsin alumni who had been Peace Corps volunteers. Even though returned volunteers receive a readjustment allowance and some job-hunting help, they come home as different people, and others may have a difficult time relating to their experience. One volunteer explained that he had changed from a type A to a type B personality because of his two years in Niger and said, "You have to learn to put that [experience] away in a basket in your house somewhere and not cart it out very often."[1]

Returned Peace Corps volunteer Craig Storti, who served in Morocco, has written about cross-cultural adjustment to both other cultures and the one back home. In *The Art of Coming Home,* he cites a 1985 survey in which returned volunteers reported, by a two-to-one margin, that reentry was more difficult than the original adjustment to the foreign culture.[2] Storti goes on to explain that the intensity of the volunteer experience in the local culture—in a so-called developing country and often outside an urban area—makes it difficult to adjust to the abundance of the United States, to the pace of life, to what seem to be narrow and superficial American interests and attitudes, to the loss of a new language, and to the search for meaningful work back home.[3] Storti's "Ten Ways RPCVs Know They Have Readjusted" rings true. For instance, number one is "You've stopped carrying toilet paper with you wherever you go," and number ten is "You're not afraid to swallow water while showering." In between are "Other people no longer avoid the dish you bring to potluck dinners" and "You occasionally stay in a hotel when you are in a strange city."[4]

However, before that readjustment, many returning volunteers suffer reverse culture shock. The tolerance they practiced overseas seems more difficult to practice back home. Returned volunteers have become "something of a cultural hybrid."[5] In fact, Storti writes, "you're still a foreigner (albeit for different reasons) and some of the instincts you acquire abroad won't be of much use to you back home."[6] So some returned volunteers withdraw or try to escape at first, although most eventually adjust and incorporate their experiences into their subsequent lives. As Geraldine Kennedy (Liberia 1962–1964) points out in the foreword to her collection of Peace Corps volunteer stories, *From the Center of the Earth,* "most volunteers returned to the United States and continued their lives with mainstream American pursuits. They take care of their families, they work and play and organize, own cars and lots of other things. They eat well—every day. But there is a profound difference," Kennedy points out. "The returned volunteers know—in some deep place in their consciousness—that there is another center, another definition of life, another way. Much like immigrants, they live with the complexity and the richness of another vision, and know they will never again see with only one."[7] As protagonist Harrison Shepherd, torn between the United States and Mexico, says in Barbara Kingsolver's novel *The Lacuna,* "I think most people are the same. Until they've gone somewhere."[8] Such an insight is not limited to Americans. A Pakistani returning to Pakistan from the United States writes: "Such journeys have convinced me that it is not always possible to restore one's boundaries after they have been blurred and made permeable by a relationship: try as we might, we cannot reconstitute ourselves as the autonomous beings we previously imagined ourselves to be. Something of us is now outside, and something of the outside is now with us."[9]

First, however, returned volunteers have to come to terms with coming home. A young Bill Moyers, then deputy director of the Peace Corps, warned newly returned volunteers in 1965: "If you don't think yourself special, you will simply disappear in the bog of affluent living—you won't make a difference."[10] And it is hard to return. Gary Griffin (Thailand 2004–2006) talked about missing the simplicity of his life as a volunteer and his struggle to live simply in the United States. "I came back and I was ready to sell everything. I didn't want all this stuff." However, he found some of his attempts to simplify his life artificial. "I thought, well, I can't get rid of the house and I can't get rid of the cars. I'm going to start with books. So that was pretty ridiculous." Gary went back to teach in Thailand for some months in 2009 and in China in 2011.

So, how do returned volunteers find the "happy medium" Kay Roberts describes in the epigraph? This chapter follows Kentucky-linked volunteers returning through the decades, and although there are some differences—more recent volunteers may have come home for Christmas or a wedding during their two-year tours and may have kept in close e-mail or phone contact with their families and friends—there are also many similarities. And what Joshua Mike (Nevis 2004–2006) says at the end of the chapter will sound familiar to all returned volunteers.

1960s

Paul Winther (India 1961–1963) had a difficult time readjusting. He flew from India to Denmark to meet his parents, whom he hadn't seen for two years. "They wanted to show me my ancestral home in Denmark. I got off the airplane in Copenhagen, and my father started crying. My father never cries. He said I was very, very skinny. I was down to about 124 pounds—I had had lots of dysentery. It was hard for me to get used to Denmark because everything was so clean." Paul bought a Volkswagen and ate his way through Europe for about six months. When he got off the plane at the airport in New York, "Everybody, everything was fat. There were fat cars, fat sandwiches, fat people—even the skinny people were fat. My mom and dad were so happy I came home. My mom and I had a lot in common, so she could relate to some of the things, but most people say, 'Oh! You've been overseas. Tell me about it.' And after a couple of minutes they can't relate." Paul remembered:

> I felt totally estranged from everything because I had been exposed to lots of poverty and very, very few material possessions. I was seeing the world through the eyes of my Indian compatriots, my fellow woodworkers. I had been able to go to Thailand and was in a couple bars where there were a lot of Americans talking about war. I was just turned off by that, and I began to realize my naiveté about going into the navy. If I had gone, I would probably be talking just like these people and not really thinking twice about bombing peasants, the very kind of people I was working with, only in India. It really made me begin to see myself and my background and my country in a different light, with a much more critical eye. Two of my friends, naval pilots, were killed in Vietnam. I was still eligible to go into the navy, but I said, "I can't do this because I know that someday I might be in a situation where I might be taking the life of the same kinds of people, innocent people, with whom I worked."

Paul went to Michigan State to work on a master's degree. "I talked to a friend with whom I'd been corresponding in Liberia and I said, 'I don't think I'm going to be able to live here anymore.' I can't explain the feeling. It was just a feeling of foreignness and dissonance. And if I hadn't happened to talk to him, I don't know what I would have done. He said, 'I have the same feeling, and I'm working my way through it.' I guess it's an experience of a lot of volunteers."

Tom Boyd (Colombia 1964–1966) said flatly: "I was a failure at readjustment. I went home to Westerville, Ohio, for about three days. Then I went to school in Europe at the Institute of Social Studies in The Hague. They accepted me for a program called national development. There were all kinds of people from different parts of the world and only three Americans. I caught a lot of lip because of the Vietnam War. But I was kind of like the good American. I'm learning about development studies—sociology, economics, political science, history—it's fascinating. I do okay in the program and get to stay a second year for a master's degree in social sciences. The Dutch like me, and they send me to Ghana for three years. I didn't weep when I left America. I wept when I left Colombia. I wept when I left Ghana."

Bill Sweigart (Liberia 1967–1970) didn't want to come home.

> I guess I was really liking what I was doing. I was not very happy about what was happening in our culture. I felt disconnected from the States. I would listen to the BBC and I said, "Oh, what are those Americans doing now?" I traveled. I went to Spain to meet a woman who was somehow connected to providing an operation for a local student in Kolahun, Liberia. I added on to my ticket for all these stops through Europe— Amsterdam, London, pretty much a European trip—and then I got back to New York unwillingly. I arrived back in March 1970 and had no job lined up, and the army would have been happy to have me. So I was called for the physical, and I was determined not to go. The local draft board had a lawyer working as a liaison for people who were outspoken and resistant. And I met with this person. The fellow said, "What are you going to do? What's your plan?" And I said, "I'm a teacher. That's what I do." And he said, "Get a teaching job," and within a week I found a job in Camden, New Jersey, in an inner-city school teaching math.

Another returned volunteer who became a teacher was Fred Cowan (Ethiopia 1967–1969). He remembered his homecoming as dramatic. "Between the time I left and came back, Martin Luther King was shot, Bobby Kennedy was shot. The Vietnam War was still going on. College campuses had been taken over by drugs. I wound up getting a job teaching school in Chapel Hill, North Carolina."

Other 1960s volunteers seemed somewhat less troubled by and less eloquent about coming home, but they still remembered their feelings and reflected on them. Dan Sprague (Colombia 1963–1965) came home in late October to an early snowstorm that knocked the power out. "And everybody was completely panicked. I had lived for the last few years where power was out a lot. And I thought, 'Oh man, we are really a spoiled society.'"

"Coming back, there was an illusion of normality," said Jules Delambre (Cameroon 1965–1967). "I got reminded fairly frequently over the next year or so that I had missed two years of experience. Although I had read *Newsweek* and the *Christian Science Monitor,* I had completely missed the visceral impact of the Vietnam War on college students and on the country as a whole. So I can say I had a little bit more trouble readjusting than I did adjusting to Cameroon in the first place. I plunged back into my master's program in anthropology at Louisiana State University and met my wife, who was in the Spanish program, and we both applied to enter PhD programs at the University of Kentucky."

Terry Anderson (Ghana 1965–1967) found ways to cope: "One of the things that helped me in the transition was finding something that was traditional in American society, because I'd been in a traditional society for four years. I found old-time mountain music, and we'd go to fiddle festivals all over North Carolina and Virginia. It was also an easier transition because I was in graduate school at a large university with other Peace Corps volunteers around that you could talk to about your experience. Also, the environmental movement had just started, and we had some world-class lecturers that were in the science news—it was a wonderful time. What dismayed me most when I came back and talked to my friends? They were always talking about the things they had just gotten, like new cars, all this materialism. I, on the other hand, was full of stories on West Africa."

Like Jules and Terry, graduate school was the next step for many 1960s volunteers, and the Peace Corps sent out information about universities that were actively looking for returned Peace Corps volunteers. For Bill Davig (Peru 1965–1967), it "turned out there was a professor of industrial engineering at Northwestern who was particularly interested in people who had experience overseas in other cultures and were interested in economic development, particularly technological development. So I applied." As a student, Bill had an opportunity to work in Washington, DC, with the Organization of American States and travel to Latin America to interview people and collect information from technological institutes. He did his dissertation in Brazil on transfer of technology and had a fellowship to pay part of his expenses. "But it all started with the Peace Corps. That was the beginning of my interest in economic development and led me to Northwestern, and then that led me back to Latin America." Bill stayed in Brazil for eight years and met his wife there. He then taught at Auburn for four years before coming to Eastern Kentucky University, where he taught courses in small business and international business until he retired.

Sometimes returned volunteers didn't get into graduate school or had trouble finding jobs. Jeff Kell (Dominican Republic and Ecuador 1962–1963) reflected: "You get an inflated sense of worth. You may be able to have a greater impact on what is going on [in your host country] than you would in the U.S., so when you come back, you don't adjust quickly to the fact that you're more of a number, definitely not a big fish in a small pond. Indeed, you're a small fish in a big pond, and that adjustment is not easy for some. I applied to law school but didn't get in because I had a beard. I just didn't fit in anymore. Having been a Peace Corps volunteer didn't seem helpful on applications." Jeff got his first job with Northern Natural Gas in Omaha, Nebraska, after disclosing at a presentation about the Peace Corps at the Aspen Institute for Humanistic Studies that he hadn't been able to find a job.

Marlene Payne (Malaysia 1967–1969) said, "I was disappointed because I had been gone for two and a half years, and in the meantime, television had taken over my family's life. They were so glued to the television that they didn't even have a conversation about what I had been doing. I went to Washington, DC, looking for jobs, but I wasn't Republican and I wasn't black, and that's who the jobs were going to, so I got an invitation to come back and teach at Berea College."

In terms of coming home, John Skeese (Nigeria 1961–1964) was an exception. "I could go back and have hot dogs or hamburgers in the States," he said. "I never felt readjustment problems, because I feel at ease wherever I am, more or less." After the Peace Corps, John spent a year in charge of the carpenter shop at Albert Schweitzer's hospital in Gabon, but once he came home he never traveled outside the United States again.

1970s

For volunteers who served in the Peace Corps in the 1970s, coming home was sometimes difficult because of what they had missed or because of what they saw at home through new eyes. Sometimes a job eased that early shock; sometimes volunteers tried an interlude of travel or a different lifestyle. Readjustment took time. While some returned volunteers were really happy to be home, one couple and one individual decided to sign up for second tours.

William Salazar (Guatemala 1972–1973) described coming home as "very difficult."

The phone would ring at my house and I would stare at it, and my mom would say, "Well, aren't you going to answer it?" I would go to the store probably three blocks away, and in Phoenix in July it's 115 degrees, [but] I would walk to the store and walk back. And my mom would say, "Well, what took you so long?" I missed speaking Spanish and I missed the slow life. I missed feeling important. I was just one of the seven kids in my family, just one of the kids in the neighborhood. I missed people coming to my door and wanting me to teach them English or translate something or [asking] if I was going to the city to take something for them or buy something for them. I had a hard time with the traffic, with the hustle and bustle. I would still go to bed at 8:00. I missed the clean air, I missed the beautiful clouds, I missed the sincerity of the people. When I would run into friends [who said], "Hello, how are you?" I would begin to tell them, but they didn't want to hear. I was trying to figure out how to go back. I probably would have done it, but I promised my mom that I would finish my degree. Being a student was very different because I had seen the world, I was more mature, and I had seen death and had lively political discussions.

Sally Spurr (Ecuador 1975–1977) said she "cried all the way. I really did not want to come home. I knew I was leaving what I loved and coming to something I really didn't want and didn't know what I'd be doing." She took a job as a lock and dam operator on the Ohio River. "I have often said that this was more culture shock than Peace Corps ever was. I was the token female, and they were all veterans, most of them from World War II. It was a great job for me. I loved it. Some of the guys really resented me, and some of the guys really took up for me." Sally then went back to school and got a master's degree in education and her teaching certification in Spanish and English as a second language at the University of Kentucky. She eventually took a job in Louisville at Jefferson Community and Technical College.

"It was hard coming home because I had been pretty spoiled as a kid," Gwyn Rubio (Costa Rica 1971–1973) explained. "My eyes were opened in Costa Rica. Disney World had just opened in Orlando, and we were treated to a trip to Disney World, and it was just obscene to me. I think the readjustment was pretty hard, and this is why we decided we were going to be 'back-to-the-landers,' because we had seen another way of living that we respected. The things we threw away they kept. So we took our readjustment allowances and backpacked for seven or eight months in Europe and Africa, taking a freighter over and back, and then we came to Kentucky and bought land in Wayne County and lived there for two years."

"I really didn't want to leave Afghanistan, but I did," Maurice White (1974–1976) said. "Coming back was a bit of a culture shock. I was lucky to get a job. My father got me a job at a state hospital in the Boston area. I was constantly stupefied by the two existences, like the ease of transportation here and the freedom of our society, not having to worry about accidentally touching someone of the opposite sex and having that interpreted as a sexual advance. Also, the amount and variety of goods in the stores were overwhelming."

Richard Parker (Côte d'Ivoire 1973–1974, Morocco 1976–1978) came directly back to the United States both times—the first because of his motorcycle accident, and the second because, "after two years, I was exhausted with being a foreigner, a *nasrani,* which literally means a Christian, which they call anyone from Europe. It's fascinating and educational, but I was tired of being a foreigner." Ann Neelon (Senegal 1978–1979), who much later met and married Richard, came home in a Senegalese patterned dress made by a local tailor. She landed in New York City and had to take the shuttle to Boston. "I just remember seeing all the grayness, and I stuck out like a sore thumb because I was wearing this African dress. I remember being in my mother's house and a neighbor was over. I said some basic facts about the U.S. and Africa. She took what I said like I was criticizing the U.S. and said, 'You should appreciate what you have.' I don't think you're ever the same in terms of cross-cultural stuff. I mean, I can never go back and live in Boston the way my siblings do. I probably wouldn't even be at Murray State if it weren't for the fact that our former dean had a son who was a Peace Corps volunteer. Also, at that time, Murray State was named the regional university that was going to be internationalized."

Coming directly back to the United States to take up his career, Ben Worthington (Costa Rica 1973–1975) still found those first days disconcerting. He had begun to fill out applications for the Forest Service six months before he returned and had heard about a job in Olympic National Forest, but first he went to see his parents in Washington, DC, where his father was working. Ben wanted to see the Smithsonian, so he and his father took a bus into downtown Washington. "In Costa Rica if you had a seat, you didn't get up until the bus stopped. So when we were a hundred yards from the stop, [my father] jumped up, got off, and was almost at the door of the Agriculture Building, looking around for me. I was sitting there, waiting until the bus stopped. I'd adopted the slower pace of living in Costa Rica." Ben felt "an affinity for the Costa Rican people" but said, "I was happy to come home and be an American in America."

Cecil and Sheila McFarland (Micronesia 1972–1974, Philippines 1974–1976) decided to re-up for another two years in the Peace Corps, but in a different country. "So we didn't have to worry about readjustment," Cecil said. Back in the States, "We tried to eat all the greasy food we had missed, see some movies. We didn't know any of the music or movies or TV shows. We were flying back to Honolulu after Micronesia and heard a song on the airplane that I thought was a commercial, 'Put Your Camel to Bed.' For us there was no real cultural adjustment or hardship when we went to the Philippines, as in Micronesia. I worked directly with farmers and set up a feed analysis laboratory, and the second year I was a Peace Corps rep visiting other volunteers. We had our first child there and named him after our best friend in Pohnpei. We finished up there in 1976. And by that time we knew we wanted to stay in international work."

1980s

Looking different, dealing with people who couldn't understand or hadn't changed, reacting to consumerism and "plentifulness," and considering whether one wanted to fit in were all described as part of reentering American society for volunteers we interviewed from the 1980s.

Elaine Collins (Micronesia 1989–1991) described her experience:

First, I looked very different. My hair was white from the sun. I was very dark, and my teeth were red because we chewed betel nut. I traveled for two months and got home before Thanksgiving. I remember calling my dad and telling him to make a dentist appointment for me. When I got back I decided to stay with two really good friends who had also been in Yap. One was from New York City, and her mom had this huge loft in Soho and was in and out of the country, so it was a place we could live for $200 a month. We lived there together for probably six to eight months. Mostly what we did was wake up and drink tea all morning and talk about Micronesia. It was really good to be in New York because it was a place I'd never lived before, and there was a diverse group of people, so you were surrounded by a lot of difference. But I remember finding it hard because I had this expectation that all my friends would be doing wonderful things and would have changed, and they were in exactly the same places as when I left.

Coming home from Gabon between his second and third years forty pounds lighter and with long hair, Glen Payne (1989–1992) remembered looking very different, too. Also, "the chasm between being a regular American guy growing up in Ohio and being in one of those Gabonese villages is really so broad that I hardly knew how to cross it, even with my own family. They're asking me, 'Well, what's it like?' [And I'm thinking] 'Well, how do I tell you?' If I say the word 'road' or 'bridge' or 'house' or anything, none of those things is like what you picture. The road is a red dirt track that if you drive a truck down it, it's jungle brushing up against both rearview mirrors."

Capp Yess (Fiji 1982–1984) was struck by the difference between consumer-oriented America and the simpler way of life in Fiji. "When I got back, everybody had a video player, and there were lots of satellite dishes in people's yards. I mean, technology changes so fast that you go away for a few years and you come back and stuff has changed. I remember the first time I went in a large grocery store, seeing everything so clean and bright and so organized. I had forgotten how consumer oriented we are and how many choices we have and how clean and prepackaged things are. I remember wanting to just meet my friends and sit down and talk, and they kept saying 'What do you want to do?' And I said, 'I'm doing what I want to do. Can't we just sit here and talk?' I realized that in Fiji I had gotten used to a much simpler way of life, where there was a lot of just talking and visiting people because there was no other entertainment. But I quickly readapted, and things became familiar again."

Returning from The Gambia, Sarah Payne (1989–1991) had similar feelings:

There was a lot more culture shock coming back. They tell you that, but you don't really believe them because you're coming home and it's familiar. You are overwhelmed by fat dogs and big people and cars that only have one person in them. You go to the grocery store and you are paralyzed because you're not used to having choices. The onions are huge. All you want is some soap. You're used to having one choice of soap, and now there is half an aisle of soap. And you get disgusted by the "plentifulness" of everything and our wastefulness of everything.

I had missed two Christmases with my family, so they saved up gifts for me, and my first night back in July they put up the Christmas tree at home to welcome me and help me celebrate Christmas. They showered me with gifts, with the best of intentions, but it was very overwhelming. My brother gave me a transition back to the U.S. guide—he had a picture of my pit latrine and then a picture of a porcelain toilet.

Marianna Colten (Ecuador 1981–1983) "came straight home because Lee was here and I was ready to see him. Had I not met him, I probably would have extended and stayed longer because I really liked it, or gone to another country. It was kind of scary to come home. I was really anxious to see my family and see Lee, but I had changed a lot, and I knew that things were not going to be the same with some of my college friends. It was difficult trying to fit in again, or maybe I didn't want to fit in anymore."

1990s

Again in the 1990s, volunteers who had changed themselves struggled to reconcile what they had experienced as Peace Corps volunteers in other countries with what they found back home, this time in a quite changed United States. Those who returned at the end of the 1990s discovered technological change, and those who left before the twenty-first century began and returned after 9/11 experienced a particular disconnect. Four of the ten volunteers we interviewed who chose to extend their tours for a third year were 1990s volunteers, and their reactions are described first.

Carolyn Cromer (Morocco 1992–1995) had rather rare good coming-home memories. She remembered coming back as "wonderful. I had sort of reached a point in my third year where I realized I've spent three years trying to get to know this culture and these people, investing of myself, but I've got a family, too. I've got my own people back home that deserve my energy and my time, so I was really ready mentally to go back and embrace my culture and my people, so it wasn't a big hardship to come back." She pointed out that "the hardest part was the adjustment to the isolation in our society, everybody sitting in their little box and lack of community." After living with her parents in Louisville for about eight months, she got a full-time job working for a local alderman and entered local politics. "It was more community service."

In contrast, Debra Schweitzer (Mali 1993–1996) found coming back "really, really hard. I got angry and depressed just to see so much wealth and so much waste. You come back to electricity, running water, people that have their knees uncovered. Mali is a very relaxed Muslim country, but women don't expose their knees. You come back to everything you've taken for granted before, but you don't take it for granted anymore. People are just so narrowly focused on America, and nothing else affects them. They don't know there's a country called Mali. It was just very difficult."

"America had definitely changed a lot since I left," said Robin Sither (Cameroon 1996–2000). "It was during the whole Clinton boom, and the dot-com thing had exploded, the Internet was going wild, and people were still full of optimism. And with all that prosperity, there was a lot more conspicuous consumption. And here I was. I was raised to be very frugal and thrifty, and I've never really cared for material possessions. So going to Cameroon and seeing people living with a lot less than I had to begin with and coming home and realizing that you don't need that much and seeing all this going on was disconcerting. It was pretty difficult getting the stock question: 'Well, how was Africa?' or 'How was Peace Corps?' How do you answer that question in a nutshell?"

Coming home two months after 9/11, Kristen Perry (Lesotho 1999–2001) noticed a changed country.

I flew into Atlanta the day that moron ran back through security and they had to evacuate the whole airport. You always come home and it's a different world, but I came home to a world that was radically different. And that was really hard. It's hard enough because you've suddenly had your eyes opened and you see the world in a very different way. You understand different worldviews and yet I came home to a country that was suddenly hyperpatriotic and "we're the best." And suddenly I felt like such an alien because I had had these experiences, and that was not necessarily valued. My mother had moved to Michigan, so I came home to a place that wasn't my home, and I didn't know anyone. It was almost harder to come back here than it was to go over there, because I expected things to be the same, but they weren't. Just the changes in people's attitudes—we were gearing up for war, and that was not something I agreed with. It was just shocking. It was really disorienting. I wanted to just go back to Africa and be back in my village, where things seemed so much simpler to me and more clear-cut.

Tara Loyd (Lesotho 1999–2001) remembered her friends at home asking about September 11, but that wasn't her entire Peace Corps experience. "I had traveled a lot, to Madagascar and Botswana and Zambia and Capetown [South Africa]. I wanted to show my pictures of my fun and kids I worked with." She felt left behind because her friends had gotten apartments and cars and were dating or getting married. "Cell phones had happened. I was at the video store thinking people seem to have lost their minds, talking to themselves, and realizing they have little earpieces in their ears and they're in fact asking their wives what movie they should rent. Is this for real? Basically, I just felt what sort of an isolated life we live here in America. My friends, who are very open-minded and very intelligent people, really have no idea that HIV is killing a lot of people right now. Or they know and they care, but their lives aren't affected by it in any way. I found myself out at bars talking about the rate of HIV among young women in Lesotho. I have all these visions in my mind about being at the funeral of a child, and I'm trying to be normal, I want to be normal. I want to stay connected to Lesotho and my friends there and my Peace Corps friends, but I also want to be accepted here." Tara lived for a while in a cabin on her parents' tree farm in Kentucky. Then she took a road trip to an organic farm in Alaska and worked for the Bluegrass Conservancy, a farmland preservation nonprofit organization, before going on to graduate school in public health at Johns Hopkins in Baltimore.

"One of my favorite stories," said Cori Hash (Zimbabwe 1999–2000), "which my Peace Corps friends think is hilarious but my other friends don't laugh at, is about taking a shower. When I first got back, my mom had moved into a new house, and after she left for work the first day I got up to take a shower, and I couldn't figure out how to make it work. It wasn't one of those normal ones where you pull the little thing up. I was used to taking a bucket bath, so I just squatted and showered by splashing the water onto my head from the faucet. Then I kept forgetting to ask her how it worked, until finally she had a day off after a week had passed. She showed me how it worked and said, 'What have you been doing?' I squatted down and showed her. I really think she almost thought I needed therapy at that point."

2000s

The reentry experiences of twenty-first-century volunteers were not so different from those of earlier volunteers. For instance, Blake Stabler (Russia 2000–2002) recalled supermarket shock. He had returned just in time to be best man for his college roommate. "I was staying with his fiancée's parents, and I remember them asking 'Do you need anything?' I said, 'Actually, I'm out of shampoo,' so we went to a supermarket, and there's the aisle of shampoo. I had shopped at my little outdoor market for two years. I was overwhelmed. 'How do I choose a shampoo?' I didn't know how to make a decision, because in Russia I would just ask someone else, and they would make the decision for me, as the foreigner. People would hand me something, and I'd say how much and give them money."

Besides supermarkets, the United States also has ice and air-conditioners. Like some earlier returned volunteers, Peg Dickson (Ukraine 2000–2002) said, "Americans are really very spoiled. The first time I went to an American restaurant and I could have a glass of water with ice in it was absolutely amazing. I guess I'm still adjusting, because I still like to walk. And last night when I got home, somebody was running an air-conditioner. And I thought, 'What a waste.' There were no air-conditioners in Ukraine. In the middle of summer it was hot; in the middle of the winter it was cold. You had no control over your heat, and to save money they would sometimes turn the heat off in the winter. So you took whatever it was, and you lived with it."

Coming home in the middle of one's service (not permitted in the early decades) and traveling after one's service were ways to cushion reentry. Ashley Netherton (Senegal 2003–2005) said, "I thought it might be weird to go back home to the U.S. after two years in Africa, but I had gone for a visit halfway through my service. I remember that first night at home I woke up in my bed and I didn't know where I was. I felt for my mosquito net, and it wasn't there." Jenny Howard (Gabon 2000–2002) gradually worked her way back into the United States. "I spent half of the adjustment allowance they gave me at the end, cashed in my plane ticket home, and then flew to Tanzania and went out to Zanzibar and found a little beach hut of a hotel right on the Indian Ocean. I stayed there for about five days and cried and wrote postcards and in my journal and adjusted to not being in Gabon anymore. That was good. Then I traveled in Tanzania and

Zambia, and the last thing I did was walk across the top of Victoria Falls because it was dry season, and there were swimming holes at the top of it where you could dive. People on the Zimbabwe side would look over, and they thought people were diving off the edge. It was just amazing, and I felt on top of the world."

Several twenty-first-century volunteers shared their stories of arriving back in Kentucky. Michael Geneve (Mozambique 2003–2005) thought there would be "banners and all these people at the [Lexington] airport welcoming me back. And I'm just going to get right back into what I'm doing. My parents didn't even show up at the airport. They thought it was an hour later. Things here have stayed the same, but I've changed so much. And I have a hard time communicating with people. The first month I just had to try to remember even how to speak English." In contrast to Michael, Audrey Horrall (Zambia 2000–2002) flew into Lexington to a "little reception party for me at my sister's. My aunt and uncle were there, and a few other family members. They were all really excited to see me, and I was still pretty overwhelmed and jet-lagged and happy to be home." But getting used to people's accents was an issue for her. "It was really strange to me how people sounded, and just to see white people everywhere was kind of odd. I remember my parents and my family having a very overtly hillbilly accent. After trying to speak English very clearly and deliberately [in Zambia], they just sounded like they had such heavy southern accents, I was amazed. It was really, really strange for a long time. And they thought I sounded weird because I had kind of lost my accent a little bit."

Another concern for returned volunteers was finding a job. Peg Dickson (Ukraine 2000–2002) called herself lucky. "I had an e-mail before I left Ukraine asking if I was interested in serving as director of the Thornhill Learning Center in Frankfort. I think that made the transition much easier for me because I came back to a place where people knew me, and they gave me an opportunity to share some of my experiences. If I had tried to take this job before I went into Peace Corps it would have scared me, but I gained self-confidence in my ability to do things and handle situations, because you just had to."

Lauren Goodpaster (Malawi 2005–2007) was back in the States only forty-eight hours before the University of Kentucky flew her to Lexington for interviews. She became program director for leadership and service in the Office of Student Involvement. Lauren pointed out, "Here you get stressed out about health insurance and car insurance and all kinds of stuff that you just don't think about over there." In February 2008 she and David had their first child, and in May 2010 their second.

Finding a job took longer for Sara Todd (Armenia 2001–2003). After staying with her parents for a couple of months and working for a temp agency, she decided to volunteer for AmeriCorps and went to Alaska for a year, where she was program coordinator for a youth detention and mental health facility in Ketchikan.

Lettie Heer (Senegal 2001–2003) tried VISTA for eight months, working on homeland security for the Red Cross in Louisville, but she was very unhappy and began to work with Senegalese refugees instead. She recalled coming back as a "kind of shell shock. A friend in Danville wanted $10,000 of flowers arranged for a wedding, and a girlfriend asked me if I would help. I came back from that experience just crying, just the absolute excess of it all."

Leigh White (Bulgaria 2001–2003) described what it was like to come home with a Bulgarian husband. After "leaving behind so many friends, so many students, my in-laws, my niece, my sister-in-law, I was so excited to come back and get back into things again, but there weren't that many people waiting here excited to see me. It was just a really weird transition time. I didn't have a job. I didn't have a place to live. I had this husband. The economy was terrible. I didn't know how I was going to get a job. I was stressed out about how I was going to pay for things. The readjustment allowance that Peace Corps gives you seems like it's going to be enough money to live on for about a month, two months." After living with her family in Knoxville, Tennessee, for six weeks, Leigh and her husband Nikolai moved to Louisville. Within a week she got a job in the communications department of a health care corporate office, where she had worked during college. Leigh watched her husband experience the same kind of cultural adjustment in the United States that she had been through in Bulgaria. "It was just a very weird time," she said again. "But now I'm back, and nearly two years later, it hardly seems as if I ever left. I do have a much stronger connection to other cultures now, especially Eastern European cultures. I'm so excited to meet anyone from Eastern Europe now and talk about how I was in the Peace Corps and what I did when I was there—just show them respect for the part of the world they come from, let them know that I know how hard it is, because I did the same thing."

Plus ça change, plus c'est la même chose

When Joshua Mike (Nevis 2004–2006) talked about returning from the Caribbean in 2006, he could have been a returned volunteer from any decade. He said: "I came home to a very shocking world of materialism and unnecessary pace. The abundance of stuff in America. Walking into a Wal-Mart or Meijer or Kroger the first time. Relationships seemed so artificial and superficial here. People say, 'How was your experience, Josh?' I say, 'It was great. I had an awesome time, glad to be back.' They say, 'Okay, well, let's go to Dairy Queen.'"

Chapter 10

Making a Difference

Peace Corps offers volunteers work that needs to be done, and
hopefully small changes in individuals' lives can happen—if there
are two more students in Zimbabwe who further their education,
I think that's enough—but I also hope that people get a different
view of Americans, another face of the American population.
—Cori Hash (Zimbabwe 1999–2000)

Six Volunteers in Five Decades

Martin and Patsy Tracy (Turkey 1965–1967)

Patsy described a project they started in their second town of Ürgüp.
"We took on the merchants' association, who wanted to learn business and tourism English and marketing skills. Most of the tourists
came from Scandinavia and Germany and brought in all their supplies, enjoyed the area, and left—and never left any money. So we
became like Robin Hood: fleece the rich and give it to the poor.
The poor merchants began to open up their restaurants and fix box
lunches and put out their carpets and advertise in English [with
menus translated by Martin and Patsy]. And so the tourism business
blossomed."

Rona Roberts (Philippines 1973–1975)

Rona said, "I found out when we went back three years later that
they had launched the barefoot doctor program that I had helped
write the proposal for. But I also found out that that very brief golden
era early in martial law when people were afraid to do corruption

stuff had ended. The Bikol River Basin Project had 500 employees now, and you had to be especially nice and pass some money to the accounting people to get your paycheck every month. So I'm not sure that we changed the country at all. Howell [her husband] did have some luck with backyard pig farming. Part of his job was to help people grow two pigs so they could have a little extra money and maybe buy school uniforms and books and send the kids to school. He also helped an international team work with an early mainframe computer in Manila to plan the infrastructure for the increases in rice and corn production the River Basin Project expected to generate."

Rebecca Roach (Liberia 1988–1989)

"I would talk to Liberians," Rebecca said, "and they all remembered every Peace Corps volunteer they'd ever known. I think Peace Corps volunteers are just nice people, and Liberians realize that not all Americans are rich and not all Americans want to start wars. We have other concerns. We're regular people. That was the impact I made. I think they'll remember me as being a nice girl, a good girl."

Sarah Cross Oddo (Jamaica 1993–1995)

Sarah hoped that some teachers in Jamaica found her environmental materials useful. She knew she had helped some girls personally. "At a going-away party, one girl who had been in the environmental club said, 'What I remember about Ms. Cross is that even a lady can ride a bike.' I like that because maybe riding a motorcycle taught her a little about things that women can do." But Sarah also hoped that people learned about a typical American. "All over the world, people think I'm not a typical American, and I really try to explain to people that I am very typical. I want to know people. I'm friendly. In many ways I'm very American, and by knowing me, you're knowing what America is like."

Aaron Shraberg (China 2004–2006)

"The fact that I was there and I was not Chinese affected the people in my community," Aaron said. "They were able to see something and maybe even get a glimpse of something that wasn't familiar but was there. At many schools all the foreign teachers live in the same dorm. But Peace Corps made a point, there was a rule, that we could not live in all-foreign teacher dormitories. So I lived with Chinese neighbors. And I think that was one of the most effective ways of allowing us to get to know more Chinese—the old ladies and old men who are always crouched around your door playing mah-jongg or just chatting, and all the Chinese children that would come over each day. So that allowed me to also become a member of the community and be remembered."

The three purposes of the Peace Corps, as stated in the original act, point to three ways of making a difference. What impact did volunteers have through their jobs? What impact did they have as Americans in other countries? Finally, how did they bring the world back home and have an impact here in the United States and, specifically, in Kentucky? This chapter deals with the first two goals, and chapter 11 focuses on the third. After a short review of the Peace Corps' own evaluation of those first two goals, along with several Kentucky examples, our main focus in this chapter is on what volunteers told us in the interviews.

PEACE CORPS REPORTS

The Peace Corps has always evaluated its programs, beginning in the 1960s with Charles Peters, the first chief of evaluation and later founder and editor of the *Washington Monthly*. Peters sent writers like James Michener and Fletcher Knebel out to the field to write the early reports. Volunteers in Liberia were not necessarily happy to see themselves in Knebel's later novel about them, *The Zinzin Road*,[1] and Peters was not always appreciated by the Peace Corps country directors, although Tom Quimby, director in Liberia and later Kenya, admitted, "It's good to have a burr under the saddle."[2]

Twenty Years of Peace Corps offered the more usual overview of accomplishments. In terms of the first goal—providing technical assistance—the report cites studies documenting success in educational television in Colombia, tuberculosis control in Bolivia and Malawi, and smallpox eradication in Ethiopia.[3] Susan Simpson (Colombia 1967–1969) worked with that educational television project in Colombia, returned to rural Kentucky to teach, and became the teacher representative on the statewide Council on Education Technology in the early 1990s.[4] The same report quoted an analysis of the Peace Corps' role in education, which asserted: "What has been done is clearly remarkable for its sheer size, for its timeliness in helping to extend the coverage and improve the quality of nascent school systems, and for the early focus on development of human resources."[5]

By the end of 1965, 4,271 volunteers had already taught in fifteen African countries. The first 280 volunteers who arrived in Ethiopia in 1962 doubled the number of degree-holding secondary school teachers in the country and helped Ethiopia increase its secondary school enrollment by 37 percent from 1962 to 1964.[6] Harold Freeman (1965–1967), Ron Pelfrey (1966–1968), and Fred Cowan (1967–1969) contributed there later in that decade. A 1966 article in *Africa Today* pointed out how volunteers improved the quality of schooling through their attempts to go beyond the traditional rote learning to connect experience and education and to teach analysis and problem solving.[7]

Peace Corps teachers were not universally welcomed by host country citizens. Newspapers in Sierra Leone and Fiji complained about the bad influence of volunteer teachers on pronunciation and spelling (such as the American *program* instead of the British *programme*) and were also critical of the volunteers' appearance.[8] However, the complaints did not keep those Peace Corps programs from continuing or improving.

In terms of the second goal—a better understanding of Americans abroad—the *Twenty Years* report noted that initially skeptical American ambassadors lauded the Peace Corps' sensitive approach to foreign relations and touted the ability to speak local languages as one of the most distinctive features of Peace Corps service. It also stated, "Peace Corps volunteers have penetrated further into Third World societies than most previous Americans. In 1979 it was estimated that over 50 percent of volunteers lived in villages or small towns with 10,000 or less."[9] In the twenty-first century, some have argued that the Peace Corps ought to focus on building social capital in rising powers such as Brazil and Indonesia (the Peace Corps returned to Indonesia in 2010) rather than working in tiny countries such as Vanuatu and Cape Verde; likewise, since more than half the world's population lives in cities, more volunteers ought to be assigned to urban communities than to small towns and villages.[10] Although it is true that many earlier and some recently returned volunteers served in small towns and countries,

Aaron is an example of an early 2000s volunteer who served in a large city in China.

Today, performance and accountability reports are available on the Peace Corps Web site, providing statistics on how performance objectives have been met in relation to all three goals. The 2009 report includes as its first strategic goal: "Enhance the capacity of host country individuals, organizations, and communities to meet their skills needs." According to that report, 88 percent of volunteers surveyed said that their work transferred skills to host country individuals and organizations adequately or better. That same report included survey data from 528 host country individuals in four countries (Bulgaria, Burkina Faso, Nicaragua, and Romania): 99 percent of counterparts reported using knowledge or skills gained through their work with the Peace Corps in their work lives, and 69 percent used them daily; 95 percent reported they would definitely want to work with another Peace Corps volunteer; and 98 percent reported that the positive changes resulting from Peace Corps work were maintained to some degree after the volunteer's departure. As for meeting the second goal, 94 percent of volunteers responded that they had helped host country nationals gain a better understanding of the United States.[11]

In a December 2008 interview, then–Peace Corps director Ron Tschetter admitted, "We haven't done a good job of measuring our impact." He described a new five-year plan that includes measurements for "what we are doing, who we are touching, how we are impacting people."[12] The evidence we present here is anecdotal rather than quantitative, and volunteers were modest about their achievements.

RETURNED VOLUNTEERS TALK ABOUT IMPACT

In contrast to 1960s rhetoric about volunteers being change agents,[13] almost all the volunteers we interviewed would probably agree with the sentiments in a letter from Redeagzi, an Ethiopian. The letter was attached to a 1969 memorandum to Peace Corps staff from the regional director for Africa. Redeagzi wrote: "It is not our wish that volunteers change our country. We want to do that. The kind of help we want from volunteers is the encouraging of local initiative, and where it does not exist, creating it. We do not need much help, but just a little at a time. After all, development is a chain reaction which creates its own trend and the volunteer is requested and required only to make a start."[14] So a little help might be enough; in fact, it might even be best.

Caroyl Reid (Philippines 1964–1966) said it took her "ten years to sit down and say, 'You know, I did leave something behind. I did have some kind of positive influence on some individuals.' But there are not great monuments that I built." Bill Sweigart (Liberia 1967–1970) "provided services as a good teacher, as a cultural liaison, sharing experiences, sharing stories." And he enjoyed writing a play with a Liberian teacher based on a Gbande folktale and producing it for their school.

Joyce Miller (Chile 1964–1966) hoped that after "working with the men and some of the women, they realized that they could do things, they could pull themselves up. They knew that I had no fear. That I would talk to the governor, I would talk to the mayor, and carry their complaints. They eventually would come with me, and they would do the talking and get what they wanted. They could do it. That's it." And that's the "little" help the Ethiopian letter writer was talking about.

The tension and debate between Peace Corps work as technical assistance and Peace Corps work as relationship building (described in the earlier chapter on jobs) reverberates in a discussion about impact, too. Elizabeth Greene, just back from Niger when she was interviewed in 2005, concluded:

Hopefully, I touched some people's lives in my village. Development work is hard. It's very slow. You don't see results right away. And I've always believed that building things is not the way to go in Peace Corps. We lost small projects assistance funding from USAID, one of the biggest funding sources for volunteers in Niger. It was kind of an issue because volunteers were freaking out about what are we going to do. Our country director responded by printing an article written by another country director saying, "Don't think you have to build memorials to yourself." That article really put my experience in perspective and affirmed what I had always been trying to do. The biggest impact you're going to have is on people's lives. I did a couple training projects, and I don't really know how lasting those are. I taught people in my village a lot about America and about me, and that's all I can ask for. I think Niger has a great view of Americans because of Peace Corps probably. They're a 90 percent Muslim country, and they're not hostile at all to Americans.

Kay Roberts (Ecuador 1982–1984) said, "I think many volunteers—and I'm certainly one of them—tended to focus more on the technical aspect of our volunteer assignment and the Peace Corps goal that is supposed to be measurable: Did you provide technical assistance? And the part of Peace Corps that's equally important but so much harder to measure is: Are people learning about the United States through you? And are you learning about other countries through your experience? Clearly that was happening, but it's a lot harder to actually count."

Of course, volunteers often couldn't be sure of their impact. Ashley Netherton (Senegal 2003–2005) said: "I wondered as I was leaving if I had any impact because so many projects fail. And you get excited about doing a project and then the goats eat all of your trees, and all this hard work is down the drain. And being a female is tough because they're not used to listening to a woman tell them to do anything. Then a couple months after I was home, my brother [in her Senegalese family] called me on the phone in Kentucky—I can't believe he did it because it must have cost him a fortune—to let me know they had just planted some more trees in the village. He did it with some guys on his own."

Sometime impact just takes a while. Older volunteer Lettie Heer (Senegal 2001–2003) returns to her Senegalese village for several months each year and built her own house there. By 2010 she could report that there were seventy students and four teachers in the village school, for which she had built two classrooms. Three village students had gone on to secondary school—one girl and two boys.

THE JOB'S IMPACT ON HOST COUNTRY

Several volunteers talked about the specific results of their jobs. For example, Rachel Savane (Guinea 1990–1992) and Debra Schweitzer (Mali 1993–1996) facilitated the building of health centers in their villages. Carolyn Cromer (Morocco 1992–1995) thought teaching people about contraceptive use was her most successful program, and Elizabeth Greene (Niger 2003–2005) helped organize midwife training. Marianna Colten (Ecuador 1981–1983) worked with parents to start a kindergarten. Glen Payne (Gabon 1989–1992) was pleased that his school construction program trained village workers who could move on to their own job sites.

One program with very concrete results trained thirty-six

young female Peace Corps volunteers in 1969, including Charlene McGrath (Afghanistan 1969–1971), as vaccinators to join teams of male Afghans as part of a World Health Organization campaign to vaccinate women and children against smallpox. Their story is told in the 2008 film *Once in Afghanistan*. As their Peace Corps training director Kristina Engstrom concludes in the film: "They were part of something unique in human history, the eradication of a disease."

Working in agriculture, Sally Spurr (Ecuador 1975–1977) knew that her intensive gardening project had been successful because "everybody did the raised beds wherever they were." Another agriculture volunteer, William Salazar (Guatemala 1972–1973), had some success in organic farming—a lot of composting and getting farmers to grow beans between the cornstalks. But William was most proud of his secondary project: "Building the basketball court, which really was a lot of fun getting a lot of different people involved and then setting up the basketball team. I think that was probably the most important thing I left in Guatemala."

Audrey Horrall (Zambia 2000–2002) still gets letters from farmers in her village. "They're definitely still fish farming. Their ponds are still going. There's a volunteer who replaced me in a different location but the same general area. He's opened up a new area of fish farming. At least with the core group of farmers I worked with, they were convinced of the benefit and indicated to me that it was definitely something that had helped their lives, either just having that extra food/protein available or being able to make that extra little bit of money for school fees. I really got the sense that these farmers felt it was a worthwhile project, and this is a program that the Zambian government feels has been very beneficial to the rural areas."

Other volunteers explained the effects of their jobs more generally. Said Kay Roberts (Ecuador 1982–1984): "I was someone who could help them get their ideas together and develop project ideas and find the technical assistance in agriculture that they needed. People in the community would never have felt comfortable walking into a government office and saying, 'My corn isn't doing well and I don't know what's wrong with it.' They would never have taken a soil sample in and said, 'I need my soil tested,' so I tried to act as a bridge between the government entities that were there supposedly to provide services and the people who were reluctant to go ask for those services."

Lloyd Jones (Colombia 1973–1975) was proud of what his group had done: "A lot of the activities we did in terms of developing businesses and starting accounting co-ops and working farming co-ops are still going on. I've been back several times on business and talked to people in the accounting co-op that we started in 1973, and it's still there."

Robin Sither (Cameroon 1996–2000) said, "One of the great successes of Peace Corps in my part of Cameroon was introducing the cultivation of vegetables such as carrots, cabbage, market-type vegetables. As they've grown these crops, they've grown to enjoy them, and that's varied their diet, too."

The Peace Corps volunteers who were teachers usually felt good about their jobs. Nancy Dare (1965–1967) said: "Malaysia was one of the ideal places for Peace Corps. We were invited in for a specific purpose—to staff schools until they could train their own people. They were doing that at the time. We were doing some of the training, and when they got them trained, they asked us to leave." Similarly, Terry Anderson (Ghana 1965–1967) said: "I felt really good about my experience and the job I had because I knew we were filling a real gap and that having experienced, knowledgeable teachers was something that Ghana really needed." Don Stosberg (Malawi 1965–1966) explained that the Peace Corps was supplying about half the secondary school teachers in the country. He also remembered Malawi's first national track meet, where half the coaches were Peace Corps volunteers. Ron Pelfrey (Ethiopia 1966–1968) returned to his town five years later and saw his headmaster. He asked how his tenth-grade students had done on the national exam and learned they had scored number one in the country, beating even the American school.

"At my school, with my students and fellow teachers, I think I did make a great impact," Maurice White (Afghanistan 1974–1976) said. "They were exposed to an American for the first time. They were exposed to some different ways of thinking, some American customs and politics. And I know for a fact that many boys learned a fair amount of English because of my teaching." Capp Yess (Fiji 1982–1984) said, "Most of my students were able to take the experience with me teaching in the upper program and pass tests at a level where they went on to a professional school. The first year, one of my students got the only A grade on the whole island—which means they were better than any student at the elite government school."

Jules Delambre (Cameroon 1965–1967) concluded: "The students I taught got introduced to algebra and got acquainted with an American. The faculty were all Cameroonians, and I got to know them and they got to know me." Bill Miller (Dominican Republic 1968–1970) found teaching more rewarding than the community development work of his first year. "During my second year at the Catholic University in Santiago, I think I made more of an impact working with students in social research and with their field placements."

Teacher Leigh White (Bulgaria 2001–2003) quickly learned that "making individual connections with individual people" was most important. She modeled enthusiasm and promptness and different ways of teaching for fellow teachers. Her students now have a strong background in English. In addition, the local community saw "who an American is and what an American is like." The morning she was interviewed, Leigh had been on the phone with a fellow teacher in Bulgaria to wish her a happy birthday. The teacher told her about a successful fund-raiser that allowed the school to buy a van to pick up children in surrounding villages.

Michael Geneve (Mozambique 2003–2005) was pleased that, "after two years of these kids learning English with me, there were fifteen of them who spoke English. They could come over to my house, and we would speak English together. That was just a really great feeling." He had a "bricks and mortar" impact as well. Using his architecture background, he designed a library for his school, worked with the school director to write a proposal, and got approval for $7,500 from USAID to build it.

George Miller (Washington staff, Tonga 1979–1982) summarized his view of the Peace Corps volunteer in terms of both doing the job and working with people. He called it "an American brain on the loose. We're not locked in to the way things work. We collectively and individually seem to walk in and look at a mess and say how can we fix it, and proceed to do it. We're just not satisfied. And this is in a village in South Africa or Asia, and now villages in Eastern Europe, a real valuable thing. That brain gets toted around by the individual Peace Corps volunteers, who go in as experts in their field, but then they expand immediately into different fields." George believed that volunteers have an impact because "we sit down and talk, it's nose to nose. It's not a tool of the government, not a tool of anybody except this individual. They're an integral part of the community as individuals."

IMPACT ON HOST COUNTRY AS AMERICANS

Sarah Payne (The Gambia 1989–1991) came down on the side of personal relationships as being most important. She remembered: "Because I was there when the first Gulf War erupted and people were very scared, I said, 'There's lots of people like me. Yes, I'm a *touba*, a white person. But we all eat, we all need basic clothing.' The math I taught? The woodworking project? The donated books? Not a lasting impact. I think it's really the personal relationships that you develop."

Both Terry Anderson (Ghana 1965–1967) and Kay Roberts (Ecuador 1982–1984) saw an impact beyond their jobs; what mattered was who they were as Americans. Terry pointed out that Americans went to Ghana without any of the colonial baggage. "I was told by several people they like the way Americans deal with other people—they're honest, friendly, with a lot of goodwill." Kay said, "I would like to think they had a more realistic view of America and Americans because I had been there. I like to think I was able to change those stereotypical ideas from the three television programs in Ecuador at that time—*Dallas, Three's Company*, and *Daniel Boone*. I gave them an opportunity to know firsthand what a particular American was like and to distinguish what they would read in the newspapers and see on television from what a real live American was all about."

Many returned volunteers mentioned their impact as ordinary good Americans who were there to respect the people, to learn, to care. Angel Rubio (Costa Rica 1971–1973) said, "We acted right as people." Debra Schweitzer (Mali 1993–1996) said, "I'm just a regular person with the same hopes and dreams they have for their children." Kathleen McFarland (Jordan 1999–2001) showed Jordanians that "there are Americans out there who can be respectful of their culture and their religion. They saw a woman who could live on her own without her father, and I was still a good woman. Maybe that will change their attitudes."

Teacher Dianne Bazell (Zaire [Democratic Republic of Congo] 1975–1977) was "someone from another country who wasn't there to either avoid the draft or preach to them, [someone] who said she was there to learn and who really appreciated everything they were doing. I think that was a stunning shock. I think that had a powerful message about Americans." Joan Moore (Swaziland 1979–1981) said, "I think that one thing I left behind was a white person who wasn't racist, who cared about and loved them as people. I think that was a big hurdle for the students and my friends."

"They saw a different kind of European [or American]," Phil Dare (Malaysia 1965–1967) pointed out, someone "who would go to the movies with them and afterwards come back to a coffee shop and talk. Sometimes we would get a *National Geographic* and show them pictures of things back in the States. And you'd try to get pictures from home of people playing in the snow. I guess if we made any difference it would have been just making their world a little bigger."

Ken Wilson (Malawi 1997–1998) showed his villagers an American different from those they might have heard about or met before. "I was very conservative," he said, "and I was very quiet. I was thirty-three, I wasn't married, and I didn't have any children. I taught the women in my health center how to make tortillas with an empty Coca-Cola bottle from the bottle store. Coming from Texas, I made tortillas three times a week because they kept. They didn't spoil like the stale, hard yellow buns because it was basically flatbread."

Michael Geneve (Mozambique 2003–2005) was different because, in addition to Portuguese, he learned Xitswa, a Bantu language similar to Shangana and other languages spoken in southern Africa. "If I really wanted to integrate into my community," he said, "I needed to learn at least some of the dialect and mix with the people who didn't speak Portuguese. You're going to just bond with people a whole lot more if you learn the dialect. So I would go around town and practice. I asked one of the [Mozambican] English teachers if he could show me how to conjugate the verbs, tell me about pronouns, and I'd take care of the vocabulary on my own. And I would walk around the town and write vocabulary in my little book and study it." Michael became known as the dialect-speaking guy. "I had a blast with that language. It was great to practice speaking a language and then great to interact with the people."

"There are all types of people in American culture—that was a new idea to a lot of people," Jenny Howard (Gabon 2000–2002), said. "You know, a lot of people thought I was crazy—you have a college degree from America and you're sitting here pounding *feuilles de manioc* with us?" She was pleased to learn after her return to the United States that one of the high school teachers with whom she had developed an ecology club had organized an environmental scholarship named after her. As William Salazar (Guatemala 1972–1973) explained, "Peace Corps, on a one-to-one level, gets people to understand what Americans are like and that Americans are from A to Z. They can be black Americans, they can be someone like me who is a child of migrants, immigrants, and then they can be white kids."

Philip Curd (Guinea 1963–1965) perceived the opportunity for Guineans to get to know Americans as a positive thing, allowing them to see how different Americans were from the communists in that country in the 1960s. Serving forty years later, Blake Stabler (Russia 2000–2002) said, "There are people who decided after Peace Corps that they really liked Americans based on you and the one other volunteer who came to visit you once and your parents, who were there for two days in the summer. They like Americans now." He pointed out the contrast to Russians' previously held ideas: "a complete distrust of America as the enemy during Soviet times, and afterwards just not knowing what to think." He also thought it was "very valuable to have this set of people in the United States who are comfortable in areas where most Americans—and where lot of people even from these host countries—are not comfortable. The central government of Russia is clearly uncomfortable with these country hicks in the Volga Valley. I think having a comfort level is such a valuable skill for our country because there are opportunities in these parts of the world. Growth in the developing world is where a lot of international business expansion is going to be."

After serving in another formerly communist country, Mimi Gosney (Slovakia 2000–2002) reflected: "I think Peace Corps had a very positive impact. During communism they didn't know a lot about Americans, except what the communists wanted them to know, so there was a whole generation of people that had never had any ties with the West. After 9/11 my neighbors and people I did business with would come up and say, 'We're so sorry.' It was amazing. I think we've made a difference."

A LITTLE HELP AND CHANGE IN SOUTH AFRICA

A final story illustrates how the Peace Corps' American "brain" described by George Miller can help a little, as Redeagzi suggested, by coming up with small ideas—some that work, and some that don't—and developing personal relationships that lead to a little change in a nation that, like ours, has a long history of serious racial issues.

Harry Siler (South Africa 2001–2003), a retired architect and professor of architecture at Howard University who grew up in Williamsburg, Kentucky, was a support person to five primary schools in Limpopo province. He began by visiting all five schools at his assigned site in Mahlaba Cross, sitting in the back of classes in reception grade (kindergarten) to sixth grade. "I'd sit in whatever chair, no matter what size," he recalled, "and in many cases there was no furniture. There would be a teacher usually lecturing. I would have my pad and try to take notes. The kids would be copying off the board. There was no paper, so I went and asked businesses for scrap paper, and then I would come to a school with a backpack of scrap paper and give it to teachers. I was an absolute failure at institutionalizing an organizational structure that would allow a teacher to go to a shop on a regular basis and pick up the scrap paper."

However, his library idea was more successful. "On my trips to Pretoria, I went to a flea market and bought bargain books, and I would go around to the schools and distribute ten books to each classroom. Then I introduced the idea of a library. I discovered in the trash at a ShopRite grocery about sixty old rubber baskets and took two to each classroom. The teacher would write 'library' on them, and then I brought books. I subscribed to *Time* and several other magazines while I was there, and I would move those magazines around school by school to be in the teachers' lounges. Of course, I had professionally been getting things done for a long time, so I was able to help the schools get things done, get things planned, built. I was of some help to the high school because I helped them plan and provided the drawing so they could get a grant to build a science building and a library."

Harry also described a particular event in which he linked one of the Mahlaba Cross schools with a school in a neighboring town.

I went to a primary school in the nearby Afrikaner farmers' town of Tzaneen and found a man named Victor Rijnen absolutely waiting on me to show up—an Afrikaner trying to figure out how to have his white kids make some sort of a connection with African kids. So I organized every one of my classrooms in Ponani School to be represented by three students to visit—first grade with first grade, second grade with second grade—and spend the day at this primary school. I wanted to get folks to rub up against each other, let folks see you can survive, people are kind, you don't have to be afraid. Vic, the principal, supplied their giant bus, and about fifty kids and teachers and administrators went. We were part of the assembly, and then we went to classes. I couldn't quit with that, so after school, when the Afrikaner kids went home, we went to the Tsongan museum near the school and then to the public library. These kids hadn't been to Tzaneen, and it's fifteen minutes away. The most memorable thing happened as we were riding back: a fifth- or sixth-grade girl said, "Can anybody go to the library?" It was glorious to say, "Yes."

In the seven years since he returned to Kentucky, Harry has kept in contact with Shalati, the principal of Ponani School, including trying, via e-mail, to help her learn to write grants. Once she reported that there had been a meeting where participants admitted that people had died of HIV/AIDS. She had told them, "Harry would be so happy." He had pleaded at village meetings that teachers needed to be able to talk about HIV/AIDS. He has also continued to send books, sometimes multiple copies with a teacher's guide. In 2010 Harry worked with the International Book Project in Lexington, Kentucky, to send a sea container of more than 33,000 books to the five village primary schools, the two village secondary schools, and the primary school in neighboring Tzaneen.

Chapter 11

Citizens of the World
for the Rest of Our Lives

I'm a citizen of the world, thanks to the Peace Corps.
            —Tom Boyd (Colombia 1964–1966)

My real Peace Corps job was the rest of my life. You can work the
rest of your life to try to help people understand each other.
            —Richard Parker (Côte d'Ivoire 1973–1974,
                                    Morocco 1976–1978)

SIX VOLUNTEERS IN FIVE DECADES

Martin and Patsy Tracy (Turkey 1965–1967)

Martin began by talking about the Peace Corps' influence on his and
Patsy's professional career choices.

Political science came out of that for me, as did Patsy's social work, and
then eventually I went into international service in the Social Security
Administration. I traveled all over the world with the International Social
Security Administration. We were in Geneva for two years. Then I got
a doctorate in international social work and taught at the University of
Iowa and Southern Illinois University and finally came back to Kentucky
to be associate dean for research in the School of Social Work at the
University of Kentucky. Now I'm retired back in Murray, where I grew
up, but still doing training in southeastern Europe using models that
are community based and sustainable and get us back to Günaydın
Günaydın's message about the water [in chapter 7]. It all sort of comes
together. So Peace Corps was profound.

285

I think our perspectives about relationships with other parts of the world and how other societies live have been strongly influenced by our Peace Corps experience. I had the opportunity to do studies in Malaysia and China and Costa Rica when I was at Iowa and at Carbondale. When I go into those cultures I'm there to see things from their perspective and not to impose my Western views or judge their culture by using the Western world as a benchmark. Like a lot of people, I think the biggest impact of returned Peace Corps volunteers is that we have come back and gone into so many different professions and influenced community development, influenced policies.

Patsy used her Peace Corps experience when she taught English as a second language in Chicago and Washington, DC, after returning from Turkey. She later got a PhD in education and taught at the university level until she retired. Now she and Martin work together on international consulting. They also volunteer in Murray, raising thousands of dollars for cancer drives and for the United Way, helping settle families displaced by Hurricane Katrina, and hosting international friends. "So here we are at the end of our life doing the same thing we did when were young."

Rona Roberts (Philippines 1973–1975)

For me, first of all, I found the kind of work I wanted to do for the rest of my life—to work in a developmental way in a communications field and to work on positive and progressive interests. When I came home I began working as an organizer, which is what I had learned to do. I got a job organizing new legal services programs—three in Kentucky. It was kind of like that Philippine community development work, and I liked working with people who were passionate about social change. Then I was a consultant for legal services and helped start the last two or three legal services programs in the country and organize new state support programs for legal services in about thirteen other states. Eventually I got a doctorate in organizational communication—how organizations are put together and how they function as cultures with their own language and value sets. I've been the organizer of many, many community efforts, but they have come closer and closer to home so that now I am completely absorbed in neighborhood-based organizing work [in Lexington].

Professionally, Rona has been the Roberts half of Roberts & Kay, Inc. (RKI) for twenty-five years. She and her business partner, Steve Kay, married twenty-two years ago. RKI, which is dedicated to advancing democratic practices in workplaces and communities, provides organization development, facilitation, and research services for nonprofits, foundations, and government groups. Nationally, Rona and Steve have worked with groups such as Everyday Democracy and Southern Sustainable Agriculture Research and Education. In Kentucky they have worked extensively with citizen action groups, including the Prichard Committee for Academic Excellence, and public engagement projects such as Fayette County Public Schools' 2020 Vision. In 2009 Rona and Steve began hosting Monday night cornbread suppers at their home every week as a way to encourage the consumption of locally produced food and the building of community.

Other aspects of Rona's life have also been affected by her Peace Corps experience.

I saw the value, like other volunteers who were in Asia, of being happy, and I became committed in my life to making choices that would make me happy and other people happy. I haven't had any other international experience, other than the visit back to the Philippines, but I'm a supporter of international efforts like the Foster Plan for Children and Save the Children and Catholic Relief Service, and I've gotten particularly excited about and interested in the Heifer Project. I'm more skeptical about how I look at the world and possibilities for goodness in the world. Recently my great effort is to try to figure out how to be realistic. I believe in a very mild way that Peace Corps has put a whole bunch of people in a whole lot of countries in touch with U.S. citizens who have a more global view of the world and a big heart, so they have more widespread knowledge about Americans. But the biggest difference is in how Peace Corps volunteers behave at home. The Peace Corps advocacy effort at home is still in its infancy and will become more important. I think and hope that.

Rebecca Roach (Liberia 1988–1989)

The impact on me was huge. I had never even flown before in my life. I had stayed within the tristate area of Ohio, Kentucky, and Tennessee. I learned so much about myself because everything that you are is questioned. When you live in a culture that may have completely different values than you do, you get to pick and choose what values you want to keep and throw away. My parents were very liberal and open-minded, but I think when I came back to the United States I looked at everything through different eyes. Living at a village level and having the events of a developing country shape your life in ways that you can't control, and being a very small person in a country that's sometimes out of control, makes you understand what people within that country feel like and what they're going through. When I hear about big events in small countries, I don't think about politicians there. I think about the women who are trying to nurse their children and take care of them. It made a huge impact on me. I realized I couldn't change the world.

Rebecca met her husband in graduate school; he was also studying international development at Ohio University. She worked in teacher training in Pakistan, Cambodia, and Thailand for the World Bank, USAID, and Save the Children, while her husband worked for Save the Children and UNHCR (the UN's refugee agency). "If I hadn't been in the Peace Corps," she said, "I don't think my son would have been born in Pakistan, and my daughter wouldn't have been born in Thailand. They are very open-minded people. My son wants to go into politics. My daughter is fascinated with China." When she and her husband returned to Kentucky, Rebecca worked for Save the Children and VISTA and then became an elementary teacher in eastern Kentucky. In 2008 she became the professional development associate for the 21st Century Educational Enterprise Center at Morehead State University. She said, "My role is so similar to the one I played in Liberia. I travel to schools and partner with teachers to improve instruction, and I also facilitate workshops." Rebecca described how she focused on social justice when she taught third grade: "I think that has to do with my Peace Corps experience. I had my kids—and I've done this with other teachers, too—do an activity from a program called 'Chocolate Economics.' It's about limited and unlimited trading. When we processed that activity, someone said, 'I don't think it's fair that she got a big Cadbury bar and I started out with just Hershey kisses, and the market was already flooded with Hershey kisses.' I said, 'Welcome to the real world. How do you think developing countries feel when they start out with Hershey kisses but they've got satellite television and see everybody with Cadbury bars?' Without my Peace Corps experience I wouldn't have drawn that connection between social justice and economics and made the point that the playing field is not level."

Rebecca began a doctoral program in fall 2009. Once her children are through college, she would like to learn French and go to Francophone Africa as a Peace Corps director or associate director.

Sarah Cross Oddo (Jamaica 1993–1995)

Because of Oghale's Peace Corps jobs, the Oddo family lived in Jordan, Swaziland, and Fiji over a ten-year period. When the family returned from Fiji in January 2008, their three sons were eight, six, and two. Sarah explained, "It's been a fantastic way to live because we don't have a lot of the things other kids are used to here. Fiji was sort of the best for us as a family, because I think in America you can get so caught up in this competitive drive with your children—wanting them to be the best in school in this activity and that activity, and making sure they have the finest education. In Fiji I started to get a little caught up in worrying, is the school good enough? Finally I realized the Fijian people are just the gentlest, sweetest people. He's [her oldest son] getting something here that he could never get in America. All of them had a great experience there, just playing on the beaches and going to Fijian villages and running around with Fijian kids. I want to keep going other places. I definitely don't feel like I'm done living abroad."

In terms of the impact on herself, Sarah said, "I'm more aware of the human aspect of the news. For example, having lived in Jordan, when I see a family's home was bombed in Iraq, I can picture what that family was like and know what they were sitting around there eating. I can put faces on those people. When I hear about AIDS orphans, I know what they look like because of living in Swaziland. I know the look they have in their eyes."

Sarah has shared her experiences with others, too. "I've written letters to classrooms from various countries and corresponded with family members of friends and acquaintances who were considering joining the Peace Corps. I think one of the most important things about Peace Corps is coming back and teaching Americans about other places in the world."

After their return from Fiji in 2008, Oghale got a job working for USAID in Iraq, where he spent two years without his family. For their Kentucky home, the family bought and moved into a house several doors away from Sarah's parents in Lexington. In spring 2010 the Oddos learned that their next posting—together—will be in Malawi.

Aaron Shraberg (China 2004–2006)

Aaron talked about gaining "a lot of respect for the Chinese. And I ended up coming away with a tremendous sense of interest in China, interest in Chinese culture and language, but also more understanding of what went on in the country before I was there and what's going to go on after I leave. I feel like my perspective was generally broadened. Being in a country like that . . . I said before I went that people do things differently, and that's okay, but now I've seen it in action. And there's actually some things I didn't agree with and I didn't think were okay. I would complain to Chinese about them sometimes, and they would agree with me. So being an impetus for change, teaching me how to be outspoken but not offensive, to be proactive but not in a disrespectful way—that is something China taught me." Aaron also learned "how to choose where I want to be the most effective, how to prioritize things and focus on certain things, to feel your limits. It taught me how to be a good public speaker. It gave me confidence, just like it gave my students confidence. Ultimately, it made me a more experienced person."

Aaron concluded: "The world is bigger than just this place we live in. And the people who can institute change? I think Peace Corps volunteers are some of the most informed people, some of the most culturally sensitive, and can be very well suited to helping to keep the communication between cultures open and to teach people about other cultures and also to help communities get where they want to be in their own way. I'm glad I went to China and that I can tell people a little bit about that. And I'm also glad when I was in China that I was able to tell people about our country."

Aaron completed a master's in Asian studies at George Washington University in August 2010 and was in China on fellowships during the summers of 2009 and 2010.

The six volunteers in five decades make clear how important the Peace Corps experience was to the rest of their lives. They discovered their lifelong careers, like Martin, Patsy, and Rona. They became interested in continuing to learn about other cultures, like Aaron. They taught their students and their families about other countries, like Rebecca and Sarah.

As in the previous chapter, we first cite Peace Corps reports, this time on the third goal of the Peace Corps bringing the world back home with some Kentucky examples. Then we focus on returned volunteers' explanations of how the Peace Corps affected the careers they chose, their view of the world, and their personal lives and those of their families. Next, volunteers talk about their contributions to the United States and to Kentucky in particular. The final sections profile a Kentuckian serving Kentucky and a Kentuckian serving in Uganda and describe Kentucky returned volunteers as a "cosmopolitan community."

PEACE CORPS REPORTS

Over the decades, the Peace Corps as an agency has focused most on the first and second goals of making an impact through jobs and as Americans in host countries. However, several directors have talked about the third goal of bringing the world back home. In 2010 director Aaron Williams listed that goal, as well as growth of the Peace Corps and the creation of a new Office of Innovation, as his own three goals.[1] Earlier, in 1981, Peace Corps director Dick Celeste (later governor of Ohio) told volunteers: "There is a third goal, and in many ways it may be the most important. . . . It's a sad fact that, despite modern technology, the United States remains culturally isolated from the rest of the world. In this sense, we ourselves are citizens of an underdeveloped nation."[2] Loret Ruppe, Celeste's successor and the longest-serving Peace Corps director, asserted in a 1988 speech to the National Press Club: "I know Peace Corps brings back an American who (in an electronic age) is user-friendly, literate, speaks the language, opens windows on the world."[3] In 1989 director Paul D. Coverdell funded a specific program, WorldWise Schools, to support the third goal. According to the 2009 performance and accountability report, 57 percent of volunteers participated in WorldWise Schools.[4] Volunteer Jenifer Payne (Gabon 1990–1992) was one of those, becoming a pen pal with students at the junior high she had attended in Somerset, Kentucky.

Associated with both the first and third goals, the Peace Corps Partnership Program encourages individuals and organizations to support community-initiated, volunteer-led projects. In 2009, 10,595 people were involved in that support, with U.S. donors contributing $1.7 million.[5] With money from the sale of a calendar created by the returned volunteers of Madison, Wisconsin, the Kentucky Returned Peace Corps Volunteers have supported Partnership projects over the years, such as painting a world map in a primary school in Mali, organizing an HIV/AIDS workshop in Nicaragua, and developing a computer lab in Costa Rica. In 2007 Kentucky returned volunteers and others gave more than $1,500 to the Slavery Memorial Project in Bangou, Cameroon, as a special memorial in honor of Jules Delambre (Cameroon 1965–1967).

Both WorldWise Schools and the Peace Corps Partnership Program are meant to educate Americans, especially schoolchildren, about the rest of the world. But from the beginning, the Peace Corps was expected to have impact on the government itself. In 1964 President Lyndon Johnson told governmental agency and department heads to hire returning Peace Corps volunteers, and within a year, the civil service had hired nearly a fourth of returned volunteers.[6] By 1981, at the twenty-year mark, 15 percent of returnees had taken positions with governmental organizations, fulfilling President Kennedy's hope that the Peace Corps would provide personnel to the Foreign Service and USAID.[7] In 1990 in Nepal, all the heads of all the U.S. civilian agencies, including the ambassador, had been Peace Corps volunteers.[8] At the Peace Corps' twenty-fifth anniversary in 1986, Peter McPherson, administrator of USAID, could point to himself and 500 other returned Peace Corps volunteers on the agency's staff and could cite cooperation between the Peace Corps and USAID in the field.[9] One of those returned volunteers who made USAID his career was Cecil McFarland (Micronesia 1972–1974, Philippines 1974–1976). In 2008 Joshua Mike (Nevis 2004–2006) took a job with the USAID, going to Thailand as his first post. George Miller (Washington staff 1979–1982), who traveled all over the world as director of overseas administrative support and was also acting director in Tonga for five months, said, "By the time I retired I could walk into an embassy anywhere in the world and be introduced around the table, and there's Willy Jones, Peace Corps volunteer, Tonga, or Sarah Smith, Peace Corps volunteer, Ecuador. They're there. Why? Because the Peace Corps volunteer can deal in foreign environments."

As well, returned volunteers have served in state governments and state agencies. For example, returned volunteers Terry Anderson (Ghana 1965–1967) and Lee Colten (Ecuador 1981) made their careers in the Division of Water in the Kentucky Natural Resources and Environmental Protection Cabinet, and in 2009 Jenny Howard (Gabon 2000–2002) joined that division to work in environmental education. Jeffrey Kell (Dominican Republic and Ecuador 1962–1963), Bill Miller (Dominican Republic 1968–1970), and Don Stosberg (Malawi 1965–1966) worked for the Legislative Research Commission.

The 1968 annual report highlighted the work of Bill Bridges (East Pakistan [Bangladesh] 1963–1965) in a four-page profile entitled "Small Miracles in Appalachia."[10] Bill, who was fifty when he joined Peace Corps, later got a job with the University of Kentucky Extension Service, doing the same thing he had done in the Peace Corps. He was a specialist in community development in Quicksand in Breathitt County.

According to *Twenty Years of Peace Corps*, 26 percent of 1960s returnees went into teaching, and 27 percent were employed by educational institutions in the 1970s. It concluded that, "perhaps the most exciting and profound impact of returned volunteers has been in the field of education," and "one of the primary benefits of the volunteers' sharing their experiences has been to take some of the fear and mystery out of the American view of the Third World."[11] Not surprisingly, given the percentage of volunteers who served as educators in the Peace Corps (still 35 percent in 2010), more than a third of the returned volunteers we interviewed found their calling back home to be in educational institutions. Many have taught in schools, colleges, and universities in subject areas ranging from Spanish and English as a second language to physics and theater. One example is Richard Bradshaw (Central African Republic 1977–1979), who became a professor of history at Centre College in Danville, Kentucky, in 1995. He continued to do research in Central African Republic and has taken students on trips there. He also opened a study abroad program in Mexico and in 2006 was a teaching and research Fulbrighter in Cameroon.

IMPACT ON VOLUNTEERS' CAREERS

Returned volunteers chose many different careers. Although education and government attracted more than half of our sample,

other volunteers joined businesses, and some became social workers, nurses, and lawyers, among other careers. Some returned volunteers talked about the relationship between their Peace Corps
experiences and their jobs. It was perhaps most obvious for those
whose careers took them back overseas, or for educators, but others
saw the relationship, too.

Sheila McFarland (Micronesia 1972–1974, Philippines 1974–
1976) said, "Peace Corps gave us a life of service overseas with the
federal government with USAID for twenty-six years. We feel like
we've seen it from the bottom, from the top, from the middle: Guyana, Guatemala, Kenya, Washington, DC, Egypt, Rwanda, Malawi."
Her husband Cecil added, "I would not have had a career in USAID
without Peace Corps. I went into those interviews having had four
years' overseas work, two languages, and a master's degree. Peace
Corps gave us an introduction to the rest of the world. I can't imagine
how one could sit back here and use the *Lexington Herald Leader*
and CNN as your window to the world—it's so limiting. Overseas
experience provided understanding of things like the serious impact
of HIV/AIDS, which you cannot pick up in the press, the impact of
high child mortality, lack of women's rights, influences of religions
and cultures, why some ethnic groups do certain things. We keep up
with host nationals from Guyana, Guatemala, Kenya, Philippines.
This morning's e-mail was from Uganda, Congo, Kenya." Cecil continued to do short-term work for USAID after retiring in Anderson
County, Kentucky, where he and Sheila grew up.

Oghale Oddo (Jamaica 1994–1996) explained that "one of the
reasons I decided to go back to the Peace Corps [as an adminis-
trator] was because I had enjoyed my experience so much and I
thought this is something I would love to do—go out, see the world,
and help other people who come in to become volunteers as well. In
1999 Sarah and I went to Jordan." Oghale stayed there until 2002,
when the program was suspended a few months prior to the war
in Iraq. In 2002 he went to Swaziland to set up that post again; it
had been suspended in 1997 but was restarted because Swaziland
had the second highest prevalence of HIV/AIDS in the world. From
2005 to early 2008 he was country director in Fiji; then he joined
USAID, working for two years in Iraq.

Two other returned volunteers found that the Peace Corps
turned their career goals toward international development. Former graphic artist Michael Geneve (Mozambique 2003–2005) said,

"I want to continue working with development." Michael completed a master's degree in community and leadership development in the University of Kentucky College of Agriculture, doing a thesis based on a community development course he led in Banda Aceh in Indonesia. He wants to work with an international nongovernmental organization. Blake Stabler (Russia 2000–2002) said, "The entire idea that I'd work in international development or that I'd be interested in agriculture as a way to make money for especially marginalized rural people is kind of weird." His interest in solving the problems of rural poverty evolved from the time he spent as a Peace Corps volunteer in rural Russia. After working for the U.S. Department of Agriculture for several years, including a return to Russia, he completed a master's degree at the Patterson School for International Diplomacy and Commerce at the University of Kentucky. "I really like going out to farms in these remote places and talking to people about what it is they actually want to do with their enterprises, and what they want to grow, and what they see as the future and trying to see what I can do to help out with that."

For several returned volunteers, the Peace Corps helped them decide what kind of work to pursue in the United States. Elaine Collins (Micronesia 1989–1991) said, "I realized I wanted to work with people and went back and got my degree in social work. I have more of a global perspective on things and can see the bigger picture a lot more than people I work with or talk to. Having had a lot of time to just think and being in a very different place has been a gift, and the way I work with kids now is different because of having those experiences. Most of the kids I work with in New York City do not come from the culture I came from, but I have a perspective that I can learn from them." She worked for the Fresh Air camps and then began working with a charter school.

Cori Hash (Zimbabwe 1999–2000) called the Peace Corps' impact on her life "immense, even though it was cut really short. It led me to my career. I'd always wanted to do international work, but it turned me back to issues of poverty and human rights in my own country. There's an enormous poverty rate and a lot of people being denied rights within our own country. Immigration work is a nice compromise, in that I'm working with the American legal system and helping people escape from economic hardship and persecution." Cori attended law school in Texas, spent a semester at a Brazilian law school, and also went to Cuba with Global Exchange.

She came to Lexington to work for Maxwell Street Legal Clinic. In the interview, she reported that "several months ago a minister from the very same place I did my training in Zimbabwe walked into our office, and we helped him fill out an application to get his green card."

Several returned volunteers found careers that linked them directly to the countries where they served. One was Bob Olson (Turkey 1963–1965), a longtime professor in the University of Kentucky History Department and a specialist on the Middle East. "Being in Peace Corps introduced you to international politics. I got introduced not only to the Turks but also to the Kurds, who subsequently became my academic career. I got a fellowship to study Turkish as one of the happy recipients of the National Defense Language Act. I left graduate school with no debt, thanks to Peace Corps. I owe Peace Corps a lot. Peace Corps interested me in another country, a country that happened to be a Muslim country, a country in which in two years I was able to become fairly familiar with the language. It ended up choosing my profession and so was the most significant thing in my life." Bob's commentary about Middle East policy often appears in the *Lexington Herald Leader,* and he has spoken regularly to local groups. His most recent book is *The Goat and the Butcher: Nationalism and State Formation in Kurdistan-Iraq since the Iraqi War.*

Another person whose job is directly connected to her host country is Sara Todd (Armenia 2001–2003). As Sara's post–Peace Corps AmeriCorps experience in Alaska was ending, "friends in Louisville who I had served in the Peace Corps with said, 'Well, you could come to Louisville. We have a lot of connections because we work in the nonprofit community, and we could probably find you a job.' My friend called me a week or two later and said, 'You will not believe this, but I just met this guy who works for an Armenian development organization in Kentucky.'" So Sara came to Louisville to work for the Jinishian Memorial Program at the national headquarters of the Presbyterian Church (PCUSA), which does development and relief work with Armenians and in Armenia. When she was interviewed in 2006, she had been back to Armenia six times that year and had traveled to Lebanon and Syria, too. "One of my dad's concerns was that I was going to learn a language I would never use, and here I am, using Armenian almost every day. One of our big community development projects in Armenia is with an organization I worked with during Peace Corps. We're doing a big project in Goris [her Peace

Corps site]. I've been to Goris a couple of times with the job to work with some of these people."

Richard Parker (Côte d'Ivoire 1973–1974, Morocco 1976–1978), who now teaches English to people all over the world through the Internet, went back to his Peace Corps experience to explain why he took a "fundamentally different direction" from being an electronics technician to being a teacher. "Seven months into my experience in the Ivory Coast, I had a dream in which I burst out speaking fluently in French, like a dam bursting, and it rushed through me like glossolalia, like automatic writing, only verbally. That was the key: that after seven months, this language was incubating on a very deep, subconscious level. An experience like this had a lot to do with my later career teaching English as a second language because it gave me the really authentic experience of what students go through when they have to go to another country or come here and learn English." Richard got his bachelor's degree at age forty-nine and then a master's degree from Murray State University, where his wife, Ann Neelon (Senegal 1978–1979), is a professor. In his 2006 interview, he said he saw himself as fulfilling the "role of an international bridge."

Marianna Colten (Ecuador 1981–1983) switched from special education and got a master's degree in Spanish literature at the University of Kentucky. She taught Spanish at Good Shepherd School in Frankfort. "I wouldn't have been able to do that had it not been for my training with Peace Corps in Ecuador. It opened up a whole new job market and has enabled me to keep up on my language skills. I started a project called Global Village Day at my school, which has become an annual event. Every year I keep thinking, 'Maybe I won't do this next year.' But then the kids say, 'When's Global Village Day?'" In fall 2010, Marianna began teaching at Winburn Middle School in Lexington.

Many educators talked about the relevance of Peace Corps to their jobs. A theater professor at the University of Kentucky, Andrew Kimbrough (Sri Lanka 1984–1986) found the Peace Corps helpful in applying for a teaching job. "One of the questions I was asked was, 'How do you think you'd be able to support our efforts with multiculturalism?' Well, how much time do you have? One of the degrees I earned overseas was with the Peace Corps. My wife is from China. I might be some middle-class, middle-aged white guy, but the Peace Corps puts all of us ahead of the curve in that respect. We just have the global multicultural perspective that I think makes us much more compassionate and understanding and aware of cross-cultural differences and difficulties. I think it's made me a much more tolerant and understanding person. I think that fifteen months made me bicultural." Andrew has worked on a film project in Mexico and Argentina. He did his master of fine arts degree in theater in Moscow. He teaches a course in Asian theater that includes the *bharata natyam,* an Indian dance form he first became acquainted with in Sri Lanka. With his wife, who is from Shanghai and whom he met while doing his PhD in theater, he taught in China for a year, and they visit family there every year. Andrew concluded: "What I learned in fifteen months with the Peace Corps far exceeded whatever I learned in four years at university. [It was] just an enriching, maturing, life-altering, really fantastic experience. And it's always great conversation."

For Kristen Perry (Lesotho 1999–2001), a professor in the College of Education at the University of Kentucky, wanting to maintain her connection to Africa led to tutoring Sudanese Lost Boys, "and that ended up leading into my research." She did her dissertation at Michigan State on "what's called literacy brokering, where people don't understand some aspect of the text, so they go ask somebody to help them with it. Usually people think about it as just translating, but I found that was not the issue. The big issue was that these were genres the parents had not ever encountered in Sudan, and suddenly in the U.S. they had to use them—like phone books. Or the schools would send home order forms for yearbooks, and the parents thought they were study guides. I thought I was going to go back to Lesotho and do some research there, but this was such a wonderful opportunity that I could see so much need for, because we have more and more refugees coming into the country, and we need to understand that we need to help our schools figure out how to work with these children." Kristen's dissertation won an award for its contribution to adult literacy research.

Kristen credits the Peace Corps for helping her define what she wanted to study.

I knew I wanted to look at literacy. And I knew I wanted to look at culture and how that impacted. One of the things that always stuck out in my mind is this story: I was sitting on the bus, and I greeted an old man in Sesotho. He was so amazed that I could speak some Sesotho, and then he said, "Well, that's because Sesotho is easy." And I said, "Well, I don't think it's easy." And he said, "No, it's easy. I can prove it to you. Even little babies can learn how to speak Sesotho, but you have to go to school to learn how to speak English." It was beliefs like "English is hard" that really made me want to study literacy and culture and understand why this is happening. I was also surprised to see someone standing in line at the bank reading a romance novel in Lesotho, because people there didn't read for pleasure. That was not something they valued, the way we do, and yet they were very functionally literate. So it was those sorts of experiences that made me think I really need to figure out how culture impacts literacy development.

Returned Peace Corps volunteers became high school teachers, too.[12] For several decades the chair of a high school social studies department in Lexington, Bob Leupold (Indonesia and Thailand 1963–1965) explained that he learned from the Peace Corps, as well as his Vietnam experiences and his doctoral studies, to see things in a broader context and to teach that way.

For example, when we talk about early American history, we read a book about John Winthrop and talk about his idea of a city set on a hill. I take that and expand it. Do Americans still think of themselves as a city set on a hill? What implications does that have? I pull down an old map with the U.S. in the middle and Eurasia split. That leads into geography. The students have the problem of not knowing where Africa is, let alone Sierra Leone. When we talk about exploration, I ask why, if Europe was on the east coast, China wasn't on the west coast. We talk about the Chinese thinking they were the center of the earth, the middle kingdom. We talk about our ethnocentrism and some of the dangers of seeing the world that way. The injection of a worldview is constant. I stress that American culture is not the only culture. When some student has his feet up on the desk pointing toward me, I point out that pointing the sole of your foot toward someone is a deep insult in some cultures. I show how you call someone in Indonesia—the hand turned down. You only call animals the other way. I end up talking about Indonesia several times a week. I'm always on the kids for just eating hamburgers and Coke. We talk a lot about current events. I'm always saying open up, take a taste—eat artichokes and crepes—and travel.[13]

Thinking about the relationship of his Peace Corps service to his life as an educator, Ron Pelfrey (Ethiopia 1966–1968) said, "The biggest part of it was just the opportunity to grow, and grow into a level I would not have done here. If I'd gone straight into a teaching position, I would still be teaching. I would not have gotten the experience of scheduling, of teaching other teachers, the professional kinds of things with new math, the experience in working with large classes and meeting individual differences. I certainly wouldn't have gotten to the point where I was writing curriculum and developing textbooks without that kind of experience. Basically, that's what I was doing in Ethiopia, writing curriculum." Ron returned from the Peace Corps and then Vietnam and took a teaching job with Fayette County schools in Lexington. After teaching math in junior high, becoming a department chair, and completing a master's degree, he became the supervisor in math education for Fayette County, a position he held from 1975 to 1995. Later he earned a doctorate and then worked for the Appalachian Rural Systemic Initiative, doing math specialist training and developing math standards, and he also wrote middle school math textbooks.

Sometimes the Peace Corps impacted not the choice of a career but how a returned volunteer worked in that career. For example, Caroyl Reid (Philippines 1964–1966) spent the rest of her life working for IBM. She thought she brought a better understanding of minorities to the table. "I think there is a direct correlation between my experience over there and really learning that the more I learned about the culture, the more I knew there was so much to learn that I would never learn. I think that made me much more aware from a management standpoint in developing people who were minorities that worked for me." She felt she had the sensitivity to help them with their futures.

Glen Payne (Gabon 1989–1992), the rural village school construction volunteer who translated a Norse saga, became a writer in the corporate communications department of Roadway Express, a trucking company headquartered in Akron, Ohio. As time went on, he "morphed into a software guy." Then in 2003, he and wife Jenifer (Gabon 1990–1992) decided to move to Kentucky. "We have three young boys, and we were looking for something new and wonderful to do, so I quit the software career and we sold the house in Ohio. We came to Lexington [Jenifer is from Somerset, Kentucky], and I started in the graduate program in historic preservation at UK. I'm kind of full circle. I'm back to buildings again, but I'm not building them. I'm looking at old ones." Glen has "an independent consulting business doing preservation planning work with cities, design review boards, engineering firms, and architecture firms. We write design guidelines for towns and work with a planning group as it moves forward to get what it wants and preserve what character they think they have in its historic building environment." What does Glen's job have to do with the Peace Corps? "Among volunteers in Gabon, there was a rule that you weren't allowed to complain. I'm never going to point out a deficiency in something without having some chunk of a solution or at least an avenue to try in my pocket already. That's how I approach every problem still today. And I would say that we developed that on those long nights talking on those wooden benches in Gabon."

Lloyd Jones (Colombia 1973–1975), vice president of Fire King Securities, explained how the Peace Corps affected him as a businessman by telling a story:

> We [Fire King] had a deal in Nicaragua when Somoza was still in power and the Sandinistas were fighting. We sent a bunch of containers of goods, and I went into Managua, which was basically a war zone. People looked at me and said, "What in the world are you doing here? We're in the middle of a civil war." And I said, "Well, you know you need to buy these security products." I came back after that visit, Somoza was kicked out, and the Sandinistas took over. Everybody up here is going crazy because we just sent all these containers. How are we going to get paid? And I said, "Well, you're only as good as your distributor." I picked up the phone to call the guy, and he said, "Yeah, it's kind of business as usual, despite all these problems, but we couldn't get the money out because the Sandinistas came in and froze all the assets in the bank." They were trying to get Somoza's money, which he'd taken with him because he's out on a boat in the Caribbean, and they're trying to chase him down and kill him. I told everybody, "Don't worry, we'll get our money back." Well, they weren't granting any visas. I went to Panama and was there with my distributor, who was a former East German living there with his own business—great guy. We talked about it, and he said, "Well, you know they ransacked the Nicaragua embassy. Everything's gone. The Sandinistas are over there running around with those little banners of theirs. Let's go talk to them." So we go over there. There basically was a chair and a desk; everything else is gone, bullet holes, they'd shot this place up, even in Panama. Anyway, I go in there and start talking to this guy, and he's a *campesino* from the countryside. I can tell by his

accent in Spanish. So I start talking to him the way I learned Spanish in Colombia. And we just clicked. Here I was in my expensive suit and tie talking to this guy, and after telling him about these security products and so on, and saying you've got a lot of my money and I can't get it out, he gave me a visa. I'm convinced to this day the only reason he gave me a visa was because I was able to speak with him with just a little bit of a country accent like a *campesino*. It was just connecting to people. That was the biggest, most important thing of the culture in Latin America that you learned: you didn't go in there and start talking about business. You had to go in and get this personal relationship built up with these guys. Forget about this being on time, the sense of urgency. It's not going to work.

I got to Nicaragua and my distributor says, "I can't believe you got a visa." So we go over to the Banco Nationale. The place is pretty well ransacked, and I go in and talk to this guy with his little red bandana. He's the Sandinista in charge of releasing any funds out of the country. I had to say, "I'd like to get paid." But I didn't say it that way. I went in there with my distributor, and we talked with this guy for two hours and had coffee and drank and talked. But when I went into his office, right behind him was one of our Fire King fireproof filing cabinets. He said, "We're only going to release money and approve expenditures for imports on essential products for food, shelter, and clothing." I sat there and convinced him that the product right behind him was an essential product. He had to have it to store his important documents. He understood. He got it. He said okay. And not only did we get the money out, but we sold him a bunch more products.

Anyway, the Peace Corps experience helped me a lot in being able to deal with situations. Peace Corps did a great job of saying—and I'll never forget this—it takes just as long to learn it the wrong way as it does the right way. When you're dealing with these people, you just have to learn that there is no right way all the time. There is no right way to do it except for coming up to the end of the mutually beneficial deal.

PERSONAL IMPACT: HOW WE SEE THE WORLD

Returned volunteers are more likely to see the world from what is often called a global perspective, and they understand the meaning of the Igbo proverb that Chinua Achebe used in his novel *Arrow of God:* "The world is like a Mask dancing; you cannot see it well if you stand only in one place."[14]

"I always tell people that I certainly gained far more than I ever left there," photographer Jim Archambeault (Philippines 1966–1968) said. "Just in a general sense of how I looked at the world and how I looked at other cultures after this experience. America was not always right. And America was not necessarily the best; they didn't have all the answers to all the world's questions. I looked at the world from a narrow viewpoint, a narrowness that was the result of being born and raised and educated in the United States. Everything is funneled through that tunnel. Then having lived overseas in another culture, and immersed myself in it as best I could for two years, I realized that there are more ways to look at things than just the American way. And other people have opinions and ideas that are just as viable as ours, if not more so, in some cases."

Paul Winther (India 1961–1963), who completed a doctorate in Indian studies and began teaching anthropology at Eastern Kentucky University in 1974, reflected:

> I was never the same after I came back. I wasn't that sophisticated, but I was not as naïve as I was before, especially about politics. The CIA had interviewed me [for a job] in 1960 and told me they wouldn't go through with it because I had relatives living in Denmark. But they wrote me a letter at my home in the U.S. while I was in India and said, "We want to talk to you when you come back." And when I came back from India I just could not do this. I could not work for this organization which might in some small way put the people whom I came to respect, who had nothing, in some kind of danger. I'm honored to be an American citizen, I appreciate the society, but I feel very much at home in many other places. We're all brothers and sisters; we're all the same. You cut anybody's finger, they bleed red. Just by luck we have white skins. Peace Corps crystallized this in my consciousness. Peace Corps was metaphorically like pouring water on a plant that had not really blossomed yet. Now that plant has grown into a tree, and I have some firm beliefs.

From her service in Costa Rica, novelist Gwyn Rubio (1971–1973) learned a similar lesson: "I'm more progressive. My eyes were just totally opened. The major lesson is that we're all human beings. We want to keep our families safe, we want to feed our families. I think if we can tap into those likenesses and exploit that in a positive way, that's what will change the world. My Peace Corps experience was a mixed bag in many ways, but it opened my eyes to much. I saw how in friendship and working on development—it's all one in the same to me—you try to overcome the differences and see the commonality."

A twenty-first-century volunteer, Ashley Netherton (Senegal 2003–2005), who recently completed a doctorate in crop science, said something similar: "It was such an incredible experience to live for two years with these people who are so different and yet still have the same wants and needs as the rest of us." She reflected, "I had never thought of problems of developing countries from an economic perspective. I never realized how day-to-day life is just so hand to mouth and how that just shapes everything that you do. Folks in Senegal probably would plant more trees or cut down fewer trees if not cutting down that tree didn't mean I don't eat tonight. I didn't fully appreciate what poverty can do to you in terms of just framing the way you view everything about life."

Tom Boyd (Colombia 1964–1966), a professor emeritus of sociology at Berea College, looked back to his Peace Corps experience as the genesis of his initiation as a world citizen. "Thank God John Kennedy and Shriver set this thing up that allowed somebody who was working class to go out and connect with working-class people in Colombia and other places. It's John Fee's thing for starting Berea College—God has made of one blood all people of the earth. It's not like America is on top and the rest are down. We can learn a lot, as I did, a lot from other cultures and other people. Peace Corps made me an internationalist. The returned volunteers are my reference group, and when we get together we don't talk about our investments, we don't play golf; we talk about international affairs."

Returned volunteers look at international affairs and the news in a different way. Joyce Miller (Chile 1964–1966) said, "I want to know what's going on, I'm curious. I get annoyed with newspapers when they say there's been a revolution in Congo. Which Congo? There's an earthquake in Chile. Any special part of Chile? My news basically is BBC to find out what's going on in the world."

Sara Todd (Armenia 2001–2003) explained that she seeks out more information now. "If I hear a story in the news, I want to hear the story in the British newspaper. I want to hear the story on Al Jazeera. I think I'm not as quick to judge on an individual or on a group basis. I'm definitely more open to say there's always the other side of the story."

Phil Dare (Malaysia 1965–1967) pointed out: "You certainly don't read the news in the same way because you can no longer just think of an ethnic group or a national group. It's Mrs. Pohghee, it's Anso and Jimbun. You hear about an earthquake, and you want to be sure they are okay. It gives faces to the culture."

Talking in 2005 and 2006, some volunteers were frustrated and concerned about the way the United States was perceived by the rest of the world. Marlene Payne (Malaysia 1967–1969) recalled: "I loved being in the Peace Corps. I loved being a part of that time when there was hope. Peace Corps was one way of being aware of the greater world, and I very much value that time in life. I'm much more aware of the world, and it definitely changes how I view my own country and how it fits into the world. But," she said, "I'm feeling very frustrated now that we've become so insular and act like we know so much as a country, as a government, and I am very aware that there are other countries who have a lot of things to teach Americans, like generosity and graciousness and spirituality and sharing."

"I think we need to do more in the area of foreign policy to create bridges [rather] than burn bridges," Marianna Colten (Ecuador 1981–1983) said. "It really frustrates me to see the U.S. portrayed as the big bully because there are so many of us that really do care and really want to see things differently. I'm concerned about the right-wing conservatism in this country and seeing things as black and white and not being more accepting of other cultures. I'm thinking that what I can do now is try to raise my kids to be more open-minded and more worldly and to care about people from other places."

Occasionally, returned volunteers became activists. Joan Moore (Swaziland 1979–1981) said that her Peace Corps experience helped her "learn more about the United States government and questions that we raise in our country, and war, and our role or no role in how apartheid continued for so long." Joan went to Iraq with a group called Academics for Peace both before and after the war there, bringing medicine and hoping to work in clinics. She has traveled to Nicaragua, studied alternative medicine in China and Sweden, and paid for a Swazi friend's daughter's schooling. "All of us are in this together," she concluded.

Some volunteers talked about having a broader awareness of other cultures—their literature, language, songs—because of their Peace Corps experience. Ann Neelon (Senegal 1978–1979), a poet and a professor at Murray State University, explained that Peace

Corps "introduced me to cultural richness. After Peace Corps I taught at a prep school in Boston where there were a lot of Caribbean black students, and I could speak French with some of their parents. I read a lot of literature from around the world that a lot of my fellow writers don't. And I have this relationship with Africa that most of the people around me didn't have watching the dead bodies in Rwanda in 1994. So somehow that came together in a poem."

Rachel Savane (Guinea 1990–1992) said, "I love how different languages have some words that are so special to that language, and what these words describe can give me a feeling that can only exist in that language. The translation isn't even worth it because you can't grasp it again. That's beautiful." For Carolyn Cromer (Morocco 1992–1995), one question was: "How do you hold on to culture and some of the wonderful songs that are sung by people while they're hand harvesting the field? What happens to those songs when you get a combine?"

Finally, some returned volunteers thought about being an American and about the definition of patriotism. "I was able to reflect on being an American and our country with all its faults and all its problems, Maurice White (Afghanistan 1974–1976) said. "I felt lucky to be an American, and I feel that as an American now, America does have a role to play in the larger world. I want to work towards making sure that we do impact the world in a more favorable way. The Peace Corps experience really helped me to become much more interculturally aware, more sensitive to the real disparity that exists in the world, and how each of us can make a small difference in changing some of that."

As an American by birth but not by upbringing or, for the most part, schooling, Oghale Oddo (Jamaica 1994–1996) became "more aware about being an American and appreciated the U.S. even more than I had prior to joining the Peace Corps. It really defined my Americanness and America in general for me. I think I needed to interact with that smaller community of Americans outside the U.S. and to see people treat me as an African and an American."

Returning more appreciative of the United States, Robin Sither (Cameroon 1996–2000) said: "I don't think I ever was a very big American patriot. I appreciate my country and I know the value of the good things, but I kind of expected my experience overseas to corroborate my bad attitude about this country, and it didn't. It actually made me appreciate my country more, and that was not what I expected."

Lee Colten (Ecuador 1981) broadened his ideas about patriotism. "People who haven't been out of the country maybe have this notion that their loyalty and patriotism stop at the U.S. border. You have a loyalty to your family, another loyalty to your neighbors, to people in your community, to your county, to your state, and then to your nation. Why should it stop there? Why not international? So I think by living and traveling, it helps you see that next step, that larger picture. If I could wave a wand, I would like to see it mandatory that everybody at some point in their young adult life has to spend at least a month in another country just to see the culture, to feel what it's like to be the minority, to not understand what everybody's saying very well, and understand that humanity exists in every country, even though we don't always agree on things."

Harry Siler (South Africa 2001–2003) said it a bit differently. "Mahlaba Cross changed me. I'm trying to see who I am and if maybe I am of enough worlds that I can be in several. It gave me the chance to be an American, identified as such, to go somewhere and do something I feel really good about."

Personal Impact: Who We Are

The Peace Corps experience influenced more than returned volunteers' careers and worldviews. It also affected their personal development. Volunteers talked about becoming more confident; learning the lessons of tolerance, empathy, and humility; and becoming more willing to take risks, including reaching out to people of other cultures.

As William Salazar (Guatemala 1972–1973) said, "That was a time in my life that helped define who I was." Carol Conaway (Jamaica 1965–1966) agreed: "Peace Corps was probably the most crucial experience in our young adult lives." Ruth Boone (Philippines 1962–1964) said simply: "Peace Corps changed my life." She credited the Peace Corps for making her "more tolerant, having been a minority," and added, "It made me more of an individual within my own family of twelve children and more outgoing. My family laughs and says I haven't stopped talking since. When I came back I wanted to travel more. I found out I could do a lot of things I didn't think I could do. I could get along on my own." Two of her sisters joined the Peace Corps, and when Ruth retired from teaching elementary school in Louisville, she led U.S. and international trips for teachers.

Glen Payne (Gabon 1989–1992) described "a kind of confidence and fearlessness that you grow, because most of what you're doing on a day-to-day basis is utterly unsupervised. Everything you do is because you somehow found the get-up and energy and commitment to try to make something happen." Perhaps that self-confidence was especially important for women. Kristen Perry (Lesotho 1999–2001) said the Peace Corps "showed me what I was made of. I could live with no electricity and no running water, and I could stand up to the South African army [a South African soldier had come over the border and asked her about illegal activities they thought were going on in her village], and I could deal with sexual harassment and go spend two days in a village with people I didn't know. Every day is a challenge. And you meet that challenge every day. And that's really empowering." Dianne Bazell (Zaire [Democratic Republic of Congo] 1975–1977) was very specific: "I know how to travel and how to do it alone, how to be a woman alone on the road and put almost like a bell jar of light around myself psychically to make sure I give off an aura of it being much too difficult to be worth anyone's while to mess with me."

Tolerance and empathy were other lessons. Sarah Payne (The Gambia 1989–1991) said, "I think I am more tolerant of different points of view. It is rare that I will start out a conversation saying, 'I know the right way.' I think I'm much more open to being influenced by other people and their ways of thinking. I seek that out more on the front end as opposed to getting surprised on the back end." Jenny Howard (Gabon 2000–2002) said, "I'm a lot slower to respond to things because I know that my perspective is not necessarily the perspective of the person who's angry or happy. I'm a little more moderate in my responses because I don't know where they're coming from. I pay attention to people as individuals, and that helps me relate to, understand, and empathize with people." Debra Schweitzer (Mali 1993–1996) said, "I tend to be more tolerant of people's differences. I'm very interested in other cultures. We've got a big Hispanic population in the United States, and I think I can feel in part what it feels like to them. I always try to talk to the Hispanic janitorial service people at work [Toyota Motor Manufacturing in Georgetown, Kentucky], say hello, and ask them how they're doing. I just gained so much knowledge and humility and strength."

Humility was also mentioned by Capp Yess (Fiji 1982–1984). He cited the example of his changed attitude on arranged marriages. At first he found them "problematic, difficult, even abhorrent. Many of my friends and some of my students got married in the two years I was there, and I saw how their lives changed, I saw how the arrangements were made, and I found it very perplexing and often disturbing. But—and I'm really glad for this—I lived there long enough to see those marriages through and to know enough people who had been married for years under that same sort of arrangement and system. So as I became wiser and certainly more informed, I began to realize that, in the end, their system worked about as well as ours did. They had as many criticisms of the way I was used to as I probably did initially of their system. I realized I wasn't as superior as I had thought I was."

Being willing to take risks was one of the things the Peace Corps taught Don Stosberg (Malawi 1965–1966). He remembered calling his mother for the last time from Kennedy Airport before flying to Malawi. "It seemed so massive, knowing that I was going to take that jump across the ocean and there wasn't going to be any leap back. I never regretted taking that risk, and that experience stuck with me at other times when I had a difficult or challenging decision, [such as] when I made a decision to leave my safe job and run for [the Kentucky] Senate from a minority party against an incumbent legislator in 1990. I believe in the importance of taking not wild abandoned risk but psychological risk as an important element in personal growth." Don ran as a Republican for the Kentucky House several times after that and in 2007 for commissioner of agriculture. "I feel that by giving competition, I made the system a little more accountable."

Don also noted he was more willing to reach out to others. He said, "Whenever I hear African drumming it touches some feeling down in my gut. I think it probably makes me able to reach out to people that are of different colors, different cultures, in a way that's more comfortable than I would have been had I not had that [Peace Corps] experience." He told a story about going into a Chinese restaurant for lunch while attending a conference in Washington, DC, in 1992.

> I sat down next to this dark-skinned man and started a conversation. He was from Mauritius, which is an island in the Indian Ocean. He started to tell me his story. He had just enough money to get an airline ticket to America, and he got here on a tourist visa because he'd worked on

a naval base. His objective was to make it here in America. I started talking to him and giving him a little advice, and after the conversation I gave him my business card and said, "Well, I wish you luck." He got this lightbulb in his eye and said, "Thank you." I didn't think much of it. About two weeks later he called me up at my office [in Frankfort] and said, "I don't know what to do." And I said, "You can come and spend some days at my house." So he did that, ended up spending the summer helping take care of my house and my yard while I was traveling a lot. I got him into Kentucky State University, and he is still living in Frankfort. I probably would have never responded in that way to that man had I not been in Malawi. It wasn't guts or courage or Christianity. It was a human thing, and the experience of Peace Corps allowed me to respond in that way."[15]

The Peace Corps affected older volunteers, too. Lettie Heer (Senegal 2001–2003) changed her will when she returned. She wanted to do something that made her feel good, so she is sending some Senegalese kids to school. "I'm living on much less money. Almost all my clothes now come from Goodwill. I bought a little car after I got rid of the Mercedes. I eat more Senegalese-oriented things, cereals like oatmeal and grits, rice, and a little fish. Lots of vegetables. I lost forty pounds over there. I feel healthier, and I want to stay out of the clutches of the American medical system. I don't worry about things. If it's going to be, it's going to be."

IMPACT ON FAMILIES

Sometimes parents were unhappy when their children joined the Peace Corps, but usually they were supportive or became supportive. They learned a lot, too. Occasionally, parents visited. Then returned volunteers had their own families who were sometimes influenced by their experiences, and some of their children even joined the Peace Corps themselves. Older volunteers weren't always sure their children understood why they went.

Jim Archambeault (Philippines 1966–1968) thought the Peace Corps was a singular, individual experience that was difficult to communicate to others who hadn't had that experience. "There's no way to connect. My family heard a few stories, but they actually just got bored with it. They couldn't relate." Marianna Colten (Ecuador 1981–1983) recalled that her mom and dad were shocked when she told them that she wanted to join the Peace Corps. "My mom even said, 'Well, I hope you're happy. You almost gave your father a heart attack tonight.' I think it was a shock to them, but they were proud, my brothers and sisters especially. It was interesting, because my brothers and sisters said, 'Mom talked about you over there all the time to everybody.'" Cori Hash's (Zimbabwe 1999–2000) father thought she was crazy. "He said, 'Why don't you just go to Paris?' Surprisingly, when I came back, he had learned quite a bit about the country." Maurice White's (Afghanistan 1974–1976) parents wondered "why I wanted to go so far away and was so eager to go to a country as exotic as Afghanistan. People wondered why was I going to a country to help others and there were so many things that had to be done here in the States. As a black person I understood that, but I also knew that I had to do something as different as Peace Corps for myself."

Their children's participation in the Peace Corps affected parents, too. Sarah Payne (The Gambia 1989–1991) said, "I think my mom's appreciative that I'm home safe. I think when she hears news of what's going on in different countries, she associates it with people that took care of her daughter when she couldn't and feels a lot of empathy and compassion." Tom Boyd (Colombia 1964–1966) remembered that his mom and dad were honored to be invited to a parents' group in Columbus, Ohio, where they met other people who had children in the Peace Corps. Tom said, "My father liked the idea that at least I was going to go out and fight communism, that Peace Corps was related to that." Robin Sither (Cameroon 1996–2000) learned that his dad, an army veteran, couldn't sleep for days after he left for the Peace Corps. "But they are definitely proud of me for my service, and my brother has confided to my parents that he is kind of envious. Of course, he's a marine, and that's kind of the polar opposite." Philip Curd (Guinea 1963–1965) remembered his dad sending "a letter while I was in Peace Corps telling me he was proud of me, and that meant a lot, because he was not a real expressive person."

Parents occasionally visited their children. When Ashley Netherton's (Senegal 2003–2005) parents came to visit, "it was a very rapid trip, and they both got sick. And it was a very intense invasion of culture. I was afraid that they were worn out and had not really enjoyed themselves, and as they were getting ready to leave, my mom turned to me and said, 'This is the best vacation we've ever had.' That meant a lot to me because I was sharing with them something that had become very special to me. After they went home, it was such a relief because I could call them on the phone and they knew who I was talking about and they could appreciate my stories."

When Gwyn's mother came to visit, Gwyn and Angel Rubio (Costa Rica 1971–1973) took her to the beach at Manuel Antonio. "There was no development then, a little bitty restaurant and maybe a few bungalows. You had to park your jeep at the bottom and hike to get there. She walked on the beach and she was talking, and I asked her later, 'To whom were you talking?' And she said, 'I was talking to your dad.' [Gwyn's father had died a number of years before.] The jeep got stuck in the mud, and she tried to push it out and got covered in muck and mud. My mother was a very sophisticated woman, and I don't remember her ever doing anything that she wasn't in high heels, but she was covered in mud and laughing about it. I got to see my mom in a whole different way, and I thought she was pretty cool. She wouldn't stay in our house at night because I had spoken too often about the rats, but the visit was wonderful."

Even though her family didn't come to visit, Audrey Horrall (Zambia 2000–2002) found that relatives she wasn't particularly close to were interested in writing to her "because it was such a strange experience for our family. No one else had really done anything like that. So I became closer to some family members that I wasn't before. And definitely people had lots and lots of questions for me, so I think that I was able to try to convey the way things were in Zambia and maybe dispel some of the ideas they may have had about Africa. I did a lot of talking in the months after I came back about my Peace Corps experience. And my family was really into it."

In terms of volunteers' own children, sometimes having two Peace Corps parents made a particular impact. Marlene Payne (Malaysia 1967–1969) said, "Our children didn't have any choice. They have been dragged off to different places in the world. They've been to Malaysia and they've got a feeling why we love being there." Cecil and Sheila McFarland's (Micronesia 1972–1974, Philippines 1974–1976) children grew up overseas because of his career with USAID. Cecil explained: "Growing up overseas had a direct impact on our kids because they grew up learning languages. I have a daughter who speaks Arabic and Spanish and was a Peace Corps volunteer in Jordan. I have a son who speaks Spanish and has lived in Spain. Our other daughter also speaks Spanish. They like to travel, and they understand how to travel and get around. Their political views are a bit broader and probably a bit more liberal because of their experiences."

Both of Tom and Susan Samuel's (Liberia 1965–1967, 1964–1967) daughters joined the Peace Corps, going to Turkmenistan and Namibia. Susan said, "They grew up with the Peace Corps. I was employed by the Peace Corps doing training. Mom went overseas, and Dad stayed home and took care of the kids so Mom could do Peace Corps things. Peace Corps was all over the house—artifacts, different foods that they never touched. In fact, they disliked the smell of palm oil so much that they would leave the house whenever I was cooking Liberian food. But they grew up with it. No one ever told them they should go into Peace Corps. But they told us later that it was sort of a given. You go to high school, college, then Peace Corps. It's just part of what you do. You're a Samuel; you just can't change that. I think part of the reason they thought it was such an okay thing to do was that we both continued on the international trail. There were times when we did nothing, but then Tom got involved at the University of Kentucky with international programs, and the international piece was in the forefront again."

Joyce Miller (Chile 1964–1966) married George Miller (Washington and Tonga 1979–1982) in 1971 and lived in Thailand, where their son was born, and then in Japan. After five years overseas, Joyce convinced her husband, who had been working as a comptroller for the navy, to apply for a staff position in Washington with the Peace Corps. He became the director of overseas administrative support. They got to travel some more, including living in Tonga for five months while George was acting Peace Corps director. Joyce told her son from the time he was a small child, "When you get out of college, you'll go to the Peace Corps and then get your master's degree and then get married." So he did. "My son was a Peace Corps volunteer in Congo Brazzaville in '97, and my daughter-in-law was [a volunteer] in Mali. She and my son met when, as desk officer, she handled his evacuation from Congo. Congo had a coup, and my son and two others were missing for several weeks."

Other volunteers have introduced their young children to international experience. Capp Yess (Fiji 1982–1984) has taken his son back to Fiji several times to visit his mother's family there. Jeff Kell (Dominican Republic and Ecuador 1962–1963) has taken his children to Mexico. Ann Neelon (Senegal 1978–1979) and Richard Parker (Côte d'Ivoire 1973–1974, Morocco 1976–1978) took their children to Costa Rica for a sabbatical year and to Mexico for a university-sponsored summer program. Debra Schweitzer (Mali 1993–1996) plans to take her son back to Mali to meet his Malian father when he is older. Lee Colten (Ecuador 1981) described his family's trip to Costa Rica in 2005: "We were staying at a hostel in a town called La Fortuna, mostly inhabited with college-age folks. We're sitting there one evening, and our sons Matt and Ian are watching these young people talk in multiple languages, sharing stories. Suddenly the lightbulb's going on for them that it's cool to go overseas and it's cool to experience different things. A couple of the guys there said, 'You can't believe how fortunate you are to have parents who give you this marvelous experience.' So I think that made a real impression on them."

Jenifer Payne (Gabon 1990–1992) described "a huge impact on my whole family." Her parents and brother visited her in Africa, and "my mom and brother and I still talk about it. It was one of the last trips my father took, and he had such a great time, he just loved it. And my best friend from high school came with them, too. Glen's family also came to visit, his dad and uncle and cousins. Now we have three boys. We have a lot of African art in our house. We talk about Africa a lot." She and Glen use French as a sort of private language, although their sons understand some, too, especially since they have neighbors from France in their Lexington neighborhood. Jenifer was also excited that her youngest was learning Japanese in first grade in his school in Lexington.

For older volunteers, the situation can be different. Peg Dickson (Ukraine 2000–2002) thought her children were just glad she was home. "I'm not sure they really understand why I wanted to do it or what impact it's had on my life. It's just, 'Oh, there's Mom. She's doing her thing again.'" Lettie Heer (Senegal 2001–2003) said, "I did notice my kids truly respect me for Peace Corps."

Bringing the World Back Home to the United States and Kentucky

As Tom Samuel (Liberia 1965–1967) pointed out, and as the volunteers' stories illustrate: "The primary benefit is what the U.S. gains, that we learn languages, have exposure to cultures, and people then come back and live as normal Americans in everyday places doing everyday things, but with a remembrance of something that really is for them very significant. A good bit of your life is filtered through that experience. I think that makes the United States a richer place. Without the Peace Corps experience, I doubt I would have gone on early trips to the former Soviet Union, where you weren't afraid but not real sure what was going on." Among other positions, Tom served as executive vice chancellor of the Medical Center of the University of Kentucky and as the interim director of its School of Public Health; he has also worked on grants in Kazakhstan, Russia, Romania, and Uzbekistan.

Elaine Collins (Micronesia 1989–1991) was reminded of the common bonds of Peace Corps volunteers when she met other returned volunteers working in New Orleans with Crisis Corps (later called Peace Corps Response) for several months after Hurricane Katrina. "It was nice to get back involved and meet people who went to Peace Corps in a lot of different years. The Peace Corps volunteers I meet think differently than other people who haven't had a similar experience, and I think that's a real benefit to this country."

While the connection between the Peace Corps and their careers was direct for some returned volunteers, others found ways to internationalize their jobs or became involved in outside activities that offered opportunities to continue their international interests and to make a difference. Jules Delambre (Cameroon 1965–1967), for example, said the Peace Corps "solidified my interest in international [issues] and in being bicultural to the extent that I can still speak Pidgin and I look for opportunities to use it." Until his death in 2007, Jules was the perpetual program chair for the United Nations Association in Frankfort and the "glue" for the Kentucky Returned Peace Corps Volunteers. He also taught a course in economic development at Kentucky State University and counted Indians, Bangladeshis, Nigerians, and Cameroonians among his friends.

Bill Miller (Dominican Republic 1968–1970) is very active in the United Nations Association, including at the national level, and in Rotary International. In his job with the Kentucky Legislative Research Commission, he founded the Office for International Relations in 1983 and headed it from 1983 to 1997. Now retired, he still does a regular Global Connection program on Frankfort's local public-access television station, which is also available on YouTube, and he often writes opinion pieces for newspapers and speaks about the United Nations. He has traveled to at least seventy-eight countries, including back to the Dominican Republic regularly, since his volunteer days. Bill said, "If it hadn't been for Peace Corps, none of this would have happened."

Now retired from Eastern Kentucky University, Bill Davig (Peru 1965–1967) said, "I've taught international business, but I've also looked at the other side, which is the Peace Corps. You get sort of mixed feelings about what's going on in the world in terms of economic development and the impact of the economy and big business in these developing countries, and that's one of the reasons I think that I got interested in working with the PeaceCraft store [in Berea, which sells fair-trade items through its partnership with Ten Thousand Villages]."

For 1960s volunteers Dan Sprague (Colombia 1963–1965) and Fred Cowan (Ethiopia 1967–1969), the Peace Corps experience impacted their careers in public service. Dan tries to engage his organization, the Council of State Governments, headquartered in Lexington, internationally. He began an annual trip to take legislators to specific countries. "We have a project going with the Mexican border governors and legislators on border issues and the environment. Now all the Canadian provinces are linked with our regions on trade, environment, and fishing issues. We held our annual meeting in Quebec. No other state-funded group had ever met outside the continental United States." Fred was Kentucky's attorney general from 1988 to 1991 and ran for lieutenant governor in 1991, county judge executive in Jefferson County in 1998 and U.S. senator in 2003. In 2006 he was elected circuit judge in Jefferson County. As attorney general, he took a trip to West and East Germany and went to Namibia to evaluate election procedures. He also went to Israel, where he met some Ethiopian Jews and talked to the young men in Amharic. In 1996 Fred went to Bosnia for the elections after the Dayton Accords. "I think in the future potentially I can work in the legal arena with countries that need help with rule of law projects. Recently I was somewhat involved in the effort to save Darfur through the Dartmouth Lawyers Association."

The list of returned volunteers' contributions to and activities on behalf of Kentucky education is long. Dianne Bazell (Zaire [Democratic Republic of Congo] 1975–1977) was assistant vice president for academic affairs at the Council on Postsecondary Education from 1999 to 2008, before becoming deputy director for academic affairs at the Illinois Board of Higher Education. She spent much of her time in Kentucky starting P–16 councils throughout the state and bringing together K–12, college, and university leadership and employers to raise the level of educational attainment and quality of life in the commonwealth, including examining the education and workforce training this would take. A historian of religion in medieval studies, Dianne did her doctoral dissertation at Harvard on monastic dietary practices and disciplines after living with Ursuline sisters in Zaire. She has thought a lot about what education can and can't do and how best to promote education. "Sometimes basic medicine and basic literacy are better than either nothing or waiting for all the exotic medical techniques," she pointed out, and "basic economic and educational infrastructure—little wells, rather than great dams—makes such a difference in people's lives. Just eradicating malaria or controlling it. Just basic dental care, just basic public health, distributing folic acid to pregnant women in Kentucky." Dianne credits her Peace Corps experience for giving her a reference point when she deals with education and literacy. "While education can certainly improve the quality of life and health of individuals and communities, the lack of formal learning doesn't diminish the dignity and moral sensibility of the people you work with."

Wearing two hats—as executive director for Kentucky Ecuador Partners, and as community liaison in the University of Kentucky's Office of International Affairs—Kay Roberts (Ecuador 1982–1984) has contributed to the education of both the public and schoolchildren for more than twenty-five years. Kentucky Ecuador Partners (part of Partners of the Americas, formerly Alliance for Progress, President Kennedy's initiative to bring people of the Americas closer together) has committees working in agriculture, health, cultural exchange, emergency preparedness, rehabilitation, and cultural exchange. Since 1989, Partners has brought annual art exhibitions to Kentucky; in 2010 artifacts from indigenous groups of the rain forest were displayed at Lexington's Central Library gallery and at the Owensboro Art Museum, and the Louisville Free Library hosted an exhibit of indigenous embroidery. Over several decades, painters, sculptors, weavers, and potters have visited Lexington and Bowling Green to share Ecuador's culture. For Kay, "Bringing the world back home has been something I've worked very hard at." In particular, she described the 1991–1992 Wavelengths to the World curriculum project, developed with Kentucky Educational Television (KET) for sixth-grade geography teachers. The project included short stories and classroom activities written by returned volunteers. Kay also organized three telecasts featuring returned volunteers and international students, and she recalled sixth graders calling in to KET to ask questions about guinea worms from a Peace Corps volunteer who had worked in the health area. In addition, she sent teachers information on WorldWise Schools and the Peace Corps Partnership Program.

Besides writing grant proposals and teaching Spanish at Morehead State University, William Salazar (Guatemala 1972–1973) has been involved in multicultural activities on campus. "I'm a great proponent of cultural diversity, for others to get to know somebody else who they would normally not know or feel comfortable with. So I've done a lot of presentations and some writing in that area." William is concerned about how universities can increase retention rates for minorities and how African Americans and Hispanics can fit in on campus without being singled out. He believes the motive for recruiting minorities is misplaced. "We're doing this because you're African American or Hispanic as opposed to having open arms, welcoming. We don't know how to be welcoming because people have never lived overseas. People don't have that ease of traveling and going from one culture to the other."

It can be a challenge for returned volunteers to share their passions, whether about our own multicultural society or their Peace Corps countries—and perhaps especially about world issues. In fact, that may be more difficult in the twenty-first century than it was in the 1960s. According to the Pew Research Center, in 2009, "49% of survey respondents agreed that the United States should 'mind its own business internationally and let other countries get along the best they can on their own.' That's up from 42% in 2005, 30% in 2002, and a mere 18% in 1964."[16]

Tara Loyd (Lesotho 1999–2001) had hoped people back home would support her friend's orphanage for children with HIV/AIDS in Lesotho by buying Lesotho women's weavings at the Woodland Arts Fair in Lexington, but no one wanted wool weavings in August. Her front-page article in *Ace* magazine, entitled "The Toughest Job You'll Ever Love, A Lexington Native Comes Home," proposed that people donate one hour of work to child-headed households in Lesotho. But only her best friend made a donation. Then, encouraged by the Kentucky Returned Peace Corps Volunteers, Tara wrote letters to friends and family asking them to donate to the orphanage. Only a few Peace Corps friends and one uncle, an unemployed teacher, responded; her physician uncles did not. After she returned from a four-month trip back to Lesotho to work at the orphanage, Tara spoke a dozen times about her experience at churches, at the University of Kentucky medical school, and in front of different non-profit groups and women's organizations. The church in which she was raised, First Presbyterian of Lexington, gave her $6,000 after a three-minute plea: "Here's where I've been. Here's what I've seen. Here's how I think you can help. I can take the money myself. Not a penny of it will be spent on anything but the kids."

In July 2004 Tara took a second-year medical student and a reporter and a photographer from the *Kentucky Kernel*, the University of Kentucky's student newspaper, with her to Lesotho. That fall, the *Kernel* published an award-winning special section entitled "Not So Far Away" about their trip to Lesotho. She also recorded interviews on her trip and used them during a three-part series that aired on the university's public radio station for World AIDS Day. Tara was quoted in the *Kernel* as saying, "I'm just trying to figure out how not to ignore this incredible problem." Many returned Peace Corps volunteers can relate to that statement in terms of their own experiences, especially in countries that have been devastated by HIV/AIDS or war.

SERVING KENTUCKY, SERVING THE WORLD

In September 2008 a group of returned volunteers sat around a picnic table at Camp Andrew Jackson in eastern Kentucky for the annual business meeting of the Kentucky Returned Peace Corps Volunteers. Five of the founders of the group were there: Tom Boyd (Colombia 1964–1966), Philip Curd (Guinea 1963–1965), Lowell Wagner (Bolivia 1964–1966), Marlene Payne (Malaysia 1967–1969), and John Skeese (Nigeria 1961–1964). We looked at a newspaper clipping that pictured those present at the first meeting in Berea in 1981. There was talk of the 1980s, when as many as thirty-six adults and twenty children would come to the camp for the weekend to play volleyball, dance, eat Peace Corps country food, and sit in the rocking chairs and talk. Tom pointed out that the peace pole the group had erected in 1993 in front of the dining hall was still there.

The group was smaller than usual, even for the 2000s. It consisted of all 1960s volunteers except for William Salazar (Guatemala 1972–1973), who ran the business meeting. The organizer of the meeting was Philip Curd (Guinea 1963–1965), who lives in nearby Sand Gap. At our request, he brought the National Peace Corps Association booklet that describes the honor bestowed on him in 1992, when he received the prestigious Sargent Shriver Award for Distinguished Humanitarian Service for "his commitment to bringing a broad range of health care services to those in need and his many years of compassionate care to his patients in rural Kentucky."[17] That commitment probably began "as a child in church," Philip said, where "I became familiar with a missionary named Albert Schweitzer who was in Africa, so I thought maybe I would like to go to Africa when I grew up. That at least got me thinking about going to medical school, and then when I was in college at the University of Louisville, I heard about Peace Corps in 1961."

The eastern Kentucky part of the story began in 1972 when, as a young physician, Philip established a nonprofit health clinic in a small, white house in the town of McKee in Jackson County, which eventually grew into several clinics. Philip left family practice in 1996 and returned to the University of Kentucky to complete a preventive medicine residency and get a master's degree in public health. He then became an assistant professor in the medical school's Department of Preventive Medicine and Environmental Health and also founded a company that helps employers develop comprehensive wellness programs for employees. In February 2010 he wrote an opinion piece for the *Lexington Herald Leader* entitled "Coal-Burning Plant Would Add Pollution," with the subhead "Poorer Air Quality Means More Disease."

When we interviewed Philip, we asked, "What did your work in Kentucky have to do with Peace Corps?" He said, "I think the Peace Corps allowed me to not feel like I had to, right out of medical school, get a job making a lot of money to pay off medical school debts. What we were trained to do in the Peace Corps was community development. How do you go into a community? How do you do a needs assessment? How do you find out who the decision makers are in a community, and how do you get support for your ideas about community change? I think all of that probably really relates to what I was doing in Jackson County, in many ways a Third World community as far as being economically depressed." Philip's experience as a medical student in the Department of Community Medicine at the University of Kentucky was consistent with his Peace Corps experience. "So I went into Jackson County thinking in terms of the community health needs. One of the first things I did was just have a community meeting at the high school, and I said, 'I'm interested in doing health care here. What do you all think about that?' There were over a hundred people there, so it built some enthusiasm for our having a community health center. So there was a real continuum in terms of the White House Clinic, what it does and still does in the community, and the way it got started probably did relate back to some of my Peace Corps experience."

The conversation around the picnic table at Camp Andrew Jackson turned to the $500 the Kentucky Returned Peace Corps Volunteers had given to a Peace Corps Partnership Program project in Uganda for a bio-sand filter. The Peace Corps volunteer requesting the money was Deborah Payne (Uganda 2007–2009), daughter of Marlene (Malaysia 1967–1969) and John Payne (Peace Corps doctor in Malaysia). They had visited her the previous January and proudly reported that Deborah had just returned to Uganda from Sweden, where she had presented a poster session at the World Water Conference. Deborah lived and worked in a fishing community on the northern shore of Lake Victoria. In her job as public health officer, she was developing programming around water and sanitation, building bio-sand filters, making soap as an income-generating activity, promoting hand washing, and leading health clubs in schools. The Katosi Women Development Trust, with which she worked, had been established in the late 1990s when a small group of fishing women decided they wanted to improve their own lives by developing skills in income generation. The initial group of about 10 women had grown to more than 250 members in twelve groups across two subcounties. Their goals included increasing skills in agriculture and income generation, accessing microfinance, and improving water and sanitation.

In a November 2008 e-mail, Deborah was clear about what a Peace Corps volunteer might be able to do. "The gift that Peace Corps offers is time and experience, not money. Within the two years of our service, we have the time to offer skills, education, and knowledge. Though we might offer some money, that money is directed at a project that is home-grown. We are here to stimulate projects from the ground up."

Deborah also described her counterparts who became her friends. "My experience as a Peace Corps volunteer has been successful in large part because I work with a collective of tremendously motivated, engaging women. My relationships with the women have deepened into those of aunties, sisters, and the closest friends. The obligatory greetings we exchange when we gather have become full of love, laughter, and sincerity." And she was clear about what she had learned. "For me," Deborah concluded, "Peace Corps has opened a door to the rest of the world. While I have always appreciated other cultures as a member of a well-traveled family, never before have I had the opportunity to immerse myself in an experience that has given me time to understand our positions as Americans, our tremendous opportunities, and the responsibilities we in turn must address. I am sure that my experiences in Uganda will shape not only my next career steps but my path in life, to live modestly, to be aware of my role as an American, and to value relationships and a development approach that comes from the bottom up."

Coda: Peace Corps Volunteers as a Cosmopolitan Community

In her e-mail, Deborah also wrote that she looked forward to seeing Kentucky returned volunteers when she finished her tour in Uganda in 2009—and she did. She presented the program for the fall 2009 get-together at Camp Andrew Jackson, a place she had come to as a child for Peace Corps gatherings. Deborah is, we believe, part of a Peace Corps community that, in Kwame Anthony Appiah's words, is "cosmopolitan," acting out of universal concern for human rights and also respecting and learning from legitimate differences. It is a community that "takes seriously the value not just of human life but of particular human lives."[18]

Except for regular contributions to Peace Corps Partnership Program projects like Deborah Payne's, Kentucky returned volunteers tend to act as citizens of the world individually or in other groups rather than as a group of returned Peace Corps volunteers. However, in fall 2008 volunteers came together twice to lobby for and talk about the future of the Peace Corps specifically. On September 6 about twenty returned volunteers and some nonvolunteer but supportive spouses representing all five decades gathered for a "More Peace Corps" house party to lobby for doubling the number of Peace Corps volunteers. We signed letters to our members of Congress and listened to Harris Wofford, one of Shriver's aides at the beginning of the Peace Corps, on a conference call from Washington, DC.

Lauren Goodpaster (Malawi 2005–2007) brought baby Sam to the party and met Don Stosberg (Malawi 1965–1966) and Kristen Perry (Lesotho 1999–2001). Glen and Jenifer Payne (Gabon 1989–1992, 1990–1992) had recently returned from a reunion of their Peace Corps groups and met another unrelated Payne, Sarah (The Gambia 1989–1991). Austin Cantor (Chile 1965–1968) and Dianne Bazell (Zaire [Democratic Republic of Congo] 1975–1977) realized they both went to the same synagogue, and Dianne took new Kentuckian Blake Stabler (Russia 2000–2002) home when we discovered he'd walked several miles from a bus stop to our house. Michael Geneve (Mozambique 2003–2005) reported that he was completing his thesis on an international development seminar he led in Banda Aceh in Indonesia. Bill Davig (Peru 1965–1967) bought Peace Corps calendars to take to the PeaceCraft store in Berea to sell, and others bought calendars for gifts. Paul Winther (India 1961–1963) told us he was leaving for Oregon the next morning to go hiking with Gary Griffin (Thailand 2004–2006). Debra Schweitzer (Mali 1993–1996) didn't bring her son Beau, whose father is Malian, and Kay Roberts (Ecuador 1982–1984) didn't bring her daughter Claire, whom she adopted from China. Both often attend Peace Corps events with their mothers, and we missed them.

On November 16, 2008, buoyed by the election of Barack Obama, who promised to double the size of the Peace Corps by 2011,[19] a group of thirteen—six returned volunteers from the 1960s, one from the 1980s, three from the 1990s, two Peace Corps applicants who had just returned from teaching in China for six years and were visiting from Virginia, and one potential volunteer (the ten-year-old daughter of one couple)—got together to eat chili and list our ideas about a bigger, better, bolder Peace Corps, which would then be passed on to the National Peace Corps Association. The Kentucky Returned Peace Corps Volunteers' new president, John Mark Hack (Costa Rica 1992–1994), suggested a Western Hemisphere initiative on extreme poverty in countries such as Haiti, Dominican Republic, and Bolivia. Other ideas, beyond those suggested in the National Peace Corps Association's *WorldView* magazine, included organizing a mentoring program involving returned and current volunteers; appointing a secretary of peace; prioritizing natural resources management, sustainability, and regenerative development; and creating a group of returned volunteers to participate in the formulation of American foreign policy. Five people sat around the fireplace for another hour after the official discussion, pondering the question of one Peace Corps applicant: How would the Peace Corps look if it were created today, with the same goals? How, for instance, would technology be used?

Perhaps what the cosmopolitan community of returned volunteers in Kentucky likes to do most is to eat—all kinds of food—and to talk. Undoubtedly, we learned to value both from our Peace Corps experience. Also in fall 2008, returned volunteers gathered at a Mexican restaurant in Lexington on the first of October and the first of November for their regular get-togethers, first organized in 2003 by Tara Loyd (Lesotho 1999–2001), then by Brian Arganbright (Slovakia 1991–1994), and then by Bennett Stein (Dominican Republic 1975–1977). Only six volunteers ate together on October 1, but on November 1 there were twenty, including Steve Sherman (Uganda 2006–2008), who was recently back from Africa and knew Deborah Payne. His wife Erin, also a volunteer in Uganda, had given birth two weeks before; Steve was studying at Lexington Seminary, planning to be ordained as both a Disciples and a Unitarian minister.

For our December 1, 2008, dinner, our organizer arranged a special treat. Mamadou Savane, husband of Rachel (Guinea 1990–1992), had launched Sav's Grill and West African Cuisine as a lunchtime eatery near the University of Kentucky campus in September, and he agreed to open at night just for Kentucky returned volunteers. So Sav and Rachel, who designs jewelry and owns Savane Silver in downtown Lexington, served about twenty of us deep African rice bowls with leaf or peanut sauce.

Cecil and Sheila McFarland (Micronesia 1972–1974, Philippines 1974–1976), who had driven in from Lawrenceburg, sat next to Sarah Cross Oddo (Jamaica 1993–1995). Cecil, just back from a short stint in Mozambique with USAID, had advised Sarah's husband Oghale (Jamaica 1994–1996) about working for USAID. Sarah and their three sons were looking forward to Oghale's Christmas leave from USAID in Iraq. Sitting on the other side of Sarah, Rona Roberts (Philippines 1973–1975) talked about a report she was working on for a meeting the next night on the 2040 Lexington visioning process. Peg Dickson (Ukraine 2000–2002), who had driven over from Frankfort, sat next to Blake Stabler (Russia 2000–2002). Bill Davig (Peru 1965–1967) had brought her Peace Corps calendars from the PeaceCraft shop in Berea and also sold one to Rona. David and Lauren Goodpaster (Malawi 2005–2007) brought baby Sam to his second Peace Corps event and talked with Harry Siler (South Africa 2001–2003), who had driven up from Williamsburg. Kay Roberts (Ecuador 1982–1984) commented on Philip Curd's (Guinea 1963–1965) unusual appearance in a suit and tie; Dr. Curd was in town from Sand Gap. Also present was Eric Brooks (St. Lucia 1993–1995), curator at Ashland, Henry Clay's home; he has researched the eminent nineteenth-century U.S. senator's connection with the American Colonization Society and Liberia and presented that information to a Liberia I Peace Corps reunion we organized in April 2008. Robin Sither (Cameroon 1996–2000) brought his wife Amy, but connecting them with a newly arrived Cameroonian that night proved impossible. Dianne Bazell (Zaire [Democratic Republic of Congo] 1975–1977) was there too, talking excitedly about her new job in Illinois.

As we left in unexpected snow, we thanked Sav and Rachel. We wished Sarah Oddo a good December. We thought about the three Savane children and the three Oddo children, who, like President Barack Obama, have fathers with African—Guinean and Nigerian—names. We thought about baby Goodpaster, too, who will learn about Malawi from his parents. The future is always the children, but it seems to us that we—especially we returned Peace Corps volunteers in this cosmopolitan community not only in Kentucky but also in the United States and across the world—have the particular job of helping to create a just and welcoming world with opportunities for all, for the children we know and for the children we don't know in Guinea and Nigeria and Malawi and the United States and nations all around the globe.

President Barack Obama was born in the year John F. Kennedy spoke his famous lines: "And so my fellow Americans, ask not what your country can do for you, ask what you can do for your country. My fellow citizens of the world, ask not what America will do for you, but what together we can do for the freedom of man." Obama talked to young people about service in his May 2008 commencement address at Wesleyan University. Filling in for Senator Ted Kennedy, then–presidential candidate Obama said: "At a time when our security and moral standing depends on winning hearts and minds in the forgotten corners of this world, we need more of you to serve abroad. As President, I intend to grow the Foreign Service, double the Peace Corps over the next few years, and engage the young people of other nations in similar programs, so that we work side by side to take on the common challenges that confront all humanity."[20]

We believe the Peace Corps community, in Kentucky and elsewhere in the United States and around the world, would say, "May it be so." Let us engage the world together.

Postscript

Our Story

We know so many Liberians and other Africans that we have to be optimistic about Africa.

> —Angene Wilson (Liberia 1962–1964)

We came back with an attitude about the importance of public service.

> —Jack Wilson (Liberia 1962–1964)

Why We Went

In March 1961 we were idealistic seniors at The College of Wooster in Ohio. We had heard John F. Kennedy's inaugural address and wanted to see other parts of the world, to learn about other cultures and peoples, to travel—and to serve. We thought Peace Corps would be an exciting and a good thing to do.[1]

Our life experiences influenced why we joined. We grew up with strong roots in our families, who also encouraged us to spread our wings. Angene remembers wearing flags representing countries of the United Nations as a costume in a 1946 Fourth of July parade. As a counselor at a settlement house camp serving poor black and white children, she became acquainted with social workers who had come from Germany as part of the Cleveland International Program. Jack worked with the minister of an African Methodist Episcopal church one summer during college. We were both moved by the testimony of participants in the first civil rights sit-in in Greensboro, North Carolina, who spoke on our campus in 1960. Although our college classmates were mostly white and midwestern, one of Angene's freshman roommates had grown up in Iran. In 1959 Angene went by ship to participate in a summer study-abroad program in France; she told her parents it was worth a year of college.

Getting In

President Kennedy established the Peace Corps by executive order on March 1, 1961, and we applied that month, stapling our applications together because we were planning our wedding for August. Later we learned that ours were among the first 100 or so applications received, but we heard nothing until we returned from our short honeymoon in Michigan in early September. A telegram was waiting, asking us to report for training at Pennsylvania State University on September 14 with the first group going to the Philippines.

Since Jack was starting graduate school in communications at Michigan State University and Angene had signed a contract to teach social studies at a small high school outside East Lansing, we asked if our acceptance could be delayed until the following spring, and we began our ordinary lives. Although Peace Corps seemed a rather improbable alternative to a future living and teaching in Michigan, we did take the six-hour battery of tests—psychological, language aptitude, and American studies.

In April 1962 a second telegram arrived, inviting us to train as teachers for the first Peace Corps project in Liberia. We remember the week: Angene was giving six-week exams and had 1,500 pages to read for a graduate course in medieval history. Jack had a major role in Samuel Beckett's *Waiting for Godot*. We sat down and developed a pro and con list—we still have the list—but it came down to these questions: Do we want to take a giant step into the unknown, or do we want to climb the usual ladders? Do we want to do something we believe in, or do we want to be like everybody else? We said yes to Peace Corps, broke our contract to work at a summer camp, and forgot about our plan to buy a sailboat. Although his professors thought he was crazy to leave in the middle of a graduate program, Jack knew he had five years to finish his master's. Angene's superintendent thought she was crazy, too, and offered her a raise in her $4,300 salary. In a letter to her parents, Angene wrote: "To be practical, we'd leave the Corps in two years with $3,600 [readjustment allowance] some of which we'd splurge traveling and buy a car in Europe and still come out ahead." Our parents, though wary, were proud of us. We were so excited! We took books out of the library on Liberia and, inspired by a magazine picture of a trainee climbing rocks in Puerto Rico, where we were to report on June 18, started doing push-ups every night.

TRAINING

The training camps in Puerto Rico were full, so Jack took his first commercial airplane ride to Pittsburgh in June 1962, where we joined about 100 others at the University of Pittsburgh. Jack remembers learning more academically in eight weeks than in any year in his college career. We had cultural studies every day with two anthropologists who had lived in Liberia, several sessions with Liberians, and also lectures on American history and democratic principles. In fact, we role-played conversations in which we had to demonstrate how we would talk to a communist. Following the Royal Canadian Mounted Police fitness book, we had significant but not rigorous physical training and also walked up and down the hills of Pittsburgh. We attended a teaching methods course that introduced the new technology of overhead projectors. In Liberia we used blackboards that were black paint on a board.

One memorable event during training was the Saturday morning when a doctor in shorts sat on a lab table in the lecture hall, took out a syringe, filled it, jammed it into his thigh, and left it there for five minutes while he talked about how we might have to give ourselves antivenin shots in case of snakebite. We practiced by giving ourselves one of our hepatitis shots.

Another memorable occasion involved the initiative of the twelve married couples in our group. We were the first Peace Corps group to have a large number of married couples, and the psychologists wanted to interview the spouses separately about our marriages. We remember that most refused, including us. All twelve couples went to Liberia, and over our lifetimes, half of us stayed together and half divorced, rather like the nation at large.

After a quick trip home to pack, we flew on a chartered Pan American prop plane from New York to Liberia on August 24, 1962. The flight took twenty-one hours. As was proper protocol, we took a live white chicken with us to present to the minister of education, who met us at the airport, where we sang the Liberian national anthem. We spent our first week on the campus of Booker T. Washington Institute. Angene remembers we celebrated our first wedding anniversary on separate army cots, sharing our space with what seemed like an army, or at least a platoon, of two-inch-long cockroaches.

LIVING

During that first week, the Peace Corps deputy director told us about our assignment—to teach high school English (Jack) and social studies (Angene) at a National Convention Baptist boarding school, Suehn Industrial Academy. The school was headed by an amazing African American missionary superintendent, Mattie Mae Davis, who had gotten a nursing degree from Oberlin College in the early twentieth century and started the mission at Suehn in the early 1930s. She had a reputation for saving sick babies, encouraging girls to "learn book," and shooting black cobras out of trees. The principal, Gladys East, born of African American missionary parents in South Africa, was an outstanding academic leader with whom we kept in contact until her death in the early twenty-first century. In spite of its name, Suehn prepared its students to go to college and had very limited vocational courses, although students were expected to work on campus.

We have always said we had a double cross-cultural experience—with African American missionaries and with Liberians. And the Liberian experience involved interactions both with so-called Americo-Liberians or Congo people, who were descended from the freed slaves from Kentucky, Virginia, Mississippi, and other states who founded Liberia in the early nineteenth century, and with people who were Gola, Bassa, Kpelle, Grebo, or another of the eighteen indigenous ethnic groups of Liberia. As for language, we learned "small-small" Gola because Suehn was located in Gola country, although our students came from all parts of the country and from Monrovia as well, and we learned Liberian English.

We lived on the second floor of a large, old wood and zinc house reminiscent of one style of nineteenth-century house found in the southern United States. Built on concrete block pillars, the first floor housed a classroom, a clinic, and a third room we turned into a library. We had the entire second floor, which consisted of two large rooms—one we used as a bedroom, and the other we turned into a classroom—and also a porch the length of the front of the house and another across the end. At the back were a small kitchen with a kerosene stove and a bathroom with a toilet, a tub, and a sink but no running water. Outside the bathroom and next to the stairs going down the back of the house, Jack rigged up an eaves trough, which caught the rain off the roof and came in through a window to a fifty-five-gallon drum. During the dry season, small boys living on the mission filled the drum, carrying water in buckets on their heads from the creek across the road.

Our days began at about 5:30, before it was light, especially when Jack had basketball practice with the boys. After a breakfast of oatmeal or maybe pancakes and often freshly squeezed orange or grapefruit juice, we started classes at 7:30. School ended at 1:30. Then we had a quick lunch and graded papers, prepared for future classes, worked at the library, taught woodworking and home economics classes, participated in or watched athletic events, took a walk up the road, or sometimes swam or bathed in the creek across the road. We also had our own chores to do while the students were doing their mission jobs. Angene started the morning by putting a bucket of water for drinking on the stove to boil for twenty minutes. Later the water was poured into the large crockery filter, which also had to be cleaned regularly. We hired someone to wash our clothes in the creek, but Angene ironed them with a charcoal iron that usually reached the right temperature just as she was finishing that task. Jack babied the always problematic kerosene refrigerator, and we had to clean our kerosene lamps and trim the wicks. We sometimes had electricity from about 6:30 to 9:00 at night. For supper we often ate rice and Claridge canned hamburgers, which came in two varieties—one with tomato sauce, and one with brown gravy. The school farm raised chickens and cows, but fresh meat was a rarity. We could buy huge sweet pineapples and sweet green oranges. Angene baked bread. Students often came in the evenings to visit, study, play checkers, and tell stories. Ma Becky was a favorite visitor from the village; she brought her Ritz cracker tin for rice in exchange for telling stories in Gola, using her umbrella as a canoe paddle. We all participated in her stories, joining in the chorus lines. Bedtime was soon after 9:00.

We were generally very healthy during our two years in Liberia: we took our malaria suppressant pills every Sunday, boiled and filtered our water, and got gamma globulin shots every six months to guard against hepatitis. (We have often said we received the best health care of our lives—and it was government health care—during our two-year tour as volunteers and our four years overseas when Jack was on the Peace Corps staff and our children were young. Our Peace Corps physicians in Sierra Leone, young Public Health Service doctors, were excellent, and our Fiji Chinese doctor made house calls.) As a basketball coach at Suehn, Jack developed a healthy respect for the bone specialists in a neighboring village, who were not Western doctors but could set bones, and for the local village woman who, with a few leaves, could successfully treat sprained ankles.

While living in Liberia, Sierra Leone, and Fiji for six years during the decade 1962–1972, we kept in close contact with our families through weekly air letters. We had no phone contact. However, the mail was generally dependable. Most packages, including 100 dolls made by Angene's mother, got through to us in Liberia. Our surface freight from Sierra Leone reached us in Washington, DC, nine months late, but after sitting on the New York, not the Freetown, dock. Jack's mother and Angene's parents visited our family in both Sierra Leone and Fiji. Two of Angene's brothers and her sister visited us in Bo, and her brothers still talk about driving Angene's 1949 Land Rover to Kabala in northwestern Sierra Leone.

Security was not a big issue in West Africa in the early 1960s. As volunteers we traveled—and felt safe traveling—by train, truck or lorry, and crowded taxis on two overland vacation trips to Sierra Leone, Guinea, Mali, and Senegal and then to Nigeria and Cameroon. Four women volunteers in our group made the *New York Times* by traveling across the Sahara during their vacation. We did live through three coups in Sierra Leone when Jack was associate Peace Corps director, and emergency evacuation plans, in the end not needed, were hatched in our living room in Bo. Fiji's peaceful and enthusiastic celebration of independence in October 1970 was a highlight of our two years there when Jack was Peace Corps director.

THE TOUGHEST . . .

As volunteers, we felt lucky to have each other to talk to and to have specific jobs teaching secondary school. We got upset about some of the school rules, especially disciplinary methods such as cutting grass with a machete. We were frustrated with students who memorized countries and capitals but resisted thinking and writing about substantive issues—and we had to remember that this concern was not just a Liberian educational problem. We chafed at what we saw as the too rigid rules of some of the American missionaries and sometimes let students listen to secular instead of Christian radio at our place—and occasionally even dance. The students labeled us the "new missionaries."

We were well prepared for cultural differences by our anthropology professors during training, learning about Gola society and Kpelle law. We knew enough about the importance and workings of Liberian secret societies not to give in to students who urged us to go see the bush devils (secret society members dressed in masks and raffia costumes) down in the village after dark and assured us, "They won't bother you." We began to understand the tensions between the descendants of freed slave settlers and indigenous people; we knew Liberian politics was none of our business but observed the "buying" of villager votes by Monrovian politicians. When we returned to the United States we were reminded of our own corrupt politicians.

We weren't as well prepared for sickness and death. We saw the pregnant women and the sick babies who came to Mother Mae's clinic on the first floor of the building where we lived. We couldn't count the funerals—for a dead child bound in a *lappa* cloth slung on a pole and carried on men's shoulders, and for a dead infant wrapped in a mat and carried in a dishpan on a father's head. We did mouth-to-mouth resuscitation for an hour on an epileptic boy who had a seizure while bathing in the creek; later we went with his brother to take the boy's body back to their village for the funeral. That same week, one of Suehn's graduates, in the midst of a successful college career, died of spinal meningitis, and her body was brought back to the school chapel for an all-night wake. Death was much more personal and immediate than we had ever encountered.

. . . Job You'll Ever Love

For us, our jobs teaching English and history turned into independent study courses in African literature and history. Most Peace Corps high school teachers taught English, math, and science, so Angene, who had been a college history major, considered herself lucky to be able to learn about and teach African history. She found books about African history by Basil Davidson in the Muslim bookstore in Monrovia and articles about African empires in *West Africa* magazine. Soon students were learning about famous West African medieval rulers such as Mansa Musa and Askia the Great. She organized the seventh graders to do interviews and research and write a pamphlet about the history of Suehn Town. She insisted that students memorize all the countries and capitals of the African continent and challenged them to role-play West African leaders and to keep up on current events. It was an exciting time because so many African countries had just gotten independence or were achieving it.

On our monthlong trip to Nigeria and Cameroon, we went to the University of Ibadan bookstore in Nigeria and brought back a box of books, mostly African literature—novels by Chinua Achebe, Cyprian Ekwensi, and Amos Tutuola and plays by Wole Soyinka—that we and then Jack's students read. We were also excited by vibrant Nigerian art, both traditional and modern, and bought Benin bronze figures and Yoruba thorn carvings, including a crèche set we still display every Christmas more than forty-five years later.

Peace Corps gave us a unique opportunity to grow together—it was good for our marriage. We cooperated on fixing up our new home, but we also cooperated in our teaching. Jack made Angene an easel on which to hang homemade maps. She typed his tests. We tried to coordinate class topics, with students studying South African literature in Jack's class and its history in Angene's. We worked together to identify student deficiencies and remedy them. Jack concentrated on paragraph writing, and Angene gave essay tests. We worked as a team to create a school library, soliciting professional advice from Angene's two librarian aunts and collecting books from various Stateside groups. With the help of students, Angene made book cards, and Jack's industrial arts class constructed tables, chairs, and shelves. We advised a school newspaper and tried, unsuccessfully, to guide a fledgling student council. Angene adapted several African folktales into dramatic form, and Jack produced them. His students also performed a play about apartheid in South Africa.

The highlight of our extracurricular activities was Jack's coaching of the boys' basketball team. The team went to the capital city and won the first national high school championship in Liberia, despite the fact that Suehn's backboards were attached to trees the boys had cut in the bush, their "floor" was dirt, and some players practiced in bare feet.

We found it stimulating to discuss methods of teaching and philosophies of development with Liberian colleagues and other Peace Corps volunteers. Was a national examination a good idea? Would a cannery for citrus fruits be a good investment? Our Liberian friends gave us insights into our own society, too, and forced us to reevaluate what was important in our lives. We could see that modern America seems to separate people, that even when we are dependent, it is in an impersonal way. We don't need someone to wash our clothes in a stream. We don't even need other people for entertainment.

Jack loved his staff jobs in Sierra Leone and Fiji. As associate director stationed in up-country Bo, Sierra Leone, he developed jobs for future volunteers with local officials and helped volunteers cope with job and cultural adjustment. He also delivered day-old chicks for agriculture projects and learned to clean the dirt-clogged fuel system of his Chevy Carryall on the road. He had both the joy of giving away a Peace Corps bride as a substitute father and the serious concern for volunteer safety during a succession of coups.

As director in Fiji, Jack learned the reality of being responsible for the lives of 150 volunteers when a volunteer on a remote outer island had a ruptured appendix and another was in danger because he had not paid his "bill" from a local marijuana dealer. He thrived on the challenges of developing the first in-country training for volunteers coming to Fiji, hiring the first host country staff, and developing a detailed Peace Corps country plan that fit into Fiji's own development plan. He filled the Fiji government's specific requests for an orthotist/prosthetist to design and make limbs for the handicapped, a statistician for the Ministry of Agriculture, and a fisheries biologist for the Ministry of Fisheries. Visiting volunteers on outer islands by catamaran was a special privilege. He also helped develop new Peace Corps programs in Vanuatu, New Caledonia, and the Solomon Islands. Both of us were excited to learn about the Fijian and Indian cultures of Fiji and to watch the transition from colony to independent nation. With our two young daughters, we visited Tonga and Western Samoa, and the two of us tried skiing in New Zealand for our tenth wedding anniversary.

TELLING STORIES

Like other early 1960s volunteers, we remember seminal events that affected us overseas, events we followed on Voice of America radio. We remember the Cuban missile crisis in October 1962 and wondering whether the United States and Russia might obliterate each other and thus our families, while we might still be alive in Liberia.

We remember learning of Kennedy's assassination when a gas station attendant in Monrovia, where we were filling up a jeep, said, "*Our* president has been shot." Schools in Liberia closed, and we had a service in the Suehn chapel during which Jack gave a eulogy.

One of our best stories comes from a vacation trip that was supposed to take us to fabled Timbuktu. We had not realized the Niger River would be so low when we arrived in Bamako, Mali, that boats could not get to Timbuktu, and we didn't have enough money to fly, so we never reached our intended destination. We did take the soon-to-be-discontinued passenger train eighteen hours from Pendembu in Sierra Leone near the Liberian border to Freetown, Sierra Leone's capital, and another train named after Patrice Lumumba, the assassinated first leader of independent Congo, for twenty hours from Conakry, Guinea's capital, up-country to Kankan. From Kankan we rode in the back of a huge open truck with a number of Muslim traders and their goods past magnificent savannah scenery and spent the night in the thatch-roofed home—complete with mosquito net and shortwave radio—of a kind Guinean customs official. The next morning, on the Mali side of the border, the Peace Corps volunteer traveling with us took a photograph of suitcases open for customs inspection near our truck. A gendarme in beret and spectacles immediately called him over and said this was forbidden. The customs official finally agreed to take just the film, not the camera, but then the discussion got around to the arrest of our friend. Finally, six gendarmes with rifles and pistols roared away in a jeep—with gasoline siphoned from our truck—to the next administrative post to determine our fate. Just after they left, the Mali ambassador to Liberia, who was on his way home, drove up to the checkpoint and explained the Peace Corps to the customs official, who gave back the roll of film. We were lucky; later the American embassy told us about one man who had spent three days in jail and almost died of food poisoning for taking pictures in Bamako. We climbed back onto the truck and got almost to Bamako before stopping for food and prayers about twenty kilometers outside the capital. We waited there until after the customs men at that checkpoint went to sleep so our overloaded truck could cross the long bridge over the Niger River and into Bamako.

When Angene found the journal she kept in a school notebook— it is titled "Timbuktu trip"—she rewrote an earlier draft of this story that had the gendarme calling us spies. Thus do stories sometimes grow! Was the poisonous green mamba that climbed up the table where Angene was grading papers a baby, or was it bigger? Luckily, one of the students arrived to kill the snake with a broom—and luckily, it was climbing up the other side of the table.

FRIENDS CAN BECOME FAMILY

Our friends have become family in both the American and the international sense. Angene's sister married a fellow Peace Corps volunteer she met in Afghanistan, and two cousins married fellow Peace Corps volunteers they met in Peru and Guatemala. Liberians entered our lives in 1962, and over the past five decades, they and we have become family. When our daughter Cheryl was seven in 1976, she began a conversation with Angene by saying: "Africa is different. Houses are different. People are different." Angene asked, "What about Alfred?" Alfred had visited that summer and gone camping with us in New Mexico and Arizona. With a sudden twinkle in her brown eyes, Cheryl said, "Alfred's a man." Indeed! Universality can trump difference.

Alfred Boymah Zinnah Kennedy, who became our Liberian son and brother, wrote us a letter seeking work soon after we arrived at Suehn. Eighteen years old and living with other boys in an abandoned house across the road from the school, he was attending fifth grade—without books. We hired him to do a few household tasks for us, bought him a uniform and books, and then challenged him to get As, promising we would pay his board at the mission as well as his school fees ($150 a year) through high school. He got the grades and we supported him, as many other Peace Corps volunteers have supported students. After a college degree in agriculture, he managed the government oil palm plantation in the 1980s, completed his master's in agricultural economics at the University of Kentucky in the early 1990s, spent years in London during the Liberian civil war, and is now back part-time in Liberia as a Baptist minister, working on both spiritual and economic development needs.

Bibi Roberts, biology teacher and farm manager at Suehn when we were there, married one of our students, Jemima Natt. Their son Bibi Jr. graduated from Berea College in Kentucky and lived with us for a year. Bibi and Jemima came to the United States near the end of the war in Liberia in 2003; they and Bibi Jr. and his daughters live in Lexington. For all of them, we are called aunt and uncle in the

Liberian sense. We continue to be in touch with and see other Liberians, including former Suehn student Dorothy Davis Martin, who
graduated from our alma mater, The College of Wooster, in 1966;
she then went on for a doctorate and taught anthropology and sociology at Lorain Community College in Ohio for many years.

In her last letter home from Liberia on July 16, 1964, Angene
wrote about people—Bibi, James Hubbard, Ballah Davis, and the
Scotts and Kemahs, who were our fellow teachers and neighbors.
She concluded: "Things are coming along 'small-small.' So what are
two white Americans doing in Suehn? Well, they have developed
a library and a basketball team and taught some English and history and made some friends. The last is most important. I hope the
small boys John Mark and Sopon can go to the airport to see us off. I
would like to see their eyes when the jet takes off. Edwin brought a
card: 'So long . . . good-bye . . . adios . . . see ya . . . don't go.' Francis
wrote a long letter thanking us for helping his cousin Alfred. Alfred's
mother brought Jack a beautiful country cloth bathrobe. Tarr has a
chief's robe to give him. Esther Kemah gave us country cloth. My
eleventh-grade class gave us a President Tubman shirt and a lappa
suit which we wore for their party last night to celebrate the fact
that they all made honor grades in African history. The basketball
team won two fine victories this week and is trying for 100 points
tomorrow for a send-off. Last Friday Tarr set a new league record in
points scored and the team set a record for game score—70. The pro
basketball players' clinic on Tuesday was a big success; all the boys
are demonstrating their new techniques. Jack and Bibi are down in
Monrovia now for a reception for the players. Tomorrow we will
close our bank account, have a final medical check-up and pay for
our plane tickets . . . then good-bye to Suehn."

People—both host country nationals and volunteers—were
important in our Sierra Leone and Fiji tours as well. In our last letter from Sierra Leone in September 1968, Angene wrote about the
special "Bundu mask Musu gave us (his mother's from the women's
secret society)" and continued: "How do you say thank you to so
many people, from Mr. Swaray who says 'You will turn back when
you reach Freetown' to volunteers who bring a chocolate cake to
Jack because they know it's his favorite or write a letter or cry when
they say good-bye. Peace Corps is still a pretty good 'thing' to be
doing."

In 1971, in a letter to the editor of our college newspaper

intended to rebut a professor's article entitled "Requiem for the Peace Corps," Angene wrote about the volunteers in Fiji we would miss: "Tom who talks about passion fruit all the time (he manages a processing factory); Lolly who's just started Fiji's first class for mentally retarded children; Bob, 70, who's on his third PC tour; Joe and Robin who 're-upped' to continue teaching in their bush primary school; Dick who's doing research on grass carp to save the Rewa River. I could go on and on."

COMING HOME

Coming home in 1964 reminded us, as it did many volunteers, how much "stuff" there is in the United States. We wondered whether it was all necessary. Another issue was that people always asked you where you had been and what you had done, but they didn't have the points of reference to understand—except for our immediate and some of our extended family, who had been reading our weekly carbon-copy letters for two years. *The Christian Century* published Angene's short article entitled "Can You Find Liberia?" in 1965. It was her response to church members who assumed that a missionary killed in the Congo meant that the whole African continent was "dangerous." After we'd been home six months, and before we attended the first conference for returned volunteers in Washington, DC, Jack wrote about the "creative restlessness" we had brought back, something he thought we could contribute to the United States.

Our trip through Europe, after buying a Volkswagen Beetle in Rome with one of our termination allowances, did ease our way back into the United States. We visited Angene's Greek exchange brother's family in Athens, then drove up the coast in between army vehicles to Istanbul as Greece's war with Turkey over Cyprus began. We drank plum brandy with Michigan friends' relatives in Bulgaria and eventually shipped our car from Hamburg, Germany, to Cleveland, Ohio. Our last stop was London to visit our Liberian colleague, friend, and first adviser, Florence. Back in the United States we visited Angene's sister, who was in Peace Corps training for Afghanistan in Vermont, and then college friends in upstate New York who were setting off for Peace Corps in Malawi.

Although our return home from Sierra Leone in 1968 took us only through Paris, since Angene was eight months pregnant, our return home from Fiji in 1972 took us around the world with a six-year-old, a three-year-old, and one West African trader's big soft leather bag. We visited our Peace Corps Fiji doctor in Sydney, Australia; Angene's cousins, who had been Peace Corps volunteers in Peru, in Manila, Philippines; and Peace Corps friends in Madras (Chennai) and Bangalore, India, and in Kenya and Nigeria. Then we ended up in Liberia for a reunion with friends there.

MAKING A DIFFERENCE

Like most other returned Peace Corps volunteers, we consider our achievements very modest. The school where we taught was almost totally destroyed in the devastating civil war of 1989–2003, and people we know were killed or forced to flee. When we were in Liberia we made a difference for some individuals, mostly our students, some of whom we described earlier.

Of course, like teachers everywhere, we did not always know our impact until much later. In 2005 a former student who was visiting us for the first time went to our Africa bookcase and quickly located her favorite short story in the West African literature book Jack had used with her class more than forty years earlier. Since Joetta had lost everything in the civil war, she was delighted to have a picture we had taken in 1964 of her large family, including her mother, Mrs. Clarke, who taught fifth grade in a classroom below our second-floor living quarters.

CITIZENS OF THE WORLD FOR THE REST OF OUR LIVES

Our gifts to our students were small, but the gift Liberia and Liberians gave us was huge. Two years as Peace Corps volunteers in Liberia quite simply changed our lives forever—our careers, our view of the world, our development as individuals, our families, and what we could contribute to our state and country.

Jack completed his master's degree, writing a thesis on the history of a Michigan opera house, and then went to work for our director of Peace Corps training in Pittsburgh, who was heading an educational association in Cleveland. One project was a master's program for returned volunteers who wanted to teach in Cleveland's inner city. He wrote an article about that program for the *Peace Corps Volunteer* magazine entitled "Reverse Culture Shock." After a year he rejoined the Peace Corps as staff, first as associate director up-country in Sierra Leone (1964–1966); then as desk officer for Nigeria, Sierra Leone, and The Gambia in Washington; and finally as director of Peace Corps in Fiji (1970–1972). Angene completed a master's in history and African studies, writing a thesis on the image of Africa in American schoolbooks from 1800 to 1965. In Sierra Leone and Fiji she taught history in teacher training colleges.

In 1972 we decided to see whether we could live in the United States—we already knew we enjoyed living overseas. Jack took up a new cause in public service—environmental protection—and worked as a state administrator in the Ohio Environmental Protection Agency.

In 1975, while Angene was working on her PhD in humanities education at The Ohio State University, she was offered a one-year contract to teach at the University of Kentucky. We decided to embark on a new cross-cultural experience and moved south to Lexington. Our overseas experiences prepared us to take time to learn about Kentucky as a special and complex place, quite different from the northern Ohio and southern Michigan of our roots. Although we know we can never be Kentucky natives, we are committed to what has become our home in the commonwealth, while still cherishing and helping to maintain the Hopkins farm in north-central Ohio, which has been in Angene's family since 1842. Jack began working for the Kentucky Natural Resources and Environmental Protection Cabinet in 1976 and was director of the Division of Water from 1988 until his retirement in 2001. Angene completed her doctorate and headed the secondary social studies program in the College of Education at the University of Kentucky from 1975 to 2004, always advising students to take advantage of courses about and opportunities to see the world. For twenty years she taught the course that prepared students for student teaching abroad. In 2005, with returned Peace Corps volunteer Merry Merryfield, she coauthored *Social Studies and the World,* published by the National Council of Social Studies; Merry and Angene dedicated it to their four granddaughters—ours are Erin and Allison, born in 1999 and 2003.

Angene was also associate director of international affairs at the university from 1990 to 1996, working with international student and study-abroad advisers, as well as internationalizing-the-curriculum projects and outreach to schools. She led teacher groups to Nigeria in 1980 and Ghana in 2004, and in 1997 she taught at the University of Winneba in Ghana as a Fulbright scholar. She encouraged three

Ghanaians—Naah, Theresa, and Yao—to do doctorates in her UK department. After she officially retired, she taught African history for the History Department for three years. Her research area—the impact of international experience on teachers and students—and many publications evolved directly from her Peace Corps experience. One chapter in her book *The Meaning of International Experience for Schools* (1993) is titled "Returned Peace Corps Volunteers Who Teach: Fulfilling the Third Purpose."

But Peace Corps influenced much more than our careers. As individuals, we discovered self-confidence because we found out we knew and could do things we didn't know we knew and could do. We could be helpful to others just because of what we learned growing up. For example, Jack knew the principles of how machinery worked—like a garden tractor that arrived for the mission farm— and how to take care of it and use it. However, we also learned to be dependent on others and to trust others, and our American self-righteousness got knocked down a notch because we were in someone else's country, learning and playing by their rules. We became more tolerant of ambiguity and more understanding of the complexity of situations. We can't explain Liberia in a few paragraphs, and we know that Africa is so much more than HIV/AIDS or child soldiers. We certainly learned that people are more important than things. Angene found an apt Akan proverb much later when she was in Ghana: "It is the human being that counts. I call gold; it does not answer. I call cloth; it does not answer. It is the human being that counts."

In Liberia, after the Birmingham Sunday school murders in 1963, we reported in a letter home that we were "constantly confronted with puzzled, angry, bitter, and even pitying questions and remarks. We meet face to face every day with adults and kids who have read the newspapers and magazines and listened to Voice of America. What would you say when someone asks: 'Why do white people think we have tails?' 'Aren't Americans shamed when we Africans treat them equally?' 'Are Americans Christian?' One seventh grader concluded we'd better pray for the whites in Birmingham." So when we returned home, we became very concerned about race relations and chose to protest discrimination in housing back in East Lansing, Michigan; to live in an integrated neighborhood and rent from a black teacher who lived above us in a duplex in Shaker Heights, Ohio, in the mid-1960s; and to send our daughter to an integrated preschool off Fourteenth Street in Washington, DC, in the late 1960s.

Our daughters considered themselves Peace Corps kids. Miatta went to Sierra Leone before her first birthday with a Gola and Mende name and was an instant hit. When she spent a summer in Cameroon as a young woman, she said, "This just seems familiar." Cheryl was conceived and almost born in Sierra Leone. They loved living in Fiji, and at ages six and three they returned to February weather in the northern United States and played in the snow as though it was sand. They grew up with international students and visitors as part of everyday life. When we moved to Lexington, we joined the university host family program and treasure our decades-long friendships with students, including Ezekiel, Jim, and Nkechi from Nigeria, Aida from Tanzania, Nelson from Gabon, Kiluba from Congo, Charles and Tendani from South Africa, and Mosoka from Liberia, as well as with Irene from Benin, who first came to the University of Kentucky on a Fulbright program in 1980 and ultimately became a professor at the University of Arizona. Swedish exchange student Ola lived with us for a year and remains part of our family, too. Our daughters Miatta and Cheryl were both summer exchange students—Miatta in Switzerland, and Cheryl in Norway. In college they took the same African art class, and both did senior theses on African topics—Miatta directing African folktales for children for her theater major, and Cheryl researching West African passport masks for her anthropology major. We all went back to Fiji in 1997 and introduced Cheryl's husband, Rick, to *yagona*, the ceremonial Fijian drink.

Retirement has allowed us to travel more, including inside the United States. Trips to South Africa in 2006 to see former university student friends and to Malawi in 2007, planned with Malawian friends Robert and Tambu, were particularly special. Another wonderful trip took us to China in 2008, where we visited college friends who had taught English at a university in Nanning for six years and our Swedish exchange son and his family in Shanghai. We continue to enjoy interacting with returned volunteers in Kentucky and through the National Peace Corps Association. Our own Liberia I group has had regular reunions, including one we hosted at Shakertown in Kentucky in 2008. At home we live in the material world of our Peace Corps past. For example, our living room includes palm tree lamps and an elephant table carved in Liberia, a drum used by

Muslims to call people to prayer in a Sierra Leone village, and Fijian *masi* (bark cloth) that hangs on one wall.

OUR CODA

For us, 2010 was a special year. In January we were pleased to be included in Bibi Jr.'s wedding to Rheitta from Ghana. In early July the Peace Corps returned to Liberia after more than twenty years. In late July Alfred's autobiography, *The Journey from the Village, a Liberian Life*, was published. In August we, Bibi and Jemima, and others were honored at a reunion of the Suehn Alumni Association of the Americas in Columbus, Ohio.

We think back to a November 2009 evening when we went out to dinner with Bibi and Jemima following the Black Church Coalition rally in downtown Lexington. We reminisced about our days together at Suehn in the early 1960s. "You brought us African history," Jemima said. "And basketball," Bibi said. Then, all rabid fans, we talked mostly about University of Kentucky basketball. As we walked down Main Street toward where Jack had parked the car, Angene asked, "How far?" "Na far," Jack replied in Liberian English. Bibi laughed. "We say, 'Can't you hear the rooster crow in the next village?'—and it's four hours away." There we were, four friends eating and talking, walking and talking. For us, that friendship is the meaning of Peace Corps.

Appendix

Interviewee Information

PEACE CORPS VOLUNTEERS (BY DECADE) INTERVIEWED BY
ANGENE AND JACK WILSON, MAY 2004–DECEMBER 2008

Name	Country	Years	Program
1960s			
Terry Anderson	Ghana	1965–1967	Education
James Archambeault	Philippines	1966–1968	Community development
Thomas Boyd	Colombia	1964–1966	Youth development
Fred Cowan	Ethiopia	1967–1969	Education
Philip Curd	Guinea	1963–1965	Agriculture
Nancy Dare	Malaysia	1965–1967	Education
Philip Dare	Malaysia	1965–1967	Education
Bill Davig	Peru	1965–1967	Education
Jules Delambre	Cameroon	1965–1967	Education
Harold Freeman	Ethiopia	1965–1967	Education
Jeffrey Kell	Dominican Republic, Ecuador	1962–1963	Well digging, school construction
Judy Lippmann	Morocco	1966–1968	Health
Joyce Miller	Chile	1964–1966	Community development
William Miller	Dominican Republic	1968–1970	Community development, education
Robert Olson	Turkey	1963–1965	Education
Marlene Payne	Malaysia	1967–1969	Education

Ronald Pelfrey	Ethiopia	1966–1968	Education
Susan Samuel	Liberia	1964–1967	Education
Thomas Samuel	Liberia	1965–1967	Public administration
John Skeese	Nigeria	1961–1964	Education
Daniel Sprague	Colombia	1963–1965	Community development
Don Stosberg	Malawi	1965–1966	Education
William Sweigart	Liberia	1967–1970	Education
Martin Tracy	Turkey	1965–1967	Education
Patsy Tracy	Turkey	1965–1967	Education
Angene Wilson	Liberia	1962–1964	Education
Jack Wilson*	Liberia	1962–1964	Education
Paul Winther	India	1961–1963	Business
1970s			
Dianne Bazell	Zaire (Democratic Republic of Congo)	1975–1977	Education
Cecil McFarland	Micronesia	1972–1974	Education
	Philippines	1974–1976	
Sheila McFarland	Micronesia	1972–1974	Education
	Philippines	1974–1976	
Joan Moore	Swaziland	1979–1981	Education
Ann Neelon	Senegal	1978–1979	Education
Richard Parker	Côte d'Ivoire	1973–1974	Education
	Morocco	1976–1978	
Rona Roberts	Philippines	1973–1975	Community development
Angel Rubio	Costa Rica	1971–1973	Community development
Gwyn Hyman Rubio	Costa Rica	1971–1973	Education
William Salazar	Guatemala	1972–1973	Agriculture
Sally Spurr	Ecuador	1975–1977	Community development, agriculture
Maurice White	Afghanistan	1974–1976	Education
Benjamin Worthington	Costa Rica	1973–1975	Forestry

* Wilson was also associate Peace Corps director in Sierra Leone, desk officer for Nigeria and The Gambia in Washington, and director in Fiji.

1980s			
Elaine Collins	Micronesia	1989–1991	Community development
Lee Colten	Ecuador	1981	Agriculture
Marianna Colten	Ecuador	1981–1983	Education
Andrew Kimbrough	Sri Lanka	1984–1986	Education
Roy Glen Payne Jr.	Gabon	1989–1992	School construction
Sarah Payne	The Gambia	1989–1991	Education
Rebecca Roach	Liberia	1988–1989	Education
Kay Roberts	Ecuador	1982–1984	Community development
Capp Yess	Fiji	1982–1984	Education
1990s			
Brian Arganbright	Slovakia	1991–1994	Education
Patrick Bell	Costa Rica	1997–1999	Youth development
Carolyn Cromer	Morocco	1992–1995	Health
Cori Hash	Zimbabwe	1999–2000	Education
Tara Loyd	Lesotho	1999–2001	Education
Kathleen McFarland	Jordan	1999–2001	Education
Oghale Oddo*	Jamaica	1994–1996	Agriculture
Sarah Cross Oddo	Jamaica	1993–1995	Environment
Jenifer Payne	Gabon	1990–1992	Education
Kristen Perry	Lesotho	1999–2001	Education
Rachel Savane	Guinea	1990–1992	Community development
Debra Schweitzer	Mali	1993–1996	Business
Robin Sither	Cameroon	1996–2000	Agroforestry
Ken Wilson	Malawi	1997–1998	Health
2000s			
Peg Dickson	Ukraine	2000–2002	Education
Michael Geneve	Mozambique	2003–2005	Education
David Goodpaster	Malawi	2005–2007	Health
Lauren Goodpaster	Malawi	2005–2007	Health
Abby Gorton	Jordan	2005–2006	Education
Mimi Gosney	Slovakia	2000–2002	Education

* Oddo was also associate Peace Corps director in Jordan and Swaziland and director in Fiji.

Elizabeth Greene	Niger	2003–2005	Health
Gary Griffin	Thailand	2004–2006	Education
Lettie Heer	Senegal	2001–2003	Environment
Audrey Horrall	Zambia	2000–2002	Agriculture
Jenny Howard	Gabon	2000–2002	Environment
Gwenyth Lee	Cameroon	2004–2006	Education
Joshua Mike	Nevis	2004–2006	Youth development
Ashley Netherton	Senegal	2003–2005	Agroforestry
Aaron Shraberg	China	2004–2006	Education
Harry Siler	South Africa	2001–2003	Education
Blake Stabler	Russia	2000–2002	Education
Sara Todd	Armenia	2001–2003	Business
Leigh White	Bulgaria	2001–2003	Education
Wini Yunker	Ukraine	2000–2002	Education

PEACE CORPS VOLUNTEERS INTERVIEWED BY WILL JONES, SUMMER 2004

Name	Country	Years	Program
Richard Bradshaw	Central African Republic	1977–1979	Health
Lloyd Jones	Colombia	1973–1975	Business

PEACE CORPS VOLUNTEERS INTERVIEWED BY ED WARDLE, 1993–1996

Name	Country	Years	Program
Ruth Boone	Philippines	1962–1964	Education
Bill Bridges	East Pakistan (Bangladesh)	1963–1965	Community development
Carol Conaway	Jamaica	1965–1966	Health
Linda Delk	Honduras	1964–1966	Community development
Frank Gemendin	Dominican Republic	1968–1969	Agriculture

Kenny Karem	Chile	1966–1968	Community development
Bob Leupold	Indonesia, Thailand	1963–1965	Sports, education
Charlene McGrath	Afghanistan	1969–1971	Health
Donald Nims	Fiji	1968–1970	Education
Caroyl Reid	Philippines	1964–1966	Education
Katherine Sohn	India	1967–1969	Health
Win Speicher	Honduras	1967–1969	Community development

PEACE CORPS STAFF INTERVIEWED BY JACK WILSON, 2005 AND 2007

Name	Country	Years	Program
George Miller	Washington, DC, Tonga	1979–1982	Staff administrator
John Payne	Malaysia	1967–1969	Staff doctor

Notes

PREFACE

1. George C. Herring, *From Colony to Superpower: U.S. Foreign Relations since 1776* (Oxford: Oxford University Press, 2008), 712.

2. Ibid. Elizabeth Cobbs Hoffman's *All You Need Is Love: The Peace Corps and the Spirit of the 1960s* (Cambridge, MA: Harvard University Press, 1998) is one of the best books written about the Peace Corps as an organization.

3. Ron Suskind, *The Way of the World: A Story of Truth and Hope in an Age of Extremism* (New York: HarperCollins, 2008), 147.

4. Hoffman, *All You Need Is Love*, 262.

5. Fast facts, peacecorps.gov (accessed January 22, 2009).

6. Among our favorite individual memoirs are Thomas Scanlon (Chile), *Waiting for the Snow: The Peace Corps Papers of a Charter Volunteer* (Chevy Chase, MD: Posterity Press, 1997); Mike Tidwell (Zaire), *The Ponds of Kalambayi* (New York: Lyons and Burford, 1990, 1996); Peter Hessler (China), *River Town: Two Years on the Yangtze* (New York: Harper Perennial, 2002); and Sarah Erdman (Côte d'Ivoire), *Nine Hills to Nambonkaha; Two Years in an African Village* (New York: Henry Holt, 2003). One of our favorite anthologies is Geraldine Kennedy, ed., *From the Center of the Earth: Stories out of the Peace Corps* (Santa Monica, CA: Clover Park Press, 1991). One of our favorite short stories is "'Magic' Pablo" by Mark Brazaitis, in *Voices from the Field: Reading and Writing about the World, Ourselves and Others*, a text published by Peace Corps for high school students. The Peace Corps has also published anthologies, including *To Touch the World* (1995), *At Home in the World* (1966), and *The Great Adventure* (1997), all edited by John Coyne (Ethiopia 1962–1964), and, more recently, *A Life Inspired: Tales of Peace Corps Service* (2006). The best source for information about Peace Corps literature of all kinds is the blog of John Coyne and Marian Haley Beil (Ethiopia 1962–1964), which is the successor to their newsletter "Peace Corps Writers and Readers" and is available at PeaceCorpsWorldWide.org. This Web site is the gateway to a bibliography of books published by returned volunteers, including books for children and a list of books about the Peace Corps.

7. Chinua Achebe, "African Literature as Restoration of Celebration," in *The Education of a British-Protected Child: Essays* (New York: Alfred A. Knopf, 2009), 123.

1. Why We Went

1. Gerald T. Rice, *The Bold Experiment: JFK's Peace Corps* (Notre Dame, IN: University of Notre Dame Press, 1985), 168.

2. Ibid., 169, 170.

3. Quoted in ibid., epigraph in preface.

4. Harris Wofford, *Of Kennedys and Kings* (New York: Farrar, Straus and Giroux, 1980), 456.

5. Rice, *Bold Experiment*, 169.

6. Karen Schwarz, *What You Can Do for Your Country : An Oral History of the Peace Corps* (New York: William and Morrow, 1991), 112.

7. *Peace Corps Handbook*, 5th ed. (Washington, DC: Peace Corps, 1967), 52–53.

8. Schwarz, *What You Can Do*, 120.

9. Kevin Quigley, "Not Our Corps, Peace Corps Must Break the Recruitment Link with U.S. Military," *WorldView Magazine Online* 2 (fall 2005).

10. 2009 Peace Corps Performance and Accountability Report, 9, peacecorps.gov.

11. "Life Is Calling: How Far Will You Go?" Peace Corps recruiting brochure, March 2005.

12. Norman L. Kauffmann, Judith N. Martin, and Henry D. Weaver, with Judy Weaver, *Students Abroad; Strangers at Home: Education for a Global Society* (Yarmouth, ME: Intercultural Press, 1992), and Angene Hopkins Wilson, *The Meaning of International Experience for Schools* (Westport, CT: Praeger, 1993), offer two models for understanding the impact of international experience and cite research in the field.

13. Kenneth Cushner and Sharon Brennan, eds., *Intercultural Student Teaching: A Bridge to Global Competence* (Lanham, MD: Rowman and Littlefield Education, 2007), 114, includes more recent research on the impact of international experience.

14. Jody Olson, "The Volunteer," in *Making a Difference: The Peace Corps at Twenty-five*, ed. Milton Viorst (New York: Weidenfeld and Nicholson, 1986), 51.

2. Getting In

1. Rice, *Bold Experiment*, 144.

2. Ibid., 166.

3. Hoffman, *All You Need Is Love*, 262.

4. peacecorps.gov.

5. 2009 Performance and Accountability Report, 28.

6. peacecorps.gov.

7. Coates Redmon, *Come as You Are: The Peace Corps Story* (San Diego: Harcourt Brace Jovanovich, 1986), 233.

8. "Am I Qualified?" peacecorps.gov.

9. National Peace Corps Association, "A Better, Bolder Peace Corps: A Summary of Survey Results from the Peace Corps Community," December 21, 2009, 15, peacecorpsconnect.org.

10. 2009 Performance and Accountability Report, 17.

3. TRAINING

1. Rice, *Bold Experiment,* 152.

2. Ibid.

3. Gerald T. Rice, *Twenty Years of Peace Corps* (Washington, DC: Peace Corps, 1981), 29.

4. Alexander Shakow, "Training: Almost the Real Thing," *Peace Corps Volunteer* (April 1968), 4.

5. Ibid., 8.

6. Rice, *Bold Experiment,* 160.

7. *Peace Corps Handbook,* 5th ed., 9–11; *Peace Corps Factbook and Directory* (Washington, DC: Peace Corps, 1968), 5–6.

8. Shakow, "Training," 9.

9. P. David Searles, *The Peace Corps Experience: Challenge and Change, 1969–1976* (Lexington: University Press of Kentucky, 1997), 87.

10. Ibid., 86.

11. *Culture Matters: The Peace Corps Cross-Cultural Workbook,* Peace Corps Information Collection and Exchange (Washington, DC: U.S. Government Printing Office, n.d. [c. 1990s]). Craig Storti, who was a Peace Corps volunteer in Morocco, contributed to the workbook and also wrote *The Art of Crossing Cultures* (Yarmouth, ME: Intercultural Press, 1990), *Cross-Cultural Dialogues: 74 Brief Encounters with Cultural Difference* (Yarmouth, ME: Intercultural Press, 1994), and *Figuring Foreigners Out: A Practical Guide* (Yarmouth, ME: Intercultural Press, 1999).

12. Jonathan Zimmerman, *Innocents Abroad: American Teachers in the American Century* (Cambridge, MA: Harvard University Press, 2006), 216.

13. WorldWise Schools at peacecorps.gov/wws.

14. Sargent Shriver et al., "Ambassadors of Good Will: The Peace Corps," *National Geographic* (September 1964), 308.

15. Jonathan Pearson, "Survey Says . . . ," *WorldView, The Magazine of the National Peace Corps Association* (winter 2009), 12.

16. *Building Bridges: A Peace Corps Classroom Guide to Cross-Cultural Understanding* (Washington, DC: National Geographic Education Foundation, Peace Corps Paul D. Coverdell WorldWise Schools, 2003), 33.

Voices from the Field: Reading and Writing about the World, Ourselves, and Others and *Uncommon Journeys: Peace Corps Adventures across Cultures*, published by WorldWise Schools, use the vast literature from Peace Corps writers to engage students.

4. Living

1. Peace Corps volunteer personnel policies, October 17, 1961, 6.

2. *Peace Corps Handbook*, 5th ed., 1967, 26.

3. Interview with Ron Tschetter, director, December 9, 2008, peacecorpsonline.org.

4. Hunter Dreidame, "Now I Can Help," *Lexington Herald Leader*, November 27, 2008, 1.

5. peacecorps.gov.

6. "Volunteer Fatalities by Cause of Death," December 2003, peacecorpsonline.org.

7. Hoffman, *All You Need Is Love*, 69–70; Schwarz, *What You Can Do*, 73–84.

8. Hoffman, *All You Need Is Love*, 106–7.

9. "Report on Safety of Volunteers," January 2010, 52, peacecorps.gov.

10. Hoffman, *All You Need is Love*, 122.

11. Peace Corps Memorial Project, fpcv.org.

12. Sargent Shriver, "The Vision," in Viorst, *Making a Difference*, 22.

5. The Toughest . . .

1. *Two's Company: Married Couples in the Peace Corps* (Washington, DC: Peace Corps, 1967).

2. *Culture Matters*, 191.

3. Ibid., 192.

4. Helene Cooper, *The House at Sugar Beach: In Search of a Lost African Childhood* (New York: Simon and Schuster, 2008).

5. Rice, *Bold Experiment*, 207.

6. *Once in Afghanistan*, a documentary by Jill Vickers and Jody Bergedick (Dirt Road Documentaries, 2008).

7. Greg Mortenson and David Oliver Relin, *Three Cups of Tea: One Man's Mission to Promote Peace One School at a Time* (New York: Penguin, 2006), 150.

8. *Peace Corps Handbook*, 5th ed., 37.

9. peacecorps.gov.

10. Philip N. Dare, *Sabbatical Essays* (Lexington, KY, 1996), 20.

6. . . . Job You'll Ever Love

1. Rice, *Twenty Years,* 53.

2. Robert L. Strauss, "Too Many Innocents Abroad," *New York Times,* January 9, 2008.

3. Chris Dodd, "Expand the Peace Corps," *New York Times,* January 10, 2008.

4. Jack Vaughn, "An Idea for All Seasons," in *The Peace Corps Reader* (n.p.: Quadrangle Books for the Peace Corps, 1967), 11.

5. Rice, *Bold Experiment,* 175.

6. Hoffman, *All You Need Is Love,* 98–99.

7. Scanlon, *Waiting for the Snow,* 242.

8. Kris Holloway, *Monique and the Mango Rains* (Long Grove, IL: Waveland Press, 2007), 4.

9. Joseph H. Blatchford laid out his "New Directions" in "The Peace Corps: Making It in the Seventies," *Foreign Affairs* (October 1970). They included (1) shifting more volunteer assignments to the high-priority needs of developing countries; (2) recruiting volunteers to meet higher-priority requests, including volunteers with families; (3) hiring local citizens to fill 50 percent of overseas Peace Corps staff positions; (4) encouraging service by international and multinational teams; and (5) working out internships for returning volunteers in change-oriented jobs in the United States.

10. Peace Corps Fiji's 1971 country plan; recommendations for programming, training, and volunteer support; and other relevant documents are in the possession of Jack Wilson, who was country director from 1970 to 1972. Wilson wrote a memorandum, dated April 21, 1969, when he was a West African desk officer in Washington, proposing the reduction of volunteer staff support and the transfer of that responsibility to host country agencies. He advocated, for example, that instead of a Peace Corps Chiefdom Development Project in Sierra Leone, volunteers would be part of an existing agricultural extension program.

11. Searles, *Peace Corps Experience,* 79.

12. Ibid., 142.

13. Ibid., 194.

14. Rice, *Twenty Years,* 43.

15. Searles, *Peace Corps Experience,* 196.

16. Hoffman, *All You Need Is Love,* 241.

17. Kevin F. F. Quigley and Lex Riefel, *Ten Times the Peace Corps: A Smart Investment in Soft Power* (Washington, DC: Brookings Institution, September 2008), 5.

18. The most recent information is available at peacecorps.gov.

19. "A Comprehensive Agency Assessment Final Report," June 2010, 8,

10, peacecorps.gov. See also Carrie Hessler-Radelet "Strategies to Guide Peace Corps' Future," *WorldView* (fall 2010).

20. Ibid., 10.

21. Rice, *Twenty Years*, 53.

22. Searles, *Peace Corps Experience*, 7.

23. Ibid.

24. Scanlon, *Waiting for the Snow*, 102.

25. Malcolm Gladwell, *Outliers: The Story of Success* (New York: Little, Brown, 2008), 150.

26. Rice, *Bold Experiment*, 179.

27. Ibid.

28. *Peace Corps Seventh Annual Report* (Washington, DC: Peace Corps, 1968), 27.

29. Erica Burman, "One on One with the New Director," *WorldView* (winter 2009), 14.

9. Coming Home

1. Jason Stein Ma, "The Toughest Job You'll Ever Leave," *On Wisconsin* (2004), 29.

2. Craig Storti, *The Art of Coming Home* (Yarmouth, ME: Intercultural Press, 1997), 161.

3. Ibid., 152–58.

4. Ibid., 160.

5. Ibid., 61.

6. Ibid., 62.

7. Kennedy, *From the Center of the Earth*, 11.

8. Barbara Kingsolver, *The Lacuna* (New York: HarperCollins, 2009), 397.

9. Mohsin Hamid, *The Reluctant Fundamentalist* (Orlando, FL: Harcourt, 2007), 175.

10. *Citizen in a Time of Change: The Returned Peace Corps Volunteer, Report of the Conference* (Washington, DC, March 5–7, 1965), 12.

10. Making a Difference

1. Fletcher Knebel, *The Zinzin Road* (Garden City, NY: Doubleday, 1966).

2. Redmon, *Come as You Are*, 209.

3. Rice, *Twenty Years*, 58.

4. Susan Simpson was one of the Kentucky returned volunteers interviewed for the chapter "Returned Peace Corps Volunteers Who Teach:

Fulfilling the Third Purpose," in Wilson, *The Meaning of International Experience*, 59–60.

5. Rice, *Twenty Years*, 60.

6. Stanley Meisler, "Peace Corps Teaching in Africa," *Africa Today* (December 1966), 16.

7. Ibid., 18–20.

8. "Rebuff to Peace Corps," *(Freetown) Daily Mail*, June 11, 1968, and summary of article in the Fiji newspaper *Volagauna*, c. 1970, in the authors' materials.

9. Rice, *Twenty Years*, 72

10. Quigley and Rieffel, *Ten Times the Peace Corps*, 5.

11. 2009 Performance and Accountability Report, 39, 58, 42.

12. Interview with Ron Tschetter, director, December 16, 2008, peacecorpsonline.org.

13. Hoffman, *All You Need is Love*, 120.

14. Peace Corps memorandum from C. Payne Lucas, February 13, 1969.

11. Citizens of the World for the Rest of Our Lives

1. Aaron Williams speaking to the National Peace Corps Association Directors Circle, Washington, DC, March 5, 2010.

2. Rice, *Twenty Years*, 85.

3. Quoted in Loret Miller Ruppe, *Costing Not Less Than Everything: A Commemorative Booklet* (Okemos, MI: Solar Circle, n.d.), 8.

4. 2009 Performance and Accountability Report, 47, 48.

5. Ibid.

6. Rice, *Twenty Years*, 80.

7. M. Peter McPherson, "As a Development Agency," in Viorst, *Making a Difference*, 105.

8. Searles, *Peace Corps Experience*, 212.

9. Viorst, *Making a Difference*, 105.

10. *Peace Corps Seventh Annual Report*, 50–53.

11. Rice, *Twenty Years*, 82.

12. Merry M. Merryfield and Angene Wilson, *Social Studies and the World: Teaching Global Perspectives*, NCSS Bulletin 103 (Washington, DC: National Council of Social Studies, 2005). Chapter 2, "Experience and World-Mindedness," explains the impact of international experience on teachers and offers teaching ideas. Richard Parker's comment about being an international bridge is equivalent to the cultural mediator role described in that chapter.

13. Bob Leupold was interviewed by Angene Wilson for *The Meaning of International Experience*, 50–51.

14. Chinua Achebe, *Arrow of God* (London: Heinemann, 1964), 55.

15. The story is from Ed Wardle's 1993 interview of Don Stosberg.

16. "Answers to FP Quiz," *Foreign Policy* (March–April 2010), 110.

17. National Peace Corps Association, *Sargent Shriver Award for Distinguished Humanitarian Service* (Washington, DC: National Peace Corps Association, 1999), 17.

18. Kwame Anthony Appiah, *Cosmopolitanism: Ethics in a World of Strangers* (New York: W. W. Norton, 2006), xv.

19. Barack Obama, "A Quantum Leap," *WorldView* (fall 2008), 29. This issue contains a number of articles under the theme "Peace Corps: Looking Back, Looking Ahead."

20. David Olive, *An American Story: The Speeches of Barack Obama* (Toronto: ECW Press, 2008), 300.

POSTSCRIPT

1. We interviewed each other at the beginning of our four years of interviewing, in fall 2004, and those interviews are part of the Oral History Center archives. However, we wrote this postscript using our letters home from Liberia, Sierra Leone, and Fiji and articles and speeches we have written about our Peace Corps experiences over many years, as well as the transcripts of our interviews. Thus we are not quoting from the interview transcripts.

Selected Bibliography

Achebe, Chinua. "African Literature as Restoration of Celebration." In *The Education of a British-Protected Child: Essays.* New York: Alfred A. Knopf, 2009.

———. *Arrow of God.* London: Heinemann, 1964.

Appiah, Kwame Anthony. *Cosmopolitanism: Ethics in a World of Strangers.* New York: W. W. Norton, 2006.

Blatchford, Joseph H. "The Peace Corps: Making It in the Seventies." *Foreign Affairs* (October 1970), 122–35.

Building Bridges: A Peace Corps Classroom Guide to Cross-Cultural Understanding. Washington, DC: National Geographic Education Foundation, Peace Corps Paul D. Coverdell WorldWise Schools, 2003.

Burman, Erica. "One on One with the New Director." *WorldView, The Magazine of the National Peace Corps Association* (winter 2009), 14–15.

Citizen in a Time of Change: The Returned Peace Corps Volunteer. Report of the Conference. Washington, DC, March 5–7, 1965.

Cooper, Helene. *The House at Sugar Beach: In Search of a Lost African Childhood.* New York: Simon and Schuster, 2008.

Culture Matters: The Peace Corps Cross-Cultural Workbook. Washington, DC: U.S. Government Printing Office, n.d.

Cushner, Kenneth, and Sharon Brennan, eds. *Intercultural Student Teaching: A Bridge to Global Competence.* Lanham, MD: Rowman and Littlefield Education, 2007.

Dare, Philip N. *Sabbatical Essays.* Lexington, KY, 1996.

Dodd, Chris. "Expand the Peace Corps." *New York Times,* January 10, 2008.

Dreidame, Hunter. "Now I Can Help." *Lexington Herald Leader,* November 27, 2008.

Gladwell, Malcolm. *Outliers: The Story of Success.* New York: Little, Brown, 2008.

Herring, George C. *From Colony to Superpower: U.S. Foreign Relations since 1776.* Oxford: Oxford University Press, 2008.

Hoffman, Elizabeth Cobbs. *All You Need Is Love: The Peace Corps and the Spirit of the 1960s.* Cambridge, MA: Harvard University Press, 1998.

Holloway, Kris. *Monique and the Mango Rains.* Long Grove, IL: Waveland Press, 2007.

Kauffmann, Norman L., Judith N. Martin, and Henry D. Weaver, with Judy Weaver. *Students Abroad; Strangers at Home: Education for a Global Society.* Yarmouth, ME: Intercultural Press, 1992.

Kennedy, Geraldine, ed. *From the Center of the Earth: Stories out of the Peace Corps.* Santa Monica, CA: Clover Park Press, 1991.

Knebel, Fletcher. *The Zinzin Road.* Garden City, NY: Doubleday, 1966.

"Life Is Calling: How Far Will You Go?" Peace Corps recruiting brochure, 2005.

Ma, Jason Stein. "The Toughest Job You'll Ever Leave." *On Wisconsin* (2004), 28–31.

McPherson, M. Peter. "As a Development Agency." In *Making a Difference: The Peace Corps at Twenty-five,* ed. Milton Viorst. New York: Weidenfeld and Nicholson, 1986.

Meisler, Stanley. "Peace Corps Teaching in Africa." *Africa Today* (December 1966), 16–20.

Merryfield, Merry M., and Angene Wilson. *Social Studies and the World: Teaching Global Perspectives.* NCSS Bulletin 103. Washington, DC: National Council of Social Studies.

Mortenson, Greg, and David Oliver Relin. *Three Cups of Tea: One Man's Mission to Promote Peace One School at a Time.* New York: Penguin, 2006.

National Peace Corps Association. *A Better, Bolder Peace Corps: A Summary of Survey Results from the Peace Corps Community.* December 21, 2009. Available at peacecorpsconnect.org.

———. *Sargent Shriver Award for Distinguished Humanitarian Service.* Washington, DC: National Peace Corps Association, 1999.

Obama, Barack. "A Quantum Leap." *WorldView, The Magazine of the National Peace Corps Association* (fall 2008), 29.

Olive, David. *An American Story: The Speeches of Barack Obama.* Toronto: ECW Press, 2008.

Olsen, Jody. "The Volunteer." In *Making a Difference: The Peace Corps at Twenty-five*, ed. Milton Viorst. New York: Weidenfeld and Nicholson, 1986.

Once in Afghanistan. DVD. Produced by Jill Vickers and Jody Bergedick. Bridport, VT: Dirt Road Documentaries, 2008.

Peace Corps. 2009 Peace Corps Performance and Accountability Report. peacecorps.gov.

Peace Corps Factbook and Directory. Washington, DC: Peace Corps, 1968.

Peace Corps Handbook, 5th ed. Washington, DC: Peace Corps, 1967.

Peace Corps Memorial Project. Available at fpcv.org.

Peace Corps Seventh Annual Report. Washington, DC: Peace Corps, 1968.

Pearson, Jonathan. "Survey Says . . ." *WorldView, The Magazine of the National Peace Corps Association* (winter 2009).

Quigley, Kevin. "Not Our Corps: Peace Corps Must Break the Recruitment Link with U.S. Military." *WorldView Magazine Online* 2 (fall 2005).

Quigley, Kevin, and Lex Rieffel. *Ten Times the Peace Corps: A Smart Investment in Soft Power*. Washington, DC: Brookings Institution, 2008.

Redmon, Coates. *Come as You Are: The Peace Corps Story*. San Diego: Harcourt Brace Jovanovich, 1986.

Rice, Gerald T. *The Bold Experiment: JFK's Peace Corps*. Notre Dame, IN: University of Notre Dame Press, 1985.

———. *Twenty Years of Peace Corps*. Washington, DC: Peace Corps, 1981.

Ruppe, Loret Miller. *Costing Not Less Than Everything: A Commemorative Booklet*. Okemos, MI: Solar Circle, n.d.

Scanlon, Thomas. *Waiting for the Snow: The Peace Corps Papers of a Charter Volunteer*. Chevy Chase, MD: Posterity Press, 1997.

Schwarz, Karen. *What You Can Do for Your Country: An Oral History of the Peace Corps*. New York: William and Morrow, 1991.

Searles, P. David. *The Peace Corps Experience: Challenge and Change, 1969–1976*. Lexington: University Press of Kentucky, 1997.

Shakow, Alexander. "Training: Almost the Real Thing." *Peace Corps Volunteer* (April 1968).

Shriver, Sargent, et al. "Ambassadors of Good Will, the Peace Corps." *National Geographic* (September 1964).

Storti, Craig. *The Art of Coming Home.* Yarmouth, ME: Intercultural Press, 1997.

Strauss, Robert L. "Too Many Innocents Abroad." *New York Times,* January 9, 2008.

Suskind, Ron. *The Way of the World: A Story of Truth and Hope in an Age of Extremism.* New York: HarperCollins, 2008.

Tschetter, Ron. Interview. December 9, 2008. peacecorpsonline.org.

Two's Company: Married Couples in the Peace Corps. Washington, DC: Peace Corps, 1967.

Vaughn, Jack. "An Idea for All Seasons." In *The Peace Corps Reader.* N.p.: Quadrangle Books for the Peace Corps, 1967.

Wilson, Angene Hopkins. *The Meaning of International Experience for Schools.* Westport, CT: Praeger, 1993.

Wofford, Harris. *Of Kennedys and Kings.* New York: Farrar, Straus and Giroux, 1980.

Zimmerman, Jonathan. *Innocents Abroad: American Teachers in the American Century.* Cambridge, MA: Harvard University Press, 2006.

Index

Achebe, Chinua, xxi, 302, 334
Afghanistan, xii, 23, 44, 75, 77, 110,
    115–16, 140, 142–43, 151, 173,
    188, 231–32, 259, 276–77, 306,
    311, 337, 339
agriculture programs, 112–14, 168–
    69, 184–88
agroforestry, 84–85, 91, 186–87
Ahidjo, Amadou, 215
Alaska, 264, 267
Allende, Salvador, 124
Alliance for Progress, 24, 317
AmeriCorps, 16, 267, 296
Anderson, Terry, 8, 42, 73, 105,
    116, 123, 129, 175–76, 256,
    277, 279, 293
Anderson County, Kentucky, 21,
    294
Angola, 125
anti-Americanism, 123–24
appendicitis, 147–48
Appiah, Kwame Anthony, 322
applications, 9, 38–40, 50
Archambeault, James, 9, 43–44,
    72–73, 101, 303, 310
Arganbright, Brian, 48, 103, 175,
    218, 324
Argentina, 23, 298
Armenia, 24, 30, 90, 104, 120–21,
    141, 191–92, 267, 296, 304
arrival stories, 202–8
Australia, 22, 24, 340
Austria, 24

BA generalist, 60, 160–62

Bangladesh (formerly East
    Pakistan), 8, 68, 293
Basic Human Needs, 164
Bazell, Dianne, 20, 79, 107, 125,
    145, 173, 225, 279, 308, 316–
    17, 323, 325
Belize, 22
Bell, Patrick, 29, 85–86, 115, 181–82
Bellarmine University, 32
Berea, Kentucky, xv, 208, 323
Berea College, 2, 29, 145, 257, 304,
    337
bicycles, 122, 210
Birdwhistell, Terry, xii
Birmingham Southern College, 27
Blatchford, Joseph, 162
Bokassa (emperor), 79
Bolivia, 271, 319, 323
Bond, Julian, 73
Boone, Ruth, 151, 307
Bosnia, 316
Botswana, 264
Bowdoin College, 21
Boyd, Doug, xii
Boyd, Thomas, 11, 30, 42–43,
    71–72, 143, 181, 230, 254–55,
    285, 304, 311, 319
Bradshaw, Richard, 25, 188, 293
Brazil, 20, 24, 53, 256, 272, 295
Breathitt County, Kentucky, 293
Bridges, Bill, 8, 68, 293
Brooks, Eric, 325
Bulgaria, xiii, xiv, 32, 51, 104–5,
    121, 175, 204, 242–43, 267,
    273, 278

Ruby
&
Emma

Burkina Faso, 273
Burundi, 83
Bush, George W., 16
business programs, 191–92

Cambodia, 288
Cameroon, xii, 8, 19, 22, 42, 84,
    105–6, 118, 121–22, 136, 147,
    176, 186–87, 215, 224–25,
    235–36, 255–56, 263, 277–78,
    292–93, 306, 311, 315, 325,
    332, 334
Canada, 15, 316
Cantor, Austin, 323
Cape Verde, 272
career
  impact on, 293–302
  Peace Corps as preparation for,
    16–18
Celeste, Richard, 291
Central African Republic, 25, 188,
    293
Centre College, 293
Chamberlin, Wendy, xi
Chao, Elaine, xv
Chile, 20, 23, 42, 69–70, 100, 124,
    139, 165, 167, 182–83, 274,
    304, 313, 323
China, 5–6, 23, 38, 46, 62, 98–99,
    127, 131–32, 158–60, 201–2,
    229, 250–51, 253, 270–71, 286,
    288, 290, 298–99, 305, 323,
    343
CIA (Central Intelligence Agency),
    124–25, 195, 303
civil strife/civil wars, 122–26
  See also individual countries
Clinton, Bill, 215, 217, 263
Cold War, 123–24
College of Wooster, 18, 327
Collins, Elaine, 20, 27, 140, 184,
    208, 213–14, 260–61, 295, 315
Colombia, 8, 11, 16, 18, 20, 23–24,
    30, 41–43, 71–72, 76–77, 124,
    128, 143, 162, 181, 191, 230,
    254–55, 271, 277, 285, 301–2,
    304, 311, 316, 319
Colten, Lee, 65–66, 80, 148, 240–
    43, 307, 314
Colten, Marianna, 20, 66, 79–80,
    101, 116, 143, 180, 240–41,
    262, 275, 297, 305, 310–11
Columbia Teachers College, 77
commercials, 1, 5, 18–20, 132
communication, 119–21
communists, 124, 169, 196, 234,
    281, 311, 329
community development programs,
    112–14, 165–66, 169, 182–84
community service, prior to Peace
    Corps, 27–29
Conaway, Carol, 8, 307
Congo, Democratic Republic of
    (Zaire), 20, 79, 107, 125, 145,
    173, 225, 279, 294, 308, 316,
    323, 325, 343
Congo, Republic of (Congo
    Brazzaville), 313
conscientious objector, 15
Costa Rica, 1, 15, 17, 23, 25, 29,
    85–86, 100, 115, 138, 147,
    181–83, 186, 242, 259–60, 279,
    286, 288–89, 292, 303, 312,
    314, 323
Côte d'Ivoire, 11, 52, 107–8, 144,
    153, 163, 209–10, 240, 259,
    285, 297, 313
Council on Postsecondary
    Education, Kentucky, 316
Council of State Governments, 316
counterparts, 162, 237–38
Coverdell, Paul, 291
Cowan, Fred, 9–10, 43, 74, 106–7,
    117, 215–16, 265, 272, 316
Crisis Corps. See Peace Corps
    Response

Cromer, Carolyn, 48, 84, 109–10, 135, 189–90, 207, 262–63, 275, 306
Crozier, David, 128
Cuba, 25–26, 295
Cuban missile crisis, 335
cultural training, 59, 62, 66, 74–75, 81, 83, 86, 91, 93–94
Culture Matters workbook, 134
culture shock, 131, 133–34, 145
  reverse culture shock, 247–48, 250, 252, 261, 340
Curd, Philip, 67, 167, 230, 281, 311, 319–21, 325
Czechoslovakia, 48, 105–6, 218

Danville, Kentucky, 293
Dare, Nancy, 8–9, 42, 59, 68–69, 115, 120, 172–73, 277
Dare, Phil, 8–9, 29, 68–69, 115, 153, 172–73, 194, 222–23, 280, 305
Dartmouth College, 9
David, Kentucky, 28
Davig, Bill, 11, 24, 143, 169, 256, 316, 323–24
deferments, 13–14
Delambre, Jules, xiii, 8, 22, 42, 105–6, 118, 122, 176, 215, 255–56, 278, 292, 315
Delk, Linda, 68
Democratic Republic of Congo (Zaire), 20, 79, 107, 125, 145, 173, 225, 279, 294, 308, 316, 323, 325, 343
Denmark, 22, 253, 303
deselection, 64, 66, 71, 74, 80
Dickson, Peg, 8, 28, 52–53, 89–90, 104, 120, 126–27, 155, 218–19, 265–66, 314, 324
Dodd, Christopher, 160
Dominican Republic, 13, 15, 25, 68, 75, 93–94, 115, 123, 143, 160, 168–69, 209, 257, 278, 293, 313, 315, 323–24
draft, military, 7, 10–11, 13–15, 255
Dreidame, Hunter, 121

Eastern Kentucky University, 30, 256, 303, 316
East Pakistan. *See* Bangladesh
Ecuador, 15, 18, 20–21, 24–25, 41, 44–45, 65–66, 80–81, 100–1, 112–13, 116, 124, 138, 141–43, 148, 152, 168, 180, 183–85, 206–7, 230, 238, 241, 247, 251, 257, 258, 262, 275–76, 279, 298, 305, 307, 310, 313–14, 317, 323, 325
education programs
  English teachers, 172–75, 195
  environmental education, 61, 179–80
  math/science teachers, 175–79
  physical education and youth development, 181–82
  resource teacher/teacher training, 180–81
  typical day in, 111–12
Egypt, 21, 294
El Salvador, 50
Emory University, 73
Emperor Bokassa, 79
England, 23, 25
English as a Second Language, 51, 59, 173–74, 182, 258, 297
Engstrom, Kristina, 142–43, 276
Environmental Protection Cabinet, Natural Resources and, 293, 341
Eritrea, 28
Ethiopia, 9–10, 12–13, 28, 42–43, 74, 106–7, 114, 117, 128, 177, 214–16, 256, 271–72, 277, 299–300, 316

Falck, Ola, 343
Fiji, 101–2, 111, 116, 119, 146, 151,
    178, 194, 223, 244–45, 261,
    272, 277, 289, 294, 308–9, 313,
    335, 338–41, 343
fish farming, 187–88
Foreign Service, 18
forestry, 17, 186
Fort Knox, Kentucky, 28
France, 22, 48, 314
Frankfort, Kentucky, xv, 28, 266
Freeman, Harold, 13, 42, 74, 114,
    128, 177, 214, 272
Fulbright program, 22, 341, 343
Fulton, Kentucky, 24

Gabon, 7, 28, 46–47, 51–52, 82–83,
    90, 114, 150–51, 178–80, 192–
    93, 205–6, 221–22, 238, 241–
    42, 261, 265, 275, 280, 291,
    293, 300, 308, 314, 323, 343
Gambia, The, 23, 46, 81–82, 109,
    114, 145, 149, 166, 194, 226,
    261–62, 279, 308, 311–12, 323,
    341
Gates Foundation, 171
Gemendin, Frank, 15, 168–69
Geneve, Michael, 31, 54, 121, 147,
    150, 152, 174–75, 195, 204–5,
    236, 266, 278, 280, 294–95, 323
George Washington University, 290
Germany, 20, 22, 24, 27, 30, 316,
    339
Ghana, 8, 42, 54, 73, 105, 116,
    122–23, 129, 175–76, 255–56,
    277, 279, 293, 341, 344
Gladwell, Malcolm, 171
Goodpaster, David, 7, 54–55, 107,
    121, 129, 138, 190–91, 237–38,
    325
Goodpaster, Lauren, 27, 54–55,
    107, 121, 133, 138, 190–91,
    266–67, 323, 325

Gorton, Abby, 18, 22–24, 87–89,
    105, 139
Gosney, Mimi, 41, 52–53, 151,
    195–97, 281
Greece, 339
Greene, Elizabeth, 18, 35, 91–92,
    108, 115, 127, 137–38, 142,
    190, 274–75
Griffin, Gary, 11, 29–30, 52, 92–93,
    103, 122, 142, 169, 253, 323
Guatemala, 18, 21, 23–24, 26, 44,
    46, 75–76, 114, 141, 143, 184,
    222, 237, 257–58, 276, 281,
    294, 307, 318–19, 337
Guinea, 22, 67, 95, 105–6, 121,
    134, 167, 184, 210–12, 230,
    242–43, 275, 281, 306, 311,
    319–20, 324–25, 332, 336
Guyana, 21, 294

Hack, John Mark, 323
Haiti, 323
Hanover College, 29
Harriman, Averill, 24–25
Hash, Cori, 22, 50, 86–87, 127–28,
    166, 264, 269, 295, 311
Hawaii, 52, 63, 68
health issues, 145–49
health programs, 188–91
health training, 83–84
Heer, Lettie, 28, 31, 53, 108, 267,
    275, 310, 314
Herring, George, xi
HIV/AIDS, 21, 164–65, 170–71,
    188, 194–95, 225, 235, 238,
    264, 283, 289, 292, 294, 318–
    19, 342
Hobbs, Nicholas, 40
Hoffman, Elizabeth Cobbs, xi
Honduras, 46, 68, 169
Horral, Audrey, 18–19, 114–15,
    136, 166, 187–88, 238–39, 266,
    276, 312

host country nationals, 231
host family, 77, 84–86, 88–92,
    108–10
Howard, Jenny, 28, 51–52, 90–91,
    150–51, 179–80, 265–66, 280,
    293, 308
Howard University, 282
Humphrey, Hubert, xiv, 2
Hurricane Katrina, 286, 315

illnesses. *See specific illnesses*
immigrant parents and
    grandparents, 20
in-country training, 63–64, 76
India, xiv, 11, 23, 27, 30, 70, 123,
    153–54, 167, 253–54, 303, 323,
    340
Indiana University, 30
Indonesia, 12, 123, 272, 295, 299,
    323
International Book Project, 283
interview questions, xviii
Iraq, 143, 289, 294, 305
Irwin, Fran and Will, xii
isolation, 145
Israel, 45, 316
Italy, 24

Jackson County, Kentucky, 320
Jamaica, 4–5, 8, 26, 37, 48–49, 61,
    98, 113, 119, 131, 135, 157–58,
    179, 185–86, 201, 228, 249–50,
    289, 294, 306, 324
Japan, 25, 307, 313
Jefferson Community and
    Technical College, 258
Jinishian Memorial Program, 296
Johnson, Lyndon, 6, 292
Jones, Lloyd, 16, 20, 24–25, 76–77,
    124, 162, 191, 277, 301–2
Jones, Will, xv
Jordan, 18, 22–23, 87–89, 105, 120,
    128, 139, 230, 279, 289, 294, 312

Karem, Kenny, 69–70, 165
Kazakhstan, 315
Kell, Jeffrey, 25, 68, 168, 257, 293,
    313
Kennedy, Alfred, 337, 344
Kennedy, Geraldine, 252
Kennedy, John F., xi, 1, 6–10, 24,
    42, 128, 214–15, 292, 304, 317,
    325, 327–28
    assassination of, 8, 9, 336
Kennedy, Joseph, 65
Kentucky Council on
    Postsecondary Education, 316
Kentucky Ecuador Partners, 317
Kentucky Educational Television,
    317
Kentucky Kernel, 319
Kentucky Returned Peace Corps
    Volunteers, xx, 292, 315, 318,
    321, 323
Kentucky State University, 315
Kenya, 18, 21, 271, 294, 340
Kilimanjaro, Mount, 214
Kimbrough, Andrew, 46, 110, 111–
    12, 125, 180–81, 234, 297–98
Kingsolver, Barbara, 252
Knebel, Fletcher, 271
Kurds, 42, 296

language, acquisition of, 143–44
language training, 59, 77, 80, 82,
    84, 86–91
Lebanon, 296
Lee, Gwenyth, 121, 136, 176, 224–25
Legislative Research Commission,
    Kentucky, 293, 315
Lesotho, 22, 31, 49–50, 86, 112,
    137, 152, 170–71, 181, 194–95,
    219–20, 237, 263–64, 298–99,
    308, 318, 323–24
Leupold, Bob, 12, 123, 299
Lexington, Kentucky, 5, 266, 283,
    286, 290, 296–97, 299–300

Lexington Herald-Leader, 121, 294, 296, 320

Liberia, xii, 4, 8, 10–11, 21, 30, 37, 42, 61, 63, 73–74, 97–98, 106–7, 123, 131, 133, 135, 157, 176–77, 200–1, 206, 216–17, 227–28, 245–46, 248–49, 255, 270–71, 274, 287–88, 313–14, 327–44

Lippmann, Judy, 9, 75, 95, 117–18, 139–40, 152, 167–68

Lithuania, 5, 20

loneliness, 145

lottery, draft, 15

Louisiana State University, 256

Louisville, Kentucky, xv, 20, 29, 258, 262, 267, 296

Louisville Courier Journal, 177

Loyd, Tara, 31, 49–50, 86–87, 170–71, 264, 318–19, 324

Madagascar, 264

malaria, 48–49, 147–48, 271

Malawi, 7, 14, 19, 21, 27, 29, 49, 54, 72, 107, 121, 129, 133, 138, 142, 145, 148–49, 190–91, 202–4, 231, 237–40, 266, 277, 280, 325, 343

Malaysia, xiv, 8–9, 18, 21, 29, 42, 59, 68–69, 115, 120, 144–46, 153, 163, 172–73, 194, 218, 222–23, 257, 277, 280, 286, 305, 312, 319, 321

male-female relationships, 135–41

Mali, 47–48, 59, 83, 136, 141, 220–21, 263, 275, 279, 292, 308, 313–14, 323, 332, 336

marriage of volunteers, 240–46, 329

married couples, 129–30

Martin, Dorothy Davis, 338

Mauritius, 309

McElroy, Cheryl, 337, 343

McFarland, Cecil, 21, 102–3, 111, 120, 145, 149–50, 240, 260, 292, 294, 312–13, 324

McFarland, Kathleen, 21, 120, 230, 279, 324

McFarland, Sheila, 21, 30, 102–3, 115, 120, 163, 240, 260, 294, 312

McGrath, Charlene, 75, 140, 151, 188, 231–32, 276

McPherson, Peter, 292

medical clearance, 49

medical examination, 45

medical training, 82–83

mentors, 29–31

Mexico, 23–24, 26, 164, 252, 293, 298, 313–14

Michigan State University, 254, 328

Micronesia, 20–21, 27, 30, 102–3, 111, 120, 140, 145, 149–50, 184, 208, 213–14, 260, 292, 294–95, 312–14, 324

Midway College, 9, 29

military service, 11, 14, 16

Miller, George, 22, 278, 292, 313

Miller, Joyce, 20, 22, 42, 71, 100, 124, 139, 182–83, 274, 304, 313

Miller, Mark, 22

Miller, William, 13, 75, 115, 143, 169, 209, 278, 315

Mike, Joshua, 17–18, 20, 24, 53, 101, 142, 182, 225–26, 253, 268, 292

Moldova, 53

Moore, Joan, 207, 234–35, 279–80, 305

Morehead, Kentucky, xv

Morehead State University, 2, 4, 35, 288, 318

Morehouse College, 73

Morocco, 9, 11, 45, 48, 75, 84, 95, 109–10, 117–18, 135, 139–40, 152, 167–68, 189–90, 207, 223–24, 240, 252, 259, 262–63, 275, 285, 297, 306, 313

Mortenson, Greg, 143
motivation, to join, 6–7, 16–18
motorcycles, 61, 79, 115, 122, 131, 184, 208–10
Mount Kilimanjaro, 214
Moyers, Bill, xix, 253
Mozambique, 31, 54, 121, 147, 150, 152, 174–75, 194, 204–5, 236, 266, 278, 280, 294–95, 323
Murray, Kentucky, xv, 1
Murray State University, 1, 259, 285–86, 297, 305

Namibia, 21, 239, 313, 316
National Geographic, 9, 41, 70–71, 280
National Peace Corps Association, xx, 16, 54, 325, 343
Natural Resources and Environmental Protection Cabinet, 293, 341
Neelon, Ann, 45, 77–78, 137, 147, 174, 199, 230, 240, 259, 297, 305–6, 313–14
Nehru, Jawaharlal, 123
Nepal, 46, 292
Netherton, Ashley, 1, 22, 29, 91, 109, 113–14, 186, 233–34, 265, 275, 304, 311–12
Nevis, 17–18, 20, 24, 53, 101, 142, 182, 225–26, 253, 268, 292
New Caledonia, 335
New Directions, 75, 162–63
New Zealand, 335
Nicaragua, 23, 231, 238, 273, 292, 301–2, 305
Nicholasville, Kentucky, 55
Niger, 18, 35, 91–92, 108, 115, 127, 137–38, 142, 190, 251, 274–75
Nigeria, xiv, 11, 26–27, 29, 42, 48, 105, 122–23, 135, 175, 208–9, 257, 319, 325, 332, 340–41, 343–44

Nims, Donald, 151
Nkrumah, Kwame, 123
nonmatrixed spouse, 37, 60, 163
Northwestern University, 256
Norway, 22, 343
number of volunteers
  by programs, 165, 272
  in education careers, 293
  interviewed, xv
  peak, xiii
  total, xi
Nunn Center for Oral History, xii

Obama, Barack, xviii, 325
Oddo, Oghale, 26–27, 48–49, 113, 119, 128, 135, 185–86, 294, 306, 324
Oddo, Sarah Cross, 4, 5, 37, 61–62, 98, 131, 157–58, 179, 201, 228, 249–50, 270, 289–90, 324
Ohio State University, 70, 341
Ohio University, 25, 288
Olsen, Jody, 32
Olson, Robert, 20, 35, 134–35, 172, 212–13, 215, 296
Ortega, Daniel, 231
Outward Bound training, 63, 68, 72, 75

Pakistan, 35, 143, 163, 253, 288
Panama, 301
Papua New Guinea, 47
Parker, Richard, 11, 107–8, 144, 152, 163, 209–10, 223–24, 240, 259, 285, 297, 313–14
Payne, Deborah, 21, 321
Payne, Glen, 7, 46–47, 82, 114, 192–93, 205–6, 221, 238, 241–42, 261, 275, 300–1, 308, 323
Payne, Jenifer, 47, 82–83, 178–79, 221–22, 241–42, 291, 300, 314, 323
Payne, John, 21–22, 145–46, 321

Payne, Marlene, 18, 21–22, 69, 120, 144–45, 218, 257, 305, 312, 319, 321

Payne, Sarah, 23, 46, 81–82, 109, 114, 120, 145, 149, 194, 226, 261–62, 278, 308, 311, 323

Peace Corps
  acceptance requirements, 44
  benefits, 17
  cultural workbook, 134
  goals, 160
  health policy, 147
  homes, 99–108
  housing policy, 99–100
  performance and accountability reports, 54, 273

Peace Corps Memorial Project, 128

Peace Corps Partnership Program, 291–92, 318, 321–22

Peace Corps Response (formerly Crisis Corps), 21, 315

Peace Corps Washington, 48–49, 51–54, 166, 313

Peace Corps Web site, 39

Pelfrey, Ronald, 12, 28, 106–7, 117, 177–78, 272, 277, 299–300

Pennsylvania State University, 48

Perry, Kristen, 22, 112, 137, 152, 181, 194–95, 219–20, 237, 263–64, 298–99, 308, 323

Peru, 11, 24, 45, 143, 169, 256, 316, 323–24, 337

Peters, Charles, 271

Philippines, 3–4, 9, 20–21, 24, 30, 36, 43, 60, 65, 72, 96–97, 101, 111, 130–31, 135, 151, 156, 163, 200, 227–28, 240, 248, 251, 260, 269–70, 274, 286–87, 292, 294, 300, 303, 307, 310, 312, 324, 340

physical training, 59, 67–68, 74

Poland, 164

practical idealism, xi, 31–33

Princeton University, 59

privacy, lack of, 140–41

protests, 1960s, 9–10

psychologists, 59, 69, 73–74

Puerto Rico, 63, 67–69, 71, 75

Quimby, Tom, 271

rabies, 147–48

Radley, Larry, 128

recruiters, 38, 45, 51

Redeagzi, 273–74

Reid, Caroyl, 135, 274, 300

Republic of Congo (Congo Brazzaville), 313

reverse culture shock, 247–48, 250, 252, 261, 340

Roach, Rebecca, 4, 37, 61, 97–98, 131, 157, 200–1, 228, 248–49, 270, 287–89

Roberts, Bibi and Jemima, 337, 344

Roberts, Kay, 18, 41, 45, 80–81, 101, 112–13, 141–42, 183–84, 206–7, 231, 238, 247, 253, 275, 279, 317, 323, 325

Roberts, Rona, 3–4, 36–37, 60, 96–97, 130–31, 156, 200, 227–28, 248, 269–70, 286–87, 324

Romania, 59, 273, 315

Rubio, Angel, 15, 25–26, 100, 115, 147, 183, 242, 279

Rubio, Gwyn, 1, 100, 115, 138, 242, 258–59, 303–4, 312

Ruppe, Loret, 291

Rusk, Dean, 161

Russia, xiv, 27, 51, 103–4, 144, 164, 194, 236, 265, 281, 295, 315, 323–24

Rwanda, 83, 294, 306

safety and security, 122–28

Salazar, William, 18, 26, 44, 75–76,

114, 141, 143, 184, 222, 237, 257–58, 276, 281, 307, 318–19

Samuel, Susan, 21, 30, 63, 73–74, 135, 245–46, 313

Samuel, Thomas, 8, 11, 21, 63, 73–74, 135, 206, 227, 245–46, 313–15

Sandinistas, 231

San Francisco State University, 73

Saudi Arabia, 28

Savane, Mamadou, 324

Savane, Rachel, 22, 95, 134, 184, 210–12, 242–43, 275, 306, 324

Save the Children, 277–78

Scanlon, Tom, 167

school construction, 192

Schweitzer, Albert, 257, 320

Schweitzer, Debra, 47–48, 59, 83–84, 136, 141, 220–21, 263, 275, 279, 308, 314, 323

Searles, David, 65, 163, 166

secondary projects, 165, 193–94

Selassie, Haile, 74, 215–16

selection criteria, 64
    See also deselection;
        self-selection

self-selection, 64–65, 75–76

Senegal, 1, 22, 28–29, 31, 45, 53, 77–78, 91, 108–9, 113–14, 137, 147, 149, 174, 186, 199, 230, 233–34, 240, 259, 265, 267, 275, 297, 304–5, 310–14, 332

Senghor, Leopold, 78

September 11 (9/11), 219–20, 263–64

sexual harassment, 131, 137, 139, 308

Sherman, Erin, 324

Sherman, Steve, 324

Shraberg, Aaron, 5–6, 38–39, 62, 98–99, 127, 131–32, 158–60, 201–2, 229, 250–51, 270–71, 290

Shriver, Sargent, xix, 41, 44, 63, 70, 123, 128, 215, 304

Sierra Leone, 122, 272, 299, 332, 335–36, 338–39, 341, 343

Siler, Harry, 50–51, 227, 232–33, 282–83, 307, 325

Simpson, Susan, 271

Sither, Robin, 19, 84, 106, 147, 186–87, 235–36, 263, 277, 306, 311, 325

Skeese, John, 11, 29, 105, 175, 208–9, 257, 319

Slovakia, 41, 48, 52, 103, 151, 175, 195–97, 218, 281, 324

smallpox vaccination program, 188, 271

Sohn, Katherine, 70

Solomon Islands, 335

Somalia, 28

Somerset, Kentucky, 5, 291, 300

South Africa, 50–51, 227, 232–33, 264, 282, 307–8, 325, 334, 343

South Korea, 22, 28

Spain, 22, 24, 312

Spalding University, 56

Speicher, Win, 68, 169

Sprague, Daniel, 8, 23, 41, 43, 124, 255, 316

Spurr, Sally, 15, 44–45, 100–1, 124, 138, 152, 184–85, 230, 258, 276

Sri Lanka, 46, 110–11, 125, 180–81, 234, 297–98

Stabler, Blake, 27–28, 51, 103–4, 144, 164, 194, 236, 265, 281, 295, 323–24

Stein, Bennett, 324

St. Lucia, 325

Storti, Craig, 252

Stosberg, Don, 14, 29, 72, 145, 277, 293, 309–10, 323

structure, lack of, 141–43

St. Thomas Seminary, 29

Suchanek, Jeff, xii
Sudan, 28
Sukarno, 123
Swaziland, 207, 234–35, 279–80,
    289, 294, 305
Sweden, 22, 308, 321
Sweigart, William, 10, 42, 106–7,
    133, 176–77, 216–17, 255, 274
Switzerland, 343
Syracuse University, 72
Syria, 296

Tanzania, 214, 265, 343
Taylor, Charles, 248
technical training, 75, 81, 84, 87
Thailand, 11, 12, 29, 46, 52, 92–93,
    103, 123, 142, 169, 253, 292,
    299, 313, 323
The Gambia, 23, 46, 81–82, 109, 114,
    145, 149, 166, 194, 226, 261–62,
    279, 308, 311–12, 323, 341
Todd, Sara, 24, 30, 90, 104, 120–21,
    141, 191–92, 267, 296, 304
Togo, 32, 313
Tonga, 22, 278, 292, 335
Tracy, Martin, 1–2, 11, 35–36,
    59–60, 95–96, 129, 155–56,
    199–200, 227, 247–48, 285–86
Tracy, Patsy, 1–2, 35–36, 59–60,
    95–96, 129–30, 155–56, 247–
    48, 269, 285–86
training. See specific types of
    training
Transylvania University, 21, 54
traveling stories, 208–14
Tschetter, Ron, 119, 164, 273
Tubman, William V. S., 215
Tunisia, 32
Turkey, 1–2, 11, 20, 22, 35–36,
    59–60, 129–30, 134–35, 155–
    56, 172, 199–200, 212–13, 215,
    227, 247–48, 269, 285–86, 296,
    339

Turkmenistan, 21, 313

UCLA, 70, 74
Uganda, 22, 291, 294, 321, 324
Ukraine, xiv, 8, 20, 28, 52, 55,
    89–90, 104, 120, 126–27, 155,
    217–19, 234, 265–66, 314, 324
UNICEF, 189
University of Akron, 46–47
University of Colorado, 25
University of Hawaii, 44
University of Houston, 24
University of Kentucky, 5, 28, 30,
    36, 54, 145, 256, 258, 266, 285,
    293, 295, 297–98, 300–1, 313,
    315, 317, 320, 324, 341, 344
    Patterson School of Diplomacy
    and Commerce, 18, 24–25, 56,
    295
University of Louisville, 320
University of Michigan, 8
University of Missouri, 18
University of New Mexico, 71–72
University of Pittsburgh, 329
University of Utah, 74
University of Virginia, 32
University of Washington, 69
University of Wisconsin, 251
USAID (U.S. Agency for
    International Development),
    18, 21, 61, 156, 168–69, 188,
    238, 243, 248, 274, 278, 288–
    89, 292, 294, 312, 324
Uzbekistan, 315

Vanuatu, 272, 335
Vasquez, Gaddi, 164
Vaughn, Jack, 161
vehicular accidents, 122, 209–12
Venezuela, 22
veterans, in the Peace Corps, 16
Vietnam War, 3, 6–15, 254–55,
    299–300

VISTA (Volunteers in Service to America), 4, 28, 267, 288

Wabash College, 30
Wagner, Lowell, 319
Wake Forest University, 46
Wardle, Ed, xv
Washington and Jefferson College, 23
Wayne County, Kentucky, 3, 259
Western Kentucky University, 15
Western Samoa, 335
White, Leigh, 32, 51, 104–5, 121, 175, 204, 243–44, 267, 278
White, Maurice, 23, 44, 77, 110, 115–16, 173, 259, 277, 306, 311
Williams, Aaron, 165, 172, 291
Williamsburg, Kentucky, 282
Wilson, Angene, 14, 327–44
Wilson, Jack, 162–63, 327–44
Wilson, Ken, 19, 49, 142, 148–49, 202–4, 239–40, 280

Wilson, Miatta, xviii, 343
Winther, Paul, 11, 30, 70, 123, 153–54, 167, 253–54, 303, 323
Wofford, Harris, 322
World Bank, 288
WorldWise Schools, 93, 291–92, 318
Worthington, Benjamin, 17, 100, 186, 259–60

Yess, Capp, 81, 101–2, 111, 116, 178, 194, 223, 244–45, 261, 277, 308–9, 313
youth development, 85, 181–82
Yunker, Wini, 55–57, 127, 217, 234

Zaire. See Congo, Democratic Republic of
Zambia, 18, 114–15, 187–88, 238–39, 264, 266, 276, 285
Zimbabwe, 22, 27, 50, 86–87, 127, 136, 166, 264, 266, 269, 311
Zimmerman, Jonathan, 66–67